THE HUNT FOR ROB ROY

First published in 2004
by John Donald Publishers,
an imprint of Birlinn Ltd
West Newington House
10 Newington Road
Edinburgh EH9 1QS

www.birlinn.co.uk

ISBN10: 1 84153 483 5
ISBN13: 978 1 84153 483 6

British Library Cataloguing-in-Publication Data
A catalogue record for this book is available from the British Library

Typesetting and origination by Brinnoven, Livingston
Printed and bound by Creative Print and Design, Ebbw Vale, Wales

THE HUNT
FOR
ROB ROY

The Man and the Myths

David Stevenson

Birlinn

WIN
(Wendy, Ian, Neil)

Wha's like us?
Gey few

CONTENTS

ILLUSTRATIONS

MAPS

PREFACE

Rob Roy MacGregor became famous through being hunted, and by his reactions to being hunted. For thirteen years, first as a fugitive debtor and then as a rebel attainted for high treason, his ability to evade all the efforts of dukes, the army and the government to capture him won him fame. Thus *The Hunt for Rob Roy* is an appropriate title for a biography of the man. But there is also another hunt for Rob Roy that is central to the book, and that is my hunt as a historian to disentangle the man who once actually lived and breathed from the vast haystack of legends and hero-worship that has hidden him for centuries. Rob has been an elusive figure for the historian as much as he was for his enemies.

The Rob Roy of the modern popular image was a man unjustly oppressed and persecuted by corrupt and vicious noblemen. But he fights back. He is the outlaw who defies the great, and in the end gets away with it, humiliating them in the process. A man of valour and set purpose who unswervingly held on to his honour and survived in an epic contest of heroic individual against the powers of darkness. He served his own cause, but was also loyal to a political one, that of the Jacobites.

This image cannot be sustained by the historical evidence. There will be many reluctant to accept the 'real' Rob Roy. Some readers may wish to continue to like the traditional stories, and find in them excitement and inspiration. Why shouldn't they? But they may also be interested in the historical biography of the man who lies behind the legends.

In the past, academic historians have tended to ignore Rob Roy. There is some sense in this. He is, from the standpoint of national events and trends, insignificant. His life touches only occasionally and marginally on matters of public importance. Yet in a wider sense Rob is clearly a figure of great significance. In 1817 Walter Scott decided that *Rob Roy* would be a good title for his latest novel, even though Rob was a fairly minor character in his book. Scott's motive was simple: marketing. A book which took its title from the famous legendary figure would sell. He was right, and the novel launched Rob as a great romantic hero, persecuted but surviving against all the odds. Books, plays and operas cashed in on the novel's success and Rob Roy emerged internationally as an icon, an instantly recognisable name. Rob had already in part become 'fictionalised' in story before Scott wrote, and afterwards he sometimes becomes unrecognisable, his name used because it evoked romantic associations rather than because writers actually referred to events in his life. Thus 'Rob Roy' became an almost universally known name which inspired creative (and some notably uncreative) writers. This very success of Rob as an entity moulded and distorted to meet cultural demands, quite obviously unreal, has deterred historians from taking an interest in the man. It is tempting to avoid getting bogged down in the endless, and often quite implausible, legends and tartan flummery that have enveloped poor Rob. So the field has largely been left to writers content to recycle old legends as history. Astonishingly, it was not until 1982 that the first biography of Rob based on systematic use of historical evidence appeared. W.H. Murray's *Rob Roy MacGregor: His Life and Times* was a huge advance on anything previously available. However, as a work of history, it is seriously flawed. Murray was a noted writer on mountaineering in Scotland, and deeply loved the Highlands, but he lacked experience as a historian. The book is fascinating and evocative to read, but once it is examined closely it begins to unravel. Murray is too close to his subject, and though he accepts some criticisms of Rob, basically he argues the case for the defence, at times in defiance of the evidence.

Murray's biography helped to inspire the 1994 Hollywood film *Rob Roy*, which contributed as much to historical understanding as Hollywood films usually do. But it had one positive effect. The Scottish Record Office (as the National Archives of Scotland were then called) reacted to this new fictional Rob Roy, and to the interest in the 'real' Rob Roy that it had inspired, by compiling *The Real Rob Roy: A Guide to the Sources in the Scottish Record Office* (1995). It may be doubted however, whether this was effective in meeting the public appetite for information about Rob, for brief notes cataloguing hundreds of sources are not to everyone's taste. But to the historian it is a goldmine, an essential starting place for a new hunt for Rob.

Credit for being the first to exploit its riches goes to A. MacGregor Hutcheson, who in 1996 and 1999 produced 'occasional papers' for The Clan Gregor Society on Rob's life, though his mingling of hard evidence with implausible story is disappointing.

W.H. Murray recorded his indebtedness to those whose painstaking efforts in cataloguing historical manuscripts, public and private, helped make so much material available for his use. I am similarly in debt to the huge progress that has been made in such work in the quarter-century since Murray wrote – and to the revolution in access that has been brought about by placing catalogues of all sorts online.

Until a few years ago I had taken no interest whatever in Rob Roy. He was just one of the historical grotesqueries inflicted on Scotland by the genius of Sir Walter Scott, and the man behind the fiction did not seem interesting enough to be worth investigating. Then the *New Dictionary of National Biography* suggested that I write an article for it on Rob. My first reaction was to refuse – I knew nothing about him – but I hesitated. Since chance had brought him my way, it might prove interesting to have a look at the man I had rather snobbishly ignored in the past. It did indeed prove interesting, for it quickly became clear that there was an astonishing amount of manuscript source material surviving for Rob's life, much of it never or inadequately used in the past. For an 'unimportant' man Rob had in his time provoked the use of a remarkable amount of ink. I wrote my brief article for the *NDNB*, but then felt tempted to continue. Hence, the present book. It is not a deliberate exercise in hero-bashing, though some will inevitably see it that way. To me Rob Roy's remarkable struggle for survival, aided by his bad qualities as well as his good, is a fascinating story, far more complex but far more satisfying than that of a cardboard hero typecast as 'Scotland's Robin Hood'.

For this paperback edition, the opportunity has been taken to make a few corrections and minor additions, many inspired by Domhnall Uilleam Stiubhart.

ACKNOWLEDGEMENTS

I thank for their help: Professor William Gillies; Angus Stewart QC; Jane Anderson, archivist at Blair Castle; John Brims, Stirling Council Archives; Domhnall Uilleam Stiubhart; Ronald Black; Susanna Martins; Suzanne Olisen, Old Auchietroig, who gave me access to Rob Roy's door; Elain Stanier, Mitchell Library, Glasgow, for information on the MacGregor Dick collection; James Stewart. In addition, behind every historian there stand battalions of archivists and librarians.

CONVENTIONS

The presentation of quotations from sources raises problems which have no simple solution. Showing in print a text that sticks as far as possible to what the writer put on his pages appeals to purists, but may present a text difficult for readers, through abbreviations, random capitalisation and lack of punctuation. I have therefore, in quotation from both manuscript and printed sources, extended abbreviations, modernised captialisation, and introduced punctuation where this seems necessary for comprehensibility. Original spelling has been retained, however, though in some cases with the modern version of words added in square brackets. In a few cases missing words have also been added in this way.

Plagued as Britain is by the indecision of successive governments unable to settle fully for either imperial or metric systems of measurement, I have stuck to the former.

In dealing with money, it is specified whether pound Scots or pound sterling is meant. £1 sterling = £12 Scots.

In both Scots and sterling, the pound was divided into 20 shillings, the shilling ('s') into 12 pennies ('d'). Thus £1 Scots = £0 1s 8d sterling.

The Scots merk was two-thirds of £1 Scots: that is, £0 13s 4d Scots, just over 1s sterling. All quite simple once you get used to it.

CHRONOLOGY OF
THE LIFE OF ROB ROY

7 Mar 1671	Rob Roy baptised
27 July 1689	Battle of Killiecrankie
23 Aug 1689	Battle of Dunkeld
Aug 1689	Donald Glas 'and his youngest son' (Rob) raid Cardross
Jan 1690	Donald Glas brought to Edinburgh under arrest
1691	'Heirship of Kippen'. Rob possibly involved.
Oct 1691	Donald Glas freed from Edinburgh Tolbooth. His wife Margaret, Rob's mother, had recently died.
13 Feb 1692	Massacre of Glencoe
1 Jan 1693	Rob and Marie MacGregor give in their names to be proclaimed before marriage
9 Feb 1693	Gregor MacGregor of Stucanroy, chief of the MacGregors, dies. Succeeded by his cousin Archibald Graham (MacGregor) of Kilmannan.
June 1693	Name of MacGregor banned. Rob adopts name of Campbell.
4 Jan 1694	John MacGregor in Glengyle, Rob's eldest brother, dead by this time. Succeeded by his son James Graham (formerly Gregor MacGregor) in Glengyle with Rob as his tutor or guardian.
4 Jan 1694	Rob obtains Inversnaid from Kilmannan
1 Oct 1694	Kilmannan murders one of his own servants
May 1695	Lord Murray sends out a party to arrest Rob
1695	Earl of Breadalbane, Rob's patron, arrested
22 Jun 1695	Rob submits to Lord Murray, swearing to serve him
Dec 1701	Rob obtains feu of Craigrostan
May 1703	Montrose grants Rob, as tutor of Glengyle, a feu of Glengyle
Jan 1704	Rob gives information about Simon Fraser's plottings to duchess of Atholl

Nov 1707	Marriage of James Grahame of Glengyle and Mary Hamilton
Nov 1707	Rob acknowledges his dependency on the family of Campbell of Breadalbane
18 Dec 1711	Rob signs a disposition of Craigrostan and Ardress to Bardowie and Glengyle
June 1712	Rob denounced for defaulting on his commitments
Oct 1712	Lord Advocate issues a warrant for Rob's arrest as 'a notorious bankrupt'
July 1714	Alexander Drummond (MacGregor) of Balhaldie elected as chief
Oct 1714	Rob drinks the Pretender's health at Crieff
Sept 1715	Loch Lomond raid
Oct 1715	Inveraray expedition
13 Nov 1715	Battle of Sherriffmuir
Dec 1715	Buchanan raid
Jan 1716	Falkland raid
April 1716	Rob's house at Auch burnt
May 1716	Rob surrenders to Finab
Sept 1716	Rob's house at Inversnaid burnt
Nov 1716	Kidnapping of Graham of Killearn
Apr 1717	Rob meets the justice clerk at Cramond Brig
3 June 1717	Rob 'arrested' by the duke of Atholl at Dunkeld
6 June 1717	Rob escapes from Logierait prison
25 June 1717	Rob issues his declaration to all true lovers of honour and honesty from Balquhidder
19 July 1717	Raid on park of Buchanan Castle
19 July 1717	Permanent military presence established at Inversnaid
23 July 1717	Raid on girnals at Buchanan Castle
1718–19	Barracks at Inversnaid built
8 Aug 1718	Raid carries workers off from Inversnaid barracks (RR not known to have been directly involved)
28 Jan 1719	Attack by Rob on a party of troops quartered in Glenfalloch
10 Mar 1719	Royal proclamation for apprehending Rob Roy
2 Apr 1719	Rob refers to 'that rebellious bugger the Duke of Montrose'
16 Apr 1719	Mock challenge by Rob to Montrose
10 June 1719	Battle of Glensheil

18 Feb 1720	Attack troops at Kirkton of Balquhidder (RR not involved)
1723	*Highland Rogue* published
1725	Rob's wife reported to be collecting blackmail
19 Oct 1725	Submission of Rob to General Wade
2 Dec 1725	Rob and others granted a pardon by George I
1727	General Wade pays Rob for spying on Jacobites
Jan 1730	Reference to Rob's gang infesting 'the country'
Aug 1731	Atholl supports Rob in his dispute with 'the Breadalbane people'
28 Dec 1734	Rob Roy dies in Balquhidder

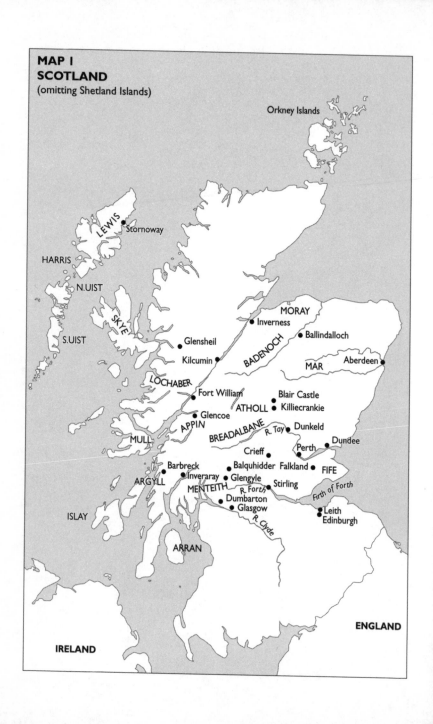

**MAP I
SCOTLAND**
(omitting Shetland Islands)

Orkney Islands

LEWIS
• Stornoway

HARRIS

N.UIST

SKYE

S.UIST

MORAY

• Inverness

• Glensheil

• Ballindalloch

BADENOCH

Kilcumin •

MAR

• Aberdeen

LOCHABER

• Fort William

Blair Castle •

ATHOLL •

• Killiecrankie

• Glencoe

APPIN

BREADALBANE

R. Tay

• Dunkeld

MULL

• Crieff

Perth •

• Dundee

• Barbreck

• Balquhidder

Falkland •

FIFE

• Inveraray

• Glengyle

• Stirling

ARGYLL

MENTEITH

R. Forth

Firth of Forth

ISLAY

• Dumbarton

• Glasgow

R. Clyde

• Leith

Edinburgh

ARRAN

ENGLAND

IRELAND

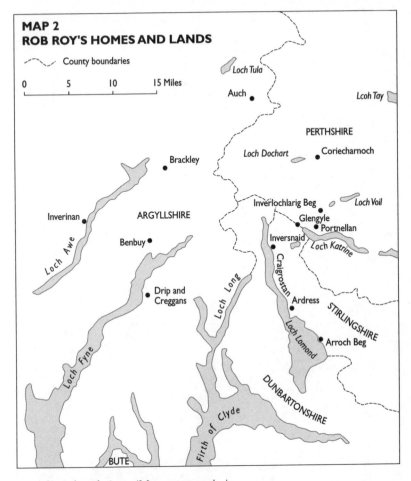

MAP 2
ROB ROY'S HOMES AND LANDS

‑‑‑‑‑ County boundaries

0   5   10   15 Miles

Loch Tula

Auch

Lcoh Tay

PERTHSHIRE

Brackley

Loch Dochart

Coriecharnoch

Inverlochlarig Beg

Loch Voil

Inverinan

ARGYLLSHIRE

Glengyle

Portnellan

Inversnaid

Loch Katrine

Benbuy

Loch Awe

Drip and Creggans

Craigrostan

Ardress

STIRLINGSHIRE

Loch Long

Loch Lomond

Arroch Beg

Loch Fyne

DUNBARTONSHIRE

Firth of Clyde

BUTE

Adress, bought 1710 (Montrose superior)
Arroch Beg, leased 1705 from Montrose for 9 years
Auch, leased 1712 from Breadalbane for 7 years
Benbuy, leased from Argyll
Brackley, leased 1714 from Breadalbane for life
Coirecharnoch, leased (from Breadalbane?) pre 1711
Craigroystan, feu 1701 (Colquhoun of Luss superior)
Drip and Creggans, bought 1711
Glengyle, RR born 1671
Inverinan, held by Rob in the mid 1690s
Inversnaid, 1694; feu charter 1701 as part of Craigrostan
Inverlochlarig Beg, leased 1720s. RR died 1734
Portnellan

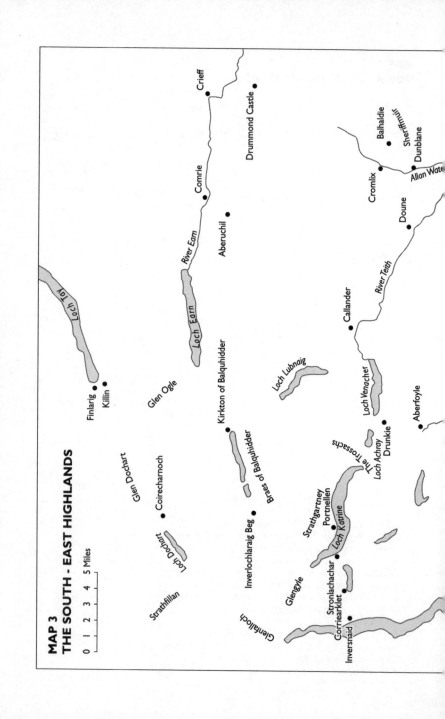

MAP 3
THE SOUTH - EAST HIGHLANDS

0 1 2 3 4 5 Miles

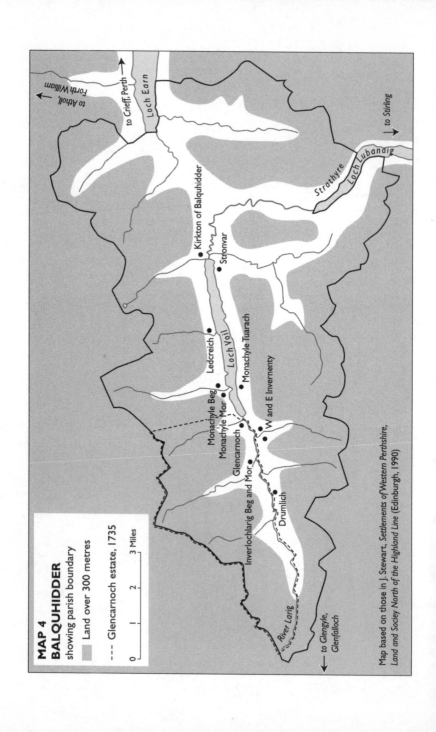

MAP 4
BALQUHIDDER
showing parish boundary

Land over 300 metres
--- Glencarnoch estate, 1735

0 1 2 3 Miles

Loch Earn

to Crieff, Perth →

to Atholl, ← Forth William

Kirkton of Balquhidder

Stronvar

Ledcreich

Loch Voil

Monachyle Tuarach

Monachyle Beg

Monachyle Mor

W and E Invernenty

Glencarnoch

Inverlochlarig Beg and Mor

Drumlich

River Larig

to Glengyle, Glenfalloch ↓

Strathyre

Loch Lubanaig

to Stirling →

Map based on those in J. Stewart, *Settlements of Western Perthshire,
Land and Society North of the Highland Line* (Edinburgh, 1990)

1

THE OBSCURITY OF CHILDHOOD

'When a male is born they put a sword or knife in his hand,' it was said of Highlanders at the time Rob Roy was born.[1] Thus advantage was taken of the instinctive grasping reflex of new-born babies when the palm is touched to have the boy symbolically accept a token of the activity basic to men in society. Men fought, or were trained to fight, and carried arms. (Baby girls were given a spindle to grasp.) It cannot be said for sure that Rob went through this little ceremony – nor whether he endured a preliminary baptism by being dunked in cold water by the midwife.[2]

Robert, the third son of Donald Glas (the Pale) MacGregor in Glengyle and Margaret Campbell (wives retained their maiden names in Scotland), is assumed to have been born in his father's house at Glengyle, at the head of Loch Katrine.[3] The first complication of Rob's life was his baptism. Glengyle was in the parish of Callander so he should have been baptised there. But his father wanted him baptised in the parish church of Inchailloch. The church of Inchailloch had originally been on the island of that name in Loch Lomond, widely used by MacGregors for burials, but by this time the church had been moved to Buchanan. Such traditional ties led Donald Glas to want his son baptised there, and permission for this was granted.[4] It seems ironic that Rob's life should thus begin with careful conformity to the niceties of ecclesiastical jurisdiction.

The baptism took place on 7 March 1671, and this means that Rob Roy had been born just a few days or weeks before, for the ceremony normally followed birth as soon as mother and child were fit to travel – though in this case seeking permission to hold the ritual in Buchanan could have caused some delay.[5] The day chosen may have been of no particular significance, but it was highly appropriate. It was Fastern's Eve, or Shrove Tuesday, a traditional day for feasting and merrymaking before the start of Lent, the season of fasting that

1

began the next day. Further, in a tradition that may well predate Christianity, Fastern's Eve was the day on which cattle were 'sained' (consecrated or blessed), a recognition that on their welfare rested that of the human community. They were the mainstay of the Highland economy and central to Highland life and culture. The cows might be blessed with the sign of the cross or, as was reported in the Western Isles, consecrated by burning evergreen juniper before them.[6] It is not known whether such practices survived in the southern Highlands as late as Rob Roy's day, but it would have been fitting if he had received the church's blessing on the day that his clan's herds received theirs, for his life was to revolve around the breeding and the buying, selling and stealing of cattle.

Other ceremonies would have surrounded the baptism. On being taken from his home on his way to the church, a few embers from the fire may have been thrown after him from the door, perhaps symbolising eternal life. At his return, he could have been laid in a basket of bread and cheese, and after he had been lifted out all present would then have eaten from the basket.[7] Was the idea that the child was to be a provider in the future? Or that the child itself was the highest form of production? A gift more vital even than food? Man might live on bread and cheese, but the continuance of mankind was only possible through children.

Rob 'Roy' or *Ruaidh*. Red Robert. Probably the epithet referred to ruddy complexion or red hair, though it is possible that 'Roy' was used fairly arbitrarily to distinguish him from other Robs.[8] More formally, Rob Roy was, for the first twenty-three years of his life, Robert MacGregor. For the remaining forty one he was officially Robert Campbell, for the name MacGregor had been outlawed. Thus the man who was to become the most famous person ever to bear the name of MacGregor spent most of his life under another name. For folk at the time, as for historians later, his nickname became the key to identifying him. Most surviving references to the man call him 'Rob Roy', or 'Robert Campbell commonly known as Rob Roy', or 'Rob Roy alias MacGregor'. He usually signed himself Robert Campbell, but occasionally and informally as Rob Roy. But everyone knew that in reality he was a MacGregor.

To Lowlanders Rob's birthplace, Glengyle and the surrounding district, seemed wild and hostile, a remote country of tumbled mountains and rocks, boggy moors, endless lochs, and streams often impassable after heavy rain – which was frequent. It was hard to reach, easy to get lost in, the few inhabitants seemed a poor and wretched lot – indeed 'barbarous' and dangerous. Men had not yet come to appreciate wilderness and see beauty in it. Those who lived in it were hardly likely to have self-consciously perceived and aesthetically assessed it, but they would have loved it. It was home, the place they knew and which supported them, and gave them refuge. To them it was not the hostile and isolated place that the glance and shudder of the stranger suggested.

Rob, growing up, would not have felt closed in and constrained by a glowering, intimidating country, but have accepted it as his world and become familiar with it and learned the passes through the hills, the fords across rivers, the ferries across the lochs. He would have learnt that some routes could be travelled only by men, but that cattle and ponies could travel others. And though he grew up in a small community, Rob would not have felt isolation. Drove 'roads' (routes, rather than artificially constructed roads) brought herds of cattle close to his glen, carrying animals destined for markets in the south from large areas of the west Highlands and the Isles. Drovers brought news and gossip from north and west. From an early age Rob probably accompanied such droves, collecting cattle deep in the Highlands and driving them to Lowland markets, visiting kinsmen. At some point Rob had also some formal Lowland-style education, for as well as his native Gaelic he could read, write and speak the Lowland Scots variant of English. The wording of his earliest surviving letters, however, indicates that he was not at ease in writing English, only acquiring the skills with the pen that he was later to show in the course of his twenties. Written English was to become central for his business life, for though Glengyle was very distinctly Highland, it lay close to the linguistic border with the Lowlands. Glasgow and Dumbarton to the south, Stirling and other market towns to the east, all less than a day's travel away, were English speaking. Closer to home, even the southern half of the parish of Buchanan was a land of Lowland farmers, very few of whom spoke Gaelic, while to the north of the mountain of Ben Lomond lay tiny scattered Highland communities, Gaelic speaking and dominated by MacGregors – called in this book the Lomond MacGregors – living in the area between the northern halves of Loch Lomond and Loch Katrine and spilling round their northern tips.

Thus through Buchanan ran part of the 'Highland Line' that

divided Scotland's two languages and cultures, but the line was not impenetrable. Frontier Highlanders traded with Lowlanders – and if they were tenants often paid rent to them. A grasp of the language of the Lowlands was necessary, as was knowledge of Lowland-based commercial and legal systems insofar as they dealt with tenancies, bonds, debts and contracts. In the most successful (if unsensational) part of his life, Rob was much more dependent on the pen than on the sword. However, training in the military skills which were a central part of the definition of a man in the Highlands was as important as formal book-knowledge. Every man carried arms, in contrast to the 'civilised' Lowlanders who carried no weapons and were not trained to fight – a distinct disadvantage when it came to disputes with their militarised neighbours. 'There games was military exercise, and such as rendered them fittest for warr, as arching [archery], running, jumpeing with and without race [racing], swimeing, continuall hunting and fouling.' Holy days, inherited from the pre-Reformation Catholic church, were marked by feasting. As he grew Rob probably, like other Highlanders, proved 'much given to tables, cardeing and diceing'.[9] Certainly skill at judging odds was a useful skill in his later life.

To be born a MacGregor was to be born with a bad reputation in both Highlands and Lowlands. In the often bloody disputes of Highland clans for land and power over the previous few centuries the MacGregors had at first seemed winners, but then turned into losers as other clans swamped the lands they had won. Their only victory was that they survived at all.

The clan had first emerged in the fourteenth century. Expanding eastward from its original homeland, it established a strong presence in Breadalbane in north-east Perthshire. However, the clan's territorial ambitions in the region were rivalled by that of another clan extending its power from the west, the Glenorchy branch of the Clan Campbell. By the later fifteenth century Clan Gregor was losing the struggle, and by the mid sixteenth it had largely been driven from its more fertile lands. But pockets of MacGregors hung on in a few districts, and individuals were scattered widely in the central Highlands. Clan feuding over resources, such as that which destroyed the MacGregors, was commonplace – it was how clans became clans, rose and fell. For there to be winners in the competitive battle there had to be losers, and the MacGregors in the end were losers. Often failing clans accepted their fates and became absorbed into their rivals – sometimes completely losing their identities and adopting the surnames of the victors, sometimes maintaining their names but accepting subordination to another chief. What made the MacGregors unusual is that so many of them refused to accept such a fate. Driven to remote areas they continued to fight back, driven by the will to survive. Dreams of past greatness and nobility of blood were deeply engrained. It was what gave meaning to the MacGregors' claim to be a clan by right. They were descendents after all, of King Alpin who had reigned nearly a thousand years before – or was believed to have, though historians now doubt that he ever existed.

As the MacGregors saw it, they were fighting in a clan feud to regain their rights against other clans. But increasingly they became regarded not only by the Campbells of Glenorchy but by all their neighbours as 'broken men' – not a proper clan whose activities were given validity by being directed by a legitimate chief, but 'masterless men' without such respectable leadership. They were merely bandits, common thieves and lawbreakers. And indeed the MacGregors, driven from their former resources of land and cattle, were increasingly forced to concentrate on raiding the cattle and stealing from the girnals (grain stores) of the chiefs and landlords around them. Their evil reputation grew, as their enemies gained legitimacy through success and political manoeuvring, winning state approval for their attempts to hunt down the remnants of the Clan Gregor. Destroying MacGregors was no longer seen as a matter of the rivals serving their own local interests, but as a service to the crown in the name of law and order. At Glenfruin in 1603 the MacGregors managed to defeat one of their enemies, the Colquhouns of Luss, in battle, but the victory was turned against them for their enemies persuaded the crown that the battle amounted to a direct challenge to royal authority. Under King James VI the Scottish regime was seeking to extend its control of outlying regions, to demand obedience in places which had formerly been left largely to their own devices. The MacGregors had not noticed – or had not cared. Their behaviour at Glenfruin was an affront to the crown, and it was decided that it must be punished in a way that would help terrify others into obedience.

The Clan MacGregor was proscribed. It was declared no longer to exist, and thus its chiefs to have no authority. The name MacGregor was banned, its use becoming a capital offence. In one perspective, the state was trying to force the MacGregors to do what many clans had done in the past, as the tide of fortune went against them and they failed in struggles against dominant neighbours – to accept assimilation with a more successful clan and thus gain security at the price of losing their autonomy and their name. Clan pressures within the Highlands had failed to make the MacGregors assimilate, so state authority from outside was now being applied. In the event, however, while the state proved ready to give its full legal backing to attempts to destroy the identity of the MacGregors, it was not ready to commit material resources to enforce its policy. The MacGregors' enemies, led by the Glenorchy Campbells, found themselves expected to do that themselves, and in spite of bitter persecution of the MacGregors over several decades, they failed. Remnants of the clan retained their identity, and this came to be tacitly accepted. The MacGregors had been weakened and fragmented, their raiding activities limited, but it became clear that totally extinguishing the clan identity would be more trouble than it was worth. So compromises were made. Men who were MacGregors at heart were accepted as tenants by the chiefs and landlords who had subdued them – provided they did not use the name of MacGregor too openly. They might often be troublesome tenants, with a taste for cattle-raiding that went beyond the Highland norm, but no one was ready to devote the time and men necessary to evict them. If their reluctant landlords couldn't get rid of them, getting them to accept the status of tenants satisfied their honour.

Thus there were still MacGregors when at last a chance of redeeming themselves in the eyes of the crown emerged. In the civil wars of the 1640s the MacGregors chose to fight for the Stuart dynasty which had proscribed them, and against their more immediate enemies, the Campbells and other Highland supporters of the rebel covenanters. The banned MacGregors became royalists, and in the 1650s, in the brief period of English republican occupation of Scotland, they again fought for the exiled Stuarts. They got their reward after the restoration of the Stuart monarchy in 1660. All legislation discriminating against MacGregors was annulled in 1661. Men could now call themselves MacGregor, openly identifying themselves and acknowledging a chief.

It was a reward, but a limited one, symbolic rather than substantial. There was no question of compensation for past wrongs or of restitution of former property. Nor could the reputation, built up over generations, that they were uniquely violent and lawless be dissipated. The MacGregors remained scattered, the clan's aristocracy of blood holding small patches of land from other landlords and chiefs, glorying in being MacGregors but now generally accepting dependence on others in order to survive. But the tradition of cattle raiding died hard. It was (as in other clans) a way for young men to prove themselves, and by many was not seen as a crime in the same sense as, say, murder or stealing money. Edmund Burt, an English official travelling in the Highlands in the 1720s, accepted that in general theft was rare – except for that of cattle, and noted that stealing cattle was often referred to as 'lifting' rather than theft, indicating some tolerance. But he also noted that the term paralleled 'shoplifting' in the way it tried to indicate that the offence was to some extent socially acceptable. It was almost a gentlemanly crime to steal cattle, whereas to steal sheep was to act disgracefully – 'the Highlander thinks it less shameful to steal a hundred cattle than one single sheep; for a sheep-stealer is infamous even among them'.[10]

Addiction to stealing cattle was of course more than cultural convention. Cattle were the main source of wealth in the Highlands, the main commodity that could be sold in the Lowlands in return for grain and (for chiefs) luxury goods. For many raiding cattle was not a matter of greed or custom but of necessity or near-necessity. If MacGregors raided more than most, it was in part the reaction of men driven from fertile to marginal land, if indeed they had any settled hold on land at all, raiding to help eke out a living. If further justification were needed, this could be provided by passionate belief that such necessity was caused by the actions of those who in past generations had stolen the clan's resources. Lifting cattle was restitution for past wrongs.

Small-scale cattle raiding was endemic in many Highland areas in the later seventeenth century, as in previous generations, and chiefs and landlords whose tenants suffered losses from raids often took to organising 'watches' to guard cattle and to pursue and recover any that were stolen. The watchers were paid by a small tax levied on tenants who wished their cattle protected, this 'mail' or rent being known as black mail. There was nothing underhand about it. Up to the 1740s even great landlords on the fringes of the Highlands had included in their accounts how much each tenant paid in rent, how much in blackmail to help pay for the protection of their cattle. But who were the watchers, the guarders of cattle, to be? In particularly dangerous times, all tenants might be called on to serve as watchers (even if they had already paid their landlords blackmail for the purpose). But generally watchers were men specially chosen and paid for the job. Clearly the most effective such watchers would be men who knew the routes likely to be taken by raiders, their methods and traditions, perhaps knowing or suspecting who they might be. They might even have knowledge, through networks of intelligence, of the plans of raiders. Indeed, in many cases they were former (or even current) raiders or associates of raiders. Cattle raiders could convert themselves into 'watchmen', being paid to protect the cattle by not stealing them themselves. Setting thieves to catch thieves was an age-old practice, but also a dangerous one. There was a blurring of identities. When did paying watchers to act as police become paying protection money? When did a watch organised by landlord or government blend into freelance enterprise with tenants forced to pay regular 'blackmail' directly to those who, it was clearly understood, would steal from them if not paid off in this way?

Whatever the dynamics beneath the surface that often meant that blackmail amounted to extortion, the public face was sometimes given an air of respectability, with stress laid on legality. A fine example of this survives from 1741 in a contract in which Rob Roy's nephew, James Graham of Glengyle, undertook to keep the lands of a number of 'subscribers' free from theft of horses, cattle and sheep for seven years. If the animals were not recovered and returned to their owners within six months, Glengyle would pay the owner their full market value, though the 'small print' specified that 'small pickeries' – defined as the theft of fewer than six sheep – would not be covered.[11] The contract was to be recorded in the register of deeds in Edinburgh: all open and above board, with what the landlords paid Glengyle presented as insurance premiums rather than protection money.

Watches became an accepted part of local policing arrangements, though even where they existed some raiding continued to take place. Raiders were usually careful to cause as little fuss as possible, avoiding violence (though an occasional head might be broken or life lost). They were not interested in taking all, or even most, of a man's cattle. That would be killing the goose that laid the golden eggs. They would take one or two, so farmers could survive – and there would be another harvest of cattle to be lifted the following year. A tradition (much later, admittedly) told of farmers or small landowners tethering a few cattle where they could be easily found and 'lifted', when they heard that raiders were around, to avoid trouble. Raiding was routine, and roused little attention except in exceptional circumstances. Men of many clans were involved at one time or another, but there was a tendency to assume that all MacGregors were cattle thieves and for government to blame all raids on them.[12] Partly this was prejudice, but there was an element of justification for such prejudice.

MacGregors were scattered widely in the central Highlands, but three geographical concentrations can be identified: the Lomond MacGregors, those of Balquhidder to the north, and those of Rannoch Moor to the north again. To rank them in terms of resources, those of Rannoch had the poorest land, those of Balquhidder had the best pastures, and the Lomond MacGregors occupied an intermediate position. But the Lomond men were the most notorious for lawlessness. This was due in part to geography. Firstly, they were closest to Edinburgh and other Lowland centres of government and commerce. When they misbehaved it was far more likely to come to the attention of government, and be seen as a threat to royal authority, than thefts deep within the Highlands. Secondly, the Lomond MacGregors were temptingly close to rich Lowland pastures and agricultural lands to the south and east, and these they raided regularly. As far as government was concerned, for barbarous Highlanders to raid settled 'civilised' Lowlanders in the heart of the kingdom was outrageous.

Raiding into Lowland areas was tempting not only because they were relatively wealthy, but had the advantage that raiders were unlikely to be met with armed resistance. As already noted, Lowlanders went unarmed, and generally lacked enthusiasm for fighting. Countrymen were not trained to arms from childhood, and they had a healthy fear of their 'wild' Highland neighbours. They were soft targets, who would hand over cattle or blackmail without attempting any resistance except bitter grumbling.

Government too grumbled and denounced, but it had not the will to do much. Had the degree of law enforcement been directly related to the number of local authorities and courts that had jurisdiction, the Highlands should have been a very law-abiding place. Like the rest of Scotland, the Highlands were riddled with overlapping networks of legal authorities. Landlords had had delegated to them by the crown, rather randomly, the rights to hold local courts of barony, regality and stewardry, with varying powers over civil and criminal cases. Sheriffs held their courts in the shires. Central government sought to impose local justices of the peace, though their failures led to the crown repeatedly appointing central commissions of justiciary for keeping, or imposing, order in the Highlands, seemingly never learning from experience that they were generally ineffective. At the top of the edifice stood the central criminal court, the court of justiciary. But the existence of so many types of court reflected not efficiency but failure and desperation. 'Lords of regality' might have power to judge and punish nearly all crimes, and the right to impose the death penalty, but landlords often shied away from using such powers. Imposing the law in these private feudal courts was expensive and troublesome. Having to maintain prisons, hold courts, summon witnesses and so on was often seen as a burden rather than welcome grants of power. Times were changing and feudal lords, though jealously guarding their traditional rights in theory, in practice increasingly regarded law-enforcement as a matter for central government. Imperceptibly over time great lords were abandoning their place as active local rulers and coming to be primarily consumers of the wealth garnered from their rents. They might find regality and baron courts useful in enforcing estate regulations and discipline on tenants, but seldom used their powers fully. Government and most landowners wanted peaceful, law-abiding Highlanders, but neither was ready to commit the resources to create such a society. Rob Roy was to demonstrate how ineffectual, for all its courts, the law in the Highlands could be. But his eventual submission to government also demonstrated that when Highland disorder came to be perceived as a direct political threat to the regime, and large-scale military intervention was authorised, Highlanders could be subdued – a message that was to be mercilessly driven home throughout the Highlands after the failure of the 1745 Jacobite rising.

If many courts but not enough will to use them provided one context in which Rob's life as an outlaw was to be possible, another was the rivalry of the landlords and chiefs who had carved up the southern Highlands between them. Had they been united in seeking his arrest, his career would have been short. But divisions between them meant that though Rob complained of persecution by great men, there was nearly always at least one great man around to offer him refuge and protection, for the noblemen concerned were fiercely competitive in terms of both local status and national politics. Make an enemy of one, and with luck and skill you could find one of his rivals ready to support you. The ability to play on the mutual hatreds of the great was to be one of the main keys to Rob's survival, and their titles will appear repeatedly in the story of his life – Argyll, Atholl, Breadalbane, Montrose. All were arrogant in maintaining status, unscrupulous in their use of power, often more interested in protecting their own interests and embarrassing their rivals than in either wider issues of law and order, or in the tracking down the most notorious outlaw of his age.[13]

Time now to turn from the position of the Clan Gregor, rehabilitated but still held to be disreputable, to Rob Roy's place within it and society as a whole. In one perspective, Rob was the son of a tenant farmer, for his father Donald Glas rented his land from Buchanan of that Ilk. But there were other perspectives. Donald in turn divided up his land among sub-tenants, who in turn paid him rent – and did most of the work. And though Donald was a tenant, he would have claimed hereditary right to 'his' land as well. He was the fifth in descent to occupy the lands of Glengyle, and no Buchanan landlord would have been foolish enough to try to evict him. Moreover Donald's influence extended far wider than his rented lands. His was recognised as the chief family of the Lomond MacGregors, and they looked to him for leadership. He was a leading member of the clan aristocracy, a *duin' uasal* or gentleman who could trace his ancestry back to King Alpin himself, and he headed the *Clann Dughaill Cheir* (Clan of Dougal Ciar) branch of the Clan Gregor. Further, though the MacGregors as a whole still had a chief, he was a nonentity. Gregor MacGregor 'in Stucnaroy' held the overall chieftaincy by hereditary descent, and was sometimes grandly referred to as 'MacGregor of MacGregor', but he was an obscure figure holding a farm on the eastern shore of Loch Lomond. He seems to have had no taste for leadership, and this left Donald Glas as the most prominent MacGregor of his age. Donald Glas's family might be, as a later tactful phrase would put it, 'in reduced circumstances', but he was nonetheless a man of importance, a gentleman and a leader in his society.

It was not an opinion that all would have shared. In the early eighteenth century the English tended to sneer at the way in which so many Scots claimed to be gentlemen in spite of living in near poverty. Lowland Scots in turn directed the sneer at Highlanders, expressing contempt at how so many of them, though impoverished and barbarous, insisted on their 'gentle' status on the basis of long (and sometimes improbable) genealogies. Rob Roy's family fits into this caricature, insisting that it was blood rather than wealth that determined status.

The anomalous status of the Glengyle MacGregors again emerges in variations in the 'designation' assigned to Donald Glas (and indeed to many others in the Highlands). Strictly according to Scottish usage he was 'in Glengyle', denoting that he was merely the tenant, not the owner, of the Glengyle lands. Yet he is frequently referred to as 'of' Glengyle, a designation indicating hereditary ownership. Here reality is subverting official measures of status. 'In' suggests low status, but in fact Glengyle was locally a powerful and influential man, with many followers who looked to him for leadership, and though he was a tenant he was a hereditary one, whose right to the land was unchallenged. Thus many thought it appropriate to accept him as a sort of honorary 'of' to reflect his status. This technical issue of 'in' versus 'of' may seem petty, something hardly noticeable, but in a hierarchical society it was highly significant. Many an 'in' dreamed of one day being an 'of'.

Donald Glas's usual home was at Glengyle among the Lomond MacGregors, but he was also a major figure among his Balquhidder clansmen. The two MacGregor pockets were very closely linked, with constant movement between them. The strength of the link was indicated by the way in which some at least of the dead of the Balquhidder MacGregors were carried over the pass still known as Bealach nam Corp and then down Loch Lomond to Inchailloch for burial. How close the two communities were has been disguised by modern methods of transport, which have for once stretched rather than shrunk the world. As the hoodie crow flies, the distance from Glengyle, where Rob Roy was born, to Inverlochlaraig Beg in Balquhidder, where he died sixty-four years later, is about five and a half miles. On foot, to cross from one to the other, Rob would have travelled down Loch Katrine to Portnellan, then struck up the Allt a' Choin, over a watershed and down the River Larig, a journey of about nine miles. He was equally at home in either place. By modern roads, the distance from Glengyle to Inverlochlarig is about forty-nine miles, more than five times the distance Rob would have walked. To modern travellers (except hill walkers) Balquhidder and the head of Loch Katrine are places distant from each other, approached from completely different directions. To Rob and his family, they were practically next-door neighbours.

The first appearance of Donald Glas in historical record occurs in 1655, by which time he had acquired the rank of lieutenant colonel, having presumably fought in the royalist cause against the covenanters in the 1640s and against the English in the 1650s. The 1650s rising ended in December 1654, and Donald Glas made his peace with the English. By February 1655 he was engaged in organising a 'watch' paid for by some parishes in Perthshire. In the aftermath of civil war cattle raiding was doubtless unusually widespread, and Donald Glas had found a time-honoured MacGregor way of supporting himself. It was reported he was claiming blackmail-type payments to support thirty men though he had only been authorised to raise twenty-four,[14] illustrating the ease with which protection could turn into extortion. However, he continued in his law-enforcement capacity, and in 1659 the English authorities ordered him to take up to thirty armed men to the hills and arrest any of the name of MacGregor, or any other broken men or disturbers of the public peace, and send them as prisoners to Edinburgh.[15] Thus though the English tolerated the use of the name MacGregor, they retained the old Scottish prejudice that MacGregors were to be assumed to be lawbreakers and arrested at sight – even though, rather absurdly, they sent a MacGregor to arrest them.

However, the English regime was collapsing, and once monarchy was restored, all legal discrimination against the MacGregors was lifted. In 1663 and 1669 Lieutenant Colonel Donald Glas MacGregor 'in Glengyle' is found being used to help track down criminals, the assumption being that he was the man in the Clan Gregor with most authority.[16] In 1678 he was listed among 'heads of branches of families' called to Inverlochy to sign bonds for peaceful behaviour, and in 1681 he was summoned to appear annually before the privy council or legal officials to answer for his behaviour.[17] Needless to say, he did not do so – such orders reflect the council's dreams of its authority rather than reality.

In these 1679 and 1681 documents Donald Glas is referred to as 'now in the Braes of Balquhidder,' suggesting that his main residence lay there. A rental of 1665 reveals details of his presence. He rented two farms from the earl of Atholl, and the fact that he paid £600 Scots (£50 sterling) 'entry money' for them indicates that he had just acquired the tenancies. For Monachayle Tuarach, a three merk land 'of old extent' (a traditional valuation) he agreed to pay £50 Scots, two kids, and two pints of butter, while for Drumlich (a two and a half merk land) the rent was to be £58 6s 8d Scots, two kids and two pints of butter.[18] In 1683 he was still tenant of Monachayle Tuarach,[19] but, perhaps predictably, a MacGregor tenant did not turn out in the long run to be satisfactory. Thirty years later, Atholl's heir was bitterly to denounce Donald Glas as a man 'who cheated my father', adding that 'he and his family have continued to doe all they coud against me'.[20] MacGregors might be tenants of other men, but had a tendency to behave as though the land were theirs if they could get away with it.

Donald had married, in 1656, Margaret Campbell, a granddaughter of Sir Robert Campbell of Glenorchy and a sister of Robert Campbell of Glenlyon. Thus the MacGregor married into middling ranks of the dominant Highland clan of the age – and the one that had done most to destroy MacGregor power. Margaret bore several daughters[21] and three sons who lived to adulthood – John (Ian), Duncan and Robert – Rob Roy.

In the early years of Rob Roy's life one of his father's main concerns must have been a change in ownership of Glengyle. John Buchanan of that Ilk had no sons to succeed him, was deeply in debt, and was ill in his later years. To try to clear his debts he arranged to sell the Highland parts of his estate to James Graham, 3rd marquis of Montrose, but his debts were so great that in the end Montrose acquired nearly all his lands before Buchanan died in 1682. Thus instead of having a declining family of only local importance as landlord, the MacGregors in Glengyle found themselves the tenants of one of the greatest families in Scotland. The Grahams of Montrose were major forces in national politics, and in the southern Highlands one of a handful of great dynasties of regional magnates who on the one hand sought to control their territories and impose order on them, and on the other destabilised the area through their expansionist ambitions and their bitter rivalries.

National events would have impinged little on Rob's childhood, with the exception of the sensational conviction for treason and forfeiture of the earl of Argyll, chief of the Campbells, in 1681. Argyll escaped abroad, and the marquis of Atholl led an army west into Argyllshire on behalf of the government, to ravage the countryside and cow the Argyll Campbells into submission, Many eagerly took advantage of the humiliation of the most successful (and therefore unpopular) of clans by joining in the plunder. A massively incompetent rebellion by Argyll in 1685 provided a further opportunity for humbling a clan that had threatened to become over-mighty, and though there is no contemporary evidence of MacGregor involvement it would have been surprising if they had not taken their share of the rich pickings on offer. A century later it was asserted that Donald Glas had 'found means to distinguish himself, first in the civil wars, and afterwards under the Marquis of Athole, in an expedition to Argyllshire in the year 1685',[22] but nothing more is known. The troubles in Argyll apart, Rob grew up in a relatively peaceful era in Scotland. Problems of order in the Lowlands were of far more concern to government than Highland disorders, as the restored Stuarts sought to suppress Lowland Presbyterian dissidents. Indeed there had been a movement in 1678 towards reviving the alliance of some clans and the crown against Lowland enemies that had been seen in the 1640s, with the brief quartering of the so-called 'Highland Host' on dissidents in the south. That was, however, like the Argyll troubles, a brief, isolated episode. But in the years in which Rob reached adulthood, the Highlands were to play their part in a civil war, and a new regime was to be established – a regime which provided the framework in which Rob lived the rest of his life.

2

CATTLE RAIDER, CATTLE TRADER

Rob was too young to take part in the raids on Campbell territory which followed Argyll's downfall, but by the time of the revolution of 1688–9 he was old enough to fight. The 'Glorious' Revolution dethroned the Catholic King James II and VII and established the Protestant William of Orange and his wife Mary (James's daughter) in his place. In the long view the MacGregors might have had little reason to love the Stuart dynasty, which had presided over their persecution in the past, but the dynasty had cancelled the laws discriminating against the clan in the 1660s, and memories of past support for the Stuarts in the 1640s and 1650s were strong. When early in 1689 Lord Dundee led a Jacobite (the word is derived from the Latin for James) rising against the usurpers, the MacGregors were inclined to support him, and from exile King James commissioned their nominal chief, Gregor MacGregor in Stucnaroy, to act as a colonel.[1] However, Gregor had little status and no wish to assert his authority. It was therefore left to the old veteran, Lieutenant Colonel Donald Glas MacGregor in Glengyle, to lead those of his clansmen who were willing to fight to the Jacobite rendezvous on 18 May. The contingent of 'the widely spread clan of M'Gregor' was regarded as too small to fight on its own, and was placed under the leadership of Cameron of Locheil.[2] As to whether Rob accompanied his father, and whether he fought at the two significant military encounters of the campaign that followed is unknown, though a reference to Rob as 'Captain' suggests that he did at least enrol in the Jacobite army.[3]

At Killiecrankie on 27 July the Jacobites were victorious, but Dundee's death in the battle was a disaster for them, depriving them of the leader who had inspired their campaign. An attempt to advance south without him was defeated at Dunkeld on 21 August, and the rising crumbled. At this point Rob, at the age of eighteen, makes his first known appearance in written record since his baptism – though he is not named directly. A week or two after the defeat of the Jacobite attempt on Dunkeld about 140 MacGregors led by Donald Glas MacGregor 'and his youngest son, who lives under the earle of Perth' raided the lands of Cardross in south-western Perthshire and drove off 162 cattle. The raiders carefully explained that this was an act of war, not theft, as they were acting 'for their masters', meaning the Jacobite commanders. The fact that Lord Cardross, their victim, was a colonel in King William's army, and the presence of two Lowland gentlemen among the raiding MacGregors gives credibility to the claim that the MacGregors were motivated by politics as well as by the desire for plunder.[4]

In the aftermath of the 1689 rising Rob's family suffered for its involvement. It has been alleged that his elder brother Duncan was imprisoned in Edinburgh in 1689–90, but there is no evidence that the 'Duncan MacGregor' who was held was related to Rob.[5] There is no doubt, however, about the arrest of his father, Donald Glas. He had signed a Jacobite 'bond of association' near Dunkeld on 24 August 1689, an attempt to rally the clans after the rebuff at the town, and he had successfully raided Lord Cardross's lands, but in a subsequent raid he was captured by William Cochrane of Kilmoranock's men while plundering his estate in Dunbartonshire. The arrest of Donald, described as 'the great robber', was regarded as significant because it was presumed that 'some persons of good note have patronized him',[6] meaning that he was thought not just to have been carrying out a private raid but still to be acting on the orders of the Jacobite leaders. Donald was brought to Edinburgh on 11 January 1690, and his notoriety was exaggerated to make his capture seem a major victory for the regime – 'he was one of the greatest robbers and plunderers that this nation has ever been troubled with either before or since the late Revolution.'[7] News of Donald Glas's arrest was even thought newsworthy in London, where the capture of a MacGregor nicknamed 'hawkett-stricks' was recorded, for this seems to have been the Scots version of the Gaelic 'Glas' or 'Pale'.[8]

Branded as a major villain, Donald Glas might have expected severe treatment, even execution, but two considerations prevented this. Firstly, Major General Alexander Cannon, who commanded the remnants of the Jacobite army still in arms in the northern Highlands, issued an offer combined with a threat. He would free all the prisoners he held in exchange for Donald Glas's freedom, but 'in case the said Mackgrigor suffers [is executed], he will cause ten of the chief prisoners in his power to be put to death'.[9] This may overstate how explicit Cannon's threat was (in order to bolster the image of Jacobite barbarity), but he clearly indicated that he would make reprisals if Donald was harmed, and the threat was sufficient to deter action against him. The other influence suggesting leniency might be best in dealing with Donald Glas was his willingness to talk and make offers to his captors, and pressure was put on him by confiscating the rents paid to him by his subtenants, as he was a rebel – though it would have been a bold man who tried to collect such rents for the government. Donald was examined by the privy council and, having asked to speak to the lord advocate, Sir John Dalrymple, had an interview with him on 7 February. He explained that he knew how several of the Jacobite chiefs could be bribed into submission by settling some of their grievances. MacDonald of Glengarry held Moidart as a feudal vassal under the duke of Argyll, and wanted the crown to buy out Argyll's rights – or alternatively would settle for £1,000 sterling in cash. Similarly the chief of Macintosh was the feudal superior of Keppoch, and MacDonald of Keppoch wanted his rights bought out, which would cost about £2,000 sterling. Dalrymple promised Donald Glas not only his freedom but a reward if he could get these chiefs to submit, though he suspected Donald would not be able to live up to his promises.[10] His scepticism was justified. The sort of grievances over the feudal land system in the Highlands which Donald discussed were certainly major causes of unrest, but his claims that he could negotiate their settlement and get Jacobite chiefs to submit was implausible. Like his son on many later occasions, Donald was trying to talk himself out of trouble, by suggesting he would be more useful alive than dead.

He remained a prisoner, however, though some of the restrictions on him were relaxed. The council quickly lost interest in him as a source of political intelligence and would-be policy maker, and he was evidently ill, for a physician later presented a bill for 'attendance upon and furnishing medicines to' Donald and his servants.[11] Yet he managed to demonstrate that even from his cell he could be a threat. At some point during his imprisonment, Sir Colin Campbell, a law lord with the title Lord Aberuchil, voted in the privy council against a motion to release Donald. Archibald Campbell, earl of Argyll, had favoured his release, and was alleged to have let it be known that if it had not been for Aberuchil's vote Donald Glas would have been a free man. Donald then sent word to one of his sons (it is not known which one) and a nephew, and they with their men descended on Aberuchil's estate near Comrie in Perthshire intent, as the unfortunate judge put it, on destroying his tenants.[12] He estimated his losses at over £1,400 sterling.[13]

Perhaps this defiance was why, in December 1690, orders were given that Donald should be proceeded against for treason, being held guilty of rebellion, theft, depredations and robberies.[14] The motives for this hardening of attitude however were, judging by what followed, mainly tactical. Donald was threatened in order to encourage his family and followers to make a deal with the regime. This emerged in February 1691. On the 9th, acts of the privy council accepted the request of the heritors (landowners, though noble, were excluded) of Stirlingshire and Dunbartonshire, led by Cochrane of Kilmoranock (who had arrested Donald Glas in 1689), to set up a watch at their own expense, and ordered that Donald Glas be freed, on his finding caution for 10,000 merks that he, his eldest son John, his youngest son Robert and his nephew Malcolm MacGregor in Marchfield (Balquhidder), would behave peacefully and not associate with robbers or rebels. Thus the price of Donald's freedom was to be the good behaviour of his family. Three days later came another incentive for them. The new watch was to be commanded by John MacGregor in Glenglye, and Archibald MacGregor in Kilmannan.[15] Lack of government commitment again meant falling back on encouraging local people to pay for their own protection by buying the services of cattle raiders as watchmen.

The watch was not an immediate success. In April 1691 MacGregors were raiding within a few miles of Stirling, plundering the countryside, going beyond the usual cattle raiding and justifying themselves by claiming to be acting for the exiled King James.[16] This was probably the great raid that was still remembered at the end of the eighteenth century, under the name of the 'heirship [raid] of Kippen' and believed to have been led by Rob Roy, 'a robber by profession'.[17] However, the connection of Rob with the Kippen raid is first made in a text written over half a century after his death, by which time the legends of his exploits had expanded uncritically,[18] so though most subsequent authors have accepted Rob's leadership there is no real evidence of it – though that he took part in the raid seems likely enough.

Whoever organised the raid may have made a miscalculation which cost the MacGregors dear, by drawing attention to their activities at a time when the government was about to take an initiative in Highland policy. The advice which flowed to King William from his Scottish ministers evidently urged that the MacGregors were the main problem in the Highlands – or at least in the sensitive Highland/ Lowland border areas of central Scotland. The king, with no personal knowledge of the situation, parroted this back to the Scottish privy council in a letter which became the basis of a proclamation which was issued on 27 August 1691.[19] All who took the oath of allegiance by 1 January 1692 were to be pardoned. Captain Robert MacGregor was among those who duly swore allegiance to King William and King Mary.[20] But though taking the oath protected Rob and other Highlanders from charges of treason, Rob Roy and his fellow MacGregors were singled out for special treatment by William, as they were held to be largely responsible for the problem of theft (essentially cattle-raiding) in the Highlands. One of the problems in trying to control them was now identified by the regime as being the fact that they had 'little proppertie of inheritance to be a pledge for them'. In other words, since the MacGregors had had their landed property taken from them in past generations, it was impossible to restrain them by threatening confiscation. Therefore a proclamation was to be issued to warn all landowners of the dangers of having MacGregors on their lands. In future, landlords would be held responsible for any 'depredations' MacGregors resident on their land committed. They must submit lists of MacGregors on their lands, and find caution for their behaviour.[21]

It looked efficient. Responsibility for the lawless MacGregors had been placed on their landlords, who could be disciplined and fined by the regime even if the MacGregors themselves could not be caught. But this failed to take into account that the lands to which the MacGregors had been driven were often remote and beyond the full control of distant landlords. They had not the resources to police the MacGregors, but would be fined for the Highlanders' misdeeds. The best thing for a sensible landlord to do would be not to allow MacGregors to live on their estates. But how were they to get rid of MacGregors already settled on their lands? They certainly would not leave without a fight. And even if MacGregors could be expelled, where were they to go? Being driven from the farms they rented would hardly encourage them to become law-abiding.

A petition to the council by Humphrey Colquhoun of Luss

revealed some of the problems inherent in official policy. He owned the feudal superiority of the land at the head of Loch Lomond called Grigoriestone (evidently Craigroston) and leased it to the chief of the MacGregors (presumably Gregor MacGregor in Stucnaroy is meant). The chief was a law-abiding citizen, and had caution from the marquis of Atholl, so there was someone the government could hold accountable for his deeds – but Atholl was not his landlord and therefore unacceptable as a cautioner for him. Moreover though Gregor was nominal chief, there were also 'broken' MacGregors living on the lands of Grigoriestone who were beyond his control. Now, by the new proclamation, Luss would be held responsible for their behaviour. He had offered a list of their names to the council, but the council had refused to accept it until he found caution for them. But no one would give caution for such broken men, and Luss, even if he had the resources to expel them, was doubtful if he could do so legally. The land they occupied was, it is true, owned by Luss, but it was rented out to Gregor MacGregor, limiting Luss's rights over its inhabitants. Would the council give him permission to burn the houses of the broken men even though the houses were on a tenant's land?[22] The council was silent. Demanding obedience to the king's orders was easy, but explaining how they could be implemented was not.

Luss was reluctant to try to control MacGregors. Lord Murray, son and heir of the marquis of Atholl, was more enthusiastic. Atholl had already shown an interest in gaining influence over the MacGregors, by becoming cautioner for MacGregor in Stucnaroy, and Lord Murray, to whom his father had handed over the running of the family estates, had been active in 1690 in restoring order among his MacGregor tenants in Balquhidder. He was quick to make use of the act ordering landlords of MacGregors to find caution for them, using it in November 1691 as a reason for insisting that his tenants sign bonds of relief, swearing that if he was penalised by the privy council for their misdeeds, they would repay him. Many MacGregor tenants signed (though usually with a mark, as they could not write their names).[23]

Donald Glas took the oath of allegiance to the new regime in October 1691, and thus gained indemnity for his involvement in the Jacobite rising. A minor problem remained. He faced demands for payment of the fees he had incurred while he had been in prison (jailors charged prisoners for their upkeep). However, he managed to wheedle a concession out of the council by emphasising his misfortunes. His wife (Rob's mother) had recently died and he pleaded that his poverty was great. The council took pity on the old man – or, more likely, accepted that getting payment from him now that he was back in the Highlands would be near impossible – and agreed that the treasury should pay his fees.[24]

That Donald had accepted the offer of indemnity was soon proved wise. It was just a few months later, in February 1692, that the massacre of the MacDonalds of Glencoe showed how ruthless the regime was prepared to be in acting against those who tested its patience too far. The massacre is remembered as an atrocity, but at the time it was an effective one, from the point of view of deterring defiance of the regime. The MacGregors, like other clans, got the message that whatever their underlying political beliefs, submission was necessary. The complications of family and political allegiances in the Highlands must have been keenly brought home to the Jacobite Donald Glas and his family. The implementation of the massacre was the work of Rob Roy's uncle, Robert Campbell of Glenlyon (his mother's brother), while the father-in-law of Rob's sister, Sarah, was Alexander MacDonald of Glencoe, a son of the slaughtered chief.[25]

A further warning that keeping a low profile was necessary was confirmation that the MacGregors were regarded as uniquely troublesome among Highlanders. An act of June 1693 made general provision for new courts in the Highlands to crush disorder, but at the end a clause was slipped in reviving all the penal laws imposed on the MacGregors in 1633.[26] Again, they were to become clanless men, deprived even of their names in order to force them to disperse and assimilate. As so often happened, there were neither the resources nor the will to put the solemn decisions of politicians in Edinburgh fully into practice. The proscription of the MacGregors was not strictly enforced. The banned name still appears frequently even in official and legal records. But for MacGregors of any status, changes of name were necessary not so much through fear of prosecution as through the fact that as their name was no longer recognised in law, no documents, from the humblest bonds lending and borrowing money upwards, were to be legally binding if the name MacGregor was used. But there is irony here. While the MacGregors had been allowed to use their own name, at least they could be identified. Making them take new names meant that there was a danger that they become invisible. The sheer stupidity of officially insisting that all the troublesome MacGregors should assume false identities, and thus be difficult to trace, was not appreciated. In the real world, outside parliament, concessions were made. The name MacGregor was still widely used to identify the clansmen, but only with some form of words that indicated that it was not the primary name of the individuals concerned. The new name would be cited, followed by phrases such as 'commonly known as', 'formerly', or 'alias' MacGregor, to make it clear who they really were. The law was being an ass again, but the historian who suddenly finds much of his cast of characters has disappeared, disguised under new names, is deeply grateful for the compromise that led to MacGregor being regarded as acceptable as an 'alias,' as it enables – in most but not all cases – the re-identification of individuals.

To be forced to change surname was humiliating, but many Highlanders made such changes voluntarily. Men who became tenants of a chief or landlord quite often adopted his name, as a way of identifying with their new master and seeking his protection through claiming a sort of artificial kinship.[27] Fixed surnames were in any case a fairly recent innovation in Gaeldom, and did not necessarily reflect allegiance. As the following generations were to show, the sense of identity as a MacGregor could survive whatever name a man officially bore.

What name Donald Glas chose is unknown – and indeed he may not have lived long enough to have to choose one. He was active enough to sign a bond of friendship and alliance with the Buchanans of Arnprior in May 1693[28] but died sometime in the months that followed. His eldest son John was also dead by January 1694.[29] Duncan, Donald's second son, is last mentioned in the same year,[30] so he too probably died around this time, leaving Rob Roy as Donald Glas's only surviving son – but not as his heir, as John had been married and left two sons, Gregor Glun Dubh (Black Knee, named from a mark on his knee, visible in highland plaid though it would not have been in Lowland breeches) and Donald. Gregor therefore succeeded to what might be called the hereditary tenancy of Glengyle. The new MacGregor in Glengyle had been born about 1689, and Rob, as his uncle, acted as his and his brother's tutor or guardian during their childhood. It is likely therefore that it was Rob's advice that led to the child's name being changed from MacGregor to Graham following the banning of the clan name. If names had to be changed, for him to adopt the surname of his landlord, the Graham earls of Montrose, made sense. In accordance with the new law the child's baptismal name Gregor also had to go, so the young Gregor MacGregor was transformed overnight into James Graham. Rob himself, however, chose not to become a Graham. He took the name Campbell. The obvious explanation for this is that, denied the right to his father's name, he took that of his mother. There also may have been a certain declaration of independence in this, deciding not to follow the rush of MacGregor tenants of Montrose to become Grahams and invoking the name of the most powerful of all clans instead, but there is no sign that Rob's choice indicated any hostility to Graham interests.

In the same year that they lost their names, the MacGregors acquired a new chief. Gregor MacGregor in Stucnaroy died unmarried in February 1693, aged thirty-two. To the marquis of Atholl this presented an opportunity for advancing his ambitions to control the MacGregors. They might form a broken clan of bad reputation, but if they had a chief subservient to the Murrays of Atholl it would not only help control MacGregors on the Atholl estates, but would allow the Murrays to exert a degree of influence over MacGregors on other men's lands, thus extending the Murrays' power. Atholl had a candidate lined up ready to succeed Stucnaroy, one John Roy MacGregor – perhaps the man of that name who had been the tutor of Stucnaroy in his childhood, and who in 1689 had been one of Atholl's 'captains' in Glen Almond.[31] John Roy had other ideas, however, for he had no desire to be chief. There are two conflicting accounts of events, one being that John Roy had persuaded MacGregor in Stucnaroy before his death to nominate Archibald MacGregor of Kilmannan (his first cousin) as his successor. Atholl, when he heard this, was incandescent with rage. John Roy had cheated him, being 'such a bruit and so timerous that he will not accept of being cheefe'. He denounced the 'simplicity and cowardice of John M'Grigor' who 'was frightened out of his little witts'.[32] It was not only that his own candidate for the chieftaincy had failed that enraged Atholl, but the fact that the successful candidate, Kilmannan, was a vassal of his regional rival, the earl of Montrose – and indeed soon changed his name to Graham. Montrose had won a point in the endless petty bickering with Atholl about influence over lesser men.

The new chief's account of his appointment, not surprisingly, differed from that believed by Atholl. He denied the story that Stucnaroy had named a successor, and claimed his death had left the chieftaincy vacant as 'the freinds has not condischendit [agreed] who should be the man to succeed the late Macgregor'. But when the 'friends' (leading clansmen) had met after Stucnaroy's death they had with unanimous voice (vote) and consent 'condeschendit I shall be the prin[cipa]ll man as being Cheaf and chiftan to that clan'.[33] Probably the Lomond MacGregors had decided that choosing a chief dependent on Montrose, the man dominating the immediate area, was safer than accepting one who was Atholl's agent.

The new chief was appointed early in 1693. Before the end of the year the proscription of the MacGregors meant that officially there was no clan for him to be chief of. Nonetheless, at first he tried to maintain his clandestine chieftaincy. His Kilmannan lands lay outside the main area of MacGregor settlement, in the Kilpatrick Hills between Glasgow and the south end of Loch Lomond, but once he became chief he purchased the lands of Craigrostan, on the MacGregor-occupied eastern shore of Loch Lomond (including Stucnaroy where the old chief had lived), from Sir Humphrey Colquhoun of Luss.[34] In January 1694 Kilmannan transferred part of Craigrostan, the farm of Inversnaid, to Rob Roy under 'letters of impignoration', an agreement whereby Rob lent Kilmannan 1,000 merks and held the land as security for repayment.[35] In this and other land dealings with local MacGregors Kilmannan was probably partly acting to raise the money to pay for Craigrostan, but doubtless he was also rewarding those among the MacGregor 'friends' who had supported his claims to the chieftaincy, for Rob Roy, acting head (while his nephew was a minor) of the Clann Dughaill Cheir, had surely been prominent among the 'friends' who had made him chief. Rob Roy now had a landed designation. Perhaps to pedants he was only 'in' Inversnaid, rather than 'of' it, but Rob soon came to be known as 'Robert Campbell of Inversnaid'.

Kilmannan also showed himself active in enforcing his position as chief by handing over one Patrick Og MacGregor, wanted for murder, to the earl of Breadalbane's men, who hanged him.[36] Perhaps he calculated that, as Atholl was opposed to his chieftaincy, a gesture of cooperation with another of Atholl's rivals, the Campbells of Breadalbane, was expedient. However, Kilmannan soon found himself in the position of accused rather than enforcer of justice. Atholl had warned that he was not suited to be chief as he was 'a hott headed fellow',[37] and this proved to be correct. Late in 1694 Kilmannan murdered one of his servants, Malcolm MacCurich, in a drunken rage.[38] What followed typified the weakness of justice in the Highlands. The murder took place on Atholl's land, in Glen Almond, and not surprisingly Atholl proved keen to see justice done. But convention dictated that a man should be tried in the court which had jurisdiction over his place of residence.[39] Therefore, as a vassal of Montrose for the lands of Kilmannan, the right to try Kilmannan was held by the court of the regality of Montrose. The usual inefficiency and apathy ensured that proceedings did not get very far.[40] After all, Kilmannan was now a Graham, so deserved protection – especially if that would infuriate Atholl.

The murderous Kilmannan escaped without punishment, but his reputation was gone and whatever his chances had been of asserting his authority as chief had now vanished. In the years ahead he occasionally appears on the fringes of events, often drunk, so the MacGregors were again without an effective chief, though the government proved slow to recognise this. A 1704 order for the chiefs of clans to find caution for keeping the peace names 'Grahame formerly McGreigor of Kilmannan' as one of the chiefs involved,[41] thus both failing to recognise Kilmannan's obscurity and ignoring the 1693 law which had ruled that the MacGregors were not a clan.

In the midst of this turmoil in the early 1690s – the failure of the Jacobite rising, the loss of both his parents and both his brothers, and the loss of his name – Rob Roy had set about establishing a family for himself.   He married Mary MacGregor, daughter of Gregor MacGregor in Comer. The proclamation for the marriage was made at Inchailloch [Buchanan] church on 1 January 1693, and the couple were married at Corriearklet on Loch Arklet, which was in the possession of his wife's family.[42] Within months Rob was to acquire land close by, at Inversnaid, but there were financial complications about his position that are not easy to interpret. Having in 1694 impignorated Inversnaid to Rob, Kilmannan then 'wadset' it in 1695 to Dougal Graham (MacGregor) in Comer, the brother of Rob's wife. This meant that Kilmannan pledged Inversnaid as security for money (£1,000 Scots) that he owed to Dougal. Dougal then took 'sasine' or possession of Inversnaid, with Rob signing as a witness to this granting of sasine.[43] Possibly Rob had failed to pay the 1,000 merks he had promised to pay Kilmannan for Inversnaid, so what was happening here was that his brother-in-law had provided the money, and taken possession of Inversnaid himself for the moment. Not until 1701 was Rob to be able to make his right to Inversnaid secure.

In the interim Rob had more than land to worry about. Details of his activities in these years are sparse. Attempts have been made to depict him as a leading figure in, or even leader of, the Highland watch which his brother and Kilmannan had been appointed to head in 1691. There is no evidence that the watch was ever active, let alone became semi-permanent – and so, obviously, there is no evidence that Rob was connected with it. This complete lack of evidence, however, did not deter one author from calling a book on Rob *Highland Constable*,[44] evoking a ludicrous image of Rob Roy as a Highland PC Plod earnestly enforcing law and order. The reality was doubtless that Rob was active, like his forbears, in trading cattle, raiding cattle, and, when occasion offered, raising blackmail contributions either to provide protection from his own activities, or to provide wider protection by agreement with landowners to provide a 'watch' against raiders in general. Partly he was law-abiding citizen, buying land and trading, partly he was operating outside the law. He must have known, or learnt, that indiscriminate raiding was folly. It had to be kept to a level that did not make it a national issue, and there was a need to discriminate among victims. It would be fatal to alienate all the major landowners of the region simultaneously. Montrose and his tenants were evidently spared, as he was the owner of Glengyle, and Rob seems to have quickly established friendly relations with the Campbells of Glenorchy. In adopting the name Campbell, Rob had honoured his mother, but perhaps more importantly, indicated readiness to identify with her powerful kinsmen.

The lands of the Campbells of Glenorchy, whose chiefs were now earls of Breadalbane, lay mainly north and west of Balquhidder. The earl, with whom Rob claimed kinship, was one of the most active figures in the dark, violent and unscrupulous Highland politics of the 1690s. He was central to the attempts to gain the submission of the Jacobite chieftains who were slow to surrender after the 1689–90 rising, attempts which included the Glencoe massacre. It was an enemy who a few years later described him as being 'as cunning as a fox, wise as a serpent, but as slippery as an eel: no government can trust him but where his own private interest is in view'. Many believed him responsible for the Glencoe massacre, and it was said that 'He knows neither honour, nor religion, but where they are mixed with interest'. This poker-faced schemer had 'the gravity of a Spaniard', and politically he was on whichever side offered him most advantage.[45] No friendly testimony survives to counterbalance such descriptions.

Among Breadalbane's roles, it emerges, was that of patron of Rob Roy. Though his power was great, he sought constantly to extend it. Rob as cattle-raider and trader might be small fry, but he was an influential man among the MacGregors, worth cultivating if he could gain Breadalbane the allegiance of the MacGregors scattered on other men's estates. Breadalbane, Atholl and Montrose all took an interest in the MacGregors. They might be despised, but show them some favour and they could be deterred from raiding your own lands and tolerated when they raided the lands of neighbours – who were almost inevitably rivals.

A newly identified group of letters throws a flood of light on Rob's life in the mid-1690s, years that are otherwise obscure. He might have acquired Inversnaid near his birthplace, but employment drew him westward into Argyll, where he set up home at Inverinan, on the west bank of Loch Awe. From there he sent letters to Alexander Campbell of Barcaldine, who supervised the running of Breadalbane's estates in Argyllshire. Rob held some position under Barcaldine in the estate's management, probably that of 'officer', with responsibility for the estate of Barbreck, which lay on the west coast at the head of Loch Craignish. The first of the letters is dated 30 July 1693, and it suggests that Rob had just settled at Inverinan. It was just a few months after his marriage, and Rob was gathering together their possessions. It is worth quoting in full –

> Sir, Be Please to wryt to Rott Stirken[?] to desire him to cause the officer gather thes lambes that my wife gotte in the thiggen. My wife will tell you how many they ar. Wryte to Mungo to send the cow that he promised my wife. Please send the cow you promised. Be pleased to send it to witht thes two men allong with my clothes. Give 12 pund Scots to my wife [that?] I m[a]y buy a plaid there with. Give money to [my] wife that I may buy cravats and sleeves out of Glasgow for I have ocation [occasion] every week.The inclosed will lett you know how yower money was disposed of. Send up the whyt hors to help to draw in the peats. Send me my sword and gune as soone as you can. Send me money to buy a belt. Send me some pudder [gunpowder]. I rest your loveing cousen and servant.[46]

Before or after his marriage, Rob and Mary had been out thigging. This Highland custom was described at the time as 'to beg assistance of friends which is very ordinary among persons of every quality. Men thig horses and corn; women thig cows, sheep and goats.'[47] What Rob describes fits this precisely: Mary, in her womanly role, had thigged a cow and some lambs; Rob had thigged a horse, appropriate for a man. Whether the monies mentioned were similar 'wedding presents' or sums due to Rob for other reasons is not said, but as befitted the family man and estate manager that Rob now was he was keen to present a suitable appearance. He was to have a new plaid – and fashionable cravats and sleeves bought in Glasgow (sleeves were often worn separate from other garments). Rob had his own gun (a firelock musket) but needed to get powder. He had a sword, but lacked a belt for it. This is a rare glimpse of the domestic in Rob's life, a peaceful picture of a young couple setting up home together.

The letter tells us much more than the outward meaning of the words. This is the earliest of Rob's letters to survive, and compared with those he wrote in later life the script lacks confidence. The language is stilted, abrupt. And the signature differs in many ways from the one he later adopted. Later he was to use 'Rob or (more commonly) 'Ro' as written abbreviations for his first name, but here he signs himself 'Rott. Campbell'. He is not yet, it would seem, known as Rob Roy. The later letters in this 1690s group see improvement in writing and expression – and a signature that becomes increasingly like his later ones. Thus Rob's childhood education had left him with some difficulty expressing himself fluently in written English, and not experienced in handwriting. Now, when he was in his early twenties, he was making up for these deficiencies.

Rob's second letter (May 1694) also starts off with domestic matters.[48] 'I have sent down some wood to make the chairs of. I'le send down the rest sometime next week. Pray in all love[?] for to cause mak the folden table as soone as convenience can serve.' Rob then moves abruptly on to a more contentious matter. 'I strange [find it strange] that you did not send up the mony for the bear [barley] as you promised. If I had known that you had caused me breck my promise as I have done, I had bought non this year.' Sharp words to his superior. 'Have mind of my breeches,' reads an afterthought at the end of the letter. Rob wanted to be able to appear in Lowland as well as Highland dress.

The third letter (Nov 1696) also suggests strained relations with Barcaldine. Rob had evidently been instructed to collect 'old rests' (old arrears of rent) from the tenants of Barbreck, but Barcaldine had then indicated to the tenants that this was not his intention, and Rob was being blamed by the tenants. These were years of harvest failure and starvation, and Rob found himself caught between poor tenants and their landlords, and was exasperated. He wrote of the Barbreck tenants that he would 'gladly be quitt of them and have my victuall [livelihood] elsewhere'.[49]

Another reason that Rob was unhappy with his position at Barbreck was that there was a dispute over possession of the estate. Campbell of Barbreck held his lands, in feudal terms, from the duke of Argyll as his superior, but he had 'wadset' his lands to Breadalbane, meaning that he owed the earl money and that, as interest payments on the capital, the earl had the rights to the rents paid by tenants on the estate. But the situation was confused by a counter-claim on the Barbreck rents by Lord Neil Campbell (a great-uncle of the earl of Argyll). Lord Neil had died in 1692, but his widow pressed her claims, and at some point in the 1690s Rob sent a hasty note to Barcaldine. 'My lady Neill' was 'lifting' the barley of Barbreck, collecting it as rent due to her, and she was summoning tenants to attend her 'courts'. Rob wanted Barcaldine to let him know immediately whether he should try to stop the tenants paying her.[50]

These letters from Inverinan show Rob the family man and harassed employee. In these same years he was, however, also an active cattle raider. The main target of his predatory activities were the huge Atholl estates, and his ability to raid there successfully doubtless owed much to the knowledge that he had the favour of Breadalbane and was safe on his territory. Lord Murray has already been quoted as denouncing Donald Glas as a cheat and enemy of his family, and Rob Roy maintained his father's stance. By May 1695 he had proved troublesome enough for Murray to send out a party of armed men to catch him. The arrangements were made in secrecy, for Murray knew there would be many ready to warn Rob of danger, and he believed Breadalbane 'indeed is his friend because he has taken his name [Campbell] and his lordship has espoused his interest when he was pursued before the justiciary court'.[51] When Rob had been prosecuted before the justiciary court is unknown, but clearly Lord Murray knew that Rob was Breadalbane's man.

Atholl's plan to catch Rob failed. As Murray had feared, his expedition was betrayed, Rob warned to flee. Investigation indicated that it was a soldier, evidently one of the men sent against Rob, who was responsible, one 'Grigor More'. Through a chain of intermediaries he had got word to Rob.[52] The Murrays of Atholl were thwarted, and Rob's policy of balancing Murray enmity against Campbell friendship was working well. But then, from Rob's point of view, disaster struck out of the blue. Breadalbane's fortunes in the murky politics of the period faltered, and he was arrested for treason. Rob was left defenceless, and how dependent he had become on Breadalbane's support is suggested by the speed with which he reacted. Within two weeks he was in Edinburgh, and on 22 June 1695 he signed a grovelling submission to Lord Murray, thanking him for receiving him into his favour 'notwithstanding of my many ungratfull deportments and undecent cariages for some yeares by past'. In return for this favour, Rob would behave as a loyal and dutiful servant to 'this present government' – a convenient phrase whereby Rob could promise to obey the government of the day without compromising his Jacobite sympathies by stating that it was legal. In addition, Rob would become an honest, faithful and obedient servant to Lord Murray, would present himself before his lordship whenever required, and would live honestly, peacefully and quietly, having found men willing to stand surety for him for £1,000 Scots.[53] Murray must have been triumphant. His plans to gain influence over the MacGregors had been thwarted when his candidate for the chieftaincy had been rejected two years before, but now a leading – and the most troublesome – member of the clan was swearing to be his man.

Rob had acted swiftly and decisively to save himself from disaster – but it all turned out to have been unnecessary. Breadalbane was soon freed, after another turn in the bitter political infighting that had led to his arrest, and Rob again could rely on his protection. But he may have felt some sense of obligation to Atholl – who could have sought to have Rob hanged rather than accept his submission. Nothing is heard in the years that followed of his raiding on the Atholl estates.[54] Signs of activity by Atholl's agents late in 1695, seeking to enforce estate regulations in Balquhidder, may well reflect the fact that with Rob subdued they had unusual freedom of action in that difficult frontier of the Murray estates. Measures were taken to protect the area from thieving. Some cattle lifting had already taken place and more was expected, and it was ordered that the tenants, or tacksmen, go out in turns each night with as many of their subtenants as necessary to guard the passes. Once a week all tacksmen and subtenants were to search all the hills for any 'louse or broken men' and arrest any they found.[55]

Though Rob had made his peace with the Murrays, his protector remained Breadalbane, and he was ready to act against lawless fellow MacGregors who threatened the earl's interests. In December 1697 two men, one of them a Campbell, awoke one morning to find themselves surrounded by a gang of MacGregors with drawn swords and cocked pistols, and they were carried off as prisoners. The kidnappers were trying to prevent one of their comrades who had been arrested, Malcolm, from being hung, and they forced their prisoners to sign a bond to have Malcolm freed, or pay a penalty of £1,000 Scots. Thus lawlessness sought to proceed by way of a legal document. The MacGregors then freed the prisoners, but Breadalbane called in Rob to help in hunting them down. Rob's reply (from Portnellan, on Loch Katrine) was that he had already been out trying to catch the fugitives and could do no more. But he assured the earl that 'there is nothing that can lye within the compass of my power' that he would not do for him.[56]

The later 1690s were harsh years for Scotland, with several disastrous harvest failures leading to starvation and widespread suffering. Over Scotland as a whole it is estimated that population may have fallen by 13 per cent.[57] Even Breadalbane came close to ruin, as he had to cancel arrears of unpaid rent and distribute food to 'deserving' tenants. Desperation led to an increase in cattle raiding, and Breadalbane is said to have suffered particularly from the depredations of the Stewarts and MacGregors, in spite of seeking to use Rob Roy against them. The usual conventions of raiding were ignored – gentlemen's houses were attacked, cattle drovers (normally spared as their trade was vital to the Highland economy) were killed.[58] How Rob's fortunes were effected is unknown. There may be a glimpse of him in the records of the sheriff court at Inveraray in 1699, for it is probable that the 'Robert Campbell in Portnellen' involved in taking action against cattle thieves was Rob Roy.[59]

At some point at about this time Rob achieved his ambition to be free from the tenants of Barbreck, and he probably left Breadalbane's employment though the earl remained his patron. A letter of 1699 from Rob to Barcaldine (written from Taymouth, Breadalbane's main residence) reads: 'I have sent home yower sword (and belt) with yower brother James, in as good condition I gote them in if not better, so I desire that yow send my sworde and belt with the bearer in as good condition as yow gott them, for I can want [lack] them no longer. Yower pistol I'le send with the next ocation, so I desire yow may send me myn, for I must send them to Edinburgh to take the mesure of them that I may have cases conformd to that.' What was going on? Perhaps this mysterious exchange of weapons had some symbolic significance, indicating friendship or respect, or was part of a game.[60]

As the country began to recover from famine, Rob was able to add to his landholdings. He already had possession of Inversnaid, and in 1701 he obtained a feu charter not only to it but to the whole of the £10 land of old extent of Craigrostan, stretching several miles down the eastern shore of Loch Lomond. Kilmannan's fortunes were in decline, due to his drinking if nothing else, and he had resigned his feu of Craigrostan to Colquhoun of Luss, who then granted it to Rob.[61] Accounts relating to 1712 show that there were thirteen tenants paying rent to Rob, five of them still calling themselves MacGregor – and having these names recorded in the records of the baron court of Colquhoun of Luss, without any fooling about with 'aliases', two decades after Edinburgh law had outlawed the name.[62] An incomplete rental (some tenants were away from home) of 1713 put the rents due by tenants annually as £455 Scots,[63] and a 1717 rental shows the total as just over £682 Scots. Out of this, however, Rob had to pay £240 Scots as feu duty to Colquhoun of Luss, and £100 in teinds (tithes) to Montrose.[64] After these deductions, Rob's net income from the land was therefore about half the gross, say £340 Scots. His total income would of course have been considerably – but incalculably – larger, as it included the profits of raiding and trading. Robert Campbell of Craigrostan had made the important step up the social ladder from tenant to hereditary landowner.

His next step was to arrange a similar move for his young nephew, James Graham in Glengyle. As his tutor in March 1703 he obtained a feu charter from the marquis of Montrose for Glengyle – a two merk land of old extent – for 1,000 merks entry fee and an annual feu duty of £60. At last the MacGregors in Glengyle – though they had lost their name – had gained a fully recognised hereditary right to their lands. There was to be no doubt in future as to whether they should be referred to as 'in' or 'of', for they were indisputably 'of'. But though they were to be the effective owners of the land, Montrose insisted on the full feudal trappings of vassalage. In name of his nephew and his heirs, Rob Roy undertook to serve Montrose in all his lawful wars and expeditions, and in hosting and hunting, as required, in the same manner as all Montrose's vassals.[65] Rob Roy thus became Montrose's sworn vassal – until his nephew came of age. The negotiation of the 1703 feu charter indicates that Rob was then on good terms with Montrose, and in the years that followed cattle-trading links suggest that Rob was a trusted associate.

When he grew up, James Graham would become head of the Glengyle branch of the MacGregors, but in terms of landed property he was outclassed by his uncle Robert. Rob Roy's Craigrostan was a £10 land, Glengyle only a £2 one. Craigrostan paid four times the annual feu duty Glengyle did. James's younger brother Donald also gained ownership of land through Rob's activities, being granted a feu of Monachayle Tuarach in Balquhidder by the duke of Atholl. As his feudal superior was a Murray, so his new vassal took that name. becoming Donald Murray.[66] There could not be a neater example of the ways in which men switched or chose their names to flatter their superiors. The uncle and his two nephews, all born MacGregor, were now a Campbell, a Graham and a Murray, a nightmare for genealogists

Rob was proving a responsible guardian of Glengyle family interests as well as his personal ones, and the marriage he arranged for Graham of Glengyle in November 1707 served both causes. Graham married Mary Hamilton, daughter of John Hamilton of Bardowie.[67] Mary brought with her a useful tocher (dowry) of 2,000 merks (about £1,330 Scots),[68] and, equally important, brought excellent connections through her kin. The Hamiltons were an old-established family based just north of Glasgow, and until 1708 the bride's brother, John Hamilton younger of Bardowie, was Montrose's factor in the barony of Buchanan, which included Glengyle.[69] Moreover, in the years ahead Bardowie younger was to emerge as one of Rob Roy's closest associates in the cattle dealing business.[70]

Rob made sure that the young couple was housed as befitted their status as 'of Glengyle'. A new house was built at Glengyle, of stone and mortar in Lowland style in contrast to the unmortared stone and turf houses usual in the Highlands. It appears to have been the only such house for many miles around. Twenty years later it was to be described as Glengyle's 'mansion house', though Glengyle's summer residence was said to be a house on the island of 'Yerick' on Loch Katrine.[71] Perhaps Glengyle fancied leading a more traditional life in an old-style house in the summer, before retreating to his more comfortable mansion during the rigours of winter. The house Rob helped build for his nephew forms the basis of the Glengyle House that still stands, and stones over the front door bear the dates 1704 and 1728,[72] the first suggesting that building may have begun soon after feu of Glengyle was obtained. Nearby is the family burial ground of the Glengyle MacGregors. The close interest that Rob took in the building of the new house is revealed by a letter he wrote to Breadalbane just weeks before the marriage. 'I presume to tell your Lordship that I have the honour to have come of your Lordship's family, and shall keep my dependancy suitable to the samine [same],' he wrote in fulsome terms. The promise of service he had given to the earl would 'be keeped while I live', and even after he was in his grave, his nephew would serve the earl loyally. That a favour is about to be requested is becoming obvious. Breadalbane had promised to send four trees to help build his nephew's new house: please would he send them now.[73] The timber would have been for the 'couples', the main roof-beams of the house, for modest though the new mansion was, it was hard to find large enough trees in many Highland areas to roof such a building. If tradition were followed, as the couples were raised into position, a woman would have helped in the work, to bring good luck to the household. Perhaps too a goat's head was thrown over the couples – though that had to be done carefully, for if it touched the beams in its flight the omens would be bad rather than good. When the first fire was kindled in the house, a piece of iron would be concealed below the hearth.[74]

From 1701 Rob Roy had been entitled to call himself 'of Craigrostan', but the established 'of Inversnaid' stuck. The property might be only part of Craigrostan, but he had held it longest, and its name had become associated with him. He had a house there, and local tradition hopefully points out a series of mounds and hollows on the west side of the Snaid Burn, close to where it joins the Arklet Water.[75] However, Rob spent much of his time in Portnellan, judging from the number of letters he dispatched from there, and he probably had a house there – perhaps he occupied the house that it is said Glengyle possessed there.[76] Portnellan lay about a mile south of Glengyle House, and Rob probably found it convenient as it was on the point on the drove road down the north side of Loch Katrine at which a path branched off over the hills to Balquhidder. It was a good place from which to keep his finger on the pulses of the Lomond MacGregors and their kinsmen to the north. A century later a visitor was shown 'a hut' at Portnellan as being the former residence of Rob Roy.[77]

In the first decade of the eighteenth century Rob Roy emerged as a solid citizen, respected and trusted – or at least trusted commercially, for there were always doubts about the underlying political sympathies of former MacGregors, as indeed of many other Highlanders. Most of the evidence about his activities that survives takes the form of bonds, contracts and other legal papers. There is no hint of the cattle-raider of younger days. He was now in his thirties, a family man with children, and may have decided to confine himself to legitimate trading. He had become successful as a cattle dealer, and was buying cattle for Montrose as least as early as 1703.[78] Perhaps through Montrose's recommendation, he gained other Lowland clients – lairds, lawyers, merchants and others – and as well as cattle he can be traced trading in horses, sheep, meal and timber.[79] In 1702 he can be glimpsed recruiting men for the army. The earl of Moray in August ordered his agent to 'remember the men for Liftenant Holburn, and send to Rob Roye for his. Let them be sent to Clakmanen where their company is quartered'. This was followed up by a sharp reminder the following month – 'I wonder you have not yet sent Liftenant Holburn the Men I promised him – pray let it be done without delay, and send to Rob: Roye for his men.'[80]

Trade must have been profitable, for Rob was able to make modest extensions to his landholdings. In 1705 he rented the farm of Arroch Beg for nine years from Montrose, with the usual promises of services as a vassal in hosting, hunting and so on.[81] About 1710 he acquired Ardress from him as well.[82] Both lay on Loch Lomond, south of Craigrostan, but Rob was also interested in land in other areas. On Loch Katrine he acquired a four year lease of east Portnellan and Cornechan in 1711, again from Montrose.[83] By 1711 he had also possession of Driep and Craigan [Drip and Creggans] in Argyllshire, with the right to the ferry there.[84] These lands lay near Strachur on the east shore of Loch Fyne, and Rob's interest may have been in the ferry, in connection with the cattle trade. It may be coincidence, but Ardress lay just north of Rowardennan, a recognised point for swimming cattle across Loch Lomond. There are also references to Rob having a tack or lease (which expired in 1711) of the Forest of Benmore, Coirechaorach and 'Invermonechell' in Glen Dochart, held from the Drummonds of Perth.[85]

In the tangles of financial deals concerning land it is sometimes hard to sort out quite who had actual possession of lands, and rights to collect their rents at any given time. A wadset of Inversnaid held by John Graham of Corriearklet was resigned to Rob in 1706, after the former's death, by his children's tutors, led by Walter Graham of Drunkie, but then in 1710 Inversnaid was handed back to Drunkie and the tutors in a feu of Inversnaid by Rob.[86] Probably this simply reflects financial adjustments within the family, but it seems odd that Rob would grant a feu of Inversnaid if, as is usually assumed, his main home was there. Whatever the precise situation, Rob continued generally to be referred to – and presumably to refer to himself as – 'of Inversnaid'.

Overall, the surving bonds and other legal papers give the impression of Rob Roy as an active business man, buying and selling, borrowing and lending. There were routine business problems too – complaints of late delivery of cattle by Rob. In 1703 one of Montrose's agents noticed a delivery was late,[87] and in 1706–7 Rob was in trouble with MacKenzie of Delvine (whom he addressed as his cousin), with whom he had financial dealings. Craving a delay in meeting his commitments, Rob explained that if he were forced to settle his debt immediately he would have to sell cattle at a loss.[88] Occasionally there are signs also of a less orderly and respectable life. In August 1702 a case between Rob and Thomas MacPherson from Badenoch was pending before the commissioners for securing the peace of the Highlands. Some 'debate' between the parties led MacPherson to complain to the magistrates of Perth. Rob was forced to sign a bond of caution not to molest Macpherson or his men, under pain of £500 Scots. Colin Campbell of Glendaruel acted as cautioner.[89] As this was exactly the time that Rob was recruiting soldiers for the earl of Moray, it is tempting to connect that with the bond. Possibly Rob in serving Moray, to the north and east of his usual areas of activity, had been raising men in Badenoch and incurred Macpherson's displeasure.

Rob's life in the opening years of the eighteenth century must have involved extensive travelling – to the west Highlands and Isles to buy cattle, to Lowland markets at Crieff, Stirling and elsewhere to sell them or deliver them to his customers or their agents. Legal and other business brought him to Edinburgh from time to time. A Gaelic epitaph was to recall:

> You were the hawk of the people,
> Rob Roy's what they called you –
> You look good wearing plaid and sword.

It was claimed that:

Well do a hat and a cloak
With trimmings of gold
Suit your name, and it's no boast to say it.[90]

It has been pointed out that this recognises Rob as a man at ease in two worlds. In the Highlands he wore his native plaid and carried arms; in the Lowlands he dressed in a cloak and hat – and no doubt the breeches which to the Lowlander marked their 'civilisation' as opposed to bare-legged Highland 'barbarism'. But though Rob was at home in the Lowlands, there is no evidence whatever that he drove cattle into England or visited London, as has often been claimed.

Rob's travelling was primarily commercial in nature, but it allowed him to keep in touch with more than just business affairs in the Highlands. Bubbling just beneath the surface there was always political ferment. These were years of endless Jacobite dreams, and occasional plots, and Rob from his position as a leading MacGregor could not fail to be involved in talk of such things, and to be invited to participate in the many confused and hopeless schemes that floated around the region. That his heart was with the Stuart cause cannot be doubted, but he was cautious and realistic, concentrating on business and avoiding involvement in idealistic folly. Yet his identity meant that he could not escape suspicion. A report in about 1705 which listed those who were discontented in Scotland included 'the whole Macgregors headed by one Rob Roy commonly called by that name',[91] a tribute to Rob's growing reputation as an outstanding figure in his clan, but an embarrassment to Rob the businessman. In fact when Rob Roy had been approached by an unscrupulous and scheming Jacobite plotter the previous year he had hastened to clear himself – and gain favour – by revealing what had happened.

Rob had long been acquainted with Simon Fraser younger of Beaufort, for Fraser had been one of the witnesses of his submission to Lord Murray in 1695. In 1697, however, Fraser had made himself the most notorious man in Scotland. Lord Lovat, the head of Fraser's kin, had died, leaving a daughter but no male heir. Fraser had a claim to the title, and decided to take drastic measures to ensure he got it. He planned first to abduct and marry the dead Lord Lovat's daughter. When this scheme failed, he abducted her mother, the dowager Lady Lovat, instead, forced her into marriage, and then bedded her while his pipers played to drown her cries. Such tactics to gain control of widows and heiresses were not unknown in the past, but Fraser's action was unusually risky. Lady Lovat had extremely powerful kinsmen, for she was Emilia Murray, the daughter of the marquis of Atholl. Her rape brought down the enmity of the Murrays on him. At first this seemed likely to be fatal, for a case was brought against Fraser for treason, as he had been involved in Jacobite intrigues. The same charge could have been brought against many in Scotland who were not being prosecuted, but revulsion against Fraser's treatment of Lady Lovat led to his being singled out and condemned to death. He escaped with his life, however, in much the same way as Rob Roy had done in the past and was to do in the future, by exploiting the rivalries of great men. If the marquis of Atholl was seeking Fraser's life, this was sufficient reason for the duke of Argyll to obtain a pardon for him. It demonstrated that Argyll's political influence was greater than Atholl's, which was far more important than seeing justice done.

Lovat's treason having been pardoned, the Murrays fell back on a charge of rape, which they might have been wise to have stuck to in the first place. Even Argyll, it seems, felt he could not support Fraser, and in 1701 he was outlawed after he failed to appear for trial. He fled to France and became deeply involved in Jacobite plotting, putting forward plans for a rising in Scotland to be supported by a French invasion. He then got himself sent back to Scotland to investigate what support there would be for such a venture, but it became clear that he was more concerned in plotting against his enemies, the Murrays, now represented by the duke of Atholl (the former Lord Murray) than with the Jacobite cause. Fraser sought to achieve his objectives by helping the duke of Queensberry, the dominant minister in Scottish politics, to discredit his rivals, the dukes of Atholl and Hamilton. This he tried to do by providing evidence that they were guilty of treasonous Jacobite conspiracies. Gratitude, Fraser presumably hoped, would then bring him pardon for absconding before his trial for rape.

The plot backfired. Fraser's schemes were betrayed, and in 1703–4 the scandal was publicised as 'the Scotch Plot' or 'the Queensberry Plot'. In January 1704 Atholl revealed to a meeting of the Scots council in London the intelligence he had gathered on how Fraser was seeking to destroy him,[92] and though Queensberry survived this debacle his reputation was badly shaken.

Rob Roy must have been watching the unravelling of the plot anxiously, for he had had contacts with Simon Fraser since the latter had returned to Scotland, and had kept quiet about them. The revelations about the plot had not mentioned his name, but he feared that it might emerge. He therefore took the initiative, to protect himself. At the beginning of February 1704, a month after Atholl had detailed Fraser's plot to destroy him, Rob appeared at Atholl's lodgings in Holyrood House. The duke was still absent in London, so Rob made his revelations to the duchess, and was questioned by the duke's agent, Patrick Scott. The duchess then wrote to her husband that Rob had given her some information 'about the plot, and that she was convinced he could tell enough if he liked'.[93] Notes on the meeting by Scott were also sent to the duke.

Rob had only just got his version of events in in time, for on 6 January the duchess's eldest son Lord Tullibardine had written to tell her that he was certain that Simon Fraser had met the earl of Breadalbane, Lord Drummond and Drummond (MacGregor) of Balhaldie, and that 'he either saw or sent to the cheif of the Mcgregoirs'.[94] It is possible that the chief referred to was the discredited Graham of Kilmannan, but perhaps more likely that it was Rob Roy who was meant.

Quite what Rob revealed to the duchess and Scott is unclear. The duke was enraged by how little Scott had told him, and his agent felt the ducal anger. Scott apologised for the fact that his notes on Rob's 'declaration' were 'so ill writt' but he had not expected them to be sent to the duke, and he had written in haste. Moreover he had not taken Rob seriously, 'for I really took it for stories of his own making and not materiall, which made me write it so carelessly and that [I believed] it was all hear say'. Rob had by this time left Edinburgh so could not be questioned further, and when Scott sought an alternative source of information in Graham of Kilmannan, who was in town, 'I either missed him or found him so drunk I could not understand what he said.' Scott tried to pull his thoughts together. As he remembered, Simon Fraser had written – or perhaps indicated that he was going to write – to Rob, but Rob had let Fraser know that he could not trust him. Indeed, Rob had told Fraser that he 'would deliver him up to your Grace [Atholl]'. This sounds a bit too good to be true. Rob self-servingly presents himself as so loyal to Atholl that he wanted to hand over to him anyone who plotted against him. Scott added, for what it is worth, that he knew that Rob had actually written to Fraser.[95]

The picture is confused, but it sounds as though Rob had had some contact with Fraser, and though he declined to take part in his schemes he had not exposed them, understandably seeking to avoid any involvement. But when the plot unravelled, he had acted to insure himself in case allegations against him were made. As when he had submitted to Atholl in 1695, Rob had shown the ability to move to deal with a threat quickly and decisively. Later in 1704 he again emphasised his willingness to protect Atholl's interests. He tipped him off that Archibald Campbell of Finab, captain of one of the independent companies of the army which were supposed to help keep order in the Highlands, had conscripted two of Atholl's men as soldiers. One had evidently escaped, but Atholl was urged to ensure the other was released as well. If he didn't, it would seem anyone might mistreat Atholl's followers with impunity.[96]

The confusion and panic of the 'Scotch Plot' soon died down, but Scotland was soon split over the momentous matter of whether the country should accept a parliamentary union with England. An anecdote suggests that Rob took a close interest in the debates. Alexander Abercromby of Tullibody recalled that when he had been the doorkeeper to the duke of Hamilton's club at the union parliament, he had known Rob Roy. Hamilton was leading opposition to the union and his 'club' comprised his supporters. That Rob should oppose the union, to which the Jacobites were hostile, is hardly surprising, and this story indicates that he was active in his opposition and mingled with some of the politicians involved.[97]

The act of union was pushed through, but hostility to it was so widespread that fears of a French-supported Jacobite rising remained strong. They were justified. Early in 1708 a French fleet entered the Firth of Forth carrying troops and the 'Pretender' James Edward Stuart, son of the dethroned James VII and thus, in Jacobite eyes, the rightful king. The timing was good, as the union was so unpopular in Scotland many might be tempted into Jacobitism in the hope of repealing it. But the commander of the French fleet was half-hearted, and the arrival of a pursuing British fleet gave him a good excuse for turning for home without attempting a landing. A few over-eager Stirlingshire gentry who had risen in arms were arrested,[98] being the only Jacobites foolish enough to rise prematurely. But the government was panic stricken by the news of the French venture, and ordered the arrest of a number of suspect Scottish nobles in March.[99] Atholl and Breadalbane were among them, but both produced elaborate excuses for being unable to travel to Edinburgh or London to surrender. For Atholl it was claimed that he had retired home after the death of his wife a year before, turned 'hectic' with grief, and had paid no attention to public affairs. Breadalbane pleaded age (with justification, as he was seventy-three), that he was recovering from a high fever, and was still in pain from earlier breaks to an arm and a leg. The government compromised, realising that trying to carry them off by force would be likely to provoke their clansmen into resistance, so they escaped with house arrest, Atholl protesting at the humiliation of having two soldiers guarding his chamber door.[100]

It soon became clear that the French threat had passed, and all the Scots nobles arrested were released in June – with the sole exception of Atholl.[101] Instead, on 26 June it was ruled that he should be brought to Edinburgh for questioning on charges of high treason.[102] He petitioned to be allowed bail, on account of his being 'verie weak by his long confinment and siknes', and this was agreed by the end of July.[103] He had been singled out for special treatment not because there was any real evidence of treasonable dealings on his part, but through political rivalry. His opposition to the union of 1707 had brought him the wrath of the new British ministry,[104] and the treason charges were intended as a warning to him to behave. The message having been delivered, the charges themselves were dropped.

The simultaneous arrests of Breadalbane and Atholl must have worried Rob Roy. When the first had been arrested in 1695, he had been able to gain the protection of the Murrays of Atholl instead, and he had been careful to remain on good terms with them. Now he had lost both his protectors, and had the hunt for suspected Jacobite sympathisers gone further he might have faced questioning himself. But the crisis passed, and Rob retained his image of respectable business man. One of his deals, however, had political ramifications that brought him to government attention. In June 1710 the earl of Leven, the commander-in-chief of the army in Scotland, received intelligence that four to five hundred firelock muskets and hundreds of pistols and swords were in the hands of a Glasgow merchant. They had been ordered some months before, and were to be sent into the Highlands – indeed a hundred (muskets) had already been sent. The carrying of firearms and trading in them was perfectly legal, so no direct action could be taken, but clearly a bulk order for arms from the Highlands was a cause for concern. The magistrates of Glasgow were therefore asked to find out who was buying the weapons, and let Leven know before they were dispatched. By October Leven had dealt with the problem. He had, he reported, inquired about 'some armes that were bought by a highland man called Rob Roy, and caried into the Highlands by him', and somehow he had got all but a few of them into his own custody.[105]

Rob had added arms dealing to his other interests. There is no clue as to the identity of his customer or customers, but it is highly likely that they were Jacobites and that he had agreed to act as an intermediary. But this does not mean that he can be classified as a Jacobite activist. He was a businessman looking for profit through a transaction that was fully legal. In the end the arms did not fall into in the hands of the intended customers, but Rob probably still made a profit – Leven had presumably had to pay Rob for them.

Rob Roy had many dealings with Jacobites. They no doubt talked of the Stuarts and drank toasts to the exiled dynasty, but there is no way of knowing whether things went any further than mere talk. The most plausible scenario is that Rob was on the fringes of Jacobite intrigues, a known figure who might be talked to and trusted to keep his mouth shut, but who kept clear of real involvement. His ideological commitment was there, but not strong enough to risk all for the cause when circumstances offered no hope of success. His business was what mattered. It is notable that when Campbell of Finab wrote to Montrose in 1710 complaining that some of the men on his lands were persistent cattle thieves, he singled out one who was a sub-tenant of Rob Roy's, but there is no sign of suspicion of Rob himself.[106] However, Rob's career as a legitimate businessman was almost at an end. Bankruptcy loomed, and with it was to come the inveterate hatred of one of the great men who dominated his world, the duke of Montrose. Survival was to depend on retaining support from other great men, and Rob was by this time an expert on their strengths, weakness and rivalries.

3

DOWNFALL

Rob's business had its ups and downs, but overall the impression is that he was thriving, and expanding his activities. Occasional complaints about late deliveries look not like omens of coming doom so much as of routine and temporary difficulties with cash-flow and cattle-flow. Sometimes legal actions were begun against him by creditors. In 1709 several 'captions' were obtained against him, orders that he be arrested as he had failed to obey previous orders to pay his creditors.[1] Rob survived, but in view of his financial collapse three years later it may be that he was already so deeply ensnared in debt that long-term viability was already impossible. In the short term, he was lucky that his credibility survived. His business very much depended on his personal reputation and credit rating. Customers entrusted him with considerable sums of money each autumn to buy cattle for them deep in the Highlands and deliver to them to Lowland markets the following spring. But though there seem to have been plenty of customers ready to do business with him, by the second half of 1711 there are renewed signs that things were beginning to go wrong again.

A customer of importance and influence lost trust in him, and in a letter of 30 August Rob showed signs of panic. As he saw it, he had been let down by a friend – and indeed a relation. John MacKenzie of Delvine was a man of some standing, a prominent advocate in Edinburgh and principal clerk of the court of session. He was owed money by Rob – evidently a significant amount. Rob had been late in payments to Delvine some years before (as noted in the previous chapter), yet Delvine had continued to buy cattle through him. Now, in 1711, payments were again overdue, and Delvine's patience reached breaking point. He passed one of the bonds (or bills of exchange) by which Rob was bound to make a payment to him to one Donald Stewart and his comrades, endorsing it so they had the right to collect the money due on it. Doubtless he sold it to Stewart at a discount, perhaps meaning this as a warning to Rob – something on the lines of 'I've sold one of your bonds cheap, which suggests doubts as to your creditworthiness, so you had better pay up on other bonds due to me.' Delvine was right to be worried about his money. When Rob went bankrupt the following year he was still owed about £50 sterling.[2]

Donald Stewart and his colleagues did not approach Rob directly for payment, but bypassed him and took legal action to make people who owed money to Rob pay them instead, to settle the bond they had taken over from Delvine. This meant not only that Rob could not collect monies due to him, but, much worse, that his credit-rating was being publicly undermined. He was horrified, and expressed astonished indignation that Delvine 'when I was on top of my business would asigne my bond to those who if they were able wid [would] brake my credit, and did all they could'. Rob continued, 'I admire [am amazed] how he [Delvine] whom is reckond the trewest highlandman did ofer to rube upon [harm] me who can recon [reckon] myself his relation and hes a dependencie on his ain name besyds.'[3] How far Rob's words are to be trusted is unclear. Businessmen, when rumours circulate about their liquidity, are always likely to claim that all is well, their business thriving, and protestations of injured innocence were to become one of Rob's hallmarks.

Rob was shocked and worried by Delvine's action over the bond, but apart from that on the surface all seemed well. Rob continued his cattle dealings, and appears in the role of a man public-spiritedly ready to help deal with local problems. In June 1711 he and Breadalbane arbitrated in a row over ownership of a cow.[4] In September he was again in touch with the earl in solving a financial dispute between other men over a bond.[5] These were minor matters, but give the impression of a respected figure trusted to sort out such problems, and in doing so making himself useful to his great patron. It was in October 1711 that Rob took sasine of Drip and Creggans in Argyllshire,[6] again suggesting that nothing was wrong.

Yet hidden beneath this public image it seems that Rob was already in deep financial trouble. No direct link between his downfall and Delvine's action can be traced, but in retrospect it seems prophetic. Why Rob's business was failing is unknown. Perhaps he had expanded too fast, borrowed too much. Perhaps he had been unlucky in his predictions of fluctuations in cattle prices. But by the end of the year he knew he faced bankruptcy. It was a harsh reality, a collapse of ambitions for himself and his family. In a broader context, however, the matter might have been no more than a routine business failure. Such cases were common – and many landowners lived in chronic debt for generations without ever actually going bankrupt. If you could not pay your debts and creditors threatened or began legal action, you negotiated with them. Usually, in cold financial terms, it made far better sense for creditors to compromise and agree to delayed payments or less than 100 per cent payments, accepting property as security, rather than to drive debtors into bankruptcy.

There seems no reason why Rob could not have taken this option. He was a skilful negotiator, usually ready to bargain and offer a deal. But in this case he changed his life for ever by refusing to take the obvious way out, letting his heart rule his head. He could not bring himself to give up much of what he built – not just his landholdings but his position as the best-known and respected man of the Clan Gregor – without a fight. In the previous decade he had escaped the stereotype of what a MacGregor was – poor and lawless. He had an inherent sense of being a member of an élite in Highland terms, being a Gregor of the blood of King Alpin, and had added to this Lowland respectability as a man of commerce and land. To give this up without a fight would be a matter of failure and shame, impossible for a man of honour.

Yet to preserve his honour he hatched a scheme which involved dishonour as well as illegality. It also involved reverting temporarily to what was seen as typical MacGregor behaviour – theft and deception. But, as Rob was a man who kept up with the times, his actions were to involve not the theft of cattle, but of money intended to be used to buy cattle. Up to this point Rob, so far as is known, had acted honestly as a businessman. He might be failing financially and unable to pay his debts in full, but he had not acted deliberately to defraud anyone. Now he decided on a grand scheme of planned deceit. He never admitted this, so it could be said that there is no direct proof of his planned dishonesty. But the circumstantial evidence, the course of action he took from late 1711 onwards, is overwhelming. It is a case of action speaking louder than words – in this case Rob's own conduct speaking more honestly than his words.

His scheme was a desperate one. He would transfer his property to friends and family, to protect it from the claims of creditors. He would continue trading, and indeed expand his activities as much as possible, collecting all the money he could in return for contracting to buy cattle for delivery in the spring of 1712. But when spring came, there would be no cattle, and Rob and his customers' money would be deep in the Highlands, beyond the reach of the law. What he expected to happen next, it seems, was that he could revert to the conventional behaviour of someone who faced bankruptcy – and negotiate a settlement. He would be able to do so from a position of strength, for he had the money and was safe in Highlands. Whatever the morality of his conduct, whatever the fury of those creditors who realised that Rob had intended to swindle them from the moment he took their money, they would surely settle and abstain from legal proceedings against him when he offered them a percentage and it seemed that they would get nothing if they refused to do a deal. Rob could then emerge from his Highland fastness, take back his lands, and, hopefully, live happily ever after. It was a bold plan, hugely risky, but, Rob decided, better than simple surrender to his creditors. The larger the sum he went bankrupt for, the cynical calculation seems to have been, the more he would be left with if his creditors settled for a percentage of their due.

The first trace of Rob's preparations comes on 18 December 1711. Rob Roy then signed a disposition of his lands of Ardress and Craigrostan. He transferred the lands jointly to John Hamilton of Bardowie and to Bardowie's brother-in-law (and Rob's nephew) James Graham of Glengyle. In return Rob was to receive payment of one penny Scots a year.[7] The transaction remained secret, not registered in Edinburgh, for if it had become public it would have immediately been obvious that he was trying to protect his estate from creditors. They would have moved in immediately and Rob's business would have collapsed. By keeping it secret Rob could continue to raise money from customers, and only when customers began to realise that they had been swindled would the disposition be swiftly registered in the official record, the register of sasines, which would give it added legal force.

The ploy of preparing for financial ruin by transferring property to friends is a timeless one. But there is a complication in this case that may well indicate that Rob was under pressure to sign the disposition. After he became bankrupt it became clear that by far the biggest of his creditors was Hamilton of Bardowie. Thus the transfer of Craigrostan to Bardowie and Glengyle was probably partly designed to keep his biggest creditor off his back for a time. When the crash

came, Bardowie would be 'most favoured creditor', in a far better
position to get his debts paid than the other creditors. Moreover,
immediately the disposition was made, Bardowie lent Rob a further
3,000 merks (about £175 sterling).[8] Rob may have needed this
immediate cash injection to keep up his 'business as usual' pretence,
and perhaps Bardowie would only advance him the money in return
for the disposition. Bardowie was later to claim the disposition of
Craigrostan in his favour was legal. Rob had owed him money, and
had made a move towards repayment by the transfer of land. It was
to take several years of legal proceedings before the court of session
ruled the disposition invalid, as it had been made in the knowledge
that Rob was going bankrupt and its intention had been to defraud
his other creditors. On the question of whether the relationship
between Rob and Bardowie was that of debtor and creditor, or of
co-conspirators it is impossible to decide: in all likelihood elements
of both were present.

Rob had now coordinated his plans with Bardowie and Glengyle.
It would be surprising if he had not also checked with his patron
Breadalbane to assure himself of continued protection. The accounts
of the earl's chamberlain, John Campbell, note payments to John
Maltman for twice carrying messages to Rob Roy in December 1711.
The use of a special messenger suggests urgency and importance, not
just routine letters. It is tempting to see in this a trace of consultation
between Rob and Breadalbane on the former's financial crisis. The
old fox, legendary for his guile, was, it may be suspected, advising
his protégé in his time of need.

The disposition of Rob's lands being settled, he continued to sign
new contracts for the delivery of cattle and to collect the money to
pay for them. The last such contract he is known to have accepted
was dated as late as 5 April 1712, and it was perhaps the biggest
of all. He agreed to deliver to Thomas Brisbane of Bishopton 200
cows and 4 bulls.[9] No wonder his creditors were later to allege
bitterly that right up to the last minute Rob used his good reputation
'for filling his hands with money'[10] before defaulting on his debts.
In these early months of 1712 Rob remained a respected figure, a
man known to have influence with the duke of Montrose. In March
1712 Colin Fairfoul, a lieutenant in Campbell of Finab's independent
company, was worried that the duke's lack of favour to him was due
to something Rob Roy had said. In April Rob intervened on behalf of
a man who couldn't get a house because of the duke's displeasure.[11]

Having a word with Rob was a good way to the duke's ear. But by the end of April cracks were beginning to appear in the facade. William Buchanan, of Tarbert on the west shore of Loch Lomond, had captions issued against Rob to enforce payment of debts of over £100 sterling, a substantial sum.[12] Perhaps no one took much notice, but the end could not be delayed for long, for the time for delivery of cattle to customers was fast approaching. None were delivered, and soon the creditors realised that none ever would be.

Glengyle was happy to help Rob delay the inevitable by maintaining the pretence that all was well. One of Rob's customers wrote to him, hoping to find out why his cattle were late. On 11 June 1712 Glengyle replied reassuringly, explaining that his uncle Rob had gone north to meet his cows, and he apologised for the fact that Rob had failed to keep in touch, mentioning that Rob had met with some 'disappointments'. However, given a little time, the customer would receive 'satisfaction'.[13] Such talk could only conceal the truth for a matter of days. Montrose, one of Rob's minor (in financial terms) creditors had already realised that he had been defrauded, and had sent the contracts he had made with Rob to his Edinburgh lawyer, George Robertson, so that action could be taken. On 12 June Robertson wrote to Mungo Graham of Gorthie, Montrose's chamberlain, to tell him that he was ready to 'raise diligence' on them – that is, to take legal action for the recovery of debt.[14]

Now the secret was out part of Rob's plan was put into effect by his nominees, who had been poised for action. On 13 June Bardowie and Glengyle, by right of Rob's disposition signed the previous December, formally took sasine (possession) of Craigrostan and Ardress. A week later the documentation for their act had reached Edinburgh and the sasine had been recorded in the register of sasines.[15]

If any of Rob's creditors had had any lingering hopes that he might have been acting in good faith and would eventually produce cattle – or repay their money – this now vanished. Rob was revealed as having laid plans six months in advance to try to defraud them. They therefore hurried to take legal action through the formal processes of diligence. The first step was to have Rob 'put to the horn' – not (as it sounds) an unpleasant torture, but a court-enforced demand for payment of debt. If payment was not made, then an order to seize the debtor's personal (as opposed to landed) property would be made by the court of session, Scotland's supreme civil court.

Rob was now technically an outlaw, though in practice many

people remained at 'the horn' for considerable periods without much inconvenience while negotiations were carried out. In effect issuing the letters was normally a threat of further action to force a debtor to bargain with his creditors. Most of Rob's movable goods were within the regality of Montrose, and the duke therefore had the power to seize them, thus short-circuiting the processes of the central courts. The lands Rob had rented from Montrose could also easily be secured, through the duke cancelling his tenancy. But the lands held hereditarily by Rob and transferred to Bardowie and Glengyle were a different matter – as Rob had intended.

George Robertson's legal advice was that Rob's disposition of his lands could be declared invalid, on the grounds that he had been a bankrupt *in meditatione fugae* (intending to flee) when he signed it. 'Rob Roy will fall under the qualification of bankrupt at the time by his absconding and by diligence being against him, so that his heretable estate will be open to diligence, and after year and day his liferent escheit [forfeiture] will fall, upon his denunciation [in court], to your grace, of such lands as he holds of you, or to his other superiors from whom your Grace will get a gift.' But overthrowing the disposition would require court proceedings, though Robertson thought there was no need for haste in this, as it might turn out that Rob's personal property, when seized, would be sufficient to cover his debts.[16] He was wrong, for it quickly emerged that Rob's debts were much greater than had been realised.

Though routine legal process to recover debt were now underway, in the eyes of Montrose's chamberlain, Mungo Graham of Gorthie, this was not enough. Gorthie's reputation generally was that of a mild man, but in this case he may have been influenced both by his master's fury at being betrayed by a man he had trusted, and by rumours that Rob intended to flee abroad to join the Pretender,[17] carrying £1,000 sterling in gold with him. On Gorthie's instructions, George Robertson sketched an advertisement to be placed in an Edinburgh newspaper publicly denouncing Rob,[18] scribbling his draft on a scrap of paper torn from a letter. Robert Campbell, commonly known as Rob Roy MacGregor, had been entrusted by several noblemen and gentlemen with considerable sums of money for buying cows in the Highlands, ran the announcement. But he had treacherously run off with the money, upwards of £1,000 sterling. All magistrates and all officers of the army were therefore urged to seize him and his money, so he could be detained until the cases against him were heard.

Anyone who apprehended him should let the keepers of the Exchange Coffee House in Edinburgh, or the Glasgow Coffee House, know, and the news would be passed on to Rob's creditors. A reasonable reward would be given for such service.[19]

The advertisement duly appeared in *The Edinburgh Gazette*, and in the *Scots Courant* (18–20 June 1712, and six subsequent issues).[20] This publicity had a clear, practical purpose. Legal proceedings against debtors took time. Rob Roy was on the run, perhaps to the Continent, so it seemed to Montrose and his servants that some incentive to swift action was needed if Rob were to be arrested and their money recovered. But his private initiative in publicising the case and offering a reward for Rob's capture had far wider consequences. What Rob had presumably hoped would be a fairly routine case of debt after the initial fuss had died down, now became a sensational case being widely discussed. Moreover, though Montrose's name did not appear in the advertisement denouncing Rob, it became well known that he had committed himself to leadership of the attempt to catch Rob Roy. This probably made it difficult for Montrose, once his initial fury at being conned by a mere MacGregor cattle-dealer had passed, to agree to any compromise. From Rob's point of view the announcement in the gazette publicising his downfall and urging that he be hunted down as a thief was a disaster. Whatever hopes he may have had of negotiating at leisure with individual creditors from the safety of some remote place in the Highlands had now been greatly diminished. The hunt had begun.

Rumours about Rob's bankruptcy spread fast. One said Rob was – or had been – with Atholl, the marquis of Huntly, and other Highland chiefs, demonstrating the fear that he was involved in a Jacobite plot. John Douglas, Atholl's agent in Edinburgh, hastened to warn his master of this. Atholl's enemies alleged that he had met Rob after publication of the advertisement denouncing him. Douglas was sure this was not true. Indeed he knew 'to my certain knowledge' that Atholl 'had no kindness for that fellow'. But if Atholl had, after all seen Rob, then John Douglas hoped 'it was only by accident, and before any thing was discovered anent [about] him', for 'Montrose is making all the search imaginable of his wayes and conversation since he went away.'[21] It sounds as though Douglas feared Atholl had indeed been in touch with Rob but, as a good lawyer, was avoiding saying so while hinting that his master should be careful to cover his tracks.

Rob Roy's own version of events first appeared in a letter he wrote late in June to James Graham, writer (lawyer) in Glasgow. Graham was one of his creditors, but perhaps one he felt likely to give him a hearing. He apologised for his unpaid debts, but urged that he could be trusted. Some people might think that what had happened was a matter of 'design' (advance planning) but he asserted his honesty. He had money with him, Rob stated, and he would use it to pay Graham. Indeed so long as he had a groat (four pennies) left he would strive to pay him. Rob claimed that the fact that he had disappeared deep into the Highlands, inaccessible to his creditors, was not in fact flight but a positive move to sort out his financial difficulties. He was pursuing two debtors to exact payment from them, one of whom was on the Long Island (Lewis and Harris), one on South Uist. They had disposed of all their goods and were preparing to flee with considerable sums of money. 'I'll never return to my own countrey till I'll know what to doe with these people ffor if they will stay in Scotland or Ireland with God's assistance I will gett a grip of them for all the highlands has such a kindnes [friendship] for me in generall that they will assist me what ever place I will gett them taken.' He hoped to return by the end of August, having at least these men's 'gear' – movable possessions – which should come near to paying off all his creditors. But, he warned, if legal processes were begun against him, this would add legal expenses to his debts, and he would be unable to pay creditors in full. Similarly, if he was imprisoned, he would be unable to track down his debtors in order to pay off his own debts. It would be much better if he were to remain a free man, able to return to his home. And both Breadalbane and Lord Drummond had offered to make a collection for him in the Highlands 'before I should goe out of the contrey'.[22]

At first sight this may seem plausible, an honest man striving to do his duty by his creditors. On closer examination inconsistencies, unanswered questions and implicit threats emerge. If there had been no advance planning, why had he disposed of his lands six months before, and continued to trade when he could not even pay existing debts? Rob provided no direct explanation of why he had brought no cows to market. That two bad debts in the Outer Isles had left Rob unable to supply even a single cow towards honouring all his 1711–12 contracts hardly seems plausible. What had happened to the over £1,000 sterling he had collected from his customers? The hint of going to Ireland suggested that if pursued too hard he might flee beyond even nominal Scottish jurisdiction. And underlying this is the wider message that trying to force him to pay up instead of negotiating would be counter-productive. If his creditors took action against him, they would get nothing. Leave him to his own devices, and he would be able to pay them at least something. The mention of two leading Highland noblemen ready to help him is another hint that action against him would not be a good idea. His creditors need not think that having Montrose to lead them would bring them advantage, because Rob had the greatness of Breadalbane and Drummond as counter-weights. Rob's reference to Highlanders in general having a 'kindness' for him also carries a message: not only have I great men ready to help me, I'm so well liked that ordinary Highlanders will not betray me to my enemies.

Neither in this letter nor in later ones did Rob ever attempt to answer the central question of what had happened to the £1,000 sterling with which he had disappeared. In all his self-justifications in the months and years ahead he never tackled the issue. Were even his powers of invention challenged? Later legend, anxious to vindicate Rob and aware of this gap in his argument for the defence, was to provide a simple solution. Rob had entrusted the money to a drover (sometimes identified as 'MacDonald')[23] who ran off with it.[24] From the start, Rob was the victim, not the guilty. But Rob himself never mentioned this mysterious drover.

Overall, Rob's letter of self-justification was cunningly crafted and evasive, with hints and hidden messages meant simultaneously to tell creditors that they would be paid, and that trying to take action against him would be fruitless – even damaging. But some of what he wrote was ill-advised. The idea that his two noble friends were founding a charitable 'Save Rob Roy' fund is bizarre, and his claim that he might have to go to Ireland in search of those who owed him money was more likely to make creditors fear that he intended to flee abroad than to convince them of his honesty.

The letter was the start of the 'Rob Roy the victim' legend that he was to propagate zealously in the coming years. It may have fooled posterity, but his creditors were not so gullible. Rob's gamble had failed. He was a man who possessed some charisma. People who met him tended to like him and trust him. In conversation he was beguiling, in argument he was convincing. His references to how popular he was in the Highlands makes it clear that he was well aware of these gifts. But perhaps, in 1711–12, his strategy relied too much on the influence of his persuasive powers – especially when he had to communicate with his creditors in writing, depriving himself of the advantage of the personal magnetism he could exercise on those in his presence. But if over-confidence in his charm had contributed to his downfall, that charisma was also to be central to his survival.

Montrose is the villain of traditional Rob Roy stories, the heartless aristocratic wretch who, through some unexplained malice, was determined to destroy poor Rob. Certainly, like any great nobleman, Montrose was ruthless in pursuit of his personal, family and political interests, arrogant in his dealings with lesser men. In his pursuit of Rob he was eventually to prove unscrupulous and ruthless. Once publicly engaged in leading the hunt for Rob he got locked into that role. Honour would not let him turn away, and risk being sneered at as having been bettered by an insignificant fellow like Rob Roy. Moreover catching Rob, as will be seen, became inextricably linked to Montrose's political ambitions. In the end, he had to back down, deeply humiliated. Yet it is not at first obvious why Montrose took a personal lead in the hunt. The sum he was owed by Rob (£230 sterling) was certainly significant, but not (given Montrose's wealth) massive. It might have been expected that the duke would have left the pursuit of the debt to the officials who ran his estates and financial affairs for him. Instead, he became publicly involved.

James Graham, Duke of Montrose, had succeeded to the earldom of Montrose (and the recently acquired lands of the Buchanan of that Ilk) in infancy, and his inheritance of the earldom of Menteith in 1694 had added to his power. He had then, in 1703, bought the feudal rights of the dukes of Lennox in Scotland. The Lennox deal brought him possession of little extra land, but a range of feudal superiorities over other landowners in Dunbartonshire and western Stirlingshire that added significantly to the dominant position he already had in the region. Thus his family was not only of the ancient aristocracy, but it was fast expanding its resources and influence. Public office, as hereditary sheriff of Stirlingshire, was added to his powers. His role was national as well as regional. Much of his time was spent in London, and when in Scotland he preferred living in Glasgow to staying in his country seats, the castles of Buchanan and Mugdock.[25] His estates extended into the Highlands, but essentially he was a Lowland magnate. In 1707 support for union with England had brought him promotion in the nobility, for it was then that he had become a duke. By 1712 he was a major figure in Scottish politics, as played out in the new British context. He headed the party or faction known as the *Squadrone Volante* (the Flying Squadron), second in influence only to the *Argethelians* – the followers of the duke of Argyll. He held the office of keeper of the privy seal of Scotland. An assessment of his political career has suggested that he 'seems not to have been sufficiently thick-skinned to make a really effective politician. He was pleasant and easy to get on with, and he brought a touch of grace and courtesy to the routine correspondence of the secretary's office [in 1714–15]. Most people thought well of him as a person.'[26] Some years before 1712 the young Montrose had been praised for his 'sweetness of behaviour, which charms all those who know him', and comment made as to his being 'very beautiful in his person'.[27] A bitter political opponent later drew a rather different picture, doubtless with considerable exaggeration. Montrose was 'of an easy, mean-spirited temper, governed by his mother and her relations and extremely coveteous . . . He was a man of good understanding, yet was led by the nose by a set of men whom he far surpassed . . . His courage, upon certain accounts, was much questioned, but his insincerity and falseness allowed by all'.[28]

All these judgements agree in one thing: he was a courteous, friendly man. His thin-skinnedness may account for what could be interpreted as his over-reaction to Rob's bankruptcy, his alleged covetousness may have contributed to his reluctance to write off bad debts. But central to Montrose's zeal in the hunt for Rob were probably personal elements. This was no anonymous debtor but a man Montrose knew well and had trusted and given his patronage. He had, at Rob's request, granted Rob's nephew a feu of Glengyle. When Rob had acquired Ardress, Montrose had become his feudal superior. Right up to his bankruptcy he had been a man whose advice the duke had taken – if only on minor matters. And, of course, he was a man whom the duke had trusted with his money to buy cattle. There was good reason here for Montrose to feel a deep sense of personal betrayal, and to react with anger.

Finally, Montrose may have been influenced by the fact that he was, socially, by far the greatest of Rob Roy's creditors, the only nobleman. It seems likely that Rob's earlier success in business was helped by knowledge that the great Montrose trusted him and traded with him. The duke may have had a sense that others who had lost their money might indirectly blame him, for leading them to trust

Rob. It became a duty and a face-saving exercise to act as spokesman
for the debtors as a whole in hunting Rob down.

Lesser villains in the hierarchy of those blamed for persecuting
Rob Roy are two of Montrose's henchmen, the men who ran his
estates. At the head of his administration was Mungo Graham of
Gorthie, the chamberlain. He was kinsman as much as servant, and
had been the young earl's companion on the Grand Tour in 1698–
1700. He had sat in the last Scottish parliament (1703–07), but then
concentrated on running the Montrose estates to leave the duke free
to pursue his political career.[29] When in Scotland he lived much of
the time in Buchanan Castle, when in London on the duke's business
he lived with him. John Ramsay of Ochtertyre was to record that
'From what I had occasion to hear from people who were intimately
acquainted with him, he was a man highly esteemed for his worth,
knowledge and strength of intellect. And his good qualities were
not diminished by his having lived in first-rate company at home
and abroad, and being well read in books.' But Gorthie suffered the
infirmity of occasional 'mental absence' and forgetfulness, which
sounds like the *petit mal* type of epilepsy. Rents on the Montrose
estate in his time were moderate, in many cases being held on tenures
'of kindness', which indicated a relationship that was more than
commercial and implied a theoretical kinship and mutual obligation.
Even these rents were often ill paid. This is a judgement from a later
age, when landlords were becoming more stringent in their demands
on tenants, and perhaps the picture of 'those favoured, I had almost
said happy, tenants' is exaggerated.[30] But the fact that Montrose was
content to have a man known for leniency in charge of rent collection
hardly suggests that he was an extortionate and oppressive landlord,
as might be assumed from stories of his relations with Rob Roy.

However, Gorthie like his master had good reason for bitterness
towards Rob. He also had been a customer of Rob Roy's, and in
January 1712 had given him a bond promising to pay him 2,500
merks (about £139 sterling) as part of an agreement to buy 100 cows.
On Rob's failure to supply the cattle contracted for, Gorthie expected
to be able to have the bill 'reduced', or declared invalid. But Rob's
planning of his default had been meticulous. Just before it became
known that he was bankrupt he passed the bill to Colin Campbell
of Glendaruel (a man he had had business dealings with in the past).
Glendarvel in turn endorsed the bill to Hamilton of Bardowie, who
then claimed to be entitled to collect the money due from Gorthie

even though no cattle had been supplied. Gorthie not surprisingly suspected collusion, and took legal action. Glendaruel's case was that Rob had owed him 2,500 merks, and 'having 500 libra [pounds] sterling in money and banknotes about him', he offered either to pay in cash, or to transfer Gorthie's bond to him. Glendaruel had opted for the transfer. This (had Rob not been bankrupt) would have been a perfectly legitimate and routine transaction. If you didn't need cash at present, it made sense to buy a bond instead, then the money would earn interest until it was paid. But in this case, Glendaruel claimed that he had then found it convenient to have Bardowie collect the cash from Gorthie for him. Gorthie argued that the timing and the transferring of the bill to Bardowie indicated that Rob and Bardowie had been acting collusively, with Bardowie as the intended beneficiary from the start and Glendaruel acting as an intermediary to try to conceal the plot. Rob had already transferred Craigrostan to Bardowie and 'if he is not Rob Roy's Trustee, at least has had considerable dealings with him upon his own account'. In the end Gorthie won his case, but having had to fight the outrageous demand that he pay for cattle he had never received must have infuriated him.[31]

One step down from Graham of Gorthie in the duke's service was the man who was to bear the brunt of the conflict against Rob Roy in the field rather than the office, John Graham younger of Killearn, who was Montrose's factor of the barony of Buchanan. Again he was a kinsman of the duke, with a family tradition of service to him. Killearn's father had formerly held Gorthie's job of chamberlain, and had sat in the last Scottish parliament. The younger Killearn was to have his turn as a member of parliament in 1722–27.[32] If you served the duke long and well, a spell in one of the parliamentary seats he controlled might be your reward. Killearn was to show himself zealous in the pursuit of Rob Roy, but, as will be seen, there is no evidence to support the tales of brutality on his part that infect the Rob Roy legend.

While Montrose organised action to bring Rob to account for his debts, Rob made another attempt to get James Graham in Glasgow to intervene for him. On 27 August he wrote from Strathfillan. He made no mention of the trip to the Outer Isles that had been supposed to solve all his problems, and now asked Graham to get a *supercedere* for him from his creditors, so he could negotiate with them. This would involve the creditors agreeing to suspend diligence, the legal processes against Rob, so he could meet them in safety to try to reach an agreement.[33] Thus Rob was still hoping for compromise, not preparing for conflict, relying on his face-to-face charm and willingness to talk to tame his creditors. Montrose accepted the offer – indicating that he too at this point was not set on confrontation – and (at his instigation) the other creditors agreed that a *supercedere* was appropriate. Rob was promised immunity from legal action so that so he could come to Glasgow for talks. At this point Rob backed away. Perhaps his offer had simply been a delaying tactic, intended to portray him as a reasonable man ready to settle, but he claimed that his friends and relatives had urged him not to trust in the protection offered. 'He could not accept the supercedere, that it had made him alter his measures and had putt him in a litle confusion as much as when he was putt in the gazett which he says was ill policie they might be sure that since he would take himself to his keeping, gazetts would not doe it.'[34] Thus having been offered the concession he had himself requested, Rob refused to co-operate and truculently aired his grievances at the humiliation of his having been publicly denounced in the gazette. His caution may have been sensible. There is no reason to doubt that Montrose and the other creditors intended to honour the *supercedere*, but as Rob had just betrayed all of them his fear that they might plan to revenge themselves by tricking him was understandable. Rob remained in the Highlands, and the chance of compromise was lost.

Legal proceedings against Rob were now well under way. The initial 'letters of horning' against him had been issued on 27 June, when he had been 'orderly denounced rebel' by order of the court of session for his failure to pay his debts.[35] The 'letters', proclaimed after blasts of a trumpet or horn, demanded payment, and at this point agreement was often reached, amicably or otherwise, between debtors and creditors, and there was no need for further proceedings. Rob's failure to accept the *supercedere* and get his creditors to agree to have the hornings withdrawn meant that they proceeded to the next stage of legal action. On 25 September 1712 George Robertson, acting for Montrose, Gorthie and James Graham, writer in Glasgow, had letters of caption issued against Rob. These ordered his arrest and imprisonment until he had satisfied his creditors. It being uncertain where Rob was, the letters were proclaimed both at Edinburgh Cross, which gave them validity if he was in Scotland, and on the pier at Leith, in case he had fled abroad. Robertson also hoped to have the letters executed at Rob's dwelling place[36] – though it would have taken a courageous messenger to venture into the Highlands on that task.[37] In practice Rob's position was unchanged by the issuing of the captions, for he was safe in the Highlands, but legally he was in much more serious trouble than before, open to arrest at any time.

The June 1712 advertisement in the *Scots Courant* had alleged that Rob Roy's debts amounted to over £1,000 sterling (£12,000 Scots). Confirmation that this was no exaggeration emerged slowly, as the wheels of the legal engine ground on. First his creditors had to register his contracts and bonds in the books of council and session (the register of deeds) so that they could be recognised by the court of session. Then decrees had to be obtained from the court ordering repayment, hornings and captions. Finally, when payment was not forthcoming, the court issued decrees of adjudication, awarding Rob's lands to his creditors. Twelve such adjudications (dated 1713 and 1714) have been traced, awarded to eighteen creditors. They show a total default on Rob's part not of just £1,000 sterling, but of over £2,500 sterling (£30,000 Scots). Debts ranged from about £50 sterling (MacKenzie of Delvine) to a massive £1,163 sterling (Hamilton of Bardowie). Montrose (£230) and Gorthie (£178 sterling)[38] were the second and third in terms of money owed. Moreover these twelve adjudications that have been traced do not represent Rob's total debt. A further £233 sterling, for example, was owed to Thomas Brisbane of Bishopton,[39] and an investigation of Rob's finances a decade later revealed other creditors such as James Grant of Grant and James Graham of Kilmannan.[40]

The contracts recorded in connection with these proceedings indicate that the main source for the cattle that Rob supplied (or had promised to supply) to his customers was Sir Donald MacDonald of Sleat, and Rob had a quarter share in a contract to buy 2,000 cattle from him.[41] South Uist, where Rob had proposed to go in pursuit of his debtors, was the property of Allan MacDonald of Clan Ranald, but he was much in debt to MacDonald of Sleat, who sometimes collected rents from his mainland properties towards payment of the debt.[42] Possibly Rob had contacts in South Uist through collecting Clan Ranald's cattle there in Sleat's name in a similar way.

Montrose led the campaign to get Rob to pay his debts, but from a purely financial point of view it was Bardowie who was most anxious to have the matter sorted out. Under Rob's disposition he could collect the rents of Craigrostan, but though thus acting partly in collusion with Rob he was unhappy with the situation and his attempts to open negotiations with Rob for further satisfaction of his claims failed. A letter of 3 October 1712 notes that Rob not turned up to a meeting that had been arranged with him at Drummond (presumably sponsored by Lord Drummond) 'and he seems to shift [avoid] doing him justice'. Campbell of Gendaruel urged Breadalbane to send for Rob and demand that he satisfy Bardowie, who was 'ane honest man and a great servant', and 'a man that hes these sevin years past suported Rob Roy with his name and credit so that he will be the most oungreat man leaving [ungrateful man living] if he will not do what is in his power to do him justice'. Lord Drummond should send for Rob and give him the same message.[43] Rob might be outlawed and beyond the reach of even a great man like Montrose, but it was assumed that men who had been his patrons in the past, like Breadalbane and Drummond, whose support he now needed more than ever, could force him to settle with Bardowie.[44] Thus opinion was that Rob's failure to satisfy Bardowie was not due simply to inability to pay, but to evasiveness.

However, from Rob's point of view, it was probably the case that he could satisfy some of his creditors but not all of them. He may have decided that the resources he had should be used to pay selectively those who were likely to cause him most trouble. He may have calculated that Bardowie would not act harshly against him because of the family links between them. Anyway Bardowie was socially a nonentity – though it would be worrying if he won the sympathy of Breadalbane and Drummond. One debt he may have found it expedient to settle was that to Brisbane of Bishopton. He sought to pressurise Rob into payment not by relying on Montrose's influence or the might of the law, but by getting the duchess of Argyll to write to Breadalbane requesting him to tell Rob to pay up. So did Lord Nairn, hinting that two of the sixteen Scottish peers in the House of Lords (Argyll and Nairn) who had agreed to vote as Breadalbane wished on matters concerning him might change their minds if Bishopton were not paid. A third writer urged Bishopton's claim, as he was 'a very worthy honest man tho' noe whigg in principles, and represents a good old family who are not the richer for their loyalty.'[45]

How Bishopton had managed to line up this impressive firepower is unknown, but it probably proved effective. Breadalbane summoned Rob, who claimed to be keen to pay, and asked for a meeting to be arranged between him and Bishopton, or between their representatives.[46] Bishopton did not proceed to obtain an adjudication against Rob Roy which suggests he was paid. Other creditors might also have been willing to try to arrange separate deals with Rob, but lacked methods of contacting him or putting pressure on him. Most, however, were ready to accept Montrose's lead. Confrontation, it was hoped, would be the best way of getting their money back from slippery Rob Roy.

The trouble was that it turned out that Montrose's leadership of the creditors, which gave them hope, was balanced by the strength of Campbell support for Rob Roy, and the result was stalemate. The duke of Argyll's influence had already probably hindered attempts to arrest Rob, by making Campbell of Finab's independent company less than zealous in attempting to catch him. Sometime around the end of 1712 one of Finab's sergeants, based in Drymen, was granted the necessary permissions to use military forces to attempt to arrest Rob, and as well as using men from the independent company Montrose authorised him to recruit local folk in Menteith. An exasperated duke recorded what happened next. The sergeant had 'made a march up to Rob Roy's house, and Robert walked up from his house to the syde of a hill for an hour or two, till he was gone, and then return'd home and so theirs ane end to that story.' There had been no attempt at secrecy – everyone knew an attempt was to be made to catch Rob. When he had heard of the approach of the troops he had simply walked out of his house. In the rough, broken hill terrain, partly covered by forest, he would quickly have been safe from anything a small party of troops could do. Finab bore the brunt of Montrose's anger. 'I'm not well satisfyed with the conduct has been in all this matter from first to last. Ye may easily consider that this treatment I have gott from R. Roy is what cannot be born with; and that on way or other I must see my self put in the right.' He had expected that Finab's company would work diligently to catch Rob, but now resolved to use other methods. In doing so he would have to cast aspersions on Finab's conduct, for no one would believe that Finab could not have caught Rob if he had really tried. 'I will make application above [to more senior army officers], but wish with all my heart you either had better officers under you, or took more of the execution [of action] upon yourself.' But if, in the meantime, Finab could capture Rob, 'I assure I would be mighty glad of it' as he had no wish to harm Finab's reputation.[47]

The influence of the Campbells of Argyll ensured that Finab never seriously tried to catch Rob. The Campbells of Breadalbane went further, openly promoting his interests. By December 1712 it was known that the earl of Breadalbane had provided Rob with a bolt-hole for use in time of need, by granting him a seven-year lease of the lands of Auch, or Auchinchisallen, a two merk land a few miles south of Bridge of Orchy in the north-eastern corner of Argyllshire.[48]

Secure in Breadalbane's friendship, Rob sought to strengthen his position by gaining Atholl's as well. In January 1713 he wrote to the duke, saying that he would have heard that Montrose 'is ofering to ruine me'. Rob had, he continued, offered to pay the whole sum he owed him, with a year's interest, but Montrose had rejected this, saying that he should use a protection (the *supercedere*) granted to him to come and negotiate directly. But at the same time that Montrose had been pretending to be ready to talk, he had procured an order from the lord advocate to arrest him and had got Finab to attempt to seize him. 'This was a most ridiculous way [for] any nobleman to treat any man after this manner.'

Rob was indulging in creative chronology. He had rejected the protection offered in August 1712, while the order against him by the lord advocate had not been issued until October. Rob's purpose, as usual, was to present himself as a wronged man, suffering from the unreasonable behaviour of others. Flattery was added, to help persuade Atholl that Rob was a good chap. God knew, his letter continued, there was a difference 'between dukes. Blessed be God ffor it that its not the Athole men that is after me,' for Atholl's authority would have been sufficient to secure his arrest whereas Montrose's had failed. In any case, Atholl would never need to send men to catch Rob, for 'if your grace would send to me the least foot boy I would come without any protection', as Atholl had always been kind and charitable to him, beyond his deservings. As in some of Rob's other letters, lavish flattery and assurances of loyalty precede a request. Rob wanted Atholl to intervene to get the lord advocate to countermand the order for Rob's imprisonment. He signed off as, 'your Grace's servant while I am alive'.[49]

Great men expected this sort of flattery from lesser men. Convention made it essential to the gaining of patronage and favour. But the letter again reveals Rob not simply as adept at conventional displays of deference but as a skilled master of the pen in stating his case and manipulating evidence. Atholl, and others before and afterwards, were presented with the picture of poor Rob whose honest efforts to satisfy his creditors had been vindictively spurned. That Rob had offered to pay Montrose in full, and that this had been refused, was to become a significant part of his legend. But though Rob claimed the offer was rejected, there is no evidence apart from his own statements that he ever actually made such an offer. There is no trace of it in the voluminous correspondence of Montrose and his servants dealing with Rob's case. But even if some such offer was made, it would have been hard for Montrose to accept it. He had led the organising and encouraging of Rob's other creditors in pursuing their money. He could not, without seriously damaging his reputation, accept payment of what was due to him personally from Rob and then abandon the rest of the creditors.

The duke continued to insist that Rob be tracked down and arrested, but it remained the case that even when it was known where Rob was staying the independent companies could not catch him. As Sergeant Andrew MacDonald explained to Montrose on 3 February 1713, he had made several attempts to hunt down the fugitive, but as soon as he tried to gather his men together Rob was informed and made himself scarce. What the duke should do, he suggested, was to get some local gentlemen to join him in Aberfoyle with six or seven men. This would not seem suspicious, as the men were not soldiers. 'I am credably informed be my spyes that he is to be at his oun house Monday and Tuesday nixt and I think I cannot miss him if ffortun favour me.' 'Young Drunky' would be 'very fit for my purpose'.[50] Montrose agreed to the sergeant's plan, and John Graham younger of Drunkie was dispatched to join him. Frustration followed. They heard that Roy had 'supped in his own house last night and we were at his house be the break of day this morning [11 February] and yet mist him'. The sergeant had been told that Rob kept a strong party of men around him, so he had taken forty or fifty men rather than the six or seven men he had first thought of, and doubtless this contributed to Rob's escape – news of such a large number of men moving through the hills was bound to spread fast.[51]

However, living in the Lomond area was proving too dangerous for comfort, and in May 1713 Rob moved north to Auch[52] to continue his fight for rehabilitation. In letters of 3 June he pleaded his case to the laird of Douglaston and his brother James Graham (sheriff depute of Dunbartonshire). He would love to settle his debts to them, but he had been advised not to settle with any creditors until he had first satisfied Montrose. He therefore begged for their help in persuading Montrose to be reasonable. He wanted to negotiate, he emphasised, and he repeated the claim that he had made to Atholl – that he had offered to repay Montrose in full, and to pay interest from the time the money had been advanced to him. In addition, Rob now offered a further inducement. He himself was taking proceedings against Walter Graham of Drunkie for a debt owed to him, and he was willing to assign this debt to Montrose to collect – and indeed would help him to collect it. This, said Rob, was all he could afford to do, or he would have nothing left for his other creditors.

In trying to enlist Atholl's help Rob had been happy to denounce Montrose as the source of his problem, but now he was writing to Grahams who were kinsmen of Montrose, and fellow debtors. They would be likely to respond with indignation to an attack on the head of their kin, so Rob's letter provided a different perspective on events. The fault, it now seemed, lay with Killearn, Montrose's factor, not with the duke himself. 'I am afrid Killearn will be my enemy upon the account of an old quarrell.' Of one of the factor's actions, Rob writes 'I know the reasone why he did this that my lord might always keep a grudge att me.' Then he reverts to an old theme. His creditors had better reach a settlement with him soon, for the legal expenses of pursuing him were rising daily. The longer they waited, the less they would get.[53]

Meanwhile his disposition of Craigrostan was working out as planned. Financial accounts show that as early as 1713 Bardowie was collecting the rents of Craigrostan,[54] and there was nothing Montrose could do about it. He was confident that in time court proceedings would overthrow the disposition and conclude that Craigrostan and its rents belonged to Rob's creditors, but for the moment all he was able to do was use his powers as lord of the regality of Lennox to get Killearn to summon the tenants of Craigrostan to attend his regality court at Drymen to give details of the rents they paid (November 1713),[55] to be sure he knew what rents were being paid to Bardowie so that they could be later reclaimed from him.

Once settled at Auch Rob could live openly. His outlawry was ignored and he became active in trade again, finding Highland friends and patrons still ready to trust and employ him. When Colquhoun of Luss decided to build himself a 'highland house' as a summer dwelling, Breadalbane promised him fourteen or fifteen fir trees as materials. In October 1713 Colquhoun asked that they be delivered by 'Robert Roy or any trustie you think fitt'.[56] Thus the feudal superior from whom Rob held Craigrostan was willing to rely on him. In December 1713 Rob can be detected discussing with an unidentified lord a cattle trading deal they were involved in and other financial matters.[57] For some Rob was an outlaw to be hunted down, to others he was a man to be treated like anyone else. Ostentatious further gestures of support for Rob Roy by Breadalbane followed.

In January 1714 Sir Alexander Campbell of Lochnell, whose widow was a half sister of Breadalbane, died. His son who 'has lately set up as a Jacobite', made the funeral a covert demonstration of support for Jacobitism with, by some accounts, over 2,000 armed men gathering under the pretext of paying their respects. Rob Roy ('a bankrupt Jacobite') was placed in command of Breadalbane's own contingent, perhaps 500 men, carrying Breadalbane's colours (banners). Thirteen bagpipers contributed to Lochnell's grand send-off,[58] and a story was to claim that Rob insisted on being one of those that had the 'first lift' of the coffin in the procession. This was agreed as 'it was apprehended if he were not gratified in his requests disturbance might arise'.[59] The wily fence-sitting earl of Breadalbane was hinting at sympathy with Jacobitism – and showing openly his attitude to Rob Roy, using him as his personal representative. It soon emerged that Breadalbane had gone further in demonstrating his trust in Rob, by an appointment that seemed to many provocative and outrageous. He employed Rob as one of his baillies on his Argyllshire lands, a position that empowered Rob to act as judge in baillie courts. Montrose's tail is surely being ostentatiously twisted here. Montrose had made Rob an outlaw, so Breadalbane had made him a judge. An old man (Breadalbane was now in his late seventies) was having a joke at a young one's expense (Montrose was in his early thirties) – and Breadalbane gained the support of Rob's MacGregor supporters even if they lived on Montrose's lands.

Breadalbane might indulge a cynical smile, but his son, Lord Glenorchy, was one of those who was not amused. The old earl had transferred running the estates to him, so his consent was meant to be necessary for all appointments, and he was furiously opposed to employing Rob. 'To make use of such a person as Rob Roy to be a judge upon our estate is what I can hardly beleeve.' Indeed it went against the advice the earl himself had given, that the family should keep on good terms with 'them' – the MacGregors – but never employ them on the estate. Further, Breadalbane was intending to leave his Highland estates for a time (presumably to visit Edinburgh), raising an even more appalling prospect in Glenorchy's mind. Was his doddery old father so crazy that he 'intended he [Rob] should command in your absence which forseth [forces] me to tell your Lordship, he, nor no man ever shall, as long as I am living and in this nation, and for my own honour I am oblidged to writt to him to forbear medling in any publict bussines in the countrie'. Incoherent but heartfelt. Centuries earlier the MacGregors had been driven from Glenorchy by the Campbells, so it was unthinkable that the chief of the Campbells of Glenorchy would now entrust oversight of his estates to a MacGregor.

Lord Glenorchy also wrote in strong terms to the outlaw-judge himself, forbidding Rob to act as baillie. Rob replied with masterful tact. He had had the pleasure of receiving his lordship's letter though it 'was not off the nature I expected', given his wish to serve his lordship and to do him all the good offices that were in his power – though without meddling in his private affairs. The 'poore family I am come of' had always served the interests of the house of Glenorchy, and he had never dreamed that Glenorchy would repudiate him because he had accepted a commission as baillie from his father. He was grateful that Breadalbane was showing him his favour and protecting him from the unjust persecution that he was suffering. Indeed, the earl had insisted that Rob accept his protection, and not that of any other man in the country of first rank. Rob urged that he stood to gain nothing while he acted as baillie for the earl, who intended only to employ him 'untill I gett my private affairs putt in some order'. The earl had forbidden him to resign his post, and if he resigned without permission, the earl would become 'my greatest enemy this would be the highest injurie done to me imaginable'. He hoped this was not Glenorchy's intention, wrote his 'most faihfull. humble and obedient servant', Rob Roy.[60]

Many must have found Rob Roy's new authority as a baillie hard to stomach. Perhaps this was why two sons of Campbell of Glenfalloch drew their swords on him without provocation – though they were drunk at the time. Was Campbells having to take orders from a MacGregor (even one calling himself Campbell) too much for the lads? But Rob had stepped back, refusing to be drawn into a fight. This counted in his favour, urged John Campbell (Breadalbane's chamberlain) in reporting the incident to Lord Glenorchy. The MacGregor baillie had acted sensibly, seeking to avoid trouble. The chamberlain further sought to persuade Glenorchy that Rob was no threat to his authority by repeating Rob's own plea. Though he was holding baillie courts he had a distaste for making his 'bread' in such a way. Only his need for protection from Breadalbane had made him accept office until he had extracted himself from his 'difficulties'. He wanted to avoid offending the earl or his son, and was unhappy at the thought he was the cause of a quarrel between the two men. As for John Campbell himself, he carefully disassociated himself from Rob's acceptance of office, just in case Glenorchy was not convinced. 'The trueth is I neither advised him to it or forbid him, being reproached before when he was persecute (be the whole country people) as the author of the ruine of himself and ffamily.'[61]

This last sentence is revealing. John Campbell had evidently at first been hostile to Rob Roy when news of his bankruptcy had broken and he had sought protection. As a result he had found himself faced with widespread hostility. Rob's confidence that popular opinion in the Highlands would support him had proved well founded. And Breadalbane showed that his son's attacks on Rob's appointment had not changed his own determination to favour him. On 10 February 1714 he granted Rob a lease of the two merk land of Brackley for life.[62] Situated deep in Glenorchy, near the head of Loch Awe in Argyllshire, Rob would be even safer than at Auch. In May Rob bought from Breadalbane at auction eight 'couples' of cows, two stirks (young cows or bullocks) four plough horses and a mare, presumably to stock his new farm.[63]

For some months little is heard of Rob. Legal proceedings against him continued, but a temporary deadlock had been reached. Safe in Breadalbane, where the earl's authority was greater than Edinburgh's law or the duke of Montrose's influence, Rob seemed to be settling into a new life. A contract to build a new sawmill for Breadalbane in August[64] indicates his continuing business interests. Perhaps Rob was reconciled to this being his life for the foreseeable future. He could make a living safe from his creditors if he confined his activities to a limited geographical sphere. The most pressing danger that threatened was that in the course of nature Breadalbane must soon die, and be replaced by the hostile Lord Glenorchy. Moreover Rob cannot have given up the dream of somehow eventually restoring his fortunes by regaining the lands that he believed were his by right, whatever others thought. Perhaps Montrose too might die, removing his driving personal rancour from the motivation of his creditors and making a negotiated settlement possible. Or there might be a political upheaval which could be worked to his advantage. Queen Anne was sickly, and all her children had died young. By law her successor would be George, elector of Hanover, the choice of supporters of the 1689 revolution. But to Jacobites her death would offer a great opportunity to right the great dynastic wrong that had been done to the senior Stuart line by dethroning James II and VII. His son, Prince Edward Francis, could ascend the throne as King James III. This might well be done peacefully, for some of the queen's ministers in London were willing to indicate that they were ready to support such a move. As each month passed the queen's health was studied obsessively, and tensions increased. Some openly declared their beliefs as to who should succeed to the throne. Most, whatever their individuals opinions, sought to hedge their bets to make sure they and their families and property would survive whichever candidate won. Among those most openly aggressive and ready to declare willingness to fight over the issue were the Highland Jacobites. Lochnell's great funeral in January 1714 was a political statement as crisis crept closer.

On 1 August 1714 (at long last, in the irreverent opinions of some of her subjects) Queen Anne died. Within weeks Rob Roy the outlaw was to be well on the way to becoming Rob Roy the rebel, openly declaring support for the Jacobite cause.

Usually in a biography the subject's actions are more important that what he does not do. But in the years of Rob's life from his downfall in 1712 to the eve of the 1715 Jacobite rising, it is worth stressing what he did not do, for the legends of his life that often pass for biography paint a very different picture from the evidence. In tradition, action by Montrose after June 1712 was brutal. Rob's house was burnt and his wife seriously assaulted by the duke's agents. But there is no trace of this in the copious historical records. Similarly it is generally assumed that almost immediately after he was declared bankrupt Rob began to raid Montrose's lands, carrying off money, cattle and grain, and justifying this by claiming to be collecting compensation for the rents of Craigrostan, which had been unjustly seized by the duke. But not only had Montrose not succeeded in gaining possession of Craigrostan, but with Rob's own agreement its rents were being paid to Bardowie. Far from further alienating the duke by raiding his lands, Rob committed no known acts of violence. It is true that, according to an account drawn up by Montrose a few years later, Rob collected rents from the tenants of his former lands, including those he had rented from the duke, by use of violence. In time some reverted to wasteland, as no tenants were willing to lease them.[65] But it is to be suspected that Montrose is here reading back into the pre–1715 years the later behaviour of Rob. Quite possibly he still tried to collect rents of the lands he had rented rather than owned, which had reverted to the duke, and put pressure on tenants, but the strictly contemporary records do not mention violence. Rob spent 1712–14 negotiating, trying to reach a peaceful agreed settlement with his creditors, and to re-establish himself as a trader in the areas of the Highlands where he enjoyed the protection of Breadalbane and others. He was, after all, not a wild young man. He was forty-one years old when he went bankrupt, and perhaps, while still hoping in time to regain his lands and escape from the technicality of being outlaw, he was ready to settle into his new life.

But this was not to be, for his reactions to the opportunities and challenges posed by Jacobite plottings and rebellion were to propel his life into a new phase. He moved from being, as it were, a passive outlaw with a fairly comfortable and settled lifestyle, to an active one, committing new crimes, from cattle-raiding to treason, very much on the run, in fear of his life.

4

CHIEFS, PENSIONS AND POLITICIANS

The previous chapter dealt with the years 1712 to 1714 in terms of Rob's downfall, his unsuccessful efforts to sort out a deal with his creditors, and his survival under Breadalbane's patronage. But there is another strand to Rob's life in these years and those that follow, and it is now necessary to backtrack to look at political developments and how they affected the Highlands. Bankruptcy in 1712 had deprived Rob Roy of home and property. It may possibly also have deprived him of a chance to make a bid for the chieftaincy of his clan. The government might have outlawed the clan, but ironically it was government policy that drove home to the MacGregors the importance of having an effective, if technically illegal, chief.

A French landing in Scotland had been avoided by good fortune in 1708. Had it taken place there was little doubt that there would have been a major (if incoherent) Jacobite rising against the government, but after it failed those in power lapsed into complacency, content to regard good luck as a substitute for a defence policy. Nothing significant was done to strengthen the regime's hold on the Highlands. It was evidently calculated that a successful outcome of the war with France (the War of the Spanish Succession, which had dragged on since 1702) would defuse the threat of Jacobite insurrection by destroying any hope of overseas support.

A change of ministry came in 1710, after a general election had produced a big swing from the Whigs to the Tories. A British ministry dominated by the Whig *Junto* and intent on pursuing the war, was replaced by a predominantly Tory one in which the leading figure was Robert Harley, who became lord treasurer and earl of Oxford in 1711. Harley's ideal was a moderate, broadly-based ministry which would restore peace abroad and defuse political tensions at home. He strove to keep the extremes in politics out of power while conciliating in the middle ground. But the virtue of moderation can have associated

70

vices, and Harley displayed them. Reluctance to upset anyone could lead him to indecision and failure to act. His habit of disguising his meaning by deliberate obscurity of language left men expecting from him more than they got. Governing Scotland was a prime example of this. The downfall of the old Whig secretary of state for Scotland, the duke of Queensberry, was eagerly awaited by his many enemies, but Harley left him in office until he died late in 1711. His reasoning was that Queensberry had many friends as well as many enemies, so dismissing him would cause controversy. Moreover, if he were to dismiss him, choosing a successor would cause even more bother, for if he made any one of those who believed they deserved the job happy, rival candidates would be left resentful. Therefore Harley simply left the office of Scottish secretary vacant. It avoided the need to make a decision.

However, though Harley's inaction can be interpreted partly as weakness, as a 'policy of drift', there were arguments in favour of it so far as Scotland was concerned. The situation was tense.[1] Most Englishmen regarded all Scottish Tories as Jacobites in disguise. Appointing Tories to office there would therefore cause alarm about the safety of the 1688–9 revolution settlement and the Protestant succession to the throne. Thus Daniel Defoe, one of Harley's most pushy advisers on Scottish affairs, argued that to appoint a Tory as commander-in-chief of the army in Scotland would be regarded as handing over the country to the Jacobite Pretender, Prince James Edward. The 1710 elections of the sixteen Scottish peers to sit in the house of lords returned four nobles who were openly Jacobite in their politics,[2] an indication of the strength of that party in Scotland which confirmed Harley's belief that doing nothing was wise. He knew powerful positions were held by his enemies, but reasoned that it was far more sensible to retain enemies in office, which would keep them quiet and prevent them leading opposition, than make new appointments which would be seen as provocative.

In effect, Harley had taken Scottish affairs into his own (inactive) hands in the hope that he, as an outsider, could stand above the political factions which split the country. He may have thought that the Scots would be flattered that he was looking after them personally, but in reality they tended to feel they were being neglected. The 1707 union had provided for the continuation of a centre of government in Edinburgh, the Scots Privy Council, but that had been abolished in 1708. There had been a Scottish secretaryship, but now that too had been abandoned. The degree to which government was being centralised in London was far greater than had been anticipated in 1707, and this was intensely resented.

To Harley the most acute problem in Scotland was the strength of Jacobitism in the Highlands. Lowland Jacobitism might be very strong in some areas, but it presented no immediate or direct threat to the regime. The days were past when Lowland nobles could call out their followers and create an effective military force. The militarised society of the Highlands was a different matter. Men were trained to arms, carried them regularly, and generally accepted that they could be called out by their chiefs to fight. If Jacobite rebellion came in Scotland, it would start in the Highlands. Harley resolved that action was needed to decrease the risk of a rebellion, and having the choice between the stick and the carrot, he predictably choose the carrot. At first, it is true, he considered an act to curb the power of clan chiefs (a bill for this had been debated in 1708 but dropped when French invasion failed to materialise),[3] but hostile reaction to the idea persuaded him to drop it. He also dismissed a plan put forward by the earl of Cromarty that the power of Whig clans should be used to counter the Jacobite Highland threat. They should be organised and trained so that 6,000 men would be in readiness to assemble quickly in the event of Jacobite aggression.[4] It is hardly surprising that Harley ignored Cromarty's scheme. Putting a militia of 6,000 men in the hands of the Whigs would undermine his own power in Scotland, infuriate the Tories on whom he relied for support, and might well provoke rather than deter a rising. He therefore resolved to try to placate, even to win the support of, the Jacobite chiefs. The fall of the Whigs from power provided an opportunity for negotiation. The chiefs knew the previous ministry had been implacably opposed to them, but expected better things from a ministry in which the Tories were strongly represented. To some extent, the chiefs involved were fooled by simplistic political labels. As Tory in Scotland meant Jacobite, they assumed the same held true in England. It was a basic error. There were certainly some English Tories who were Jacobites, and Tory politicians might be more willing to negotiate with Jacobite agents than their Whig predecessors had been. But the Tories were committed to upholding the Church of England, and few would ever be happy at the thought of the return of the Catholic Stuarts. In religion as well as politics perhaps the chiefs were naive. Episcopalians in Scotland were almost invariably Jacobite, and they may have too easily believed that the English Episcopalians of the Church of England must at heart be Jacobites like them.

Moreover, with a little sleight of hand, it was possible to persuade Jacobites that it was in their interests not to rebel, and that they should accept Queen Anne as their legitimate sovereign. It was true that in terms of strict hereditary succession she was a usurper. Her half brother James, the Pretender, should have been on the throne. But at least she was a Stuart, and giving allegiance to her could be seen as compatible with support for the Stuart dynasty in general. Combine this with the facts that she had no surviving children and was believed to be willing to bequeath her thrones to the Pretender, and the argument that it was legitimate to give her allegiance became compelling. She was ageing and in poor health, which meant that Jacobites would not, in all probability, have to put up with her rather than their true king for long. In this context, the Jacobites were anxious to arrange some sort of a deal with Harley's Tory-influenced government. Under the 1701 act of settlement, on the death of Anne the throne would pass to the family of the electors of Hanover, and Jacobites believed that cooperation with the government would be the best way to ensure that the act was ignored and a Stuart restoration implemented instead. The Jacobite clans of the Highlands were, indeed, ready to offer their military resources to support the queen and, implicitly, to help thwart the Hanoverian succession. But they would only do this in return for government favours, including cash up front.

Robert Stewart of Appin is usually given credit for being the leading agent of the Jacobite chiefs in the negotiations that followed, but it was a scheme outlined by Allan Cameron which was presented to Harley by one of his intelligence agents in Scotland, Captain John Ogilvie, in May 1711. As the second son of Sir Ewan Cameron of Locheil, and thus the brother of John Cameron who had taken over from his elderly father as effective chief of the Camerons, Allan was exceptionally well connected in the Highlands, though how many chiefs knew of his proposals was to become a matter of controversy.[5] His plans were ambitious.

His first paper[6] surveyed the Jacobites and Jacobite clans, indicating the manpower that they could put at government disposal if agreement were reached. He concluded that the Atholl men (mainly Stewarts) were a resolute, brave and hardy people, and could raise 2,000 in arms. But they did not love the duke, because after an ancestor of his had married the Stewart heiress of Atholl, the earls had retained the name of Murray instead of taking the name Stewart (and thus identifying with their new clansmen). The Atholl men were Jacobite, and would follow the duke if he rose for the Pretender, but not otherwise. This is plausible, for it was notorious that the Murray duke was felt to be an alien and little loved. On Breadalbane also Cameron is credible. The earl had a good following of his own, and there is no doubt who he was for – the Pretender. When Cameron turned to the Campbells of Argyll, however, he probably allowed his prejudices (or his hopes of Harley's ignorance of things Highland) to push his case for the extent of Jacobite support too far. He claimed that most of the duke of Argyll's great following would also serve Breadalbane, because the duke and his brother the earl of Islay were the worst-beloved men in the Highlands. Nonetheless, there was a some truth in what Allan said, as was to be proved in 1715. A number of leading Campbell lairds who normally followed the duke of Argyll's lead came to the brink of joining the Jacobite rebels before drawing back and supporting the government.

In his lists of chiefs and their men, Cameron of course had to include his own clan and he gave assessments of his father and brother. Sir Ewan was cunning and brave, but very old. His son John was not so subtle, but was a man of honour who could bring 2,000 men to the field, hardy people who were great robbers in the Lowlands. This might not be thought likely to be a recommendation to government in their favour, but Cameron wanted to emphasise his clan's military prowess. On the MacGregors, Allan Cameron was blunt. They were a very numerous and bloody sort of men, and though their name was banned they still added it to the ends of their assumed names. They lived dispersed over a wide area, but on their 'watchword' they would all assemble and follow their chief, though for the present their chief, the laird of MacGregor, was 'out'. Probably Cameron meant that the chieftaincy was regarded as vacant – one source (though late in date) states that Archibald Graham of Kilmannan had resigned the chieftaincy at some point, and indeed he may have been dead by this time. But, Cameron continued, the MacGregors had chosen a gentleman of their name to be their new chief, and they had made great offers to serve the Pretender if he restored their name when he landed in Scotland. Cameron added that the MacGregors had made another offer, but stated that he would say nothing about it at present, as it concerned some men in the government. What this other offer was remains mysterious. As to the new MacGregor chief, it seems most likely that Cameron was referring to Alexander Drummond (MacGregor) of Balhaldie, for Allan Cameron kept him in touch with his activities and three years later Balhaldie was to claim the chieftaincy (see below).[7]

Having summarised the strength of Highland Jacobitism, Allan Cameron turned to how this could be harnessed to serving the queen's interests. As a preliminary Cameron stressed that no nobleman should be used in negotiations. The chiefs put no trust in the titled nobility, and if they trusted anyone in government it would be Harley himself. He was believed to be a man of honour – because he had been so hated by the previous Whig ministry. The chiefs loved (or, it might have been more honest to say, were prepared to love at a price) Queen Anne, for the sake of her father, James VII, and they believed Harley loved her. They were anxious to reach agreement with the government while she lived, for they foresaw it might be much more difficult to do this once she was dead – a coded reference to fear of a Hanoverian succession. As to action, Cameron recommended to Harley firstly that all feudal superiorities should be abolished, so chiefs would be independent and not burdened with services and payments to great men. Secondly, the small army garrisons scattered in the Highlands should be removed – they were useless, since if there were a rising they would be swept away immediately. Thirdly, every clan should be organised as a militia, with its chief as colonel, and paid a small pension. There would be about twenty militias in all, and they would keep 10,000 men in readiness to march to serve the queen at a week's notice.

In seeking the abolition of superiorities, Cameron asked in a few words for extremely controversial and complicated reforms, requiring fundamental changes to laws governing landownership – and consequently distribution of power – in Scotland. Either Cameron and his backers were extremely naive, or they were simply reiterating a long-held position on superiorities to make it clear that removing them remained essential to solving their grievances in the long term, even if there was no hope of anything being done immediately. In the short term, the core of the policy proposed was the 'modelling' of the Jacobite clans into militias, in return for pensions paid to chiefs. Cameron made it clear that this was to be seen not just as legalising the existing military structure of the clans and giving them a vested interest in living peacefully under the queen. The clan militias were to have a far wider role. They would form, if not a standing army, an organised fast-reaction reserve that could be called up to fight for the government in any of the three kingdoms of England, Scotland and Ireland. Scotland itself could be kept in obedience without the need for any army except the Highland militias – except a few garrisons. The queen and her successors (judiciously not defined) would be secure, and the continuing loyalty of the clans would be assured by the fact that once they were formed into militias they would come under military discipline. Allan Cameron ended with a warning. It would be no use trying to enforce an opposite policy, of demilitarising the Jacobite clans. Disarming would do no good, as clansmen would hide their weapons – or make new ones themselves. It was no use trying to arrest such uncooperative clansmen, for it would be impossible to arrest all of them simultaneously, and if that were not done they would all take up arms immediately. It was best therefore to gain the clans with gentle means. Do not awaken sleeping dogs, Cameron advised.

There is in this an appeal to a strand of Stuart policy going back to the civil wars of the 1640s, when Highlanders had proved more ready to fight for the king than other Scots. The dream was of the Highlands as a religiously conservative (Catholic and Episcopalian) and politically traditionalist bastion, with the military prowess of its inhabitants no longer seen as a threat to government but as a powerful military resource, dedicated to training fighting men to keep the rest of Scotland – or even the British Isles as a whole – obedient to government. The Highland Host of 1678, sent to suppress Lowland Presbyterian dissidents, had been a blundering trial of such an idea. Clans had tried to uphold James VII in 1689, and even though they failed they had indicated their potential to play such a role.

From the point of view of supporters of the Revolution Settlement, Cameron's vision was horrific, raising the spectre of the Stuarts, restored to the throne and absolute in power, enforcing their will with Highland armed might. The existing military structure of Highland society would be regularised and strengthened by the imposition of martial law, exercised by the chiefs, on all clansmen. The clans would become a hereditary military élite dedicated to enforcing obedience to a Stuart absolute monarch – and be suitably rewarded.

Cameron's plan, a dream of despotism, was far too ambitious for Harley. If trying to disarm the clans would awake sleeping dogs, so would trying openly to turn them into a government-sponsored militia army. But he saw some potential in Cameron's approach, for it indicated that the clans were ready to negotiate about their short-term loyalties, and he was willing to buy them. He agreed that pensions should be paid to some chiefs to ensure their loyalty to Queen Anne. The matter was handled secretly, and it is impossible to know the terms of the agreement negotiated. Essentially, Harley wanted to bribe the clan chiefs not to cause trouble. To be palatable to the chiefs, however, the deal had to be wrapped up in passionate assertions of loyalty to the Stuart queen and implicit ambitions of securing the Stuart succession – and an immediate start to military preparations. Essentially Harley was hoping to fool the chiefs, to lull them into a false sense of security so they would only find out too late that their passivity had allowed the Hanoverian succession to take place. But controlling over-enthusiastic chiefs who wanted to implement, at least in part, Allan Cameron's remarkable dream of the Highlanders forming the Stuarts' praetorian guard proved difficult. This fervour was potentially fatal to Harley's devious plan. If it became known that the government was encouraging, or even allowing, the Jacobite clans to arm and organise, Protestant Whig and (in England) Tory opposition would be likely to overthrow his ministry.

On the whole, Harley got what he wanted. Chiefs got their pensions, and though some preparations to fight for 'the queen' were made they were too small-scale to cause panic. However, news of the pensions did soon begin to leak out, and caused alarm. There were rumours that the payments were connected to a military build-up. An anonymous letter of about 1712 from an intelligence agent named seven chiefs (including Locheil) who had received government money, and claimed that each had agreed to provide a certain number of men in return. More dramatically, the agent had been with a group of men newly levied by Stewart of Appin under the pensions agreement. The meeting had ended abruptly when the agent unwisely refused to drink a toast to 'James VIII' (the Pretender). At least twenty-seven dirks and daggers had been drawn against him, but he had managed to escape[8] – though it may be doubted that he had really stopped to make a careful count of the weapons being flourished at him.

By December 1711 preparations for payment of the pensions were well advanced. The earl of Kinnoull was Harley's agent for the affair in Scotland, and Sir Patrick Murray of Ochtertyre was entrusted with actually making the secret payments. Harley had sent Kinnoull a 'parchment' to be signed by the chiefs, and Stewart of Appin was just setting off to gain signatures, before the first payments were made.[9] Nothing more is known of the parchment, but presumably it spelt out the terms of the deal Highlanders and Harley had made – and as such would have turned out a few years later to be highly incriminating to all concerned, and therefore a priority for hasty burning. However, a letter of thanks from ten chiefs to Harley, dated 20 December 1711, does survive, and it seems that they were those who were to receive pensions. There were four MacDonalds among them, plus MacPherson of Cluny, Stewart of Appin, the tutor of MacLeod, MacDougall of Dunnolly, John MacKinnon, and John Cameron of Locheil. Rather cheekily, the chiefs also suggested that a 'gratuity' to old Sir Ewan Cameron would be nice as a reward for past service. The Camerons wanted two bites from the cherry of secret service money.

Four thousand pounds sterling a year had been assigned for the pensions, and payments for the first year (up to November 1711) amounted to £3,450[10] – which fits in approximately with the claim in a later account that each chief was paid £360 sterling a year.[11] Work on cementing the alliance continued. In September 1712 John Cameron of Locheil was in Lochaber on a mission for 'our great friend', a coded reference to Harley. He referred to a 'paper' that would show that the 'party' would support Harley against all factions, which he was taking round the chiefs involved for their signatures. Harley's health, he reported, was being heartily drunk in Lochaber.[12]

Crucially for Harley, though stories of the secret plottings with the chiefs leaked out, they did not leak far. Those who discovered something of what was going on chose, for one reason or another, not to exploit what could have become a major political scandal. One of those who heard of the Highland pensions was Adam Cockburn of Ormiston, a man always with a finger on the pulse of events and a staunch ally of Montrose in the *Squadrone*. He heard that arms were being landed in the Highlands, and reported that the 'honest Revolution folk' in Edinburgh were very much alarmed. That news had spread to men bitterly opposed to both Harley and the Jacobite clans, and yet failed to develop into an acrimonious national debate seems remarkable, but government intelligence work no doubt helped. When Ormiston wrote to his son about the matter, the letter was intercepted and ended up in Harley's hands.[13]

Some who heard that a deal had been done with the chiefs privately expressed shock at payments being made to Jacobites and Catholics for military service. Others, like Breadalbane, were angry for other reasons. Why had a bunch of petty chiefs been given pensions and not a great man like him? Chiefs not in on the deal also resented their exclusion from the government handout, and even some of those who had been paid were unhappy at the amount they got. Payments seem to have been made at something approaching a flat rate, but more powerful chiefs argued that the money should have been distributed in proportion to clan manpower. Stewart of Appin, who had done much to further the pensions plan, was regarded by many of his colleagues as unworthy of having a pension for himself, as he could raise very few men in arms.[14] Both Stewart and Allan Cameron were also denounced for pretending they had commissions to negotiate with government which did not exist, and for not keeping chiefs fully informed as to what was being agreed. Probably there was truth in this. Both men had committed themselves to negotiating a deal between chiefs and government, and had probably tended to tell each party to the negotiations what it wanted to hear.[15]

Nonetheless, the deal worked. For Harley it was a successful political manoeuvre which bought him quiet in the Highlands, though the enthusiasm of the Jacobites for the scheme to be more was an embarrassment. A passionate statement of loyalty and reverence for monarchy (which may have been the paper Locheil was having signed in September 1712) was agreed by the chiefs and carried to London by Allan Cameron. There Harley presented him to Queen Anne, and Cameron offered what became known as the 'Sword in Hand' address to her. Ardent desire to serve Anne and the sacred house of Stuart, even (or perhaps especially) in arms was expressed, though the comment that it was hoped that the country's divisions would be ended on her death (and the succession, it was assumed, of her half brother) was hardly tactful.[16] However ready to serve they might be, the Jacobite chiefs had not been able to resist making the point that she, by occupying thrones that rightfully belonged to the Pretender, was prolonging the country's divisions. They could only be ended by the Pretender's succession to the crown. The message was that 'we are fervently loyal to you but we are also looking forward to your death'. 'Sword in hand' referred generally to willingness to fight for the Stuarts, and more specifically to the crest of Cameron of Locheil – a mailed hand grasping a sword with the motto 'Pro rege et patria' (For king and country).[17]

Having secured the Jacobite Highland chiefs through pensions, Harley considered extending the policy to other parts of Scotland, and a list was drawn up of Scots nobles 'to whom it is proposed to give pensions'. Nearly all were Lowlanders, but Breadalbane's name was among them.[18] Nobles had of course originally been excluded from the pension plan, but the wily Breadalbane now succeeded in inserting himself between Harley and the chiefs in a new round of negotiations, acting as their representative in asking Harley to send someone trusted and independent to tell the chiefs what Harley's plans were. Breadalbane's nominee for the mission was John Ogilvie, Harley's own agent,[19] independent only in the sense that, unlike the discredited Allan Cameron and Appin, he had no vested interests in the Highlands. In June 1714 Breadalbane was back in touch with Harley, urging that Ogilvie be sent north, and stressing that an essential ingredient in making Scotland 'secure' was letting the chiefs know what was to be done for them.[20] But, cunning as Breadalbane was, Harley was fooling him, as ever happy to string the Jacobites along with promises but not fully committing himself to their cause.

In April 1714 Harley's balancing act received its most serious challenge. In the House of Lords the duke of Argyll accused him of paying about £4,000 sterling a year to the clans, 'as if that sum were designed to keep in heart and discipline the Pretender's friends'. Further, 'the Scots highlanders being, for the most part, either rank [open] papists, or declared Jacobites, the giving them pensions was, in effect keeping up popish seminaries and fomenting rebellion'. But even Argyll did not mention the most serious part of the charge against Harley, that he was sponsoring the raising of militias, and Harley explained blandly that he was simply reviving a practice followed under King William, who had paid the clans 'to keep them quiet'.[21] Harley's conduct was approved, but within two months he was to be driven from office, for as the queen's health worsened, fears grew that his contacts with Jacobites meant he might try to bring about a Stuart succession.

Rob Roy has been missing from half a chapter in his biography, but can now make his entry. The plottings of Harley and the chiefs had taken place in his world, and it is likely that, with his close links with Breadalbane and the Camerons, he knew much of what was going on. Two cryptic letters suggest that he may have been at least on the fringes of the grand plans for the future of the Highlands. In January

1711 Allan Cameron, the prime mover in the plot, had stayed for several days at Taymouth Castle with Breadalbane. In February he was at Inverlochy, strategically placed for talks with the Jacobite chiefs of the west.[22] By April he was in London, ready to present his ideas to Harley. John Cameron of Locheil reported to Drummond of Balhaldie on his brother's activities. He understood that Allan was acting for Balhaldie and for John MacLean, chief of that clan. He then makes reference to 'the drover that wes with R Roye who is to be hear shortly in order to buy cowes.'[23] Who was the mysterious drover? Drovers, travelling widely in the Highlands and meeting with people of all sorts in pursuit of their trade, made excellent gatherers of intelligence and carriers of secret messages. Rob Roy's drover may have been a real drover, but equally the name could be code for an agent active in the negotiations with Harley. It was just a month after this letter was written that Allan Cameron presented his proposal for modelling the clans into a militia to Robert Harley.

A year later, the drover resurfaces, this time in a letter from Allan Cameron himself to Balhaldie (May 1712). The letter is incoherent, evidently through excitement as well as the necessity for obscurity in case the letter was intercepted. The persons his 'near friend' had visited when last in that country (Scotland) were well thought of by some people in London – which may be interpreted as meaning that the Jacobite chiefs in the pension plan were well thought of by Harley. Allan referred to 'the great affair in hand' then switched to revealing that 'The unknown ffriende I wrote to you of is Rob R's old camarad the drover, who is right every way, let some people fancie of him as they will [yet] he is full of honor and honesty. He tells me he wrote some tyme agoe to the great man my friende he visited last year.' It seems Rob's old comrade the drover was acting as a link between the chiefs and Harley (the 'great man') – and Allan believed in his honesty though some doubted it. The great person 'ought not to slight the drover for to my knowldge there is none . . . likes him better or would be readier to venture his life and all thats dear to him for that person than the drover'. In his determination to get his point across, Allan repeats himself, urging the 'great man not to slight the drover'.[24] The question of whether the elusive drover friend of Rob's has anything to do with Rob himself remains unanswerable. If he was indeed Rob's comrade, it strengthens the argument that Rob was well placed to know all about the pensions plan.

As news of the pensions leaked out, the MacGregors joined those furious about them, for they had been left out. The reason was simple. In law, since 1693 they had not been a clan, and had no chief. Pensions were only payable to chiefs. Something must be done – especially as Allan Cameron in 1711 had included the Clan Gregor in his list of those which it would be worth the government favouring. Cameron had realised that for this to be possible a clan chief was necessary, but though he had asserted that there was a MacGregor chief he had failed to name him. As has already been suggested, he probably meant his friend Drummond of Balhaldie, But there is no evidence up to this point of any wider acceptance of a claim to the chieftaincy by Balhaldie, and when Balhaldie had petitioned Harley personally for a pension in 1712 he had made no mention of a claim to chieftaincy. Of course the situation was awkward. To claim to be chief of an outlawed clan in order to secure a pension would have laid him open to criminal prosecution. Nonetheless that Balhaldie felt his petition had any hope of success at all may indicate that it was hoped that it would be understood as implicit in his request that he was in effect a chief. He didn't get a pension – Stewart of Appin had opposed a grant as he could not even raise 100 men,[25] thus judging him a private landowner rather than a chief of all the scattered MacGregors.

Nobody among the MacGregors seems to have bothered much about not having an effective chief for over a decade, but the situation had changed. Having a chief could mean money. There was need of a recognised (if still illegal) chief if there were to be any chance of MacGregors benefiting from the pension scheme. An election was organised, and it seems that Balhaldie was the only person seriously interested in the dubious status illegal chieftaincy would bring. A decade later it was to be said that Graham of Kilmannan, his 'male issue being all dead, and those few who pretend nearest relation to him being of mean repute and circumstances', had 'made (as is reported) a formal renunciation of the chiefship' in favour of Gregor MacGregor of Glengyle.[26] As senior representative of the *Clann Dughaill Cheir*, Glengyle indeed might have had a claim to the position. Perhaps even Rob himself might, in his heyday, as Glengyle's mentor and the best known figure of his kin, a successful cattle dealer and a landowner, have had a chance of being chosen. But his bankruptcy made that impossible. In any case Balhaldie had a head start in any chieftaincy contest, as a man already involved in the pension negotiations and 'respectable' as the owner of an estate in Lowland Perthshire, rather than being perceived as a wild Highlander like most MacGregors.

Sixteen leading MacGregors signed a bond in July 1714 declaring Alexander MacGregor of Balhaldie to be their 'Rightfull, lawfull and undoubted governor, head, chief and chieftan of our clan of Mcgregor.' The chieftaincy was to descend in his family 'as long as sun and moon endures'. The 'dismal calamities, oppressions and disgraces' the clan had suffered were narrated, and blamed mainly on men who had deserted 'their lawfull sovereign [James VII] at the time of the late unhapie revolution and still continue in rebellion against him'. The clan had sealed its loyalty 'with our blood and the death of our best men in every battle fought by our thin [then] gracious sovereign'. Since the Revolution implacable enemies had sought to destroy them, so not even the memory of the clan would survive. Now they were electing a chief, and at his command would fight to the death for their lawful sovereign.

The rhetoric is heartfelt and moving, the language that of real bitterness and loss. But the document then briskly descends to wheeling and dealing about money. If the government happened to grant Balhaldie, as the new chief, 'a pension, as other Chiefs get', he was to divide it into three parts and pay them to Gregor MacGregor of Glengyle, Gregor MacGregor of Brackly, and Gregor MacGregor of Rora. The rhetoric crumbles and collapses. Balhaldie has been accepted as chief in the hope that he could squeeze a pension out of the government. And though he would get the chieftaincy, his leading supporters would get the money.

All three men who where dreaming of payments from the putative pension signed the bond, and Rob Roy was among the other signatories. Indeed the bond was first signed in his house at Auch. This suggests that Rob had played a – if not the – central role in organising the revival of the chieftaincy, though in the background the influence of his protector, Breadalbane, may be suspected. The bond sought money, but it also pledged the MacGregors to the Jacobite cause. Cameron of Locheil signed as a witness, showing the interest other Jacobite clans were taking in the settling of the chieftaincy. After being signed at Auch on 20 July, the bond was sent to Dunblane, near the new chief's estates, where other signatures were added on 27 July.[27] The bond was written and witnessed by Duncan Corrie, the former minister of Inchailloch (Buchanan), who had performed Rob's marriage over twenty years before. Though deprived as an Episcopalian he had managed, with local support, to remain in his parish until 1707.

The best laid plans aft gang awry. The MacGregor pension bid went awry more quickly than most. Signing of the declaration declaring Balhaldie chief had been completed on 27 July 1714. Five days later, Queen Anne died, and the disastrous (from a Jacobite perspective) news spread that the Hanoverian King George instead of the Stuart King James VIII had been proclaimed in her place. The pension plan was dead, for George I, not unreasonably, turned out to be damned if he would pay pensions to Jacobite chiefs who wanted to dethrone him. The chiefs, who had eagerly accepted government pensions from a usurper's regime and justified this to themselves on the grounds that the money was intended to help them cooperate with Harley's ministry in bringing about a Stuart succession, found they had been tricked. Harley, and Harley's successors in office, had conned them. The only consolation they had was that he had lost office and was to suffer for his devious dealings with Jacobites by being arrested the following year on suspicion of treason.

Balhaldie had his chiefly title, but little respect. He had been elected in the hope that he would be the conduit for pension payments to clan members, but there was no pension for him to distribute. Dreams of a militarised Highlands that would keep Britain as a whole loyal to a restored Stuart dynasty lingered for many years. In the early 1720s the exiled earl of Mar, undeterred by his glaring failures of leadership in the 1715 rising, was urging that fifteen or sixteen thousand Highlanders should be formed into regiments under their chiefs and kept armed. They would be almost as good as regular troops and at 'much less expence'. It would be the cheapest army in Europe. Chiefs would receive £200 sterling a year per 500 men, the men themselves would be paid nothing except in time of war. They should be armed and clad in Highland dress – plaids in summer, trews in winter – and perhaps each regiment should have different colours of clothes.[28]

Within a few decades Mar's dream of tartan-clan Highland regiments serving the crown would begin to be realised. But it would be the Hanoverian crown that they served, and they would be used to fight in Europe and to extend the British Empire, not to cow the rest of Britain into submission to the Stuarts.

The peaceful, uncontested proclamation of George I on Queen Anne's death was a huge shock to the Jacobites. They had built their hopes for years on the expectation of a Stuart succession only for the Hanoverian candidate somehow to slip onto the throne when the moment came. As one 'J. MacGregory' wrote to Harley, the Scots Jacobite leaders had been astounded by the speed of events. As Tories had seemed firmly in power in London, they had relaxed, confident that the Pretender would be proclaimed king on Anne's death.[29] They had been fooled into thinking that English Tories were like Scottish ones – and, he might have added, by trusting in Robert Harley, earl of Oxford. Only military action could now further the Stuart cause, and obviously the best time to challenge the new King George would have been while he was seeking to establish his new regime and was still a stranger to his new kingdoms – grudgingly accepted by many because he was a Protestant rather than through positive loyalty or respect. But the Jacobites were not ready for action. They had spoken brave words about being willing to die for the cause but had not really expected to have to take the risk of doing so. They lacked organisation and leadership, had no specific plans for action, either of their own or co-ordinated with the Pretender. That Britain and France were now at peace meant there was little hope of foreign help – and the death of King Louis XIV, just weeks after Queen Anne, left France with a child monarch and even less likely than before to intervene in British affairs. There was fury and determination to do something in the Highlands, but frustration because nobody had thought out how to act.

All these developments affected Rob Roy. Like many other Jacobites he may be presumed to have had high hopes that on Queen Anne's death there would be a peaceful return of the Stuarts. At a personal level, if the Stuarts were restored he might hope for some sympathy in sorting out his financial problems – and above all, Montrose would lose his political influence. Now, instead, the Hanoverians were in power, the activities of his protectors, Breadalbane and Lord Drummond were under close scrutiny. Worst of all, Montrose had become secretary for Scotland, the government's chief minister for Scotland. He had plenty of more important things on his mind for the moment than that minor irritant Rob Roy, but it might not be long before he thought of using his new authority, and a new readiness to send troops into the Highlands, to deal with him.

Rob's reaction was defiance. This, it seems, is the point at which he despaired of reaching a peaceful compromise settlement with his creditors. The only hope of escaping from his problems was a Jacobite victory, and that could only be achieved by force. Already a Jacobite

in his heart, Rob for the first time since the early 1690s added action
to conviction. One evening late in October 1714 he appeared at the
market cross of Crieff, a town on the edge of the Highlands whose
cattle market he must often have visited in the past. There he publicly
drank the health of the Pretender, James Stuart. There were soldiers
stationed in the town, but they were taken by surprise, and Rob
was able to escape back into the safety of the hills.[30] This gesture
of defiance was far from unique. Scattered public drinkings of such
toasts were reported from many areas of the country. Jacobite lords
and chiefs were not ready to declare themselves, biding their time,
but Rob Roy and others of relatively lowly status were ready to dare
to express their feelings in public. Hatred of union and high taxation
fuelled a dangerous wave of popular opposition to the regime that
expressed itself in Jacobitism. Another incident in Crieff illustrates the
explosive mixture of grievances. On 13 November John MacAllan, a
gauger (an official collecting excise duties), went peacefully to sleep
for the night in Crieff. He woke to find the house he lodged in under
attack by 'several Ruffians' in Highland dress, armed with swords,
dirks and pistols. They burst into his room, which was lit by a candle,
and 'fell upon me most cruelly bruising and inhumanely wounding
me in several parts of my body, And which was worst of all, cut of
the most part of my right ear, which they carry'd with them'. Excise
officers were generally hated through opposition to the high duties on
spirits that they collected. The cutting off of an ear was not a random
act of brutality, but a deliberate copying of the regular punishment for
theft. If anyone involved was a ciminal, the attackers were claiming,
it was the tax collector. But there was more than this behind the
attack, MacAllan argued. He believed he had caused offence 'by
some modest signs of joy' he had shown on news of the coronation
of George I, and by expressing his zeal for 'our constitution' (the
Revolution constitution of 1688–9) on other occasions.[31] No doubt
he was right, and certainly this was the official interpretation of the
incident. MacAllan had been attacked not by tax protestors but by
Jacobites, ten to twelve of them.[32]

Now that he had committed himself (and doubtless by doing so
added to his popularity in the Highlands), Rob Roy became actively
involved in Jacobite conspiracy. In January 1715 Sir William Gordon,
newly appointed commander of the garrison at Fort William,
reported that Rob had passed through on his way north, had met with
Cameron of Locheil and Macdonald of Glengarry, and was currently

in Badenoch.[33] Rob may have been representing only himself and the MacGregors who would follow him, but it is possible that he was on a mission on behalf Breadalbane. Another source reported in the same month that Allan Cameron, who had been so central to Harley's pension scheme, had recently arrived from France, and was spreading news in the Highlands that the Jacobite pretender was going to send money – and would arrive himself within a few months. An informant said 'he saw one well known to' Montrose – Rob Roy. He too was travelling round 'going from place to place and talking to the same purpose' as Cameron.[34] John Haldane of Gleneagles confirmed this, warning that the 'extravagancies' of the Jacobites were increasing. They were either stark mad or had some great plan in hand. Rob Roy 'has bin up and doun in severall houses of this countrie did, as I am just nou told (5 February), go to the Cross of Creif and after drinking the healths usual to these sort of folk drank a health to those honest and brave felous [fellows] cutt out the Gadger's ear'.[35] Poor John MacAllan's mutilation was a symbol of government defied.

For those worriedly trying to gauge Jacobite intentions, Rob was now a man to watch. In March reports said he was now known as 'Colonel Robert', and was 'listing' men – enlisting men ready to fight.[36] Atholl, with his jurisdictions as sheriff principal of Perthshire, lord of the regalities of Atholl and Dunkeld, and steward principal of Fife and Huntingtower, investigated the report, but his panoply of impressive-sounding offices did not get him very far. One Grigor Murray (MacGregor) was examined as to whether he had been buying or selling arms, and whether Rob Roy or others had tried to enlist him. He asserted that in February he had bought seven targes (shields) for Rob Roy, but that on hearing he was under suspicion of drinking the Pretender's health he had sold them elsewhere. No one had tried to enlist him.[37] Another report, that Rob had several times visited Dunblane and employed all the 'sword-slippers' there in making broadswords, also remained unconfirmed.[38]

While Atholl interrogated suspects, he was himself under suspicion, and trying to ward it off by being helpful to the government. He wrote to Adam Cockburn of Ormiston, the justice clerk of Scotland, that had only seen Rob once recently, and that had been before he knew anything either of Rob's alleged commission as a Jacobite colonel or of his enlisting of men, but he was sure that if Ormiston had a chance to question Rob there would be a lot to be learnt of what was happening in the Highlands. Rob had told him little except that he heard that Simon Fraser of Beaufort was back in Scotland as a Jacobite agent. Atholl, still seeking revenge for the rape of his sister more than fifteen years before (see chapter two), had ordered Rob 'to endeavour to apprehend them [Lovat and another Jacobite suspect], thinking he was fit enough for it'. Atholl sounds apologetic. It was a bad time to have commissioned Rob to act for him, for Rob the bankrupt was fast becoming Rob the rebel.

Rumours of Jacobite activity came ever thicker and faster. Early in April it was said Rob was at a meeting on Loch Katrine attended by Glengyle, Malcolm Murray of Marchfield (a leading Balquhidder MacGregor), some Skye men, and representatives of Lord Murray and Lord Drummond, and that some agreement had been reached.[39] In autumn 1714 the Hanoverian regime had been confident enough to demonstrate its power by making pre-emptive arrests of leading Jacobite suspects. In Spring 1715 it did not dare attempt to repeat the process, for it was clear that that would simply precipitate rebellion. Whether it acted or not, it was accepted that rebellion was coming, and it was clear that Rob Roy was going to be part of it.

Yet for all his activity and travelling in the Highlands for the Jacobite cause, Rob was playing a double game. He was simultaneously supplying the Hanoverian duke of Argyll with intelligence about Jacobite activity. This was not quite the same as passing it to the government, for Scottish affairs were for the moment dominated by the *Squadrone Volante*, with Montrose as secretary of state based mainly in London and Cockburn of Ormiston as justice clerk acting as his most trusted agent in Edinburgh. Argyll was their most feared rival, and he was not likely to share intelligence with them. But they heard that he had a profitable source of intelligence on what was happening in the Highlands, and worked to track it down. In May 1715 Graham of Gorthie at last identified its source. Colin Fairfoul was first lieutenant of Finab's independent company. He had known Rob Roy for at least ten years, occasionally being involved in financial dealings with him. Now, Gorthie told Montrose 'it's he that manages Rob Roy for ane intelligencer to D.A. [the Duke Argyll]'. Sir James Campbell of Ardkinglas had recently visited London, evidently for consultations with Argyll, and a day or two before Ardkinglas had left home Rob had been taken to his house to talk with him by Fairfoul. How long this sort of thing had been going on for is unknown. It may well have begun years before, even before Rob's downfall, with Rob and Fairfoul exchanging titbits of information when they met, this then developing into something more serious once Rob fell on hard times and needed protection against Montrose. Given this relationship with Fairfoul, it is no wonder that the independent company had failed to arrest Rob in 1712. Gorthie doubted that Rob's intelligence was worth much – Rob would 'not let him [Fairfoul] in very deep', though Fairfoul probably didn't realise this.[40] Gorthie later confirmed that it was reported that Rob was not an easy agent to manage: 'in short I believe Rob Roy is his [Fairfoul's] informer, and leads him a dance'. However, it was believed that intelligence received by Fairfoul from Rob had formed the basis of a report that the Old Pretender had written letters to Atholl, Breadalbane and Lord Drummond seeking their opinions.[41]

Squadrone ministers might put little trust in the intelligence Rob was supplying and therefore have the consolation of concluding that Argyll was only receiving unimportant information of Highland affairs. But Ormiston was sure that if captured Rob would be a highly valuable source of information on Highland Jacobites – 'he could tell all their intrigues'. If Argyll and his brother the earl of Islay looked into it, Rob 'might soon be outlawed, and forc'd to submit'.[42] At first sight this seems puzzling – Rob was already an outlaw. But what Ormiston probably meant was that if Argyll would 'outlaw' him in a much more serious way – denounce him for treason – then arresting him would become a much higher government priority. There was just one problem blocking Ormiston's scheme. It would mean asking Argyll to do him and Montrose a favour, and it was wildly unlikely that he would ever agree to that.

The world of informers and double agents is always difficult to penetrate. What are their motives, where does their true allegiance lie? That at heart Rob was a lifelong Jacobite in political terms it is unreasonable to doubt. But though he had publicly committed himself to that cause, he was far too intelligent to think it was certain to succeed. If it failed, then he could not rely on Breadalbane's protection as in the past, for the earl's increasingly open Jacobitism would discredit him – and, in any case, he was a very old man. So, contingency planning was necessary. Cultivate Argyll by feeding him intelligence, and thus have a claim to his protection if other protectors failed him. In making such calculations Rob was far from alone. Most Scots involved in the dangerous game of politics, Hanoverian and Jacobite, maintained some bonds of friendship with their ideological opponents. Partly it was a matter of genuine considerations of friendship and kinship taking precedence over political division, but there was also calculation involved. The world might change fast, and if you turned out to be on the losing side having men ready to speak up for you might help you save your estates – or your head.

It is possible therefore to argue that Rob's devious and unscrupulous behaviour should not be held against him. He was behaving normally, adopting a commonplace strategy for survival. However, Rob was not dealing with social equals, but with those far above him in rank and power. Friendship would not be enough to get him remembered in hard times. He had no cash or influence to offer to Argyll in return for protection. The only commodity he had to trade was intelligence. Perhaps at first the intelligence he supplied was low-grade, information that was about to become public or which the Hanoverian 'enemy' could have obtained elsewhere. But Argyll was no fool. Rob could not hope to gain and retain favour by supplying useless information. For him to have bothered keeping contact with Rob as an agent meant that the intelligence being supplied must have had some value. By secretly supplying intelligence to one side while ostensibly working for the other Rob raises a whole range of unanswerable questions about loyalty and betrayal.

Gorthie and Ormiston had unearthed Rob Roy's intelligence contacts with Argyll in May 1715. By the following month the Jacobites also knew that Rob was playing a double game. This was revealed by Graham of Killearn. He had decided to obtain his own intelligence information about what was going on in the seething centre of intrigue that the Highlands had become. A drover, 'W.G.', was commissioned to see what he could find out. His trade meant he could travel around without rousing suspicion, and he would have had many contacts with whom he could exchange gossip – and more. Much of what 'W.G.' reported may have been unreliable rumour. That Highlanders were arming, buying broadswords and pistols in Lowland towns on the fringes of the Highlands, may be believed, but that the captain of Clanranald had had over 10,000 targes made sounds fanciful. Equally unreliable was the rumour that the earl of Islay (Argyll's brother) had been appointed to replace Montrose as secretary of state. But the drover's report of Jacobites' reaction to this premature rumour of Montrose's fall from power[43] is of interest. They had been overjoyed, because they believed that if Montrose had been dismissed from office he would transfer his allegiance to the Jacobite cause. That the rumour proved untrue must have been a relief to Rob Roy. Had Montrose become a leading figure among the Jacobites, Rob's hopes of favour from them if they came to power Jacobites would have been lost.

However, the drover reported that Rob was in a different type of trouble. Neither he nor Maclaine of Lochbuie was trusted by the Jacobites, for they had been sending intelligence to Argyll and Islay. Indeed, 'Rob is obliged to live closs at home and dare not venture to goe much ffurder [further] in the Highlands.' On this W.G. signed off with a broad hint as to his expenses: he had been 'at a good deall of expense in drinking with them [Jacobites] wherever he went'.[44] There was nothing like drink to make men talk.

News of Rob's double-dealing had travelled fast. A Jacobite rising was in the making, but he had been discredited before it had even begun. He was, however, a hard man to keep down, and he was quickly to recover some of his credibility. His gift of winning folk over, in spite of his roguery, must have done him good service, and he was soon able to leave home safely and move through the Highlands again. Political animosities in the Highlands might be bitter, but men were often tolerant of a degree of double-dealing, perhaps having the honesty to admit to themselves their own lack of scruples. Deviousness might, indeed, be something to be admired.

5

REBEL

The new regime of George I realised that a rebellion against it in Scotland, centred on the Highlands, was almost inevitable once the Jacobites got their act together. That it took a year to emerge was an indication of how successfully the chiefs had been deceived into thinking a peaceful Stuart succession had been secretly favoured by Harley's government. Thus the new regime had time to consolidate itself before it was challenged. An immediate reaction by the new regime was to order the arrest of some chiefs, but they were released in October 1714 when it was realised that a rising was not imminent. Only a few extra troops were sent to Scotland, for fear of provoking instead of deterring rebellion. In some Lowland frontier areas it was feared that the change of monarch would herald immediate disorder in, and raiding from, the Highlands, and watches were hastily organised to guard against this. One was established on Loch Arklet, to prevent raids from Rob Roy's homeland.[1] But though there were isolated acts of defiance, it was to take a year for the Highland Jacobites to find a leader, in the person of the earl of Mar.

Late in 1713 Harley had revived the post of secretary for Scotland, and had chosen Mar for the job. Like many politicians, Mar was a man ready serve whoever succeeded Queen Anne, Stuart or Hanoverian, but he had close links with some Jacobites – and he was a Tory. The Whig ministers of King George impressed on the new king that all Tories were at heart Jacobite traitors, however, so Mar's position was in danger. He had written to the new king even before he arrived in England eagerly expressing his loyalty and desire to serve him,[2] and he came up with a plan to prove that he was indispensable to the stable government of the Highlands. He had a strong personal following in the eastern Highlands, and a letter was hastily organised, addressed to him by eleven chiefs, writing for themselves and in name of others who lived in places too remote for them to be consulted. The chiefs claimed that they had served Queen Anne loyally, and had always been ready to follow Mar's directions. They would be happy to join Mar in serving King George with equal loyalty. They awaited his directions on how they were to proceed.[3] Thus under the cover of expressing fulsome loyalty to George I there was an implicit threat. Mar must remain the link between the clans and the crown. The chiefs involved were at heart Jacobite, but the Hanoverians were for the moment in power so declarations of loyalty were expedient. Perhaps they could even persuade George to continue to pay them pensions.

The king probably never saw the letter, and had he done so the hint that it contained (keep Mar in office or there will be trouble) would have been more likely to have enraged than placated him. The king also never saw a rival approach from the clans. An address to him was signed by 102 landowners and 'heads' of clans in the Highlands. In this, the signatories expressed their zeal to serve a king who had the blood of their ancient monarchs in his veins – an intimation that they accepted him as a descendant of the Stuarts and therefore legitimate king, while avoiding actually stating that they would support him against the Pretender. Most were Jacobites – and the signatories included two of the leading Argyllshire Campbell lairds who were the following year to come to the brink of joining in rebellion (Auchinbreck and Lochnell), as well as many who were to rebel that year.[4] But for the moment, declarations of loyalty to the new regime were expedient.

Nothing, however, could persuade the king to trust Highlanders – or Mar, who was dismissed from office in September 1714. At first he hung on at court, hoping to regain favour, but as the months passed and the new Hanoverian regime began to strengthen its grip on the country he began to fear for his safety. Pre-emptive moves were now being discussed to forestall Jacobite rebellion and he like other Tories – especially Scottish ones – was under suspicion. Talk of a 'clan act' of the sort that had been considered in 1708 was revived, and in 1715 two acts sought to prevent rebellion and permanently reduce the powers of chiefs in the future.

First came an act for encouraging all who were doing and continued to do their duty and be loyal. It was clear that in the Highlands loyalty to feudal superiors often overrode loyalty to the crown, and custom and law gave superiors and chiefs power to enforce treasonable behaviour on lesser men. Therefore, in future, if a vassal remained

loyal, resisting his rebellious superior, then the superiority would be
cancelled and the former vassal would hold his land directly from
the crown. Similarly, if it was the superior who remained loyal while
the vassal rebelled, the vassal's land would revert to his superior. The
same sort of combination of rewards and penalties would also apply
to vassals and their tenants. Finally, from September 1715 to January
1716 the justice general of Scotland was given power to summon any
landowner in Scotland to appear in Edinburgh and find bail for their
loyalty. If they did not appear they would be fined or suffer 'liferent
escheat' – that is, have all income from their estates confiscated
for life.[5] Under this clause, sixty-two chiefs and other landowners
were summoned to Edinburgh. Only two minor figures appeared
in Edinburgh – and both were arrested.[6] Among the defaulters was
'Rob Roy, alias MacGregor'.[7] He might no longer have an estate to be
seized, but he was notorious enough to be included on the list – and
the fact that Montrose had now replaced Mar as Scottish secretary
may have helped ensure his name was not forgotten.

The act for encouraging loyalty applied to all Scotland. A second
act only covered the Highlands – the act for the more effectual peace
of the Highlands. The custom had too long prevailed of Highlanders
carrying and using arms, it was related. This obstructed the civilising
of the people and prevented them applying themselves to trade and
industry, led to riots and lawlessness, and had been one of the
causes of the 'late unnatural rebellion' (in 1689). In future, therefore,
carrying of weapons in the Highlands was to be forbidden, though
nobles and all those with an income of over £400 Scots a year were
to be exempt. Carrying of arms was thus to become a mark of social
status.

Another Highland practice contrary to good government, hindering
trade and promoting rebellion, was the obligation of men to perform
personal services for their chiefs, through obligations in charters or
by custom. These services were often arbitrary and oppressive, it
was declared, and gave chiefs a means of gathering together large
numbers of armed men. All services – hunting, hosting, watching
and warding – were therefore to be abolished with effect from
1 August 1717 as being destructive of the liberties of free people.
However, compensation would be given to the chiefs, the services
being commuted into money payments.[8]

What reaction to these acts did the government expect? Did it
actually expect Highlanders to disarm themselves and hand in

their weapons? Did it really believe the sixty-two men summoned to Edinburgh would appear? And believe that the chiefs would quietly submit to the abolition of personal services, which would destroy much of their power? If so, the government was remarkably naive – which is not impossible. But, in the circumstances in which they were passed, the acts were so provocative that there must be suspicion that the acts were passed with the knowledge that, though in the long term the policies introduced might prevent rebellion, in the short term they were likely to precipitate it. If a rebellion were to come in the Highlands, it might be better to provoke it while the Jacobites lacked leadership and plans. Yet this cannot be the whole story. Had the regime expected to provoke rebellion, surely it would have been building up its military strength in Scotland. But when the rebellion began, the army in Scotland could muster a mere 1,500 or so men. Rebellion took the ministry by surprise. The fact that George had been on the throne for a year without a revolt had lulled it into complacency.

These 1715 acts have been lost sight of by historians in the past century, but it is likely that they were very influential in persuading many Highlanders to rebel. Men who might have put up indefinitely, however unhappily, with a Hanoverian king provided that the government did not interfere in the Highlands, were threatened with the breakup of traditional structures of authority within their clans. Islay, Argyll's brother, recognised this and was to write (after the rebellion had begun) that many had feared that if they did not rebel, or if rebellion failed, 'the Government will put an end to Highland troubles' once and for all. Ending Highland troubles had become synonymous with destroying the powers of chiefs and the power structures of the clans. Islay favoured such action in principal, but admitted that in practice nothing had caused more trouble in the Highlands than this 'notion'.[9] An equally staunch supporter of the new regime, Graham of Gorthie, opposed the principles as well as the results of the act. Though a Lowlander, his job of running Montrose's estates meant he had many close links with Highlanders, and he feared official policy now aimed at making them second class citizens. Differences between Highland and Lowland society caused difficulties, he admitted. 'It's a hard matter that in one countrey their should be two different species of creatures, the one wild and the other tame, the last because civilised are not armed – the first arm'd for no other reason, but that they are barbarous.' But limiting the rights of Highlanders, which Gorthie feared was the intention, would mean 'we should be in no better circumstances, then the American plantations are with the wild Indians still under the apprehension of being ruined by these people [the colonists] whenever they think fitt'.[10] Thus to Gorthie Highlanders were barbarous, but putting them in fear of the destruction of their society was not going to help.

The earl of Mar was one of those who panicked at news of the acts and of the Whig ministry's threatening action against Queen Anne's former ministers. Mar saw his choice as lying between flight and imprisonment. When the king turned his back on him at court it was the last straw. Convinced that arrest was imminent, he fled north to Scotland. His English counterparts had chosen France as a refuge, for they had no regional power-bases in which to make a stand in Britain. Mar believed that he had – in his own Highland tenantry, and in the clans, which only needed a show of leadership to release their tensions through rebellion. A year before he had tried to persuade George I that he could command the clans in serving the king. Now he would implement the threat implicit in the offer – that if spurned he could lead the clans against him.

When he had still been secretary for Scotland, at the time of King George's accession, Mar had banned *tincels* for fear they would become pretexts for planning Jacobite rebellion, for these great deer hunts gave chiefs an excuse to gather many hundreds of armed men together through just the sort of personal service that was soon to be abolished. But now he arranged *tincels* of his own, holding large gatherings, supposedly for hunting, in late August and early September 1715. On 6 September they culminated in a formal declaration of war, the raising of the Pretender's standard at Braemar and Mar's announcement that he was the Pretender's commander-in-chief.

Mar has often been blamed for being precipitate in raising the standard, but it seems likely that he and the chiefs who supported him feared delay. The outrage caused by the accession of King George might well turn into despair if action were not taken quickly. A year had passed, but for all the brave words nothing had happened. Leadership was lacking, and the appearance of Mar in the Highlands seemed a godsend. He had status and credibility. He had been near the centre of British government up to a year before, and he was willing to lead. The trouble was that though he might have some skills as a politician, he had no military experience – and, it soon turned out, no military instinct. His confidence came from the fact that he was of noble blood. Military leadership was assumed to be central to nobility. It was something inherited.

Rebellion had begun. Rob had of course begun his own personal rising some ten months before by drinking to the Pretender's health in Crieff. Jacobite indignation at the exposure of his intelligence-gathering for Argyll in June 1715 turned out to be short-lived. Just weeks after it had been said that he was being shunned it was reported from Fort William that a considerable amount of money had been sent to Scotland to be distributed among chiefs according to how many men they were to raise in arms. The money had been sent under a guard commanded by Rob Roy, to be held in Drummond Castle. Distribution, supervised by Breadalbane, had begun in late July.[11]

By the time Mar raised the Stuart standard in September chiefs had already begun gathering men to form an army, but the process was pretty chaotic, and there is no sign of any strategy beyond determination to march south if necessary to restore the Stuarts. It was hoped that the raising of the standard and recruiting men would trigger off risings elsewhere in Britain, and the less committed would have been satisfied with forcing concessions from the government. Perhaps, even, King George would relent over the pensions that Queen Anne had paid the chiefs, and restore them. Threat of rebellion might lead to Mar being restored to favour and the new Highland policies aimed at destroying the power of chiefs being reversed. The total lack of any long-term planning is clearly indicated by the absurdity that Mar had given no indication of his intentions to the person in whose name he led his rebellion, the Pretender whom Mar had proclaimed King James VIII.

Luckily for the Jacobites their disorganisation and incompetence was at first matched by that of the Hanoverians. Though rebellion had been anticipated, there had been no attempt to reinforce the army since the previous year. As so often, it had been easier to hope for the best and do nothing. But at least the army in Scotland was provided with a soldier as commander-in-chief. The duke of Argyll was the right man in the right place at the right time.[12] Not only was he among the most powerful of the Scottish nobility, and the most potent Highland chief, in the war of the Spanish Succession he had won distinction as a general, and earned the nickname Red John of the Battles from his Campbell clansmen. For a time he had been something of a political loose cannon, accusing the government

of favouring Jacobites in the army, which suggested his support for
the Hanoverian succession, but he then introduced a motion in the
House of Lords (which was lost by only four votes) for dissolving
the union between Scotland and England, a move which might well
have proved disastrous to that succession. However, once George
I ascended the throne he proved a staunch supporter of the new
regime. The new king's favour was shown by his granting Argyll the
prestigious court office of groom of the stole to the prince of Wales. It
has been said of Argyll that 'His personality combined two qualities
rarely found together . . . fathomless arrogance and a fund of solid
common sense.'[13] He was not a man to suffer fools gladly, and he
lacked the art of telling people what they wanted to hear. His hatred
of his former commander-in-chief, the great duke of Marlborough,
was notorious, and he made many enemies.

One of these enemies, through family rivalry for regional power as
well as national politics, was of course the duke of Montrose, Mar's
replacement as Scottish secretary, but Montrose was frustrated by the
limitations of the powers he was allowed, and as rebellion in Scotland
approached attention and influence inevitably swung towards the
military man, Argyll, who was appointed commander-in-chief in
Scotland. In August 1715 Montrose resigned office. Perhaps he did
this because he foresaw disaster in the Highlands, and was glad to
escape responsibility.[14] More likely he resigned simply because he
saw his influence declining. There were, as already noted, rumours
suggesting that he, like Mar, might follow up loss of office by joining
the Jacobites. Some of his own followers may have feared this. On 2
August James Graham, as deputy sheriff of Dunbartonshire, wrote
to him that he hoped that the duke and his neighbours 'will not
only be far from doing anything against the government, but on
the contrary exert themselves with all the vigour in their power
for and in conjunction with the government.' He stressed the local
military preparations being made in case there was a Jacobite rising.
In Dumbarton all men in the town between sixteen and sixty had
been ordered to assemble to be formed into a militia (at which all
Highlanders had fled from the town), and watches at Loch Arklet
and elsewhere were to be re-established.[15]

Such warnings to the duke were in fact unnecessary. He remained
committed to the Hanoverian cause. However, in the months that
followed he and his *Squadrone* colleagues gave priority to undermining
Argyll's position as commander-in-chief. One commentator remarked

that the conflict between *Argathelians* and the *Squadrone* seemed to have been carried on with more spirit and malice than proceedings against the Jacobite rebels.[16]

The strategic keys to the civil war that followed were Stirling and the River Forth. Most Jacobite support lay to the north, and it took little effort for Mar to gain control of most of that region, but for the Jacobite cause to become credible he needed to break out into the south to encourage southern Scottish and English Jacobites to rise in arms. To do that, Stirling had to be taken or outflanked. Trying to break southwards to the east of Stirling would have involved crossing the River Forth where it was too wide and deep to ford, or crossing the Firth of Forth by boat. To break out to the west of Stirling would involve moving Mar's army through wide areas of bog. The arguments for a swift advance on Stirling, with its bridge over the river, were strong, and it was known that the Hanoverian forces available to defend the vital bridge were weak – though Mar may not have known quite how weak they were.

When Argyll reached Stirling in September 1715 he had only about 1,600 men to defend the position. His reaction was despair. He had been warning for months that preparations needed to be made in readiness for the outbreak of a rebellion, but nothing had been done. He thought it would be impossible to stop the rebels if they attacked, as he was so greatly outnumbered. His demoralisation was all the greater because he knew there were political calculations behind the failure to strengthen his army. He even asked to be replaced as commander-in-chief as it seemed that only then would reinforcements be sent. In a rare fit of modesty, he urged that there were army officers senior to him of infinitely greater abilities who could replace him. Everything seemed to go wrong. He had been advised to send £300 sterling to the duke of Atholl at Blair Castle, to help keep him loyal and give him the resources to defend himself. But Atholl's eldest son, Lord Tullibardine, who had joined the rebels, intercepted the money. Mar's army, Argyll feared, was about to attack over the upper Forth and strike at Glasgow, and they would have an advantage due to the nature of the routes they would follow, which were mainly boggy and mountainous, passable for infantry but impossible for cavalry, the military arm in which the Hanoverians might be stronger than the Jacobites.[17] To hopeless weakness in the face of the enemy and political back-stabbing as causes for Argyll's demoralisation were added unspoken forces. He knew that the rebellion might tear the unity of his own clan apart, with some of his greatest vassals possibly joining the rebel cause – as Breadalbane already had – and he feared that harsh government retaliation against them after the rebellion, added to the new acts banning chiefs from enforcing personal service from their clansmen, would destroy much of his power.

Luckily for Argyll, Mar was hesitant, waiting for more forces to be gathered from the Highlands. Another argument for delay was that it was important to coordinate action with the exiled Stuart court – and to get the Pretender to Scotland as soon as possible, as that would greatly increase confidence and thus encourage recruitment. Further, it may be that Mar and some of his advisers were among those who hoped for a political solution through forcing concessions from the government.

Mar was unwilling to fight for the moment, while Argyll wanted to act but was starved of necessary resources. He received some reinforcements, but on too small a scale for him to be willing to undertake the offensive action the government expected of him. His repeated demands for more resources and insistence that taking the offensive would be unacceptably risky was increasingly interpreted by his political masters (who were often also political rivals) as weakness. Some even hinted at lack of courage, or of treacherous sympathies for the Jacobite cause, and it is true that he had no taste for the sort of harsh treatment some talked of imposing on the rebels once they had been defeated, and had no wish to shed more of his countrymen's blood than was necessary. Nonetheless, Argyll's commitment to the Hanoverian dynasty was firm, and as the commander on the spot the veteran general's judgement that to advance north of Stirling in the autumn of 1715 would have been folly deserves respect as a cautious but realistic assessment of the situation. That he did not let himself be influenced by strident, ignorant and distant politicians is to his credit.

There was therefore stalemate, as the main Jacobite army gathered around Perth and the Hanoverians in Stirling faced each other, neither ready to advance for a showdown. Both sides sought intelligence of enemy activities, and to influence waverers. An agent of Argyll's in the Jacobite camp suggested that the MacGregors were among the latter. He told Argyll's brother Islay that he had got the MacGregors to agree to desert and bring 'a battalion of very good men' to join Islay in helping the Hanoverians to defend Argyllshire from the Jacobites. But honour required that they have some pretext for quarrelling with the earl of Mar before they deserted him. 'I shall breed a confusion mysel[f] that will make them to discord with the earl,' said the agent, if Islay agreed to this. Meanwhile, he would return to Mar's camp and send Argyll news of every Jacobite movement and council of war. Further, the agent indicated that his credibility among the Jacobites would be much improved if, on any list of men denounced as rebels, his name were included. 'Let me allways be in the first list.' Any correspondence with the agent was to 'come by Fanab [Finab]'.[18]

At first sight, what we know of this agent seems to fit Rob Roy. The man was an established Campbell agent in leading Jacobite circles. He was being 'run' as an agent by Finab. He surely must himself have been a MacGregor if he had such influence over them that he thought that he could make them change sides. Moreover in later years, Rob was repeatedly to argue that he had always wanted to fight for the Hanoverians but had been deterred from doing so for fear that Montrose would have him arrested (though when Rob said such things he had of course good self-serving interests in presenting such a picture of his inclinations). However, though Rob may be a suspect, the only evidence suggesting that he might have been this agent is circumstantial, and his activities at this time suggest that he was moving around too much to report regularly on the doings of the council of war at Perth – though agents are often prone to exaggerate their access to confidential information. Indeed the whole story of a possible MacGregor change of sides may be no more than the extravagant inventions of an agent anxious to prove his own importance – which would push Rob Roy back into the frame. Was it Rob himself who insisted on his name being on the list of those denounced as rebels and charged with treason?

Though there was deadlock around Perth and Stirling, to the west there was movement, as the Jacobites probed at Hanoverian defences – such as there were. Rob was active here for the Jacobites, though how far he was trusted is uncertain. Throughout the 1715–16 campaign there was to be a noticeable tendency to keep Rob on the periphery. This may simply have been because the MacGregors, though warlike, were undisciplined, and regarded as best suited to raiding. But it may also have reflected a feeling that he and his men were best kept away from the main army and the private discussions of generals. Even Highlanders did not have a high opinion of the dependability of MacGregors.

Montrose's agents on his estates busily collected intelligence of

Jacobite movements. There were fears of attack. Rob, it was reported, intended to march south, reinforced by Camerons and Stewarts of Appin, and camp on Drummond (Drymen) Moor.[19] On 25 September 1715, however, Gorthie wrote from Edinburgh with relief that there were no signs yet of activity in the Buchanan area. Nonetheless he and Graham of Killearn thought it was not safe for them to remain at their usual base, Buchanan Castle. Killearn had heard that Rob Roy had 'a design against him' in particular, so he ventured to Buchanan only during the day, retreating further into the Lowlands at night. Montrose's own tenants in Menteith and Buchanan, Gorthie thought, would not join the Jacobites, but they would not stop others joining them – several parties of horsemen had passed by unhindered on their way to join Mar.[20]

Gorthie's news was out of date. The same day Killearn heard that several of the clans were gathering their men in Glenorchy, where they were to join Breadalbane's men and move south. The MacGregors were to meet in Glengyle and join them, and threats to ruin Killearn were being circulated. Rob Roy and Glengyle had passed through Aberfoyle a few days before, and the news of his intentions came from there.[21] Such rumours of attack being imminent may well have been spread by Rob himself to cause alarm, but there is some evidence to suggest that he may have planned to move south, but was ordered north instead. Glengyle had gathered about forty men at Stronlachacher on Loch Katrine and waited for Rob, it was said, but Rob had sent a message that when he had reached Balquhidder he had received an order to return to his house (Auch in Glenorchy must be meant). MacDonald of Glengarry and Cameron of Locheil had reached that area with 2,000 men, and were due to march with Breadalbane's men. Glengyle was urged to bring his men to join them. Killearn was relieved. Wherever Rob and the MacGregors were moving, it was not in his direction.[22]

He was wrong to relax. The MacGregors did move south. On 27 September a hasty message indicated that Rob Roy, Glengyle and Balhaldie had reviewed their forces at Corriearklet. MacGregors who refused to join the rising were being threatened with death. Many of Montrose's men had also been threatened, but only a few MacGregors among them had joined the Jacobites. For fear that they would raid southwards, a Lieutenant Napier and some horsemen had been sent from Stirling and stationed at Drumkill, near Buchanan.[23] Then on 30 September the town of Dumbarton found people from the parishes to the north and east pouring into the town, carrying whatever possessions they could. They were fleeing a body of Highlanders who had come down from the 'head' of Buchanan – the northern, Highland, part of the parish – on the 29 August under the command of Rob Roy and his nephew. They had first attacked Montrose's tenants, making them surrender any arms they had, then tying them up so they could not spread the alarm. The MacGregors had proceeded to seize all the boats on Loch Lomond, and moved to the safety of Montrose's island of Inchmurrin in the loch for the night. Next day they had landed, and camped on the burgh moor of Dumbarton. Their numbers were unknown, but sixteen boats loaded with rebels were reported as having landed before returning to Inchmurrin to pick up more. On the burgh moor, it was estimated, there were about as many men as assembled at the Lammas Fair – a not very helpful measurement. The magistrates of Dumbarton sent urgently to Glasgow for help, warning that if Dumbarton fell, Glasgow would be next. The provost of Glasgow was away in Stirling, so the letter was forwarded to him. He in turn sent to Argyll, urging that regular troops needed to be sent to deal with the situation. But the letter didn't reach Argyll until 6 October.[24]

The crisis passed as swiftly as it had arrived, however. Ringing of bells and firing of guns from Dumbarton Castle had given the alarm, and local landowners loyal to the government began to assemble with their men. It then became clear that the Highlanders' advance was merely a raid, not an attempt to occupy and hold territory. The MacGregors assembled on Dumbarton moor turned out to be 'only some of Robroys party seeking for armes and plunder'[25] and they withdrew, first to Inchmurrin (where they feasted on Montrose's herd of roe deer) and then to Inversnaid, where they dragged all the boats they had collected out of the water and tried to hide them. Whether the raid had Mar's sanction is unknown. Quite possibly it was the MacGregors' own venture, and it is notable as the first time Rob had raided Montrose's lands. He did so as a Jacobite fighting for his rightful king, not in pursuit of a private quarrel as a debtor infuriated by an intransigent creditor, but of course the two cannot in reality be separated. The debtor must have found fierce satisfaction in having a justification for damaging the man he blamed for his ruin.

It may have been hoped that this raid down Loch Lomond would deter Hanoverians from taking action against MacGregor lands in the area while the clansmen marched off to join Mar's army. If so, the plan backfired. The swift withdrawal of the MacGregors encouraged a retaliatory raid. Warships in the Clyde provided a hundred or so seamen, three longboats and four pinnaces, and they and other boats were rowed or towed up the River Leven and into Loch Lomond. Men from Paisley and Dumbarton rallied to the cause, and filled the little fleet, which sailed to Luss under the command of John Campbell of Mamore. There it was joined by forty or fifty of Colquhoun of Luss's men, standing out among the Lowlanders in their short hose and belted plaids. On 13 October they reached Inversnaid and were able, after firing a few guns, to recapture the boats that the MacGregors had seized, carrying off those that were seaworthy and destroying those that had been damaged. The Clan Gregor's few-day command of the little inland sea was over – and the Royal Navy had triumphed in its first and last campaign on Loch Lomond.[26]

The MacGregors had offered no resistance to the attack on their boats, and the Hanoverians claimed they had fled, terrified by the barrage of gunfire. The 'Loch Lomond Expedition' quickly became the subject of exaggerated government propaganda about how easy it was to defeat rebels. It also provided a pretext for denouncing Rob Roy – and back-dating his notoriety by over twenty years. When the name MacGregor had been outlawed in 1693, it was now said, it had been the result of 'some horrible barbarities having been committed by that execrable crew [the MacGregors], under the leading of one Robert Roy Mc gregiour, yet living'.[27]

The lack of resistance to the Hanoverian Loch Lomond expedition may well not have been due to the MacGregors fleeing, but to the fact that they had marched north to join forces being assembled by Mar to march into the heart of Argyllshire. Such a move, if successful, would serve to discredit Argyll both as chief of the Campbells and as commander-in-chief, and it might be decisive in persuading the powerful Campbell lairds whose loyalties were still in doubt to throw in their lot with the Breadalbane Campbells and the Jacobites. Moreover rumour claimed that the Pretender had at last sailed for Scotland, and it was thought the most likely place for his landing would be in the west, somewhere near Dumbarton or on Loch Long, so it was seen as important that friendly forces should be in the area ready to receive him. The duke of Argyll had anticipated some such move against the heartland of his regional power, and on 16 September had sent orders to Finab, as commander of an independent company, to go to Inveraray, raise the local militia, and organise the defence of the town. He was also to 'use his utmost efforts with Locheil, or any other of the clans, or their friends, to influence them to remain dutiful' to King George, promising them the duke's friendship in return. Some unofficial contacts and negotiations may have taken place, but they quickly collapsed, and Argyll dispatched his brother Islay to take over the defence of Inveraray.[28]

The detachment of Mar's army that marched on Inveraray was commanded by Major General Alexander Gordon. His orders were to blockade the town to persuade it to surrender, rather than to storm it, presumably because Mar hoped that a show of force would be sufficient to overawe – or win over – the Campbells, and feared that actual fighting would harden local opinion against the Jacobites. A letter written by Mar of 4 October reveals that he had ordered Glenglye, Rob Roy and Balhaldie and their men to join Gordon's expedition, and he seemed to categorise them and others as 'those who ought to have been with you [Gordon] long ago'. Perhaps the Loch Lomond raid had indeed been largely a MacGregor venture rather, than part of a wider Jacobite strategy, and had delayed their march to join Gordon.[29]

Yet in spite of the urgency of the situation, ten days later the MacGregors had still not reached Gordon. Indeed Rob Roy had popped into Perth for a chat with Mar. Thus when Mar wrote to Glengyle congratulating him on the Loch Lomond raid but urging him to hasten to join Gordon, he added that 'Since your uncle is the bearer I need say no more.' The Loch Lomond raid, even if it had been unauthorised, won praise for its results, though Mar had heard that the Hanoverians were attempting to retake the captured boats and wrote 'I wish with all my heart this could be prevented'. If the Pretender did land near Dumbarton, command of Loch Lomond could become important.[30] However, with many Argyllshire lairds and chieftains still uncertain as to which side, if either, to fight on, delays continued. There is 'an absolute necessity to disperse those people with Finab' Mar urged General Gordon, and it is clear that what worried Mar most was not so much the actual military forces at Finab's command as the fact that he was acting as intermediary in negotiations between Argyll and Jacobites chiefs, offering protections to them if they remained – or became – loyal to the government.[31] Finab, however, was not without his problems. Some of the soldiers of his independent company were Breadalbane's clansmen, and had deserted as soon as he had begun raising men for the Jacobite army.[32]

Rob Roy, Glengyle and their men joined the Inveraray expedition in time for the Jacobite approach to the town on 19 October. Gordon's hopes were high that he would find strong Campbell support. Promises had been made by several leading lairds, and he expected to be able to occupy Inveraray unopposed. He might have done so, had it not been for the presence of Islay. He might be the politician of the family, his brother Argyll the military man, but in the emergency he proved energetic and inspiring in organising defences and reviving morale. Backbones of wavering lairds were stiffened. Drystone wall defences were erected outside the town, with little bastions defending them. He was prepared to fight, though he knew he was greatly outnumbered, because he believed that if his men stood firm he could inflict heavy casualties on the Jacobites, even if Inveraray were eventually overrun. In his view, however, the enemy would not fight. He was right. For several days Hanoverian and Jacobite forces confronted each other, without either attempting action, except that one night at about eight o'clock (when it would have been dark) the alarm was raised in the town. 'The occasion of it was Rob Roy came down the Wintertoun Closse by the Highland Kirke, where there was a company of men keeping guard. He thought to have tak'n it, but behold when he had fired about six shots he was so warmly received by them, and thereafter all round our wall, that upon his return he sayd he would go half way to hell before he would go back again.' Good Hanoverian propaganda, with Rob Roy put to flight. Whether it had been a serious attempt to infiltrate and take the village, or just a search for plunder, and indeed whether Rob was involved or is just named as a notorious figure, is uncertain.[33]

Other evidence suggests that Rob was in fact stationed some distance from Inveraray. A letter by Glengyle (now signing himself 'Greg. M'Gregor', having cast off the assumed name of James Graham) to General Gordon was written 'at the side of' Loch Fyne on 22 October. He had evidently been ordered to return to Inveraray, where Gordon was camped, but declared his reluctance to abandon a ship and its freight which had been captured – though of course if the general sent further orders, he would be ready to march all night. The general's reply was terse. He was to march at once with his own and his uncle's men, leaving just MacDonald of Glencoe's men to guard the ship.[34] A grand opportunity for plunder lost must have been the thought that must have passed through many MacGregor minds.

The 'siege' of Inveraray lasted only a few days, for on 25 October Gordon suddenly withdrew his forces. Jacobite hopes that threatening the heart of the Argyll empire would tip the balance among ditherers, leading them to join the cause, had been disappointed. Argyll's Campbell vassals had remained loyal to him. To try to subdue them by force would have tied up Gordon's forces in a peripheral campaign, and indeed there would be a great danger that many western chiefs would divert their forces into a Highland civil war in Argyllshire instead of hastening them to Perth. The bluff had failed, and as early as 16 October – three days before the Jacobites had even reached Inveraray – Mar had sent orders to General Gordon to withdraw at once to Menteith, where Mar hoped to join him with his main army to cross the headwaters of the River Forth and march south, outflanking Argyll – though Mar still wanted some men left to blockade Inveraray.[35]

During the brief siege there had been some contacts between Islay and the Jacobite chiefs. Islay himself said tersely that they sent him some ridiculous messages,[36] but others indicated there was more to what happened than this. Islay – or at least Finab – had met the chiefs. One, perhaps Glengarry, had proposed a sort of truce. Neither side would plunder the other, and no man would be forced to join the rival forces. Islay responded that he had no power to negotiate, and when the Jacobite forces retreated from Inveraray he sent Finab in pursuit with 700 men to harass them. He caught up with a party of 200 of Breadalbane's men under Campbell of Glenlyon, and the forces drew up for battle, the men casting aside their plaids in the traditional way, to fight in their long shirts. But in the end the two sides agreed not to come to blows. Finab was reluctant to kill Campbell kinsman to uphold distant dynasties. However, the terms of the agreement reached show acceptance that if fighting had taken place the outcome would have favoured Finab, for his men kept their arms whereas Breadalbane's surrendered theirs before marching off. This bloodless solution infuriated Islay: it was no way to win a war.[37] That, at least, was his official opinion. In his heart he was probably relieved a Campbell civil war had been avoided.

The bloodless Argyll campaign was a repulse for the Jacobites, and greatly strengthened the position of the duke of Argyll. Two major Campbell chieftains, Auchinbreck and Lochnell, had come very close to throwing in their lot with the Jacobites, only being persuaded to change their minds at the last moment. However, the legacy of these manoeuvrings in Argyllshire was to cast a long political shadow. Argyll's enemies already knew that he had contacts with Rob Roy. Even before the rebellion had begun Ormiston had longed to be able to interrogate Rob, believing this would reveal incriminating information on Argyll. Now, at Inveraray, Islay had had contact with rebel chiefs. Shortly thereafter forces under his command had failed to attack Breadalbane's rebel force. There seemed, to those hostile to the Campbell brothers, to be evidence of treason in these events – unauthorised contact with the enemy, and a failure, at both Inveraray and at the strategic centre around Stirling, to fight. An additional cause for suspicion was that Cameron of Locheil, a leading figure among the Jacobites, was Argyll's vassal.[38] Argyll, as the malicious interpreted the evidence, was allowing some of his men to serve the enemy. In the months and years ahead, the hunt for Rob Roy was to be inspired not so much by the desire to capture a relatively insignificant rebel, or by concern for law-enforcement, as by an obsession with the belief that he was the key to exposing a major political scandal that would destroy Argyll.

The little war in the West Highlands had proved a futile diversion, and General Gordon marched his men swiftly back to join Mar's main army. Islay saw the significance of this: Gordon's withdrawal had freed Inveraray from threat, but Gordon's men could be on the upper Forth within three days, increasing Jacobite pressure on the line of the river.[39] Perhaps now the long-expected Jacobite advance would begin. Meanwhile in the east the Jacobites had shown themselves more aggressive than in the west, sending several thousand men across the Firth of Forth on 12 October. After a quick advance towards Edinburgh it was realised that it was not feasible to attempt to seize the capital, so they marched to try to stir up active Jacobitism in southern Scotland and join up with English supporters in the north of England. The Jacobites had now over 12,000 men in arms.[40] Argyll would have had difficulty in mustering a quarter of that figure, and after it became clear that Edinburgh was safe he concluded that the Jacobite force to the south of him should not divert him from his position at Stirling. The main Jacobite army still lay to the north. Several weeks were to pass before Mar at last decided to use it.

As Gordon marched his men back from Inveraray to Perth one man in particular in his force was awaited impatiently. 'I wonder what

keeps Rob Roy from coming to Perth, as I ordered him,' Mar wrote
to Gordon on 4 November. Rob was to be sent immediately, 'for I
want very much to speak to him'.[41] The Jacobite commander's urgent
need of Rob was based on the fact that Mar was close to committing
himself to an advance which would involve his army in crossing the
upper reaches of the Forth, to the west of Stirling. His troops would
have to cross large areas of bog and ford the river, as there were no
bridges, and since major routes avoided the area few men had much
knowledge of the best ways through it. But some cattle drovers – and
raiders – knew the area well, and someone (knowing Rob, perhaps
the man himself) had suggested that Rob was the expert who should
be consulted. Indeed, according to the master of Sinclair (the heir
of Lord Sinclair), enquiries had revealed that no one in the Jacobite
army 'except Rob Roy' was qualified to provide proper advice on the
terrain, and he had often driven cattle across the fords. It seems likely
that Rob duly met with Mar and discussed the matter, but the plans
for a strike west of Stirling were abandoned. Firstly, it was argued,
Rob might be able to assess the usefulness of fords for cattle, but
he had not the expertise to say whether they were suitable for large
numbers of soldiers. Secondly, intelligence indicated that Argyll had
already had the fords surveyed and fortified. Finally, the Jacobites
decided that 'they could not trust' Rob Roy.[42] It would have been
folly to entrust the guiding of the Jacobite army over a treacherous
river to a man who had been providing the enemy with intelligence.

The Jacobite advance finally began early in November. After his
weeks of dithering Mar had finally decided to march south and
confront Argyll at Stirling. Argyll (well informed of what was going
on by his spies in Mar's army) advanced north to intercept him,
and in the hills to the east of Dunblane the two armies met on 13
November 1715. In simple battlefield terms the conflict at Sheriffmuir
was indecisive. The Jacobites were victorious on their right wing, but
after several hours of fighting their left wing collapsed and fled in
the face of stubborn Hanoverian resistance. In the centre Mar had a
good chance of victory, but hesitated. As darkness fell, both armies
withdrew, neither sure of what the overall result of the confused
fighting had been. The following day, however, Argyll advanced to
the battlefield, ready to renew the conflict, while Mar gave up and
began retreating to Perth. Thus though on 13 November itself the
battle had no winner, the aftermath converted it into a decisive defeat
for the Jacobites. For victory, Mar needed to have taken Stirling,

and he had failed. All Argyll needed to do for the moment was hold Stirling, and he had done that.[43] Jacobite morale was never to recover from this failure to defeat the enemy in spite of a huge superiority in numbers, followed by an unnecessary retreat. About 9,000 Jacobites had faced about 3,200 Hanoverians,[44] failed to defeat them, and then retreated.

Rob Roy's role in the battle, or rather his lack of one, was soon to become the cause of debate. He and his men had been close to the battlefield, it was known, but he had not fought in the battle. One narrative explained that 'Rob Roy MacGrigor, alias Campbell, a noted gentleman in former times for bravery, resolution, and courage, was with his men and followers within a very little distance from the earl of Mar's army, and when he was desired by a gentleman of his own to go and assist his friends, he answer'd, if they could not do it without me, they should not do it with me: That is, if they could not conquer their enemies without him, he would not assist him [them] in the doing of it.'[45]

This suggests mixed loyalties, or a waiting to see who looked like winning before committing himself. But, as neither side won, there was no winner to join. A satirical Hanoverian ballad described a battle of confusion, with both sides running away. Amidst a whirl of chaotic movement, Rob Roy does nothing.

> Rob Roy there stood watch on a hill, for to catch
> The booty, for ought that I saw – man;
> For he ne'er advanc'd from the place he was stanced,
> Till no there was to do there at a' – man.
> For we ran, and they ran and we ran,
> And we ran, and they ran awa' – Man.[46]

Another ballad confirms the aloof stance of the MacGregors – 'M'grigors they far off did stand'.[47] Rather later the duke of Argyll's biographer agreed. 'Among other causes of the rebel's misfortune in that day, they reckon the part Rob Roy M.Gregor acted to be one . . . in the day of battle he kept his men together at some distance without allowing them to engage, tho' they show'd all the willingness imaginable, and waited only an opportunity to plunder, which was it seems the chief of his design of coming there. This clan are a hardy rough people, but noted for pilfering'.[48] There has been much debate as to where Rob was hanging around during the battle, but the matter is settled by a note on a map of the battle later made

by the Hanoverians which states that 'Rob Roy and 500 men with
him were at Broomhills of Cromlix in time of the engagement at
Sherriff Muir.'[49] The lands of Cromlix lay about three miles north
of Dunblane.

All five of these Hanoverian accounts portray Rob and his men as
present but doing nothing as the hours of battle passed. But none of
this evidence is first-hand. The assumption is made that as Rob had
been in the vicinity but had not fought, he must have deliberately
abstained from fighting. That there was some doubt already about
his loyalties made this interpretation seem plausible. But if Rob had
refused to fight, there would surely be evidence of Jacobite fury at
his betrayal, and there is none. Gaelic poets were vituperative in their
denunciations of a number of Jacobite officers and clans which had
broken and fled at Sheriffmuir, but there is not a word about Rob Roy,
critical or otherwise.[50] In Jacobite eyes, he bore none of the blame
for the defeat. Moreover two first-hand accounts of his movements
on 13 November indicate that Rob was not standing around all day,
cynically calculating the odds, but only arrived in the vicinity of the
battlefield when the battle was already lost.

The best evidence comes from John Cameron younger of Locheil.
He and his men had been in the defeated Jacobite left wing. Driven
from the field, he crossed the Allan Water somewhere north of
Dunblane, and there found some of his own men and Stewart of
Appin, whose men had fought beside him in the battle. 'Fie on you,
Locheil! This is how your heroes went: running down the moor,
filled with fear and cowardice,' an unsympathetic Gaelic poet was
to comment.[51] But a letter of Locheil's describes how he had tried
to rally his men. 'I rallied there all I could meet with, and caused
such of them as had fyred to charge [reload] their pieces. At the
same time I perceived Rob Roy Mcgrigar on his march towards
me, coming from the town of Down [Doune], he not being at the
engagement.' Thus it seems that Rob Roy and his men had not been
stationed at Broomhills of Cromlix, near the battlefield, but had only
just arrived there in the last stages of the battle, having marched
there from, or perhaps through, Doune. He was perhaps marching
up the west bank of the Allan Water with the intention of crossing
the river on the bridge at Kinbuck to approach the battlefield.[52] Rob's
nephew Glengyle had been appointed governor of Doune Castle[53]
and it sounds as though Rob and his men had been serving with him
there, watching the Forth above Stirling. Once it became clear that

a major engagement was in progress at Sheriffmuir, and that Doune itself was not in danger, Rob had been sent east to the Jacobite army. But by the time he reached Cromlix the Jacobites' left wing was in full retreat. Locheil, it is true, had hoped that with Rob's help the tide could be turned. 'I marched towards him [Rob Roy] with the few [men] I had got together; perceiving Argyle opposite us, I intreated he being come fresh with these men, that we would joyn and cross the river to attack Argyle; which he absolutely refused; so that there was such a small number left when Rob Roy went off, and not knowing well then what became of our right [wing], [I] could not attempt any thing with that number'.[54]

Locheil is defensive in tone, no doubt anticipating the scorn that was to be heaped on chiefs who had fled. He would, he indicates, have renewed the attack if only Rob had agreed to join him, so his continued retreat was Rob's fault. But in all probability what Locheil proposed was folly. He wanted his own few men, exhausted by hours of fighting and then flight, to join with a reinforcement of perhaps only 250 men, and then not only advance against the triumphant enemy but do so by crossing a river with the far bank held by the enemy – and to do this not long before nightfall on a winter afternoon (it was sometime after 4 pm, and sunset was due at about 4.30 pm). Neither Rob nor Locheil are likely to have had much idea of what was happening elsewhere in this unusually confusing encounter, and there was no sign of the main Jacobite army. If Rob did indeed say that if the Jacobites had not been able to win without him, they would not be able to do so with them, it must have been at this point, and it seems a sensible assessment of this situation. He may have 'absolutely refused' to advance, but he was not disobeying the orders of a superior officer but a proposal by a fellow officer which he judged to be misguided. That said, Rob, with his divided loyalties, may well have been relieved not to have been drawn into the action.

At this point the battle was nearing its conclusion. The Jacobite right wing, which had pursued Argyll's broken left south towards Stirling, had now turned to march back north towards the rest of Argyll's army, which had to stop pursuing Locheil and the rest of the Jacobite left to turn south to face Mar's advance. The battle had swung round almost 180 degrees. Mar now faced Argyll, who was north of him. He still had about 4,000 men, greatly outnumbering Argyll. But, as in the past, he waited instead of acting, as dusk began

to fall. Rob Roy and Cameron of Locheil were arguing at Cromlix
about whether to mount a new attack. They were about three miles
north west of Mar's position, behind Argyll's left flank when he
turned to confront Mar. If Mar thought the situation too dangerous
to mount a new attack with his thousands of men, it is not surprising
that Rob Roy with only a few hundred reached the same decision.

The failure of the Jacobites to defeat Argyll at Sheriffmuir[55] and
then march triumphantly south across the Forth, in spite of a huge
numerical advantage, was intensely demoralising. Highlanders began
to desert even before Mar made retreat official. News soon arrived of
two more disasters. To the south the English and Scots Jacobites had
been defeated and dispersed at Preston. To the north Inverness had
fallen to local Hanoverians. The arrival of the Pretender in Scotland
in December did something for morale – but its main effect was to
make men who knew at heart that they were defeated fight on a
few months longer because it seemed dishonourable to submit now
their king was present. Within two months of Sheriffmuir Jacobite
strength had halved, only 4,393 being listed in musters in December
1715 and January 1716.[56] Chiefs and clansmen continued to drift
off homewards, and secret approaches to Argyll to try to secure
pardons multiplied. Personally, he was willing to negotiate with
Jacobites ready to surrender, but he was refused permission to do so,
being regarded as too soft on rebels. To government, as Sheriffmuir
turned out to have been a victory, there was no need for leniency,
but Argyll saw no room for complacency, especially as he knew how
unreliable many of his own men were. 'Some of our troops behaved
[at Sheriffmuir] as ill as ever any did in this world', he confided, but
it was important to keep this secret.[57]

Rob remained with Mar's forces – but continued to supply Argyll
with intelligence, writing to him from Inverarlich, near Dunkeld, on
21 November, just a week after Sheriffmuir. The letter is the only
one of his secret messages to Argyll to survive, but its tone suggests
it is a routine item in a series of messages. 'The bearer will give you
sufficient intelligence upon the late moves here as I cannot put down
on paper.' Rob apologised for taking the risk of sending a messenger,
suggesting that his instructions as an intelligence agent were to keep
his head down for the moment. He warned that the Jacobites had
still 'sufficient designs to make grievous injury to the forces under
you if they can'. They had issued proclamations, presenting their
position in a good light after Sheriffmuir, part of the paper warfare

in which each side claimed victory. Two Jacobite agents had been sent out the day before, disclosed Rob, to distribute the proclamation and false news, to undermine confidence in the Hanoverian cause. The agents are identified as 'M.N.' and 'G.D.' which surely indicates that Argyll or his staff were expected to know who they were. It was recommended that they be detained at 'the Bridge' as they tried to enter Stirling, or elsewhere. Further intelligence would be sent, Rob assures the duke, obscurely, 'when I get the matter on hand settled with them'.[58]

It has been argued that Rob in this letter was simply taking out insurance with Argyll against Jacobite failure, as others did, and that he was supplying the enemy with out-of-date intelligence. But insisting that all Rob supplied, here (and, implicitly, on other occasions) was simply 'mock aid' and 'useless crumbs', concocted after Rob had 'searched his mind for some . . . innocuous information', seems over-charitable.[59]

Rob was soon on the move again, on a venture probably authorised by Mar but so much to Rob's taste that he may have suggested the mission. He would go west to recruit men from his homeland – and, en route, raid Hanoverian-held areas that came within Montrose's sphere of interest. Most of those he and his men encountered were ready, as usual, to give marauding Highlanders what they wanted. Such unwelcome visitors, whether Jacobites or private-enterprise raiders, usually limited their demands to food and a few cattle, and had no taste for indiscriminate destruction. But at Auchintroig House in Menteith in the early days of December Rob met with resistance – or perhaps decided to make something of an example of a man unusually strenuous in his opposition to Jacobites. A chain of local watches had been established from Balmaha on the east shore of Loch Lomond to the upper reaches of the Forth, to prevent raiding from the Inversnaid area, with Auchintroig as the watch station nearest the Forth.[60]

John MacLachlan of Auchintroig had built himself a strong little stone house in 1702 – probably not very different from the one that Rob Roy had built for his nephew, Glengyle, at around the same time. It was not fortified, but with a single thick wooden door that could be barred, and windows protected by bars and shutters, it could hold out for some time against passing raiders armed with pistols and swords. But it could not stand against fire, and story has it that Rob smoked the owner out by building a fire against the door. Rob then carried MacLachlan and his son off as prisoners, along with his livestock. The house, now called Old Auchintroig, still stands and was recently restored after falling into decay. It is the only building associated with Rob to survive in anything like original form, and a treasured relic is the door said (in the nineteenth century) to have shown damage from Rob Roy's fire. Modern examination has failed to confirm this – existing damage to the door is probably due to damp and decay[61] – but the story of it having been scorched by Rob could nonetheless be true.

MacLachlan was later to claim that the seizure of his cattle, some arms and household furniture, plus what was stolen yearly from him 'by that same sett' had cost him at least £100 sterling, indicating that MacGregor animosity to him was long-lasting. He explained that there were two reasons for this. The first was that he had given local leadership to the Hanoverian cause in 1715, helping garrison the castle of Gartartan when his senior officers in the militia had failed to act. The fact that after the rebellion was crushed MacLachlan's son was given the job of administering a couple of minor forfeited rebel estates suggests that it was recognised that the family had some claim for compensation – though the appointment made things worse, leaving the family much out of pocket. The second reason MacLachlan gave for Rob Roy's animosity to him was his conduct at an election of a member of parliament.[62] That Rob should have taken so passionate an interest in a parliamentary election throws a new light on his range of interests. A possible scenario is that MacLachlan had supported a Montrose nominee for Stirlingshire in the February 1715 general election, thus arousing Rob's displeasure.

Having dealt with the obstreperous MacLachlan, Rob advanced a few miles to Drymen, with about a hundred men. There he proclaimed the Pretender, and tore up the gauger's books of excise duties. The proclamation was symbolic defiance to Montrose, whose Buchanan Castle lay close by, while the fate of the gauger's books was another sign of the way in which excise duties had come to be symbolic of oppressive government. After the Loch Lomond raid a few months earlier gestures had been made at defence against further MacGregor incursions. Boats on the Clyde had been moved to the south of the river, to prevent the sort of commandeering of boats that had taken place earlier on Loch Lomond, and parties of volunteers raised in towns south of the river had been marched north to establish garrisons. They had found little comfort in

Menteith, 'a very disaffected and malignant place', for though the people were Montrose's tenants many were Jacobite sympathisers, and anyway they had no wish to provoke the MacGregors. One of these garrisons was stationed in an old castle of the Buchanans of Drumakill just outside Drymen, and Rob evidently attempted to surprise it, but marched off when this failed[63] – and the garrison, prudently, showed no interest in taking the offensive. Raw Lowland volunteers were no match for Highlanders, and the local garrisons proved useless in curbing Rob Roy's activities. As Argyll remarked of Lowland militias 'a lamb is not more afraid of a lyon, than these low countrey people are of the Highlanders'.[64]

Moving north through Buchanan, Rob returned to Craigrostan, to what he still regarded as his own lands. That he only dared to remain there for few days must have been bitter. On 9 December the MacGregors took to boats and raided Luss, across Loch Lomond. The parish minister fled and his house was ransacked. At Auchengang they seized the house of Humphrey Noble of Kippermishoch, and carried his half brother off as a prisoner. Four of Rob's men were being held prisoner in Dumbarton, and he wanted hostages to exchange for them. The MacGregors then approached Tarbet House, but finding it 'pretty strong' withdrew. Next day, they raided Luss again. As an observer commented, the Hanoverians' confidence that they had captured or destroyed all the boats on the loch had proved misplaced. Malcolm MacGregor of Marchfield was noted as Rob's fellow commander on these raids.[65] By 21 December Rob Roy had occupied two islands in Loch Katrine and was raiding the surrounding countryside.[66]

Rob soon freed his prisoners. The two MacLachlans, father and son, were released along with their livestock – except for two cows and forty-five sheep, which had been eaten. But the father had to pay a ransom of £20 sterling, and swear to return to Rob whenever summoned. Also liberated were a 'Mr Leckie and Boyd', who had evidently been captured in the raid on Luss. 'These are hard termes,' Gorthie commented on the conditions for the release of the MacLachlans 'but any thing is better than them to remain prisoner with these miscreants'.[67] Rob was now gathering men from both the MacGregors and other clans, though the report that he had four to five hundred men in all on Loch Katrine ('which is a lake never freises', as Gorthie noted) was doubtless the exaggeration of fearful rumour. Rob, it was said, had control of all the boats on the loch 'and some leather guns mounted'.[68] This is the last known occasion on which these unusual weapons were deployed. They had been made in Scotland in 1650–1, to try to provide light artillery for use in battle against the English by strengthening a thin iron barrel with tightly wound cord and a thick leather casing shrunk on over it. They had never been very effective, but a sprinkling of them survived littered around Scotland. They had seen action at Killiecrankie in 1689,[69] and now served Rob Roy. It seems appropriate that Rob, often described as an anachronism, living the life of an outlaw more appropriate to earlier ages, was the last to attempt to use these outmoded cannons.

Too little had been done to try to halt Rob before he had established himself in his island strongholds, Gorthie lamented. Farmers gave what was asked of them, and let the raiders pass. Again there was the contrast between the military society of the Highlands, and the 'civilised' society of the Lowlands, where men expected others to protect them – government or landlords. Gorthie explained this reluctance to oppose or report raiders as traditional. To cause trouble for raiders was 'against the rules of Highland politicks. Amongst these people a quarrell is easily begun, but not forgott for many generations'. If you reported theft of cattle, you might lose a lot more than cattle next time the raiders passed your way. Difficult too was the position of new tenants who had been settled on land Rob had previously rented from Montrose. As they were on 'his' land, Rob forced them to join his band, and forbade them to pay rent to Montrose's agents – but they sent secret messages to the factor, Killearn, that they had left the rent with their wives, to be paid after they were forced to march with Rob to Perth.[70] Gorthie, however, may well be giving a rather distorted picture of tenant attitudes, seeking to persuade Montrose that their hearts were in the right place and the failure to oppose raiders was simply a matter of tradition. Others agreed that the country people did 'not oppose these banditti' but this was because they were 'either of their interest, or indifferent' as to the political issues.[71] This was a truth Gorthie was reluctant to tell his master, to avoid bringing the duke's wrath down on the tenants. However, he admitted the tenants had not behaved as they should have, and Killearn was ordered to give them a 'warm rebuke'. As for the MacGregors, 'I hope that clan shall never gett access to the king's mercy – I'm sure it were good for the country that they were all out of it'.[72]

Gorthie had feared that Rob intended a prolonged stay in the area, but his task was recruitment, not occupation, and he quickly moved on. On 26 December 1715 he was believed to be still at Loch Katrine, but on 4 January 1716 he occupied the half-derelict palace of Falkland in Fife, becoming its deputy governor under Glengyle. As a Jacobite muster roll carefully notes, 'at Falkland, Macgregors, 134'.[73] 'Roguish Rob's' venture into Fife has been called 'the only example of freelance profiteering' in the '15 rising,[74] but it is quite clear that he was acting on orders from the Jacobite command. It is indeed the only occasion on which he and his MacGregors appear on a Jacobite muster.

Details of Rob's 'campaign' in Fife are fragmentary. Most Jacobite forces had withdrawn from the shire after Sheriffmuir, and parties from both sides made forays into it. The purpose of Rob's advance was assumed to be 'to plunder the country and destroy the forrage', doing the latter to deprive the Hanoverian cavalry of fodder – though as Argyll commented, at that time of year there was little forage to destroy.[75]

According to an account by a candlemaker in Leslie called Archer, 150 Highlanders sallied from the palace to 'rob and plunder taking clothes and victuals'. On 6 January thirty-two 'Highlandmen (I had almost said devils)' were seen approaching Leslie from the north through the Lomond Hills. The townsmen resolved to resist, and, with drawn swords, met the Highlanders 'in the green' to the east of the town. The raiders said they wanted clothes and money, and were told they would get none, 'at which they stormed and swore terribly', though doubtless the offensiveness of the oaths to the pious candlemaker would have been mitigated by their being in Gaelic. Some blows were exchanged, but finding the townsmen ready to fight the Highlanders climbed down, and simply asked permission to pass through the town. This was agreed, and having been escorted through it by the wary locals they left, working off some of their frustration by taking pot-shots at spectators watching them from the parish minister's house.

In response to the plundering of the countryside by the MacGregors, the Hanoverians advanced a few hundred men to Burleigh Castle, mainly Dutch and Swiss (thousands of Dutch troops were landing to reinforce Argyll, and some of them were mercenaries hired from Switzerland), while local militias also assembled. The gallant Mr Archer waded through snow up to his boot-tops to supply the

REBEL

garrison with candles. A small force of Kirkcaldy men and Swiss moved to secure Balcomie Castle, but were ambushed in Markinch by the Highlanders, two of the Swiss being killed. Archer judged the time had come to flee with his family, but the storms were too great to take the risk.[76]

Argyll had judged that sending parties of troops against the few MacGregors had not been worth the trouble or risk, but William Cadogan, his second in command, had insisted that troops be detached to move into Fife – not least to protect the property of the vociferous earl of Rothes, owner of Leslie and Balcomie.[77] Argyll had the satisfaction of saying 'I told you so' after the Markinch skirmish – he had foreseen that sending men to help Rothes would cost lives – but he was bitter. He was supposed to be commander-in-chief but had been forced to act against his judgement.[78] His problem was that Cadogan might be his subordinate, but he was a *Squadrone* man, and it was recognised that he had been sent to Scotland to spy on Argyll and to supersede him in command when the time was judged right.

The duke's belief that intervention in Fife was not necessary proved correct. Mar's army was crumbling, and as Argyll began his long awaited march northwards from Stirling, Mar withdrew all his forces south of Perth, ordering the burning of Auchterarder, Crieff, Blackford, Dunning and Muthill before his men left in the hope of delaying the Hanoverian advance by depriving it of food and shelter in bitter winter weather. The 'scorched earth' policy was a sign of despair by a man who knew the campaign was lost, but not surprisingly the news of the burnings caused terror in Fife, for it was feared that Rob Roy and the MacGregors would be ordered to carry out similar destruction. Archer the candlemaker and his fellows stood to arms all night in Leslie, talking of rumours that Rob had a commission to burn all between there and Perth. At midnight on 30 January, they heard that Rob had had nearly all his men drawn up outside the palace in Falkland, and tension grew. It soon gave way to relief. Rob was on the march, but in retreat. Glengyle and the MacGregors had first been ordered to retire to the area of Doune, where they had previously been posted, to prevent the enemy carrying off forage for their cavalry horses and other provisions. But Argyll's advance meant that that area was now in enemy hands, and it was no longer possible for Rob's men to rejoin Mar's army by land. New orders therefore instructed Glengyle to march to Nauchton Castle in

Fife and join the Jacobite garrison there in crossing the Firth of Tay by boat to Dundee, to await further orders.[79]

Rob's men, it was claimed, had eaten about 3,000 sheep during their stay in Fife[80] – a figure that seems implausibly large. The Hanoverians were left puzzled as to why the expedition to Falkland had been undertaken, and concluded that it seemed to be the case that Rob's men's 'chief business is to pillage a little for themselves'.[81] A suspicion lingers that it was undertaken simply to give the restless MacGregors something congenial to do, if not indeed to keep them away from Mar's army.

Archer's narratives, written in letters to his brother, provide the best accounts of the episode, but other sources supplement them with flashes of detail. Of the skirmish at Markinch, it was said that Rob (whose father, it was alleged, had been hung as a thief) had approached by night and 'disposd of his men so as not to let the people well know of his numbers when it came day'. He then sent a decoy, a messenger who reported to the Hanoverians that there were only about twenty Highlanders around, seeking plunder. The decoy then led the Hanoverians to an enclosure or barnyard, where they found themselves surrounded by about 160 of Rob's men. Two of the Highlanders had been killed, but the Swiss and militia quickly surrendered.[82]

In the weeks that followed the MacGregor withdrawal, stories spread among Fifers of the terrible fate they had escaped. Had not the Lord protected his people, there would have been much more 'hellish barbarity' from the Highlanders. One George Swan went to Falkland to demand the return of two horses (not something he would have done, incidentally, if he had really expected hellish barbarities) which had been taken from him, even though he had paid the Jacobites the tax demanded from him. Rob Roy had told him that the MacGregors would 'set fire to the country if they [the country folk] were not more loyal and obedient,' which sounded ominous enough. Worse, he 'heard honest Robin say, that he never desired a more pleasant and satisfying breakfast every morning than to see a Whig's house in flames'. But he added that Rob 'was the fairest and most discreet among' the Jacobites, and that he would have been imprisoned if Rob had not intervened.[83] The bark of the famed outlaw was a lot more vicious than his bite.

Mar made no effort to fight to hold Perth. As Argyll approached, he and his army streamed away northwards over the frozen Tay and

dispersed. Many Jacobites hoped a stand could be made further
north, but their leaders were in full flight, with no stomach to attempt
to save anything from the disaster. Mar and the Pretender slipped
off into exile, leaving their followers to fend for themselves. For Rob
Roy, as for many hundreds of others, the outlook was bleak. Rob
was now not merely a notoriously stubborn bankrupt who had failed
to satisfy his creditors but a rebel denounced for high treason.

His quarrel with Montrose in 1712–14 had been over money. Now
his Jacobitism and his raiding of the duke's lands had intensified
the duke's animosity – and made it far more likely than in the past
that he would get official help in his pursuit of Rob. To defy one
great man, Rob in the past had relied on the patronage of others of
similar rank, but he was now left isolated. His most open protector,
Breadalbane, had at last succumbed to old age. His death was well
timed from the point of view of his family. A conspiracy of silence
about his part in the rising was undertaken by Campbell interests,
the official line being that though his men had joined the Jacobites it
had been without his orders. The family title and estates survived –
but the new earl of Breadalbane, the former Lord Glenorchy, was
no friend of Rob Roy. In any case, the earl had his own problems,
living down his father's Jacobitism and trying to ignore the fact that
he had an elder brother living, quietly removed from the succession
to the earldom by family agreement because of his disabilities, but
with a possible claim to the title. The new earl had no wish to
compromise himself by bothering about Rob Roy's welfare. Lord
Drummond, another long-time protector, was also gone – he had
fled into exile, though his estates remained in the family as he had
the forethought to transfer them to his infant son just days before
the rising had begun.

It was no use turning to the duke of Atholl either, though in
the past Rob had at times courted his favour. Though he was a
committed Hanoverian, his eldest surviving son, William, marquis
of Tullibardine, had served the Jacobites as lieutenant general, and
most of the men of Atholl had also joined the rising. The duke
therefore found it hard to persuade the government of his personal
loyalty – and, like Breadalbane, he was therefore not likely to help
Rob Roy. Of the regional magnates, this left only the duke of Argyll
as a possible patron and protector. Here, it must have seemed to
Rob, he had an ace up his sleeve, ready to play. Who was better
placed to save him than the triumphant Hanoverian commander-

in-chief, surely to be loaded with laurels after defeating the rebels? And he had a strong claim on Argyll's gratitude, as his faithful spy among the Jacobites.

However this final string to Rob's bow (to change metaphors) broke at the critical moment. Argyll had, with totally inadequate resources, stood firm in the face of a much stronger Jacobite army, fought it to a standstill, and seen it wither. But his constant complaints and demands for reinforcements, however justified, had discredited him at court. Political enemies had eagerly presented him as over-cautious and pessimistic. His reluctance to risk advancing north of the Forth for a winter campaign seemed to prove the point, for when orders had forced him to march towards Perth, the Jacobite army had dissolved without a fight. Indeed it vanished so rapidly that another charge was added to those against him – he had deliberately let the Jacobites escape. Moreover, now the danger was over, the campaign won, his enemies minimised the significance of the rising. 'Here is this formidable rebellion vanish[ed] like smoke, though it appeared terrible to some folks' wrote the snide Justice Clerk Cockburn[84] on behalf of the *Squadrone*. Folk like Argyll had panicked and made a great fuss about solving a minor problem, and deserved no credit.

In February 1716 Argyll was dismissed from command of the army in Scotland.[85] He reputation as a soldier had been needed while there was a rebel threat. Now he had removed it, he could be jettisoned and replaced by William Cadogan. Since Argyll had been blamed for being soft on punishing rebels, Cadogan was determined to make it plain that he was not, and Rob Roy and many others were to suffer for it. But Rob was to be a special case. He was to be hunted not merely for treason, but because the *Squadrone* believed it could convict Argyll of treason if it could force Rob to reveal the duke's contacts with him and other Jacobites. Rob was to be hounded obsessively not for what he had done but for what he might know.

Forty-nine Scots were attainted for high treason for their involvement in the '15, and Rob was among them. The list of those named is distinctly arbitrary. Many equally as guilty as those listed managed, through family connections or covert dealings, to keep their names from it. Others were omitted simply through oversight or because no one had had a vested interest in including them. Balhaldie had briefly asserted himself as chief of an outlawed clan by raising men and signing himself 'McGregor',[86] but he was not attainted. Nor was Glengyle, though Rob Roy had fought (nominally) under

his command. Both these leading MacGregors were able quietly to
resume their legal names, Drummond and Graham, and pick up
the threads of their lives. But 'Robert Campbell alias Macgregour
commonly called Rob Roy' was too notorious to escape attention.[87]
As a traitor, his lands were declared forfeit to the crown. Craigrostan
had been disposed of by Rob to Bardowie. Montrose was trying
through the court of session to claim it in name of Rob's creditors.
Now the crown's claim was to be asserted.[88] The confusion was to
take years to sort out. Perhaps Rob got some wry satisfaction from
these complications, but he must have known that he was now further
than ever from being able to recover what he saw as rightfully his.
There was not even a chance of returning to the peaceful outlaw life
he had lived under Breadalbane's protection. He was on his own.

6

BURNING HOUSES

The Hanoverian army moved north after Mar's flight from Perth, slowly penetrating into the north-east of Scotland and the Highlands, picking up rebels of status as prisoners, making sure all Jacobite forces had dispersed, and establishing small garrisons. Not surprisingly, MacGregors proved troublesome. Whether they should be classified as defiant rebels, or as traditional raiders and extorters of blackmail, or as the latter pretending to be the former to add legitimacy of their activities is a subjective matter. In March 1716 Graham of Gorthie was complaining that, while all other rebels were peaceable, small parties of MacGregors were still levying 'contributions' in the parishes of Kippen and Kilmoranock and other 'low country' areas. He went to Edinburgh to consult Cadogan, the new commander-in-chief, about 'the most proper way of makeing us rid of our nighbours the McGregors'. Cadogan promised to make troops available, but Gorthie proved, in spite of his complaints, opposed to harsh action. 'I'm of the opinion that no extraordinary [severe] method be taken with the common people of that clan, till once we see if they will lay down their arms peaceably as others do.' Only after most had been given a chance to submit should the remaining offenders be arrested.

Gorthie does not say that Rob Roy was among the raiders, but that his letter moves on to discussing how to deal with Rob implies that he was one of the 'offenders' to be arrested. 'The generall had form'd a project himself for apprehending Rob Roy, and I belive that gentleman will find his quarters too hott. He imploys Captain Robison who I beleive has undertaken it, and I make no dout he'l exert himself to gain merit of the generall. He asked me if Finab might not be as proper a person as any for that service; I disabused him of that notion, very soon'. Cadogan has not yet learnt the nuances of Highland politics, but Gorthie had found out the hard way that trying to get Finab's independent company to arrest Argyll's agent Rob Roy was pointless.

The army first struck at Rob's home at Auch. A garrison had been established in the castle of Finlarig at the west end of Loch Tay, and a party of troops was sent towards Auch at the beginning of April 1716. Rob knew an attack was coming, and summoned men from Craigrostan to resist, but they came too late or were too few. As the troops approached Rob and his men retreated into hiding, and he had to watch while all his goods were seized, all the houses burnt except one small barn. As the buildings were burning Rob and his men fired in frustration from the cover of rocks, killing two or three men, and wounding perhaps a dozen more. His own men also suffered casualties – one dead and several injured. As Rob looked on his goods were carried off, his cattle (about fifty, by one estimate)[1] driven away. Graham of Killearn, anxious for further action against 'these villians' the MacGregors, believed the army had also planned a raid on Glengyle, but it failed to take place, and Rob was not cowed. Reports soon came in that his men had 'just now stolen a good deall of sheep'.[2]

Before the '15 Auch had been a safe haven. Now the army could penetrate there at will, and it may have been this that persuaded Rob to make a submissive gesture, but not one that would place him in any danger, hoping that it might satisfy the government and gain acceptance that he was no longer a rebel. Argyll might have fallen from favour at court, but in Argyllshire his power remained dominant, and the Campbells must have come to realise that they had a vested interest in offering Rob some protection. It might strengthen claims that Argyll had treasonous contacts with rebels, but to let Rob fall into the hands of the *Squadrone* would be disastrous if they persuaded Rob to give evidence against him.

A deal was arranged. Early in May Rob, Glengyle and their men made their way to Inveraray and surrendered their arms to Campbell of Finab as captain of an independent company. In return, they got a promise of protection from him provided they lived peacefully at home.[3] Finab had no permission from his commanding officers to give Rob such a protection. It had, it is true, been ruled that rebels who agreed to surrender arms and live peaceably should be allowed to do so, but this did not apply to those, like Rob, who had been attainted for treason. Finab was acting as if Argyll was his commanding officer, so his protection to Rob would only be of any value in areas where Argyll's interests prevailed. Gorthie, when he heard the news, hastened to let Montrose, the justice clerk and Cadogan know of it,[4] so *Squadrone* opposition to Finab's action could be organised. Cadogan as commander-in-chief might be expected to be particularly indignant at Finab's proceedings – especially as MacDonald of Glengarry had sent him (indirectly) a warning that he was 'perfectly hated and abhorred' by supporters of Argyll, who wished all things to miscarry in his hands.[5]

It was probably at this point that Rob also gained a new home through Argyll's sponsorship. The earliest reference to this does not appear until 1721, but it was then said that he had taken 'possession of his old seat in Benbuy'.[6] Rob's safe house lay high up Glen Shira, about eight miles from Inveraray, and was thus in a place near the centre of Campbell power. Rob's family may have continued to live among the Lomond and Balquhidder MacGregors,[7] with Rob only retiring to Glen Shira when hard pressed, though Argyll may have hoped that Rob would settle quietly in the remote glen – and in time be forgotten. It turned out that Rob planned a more active future.

In the wider political perspective, the outlook darkened further. In June Argyll and Islay were dismissed from all the offices they still held, and Montrose was a few weeks later appointed clerk register.[8] And though a semblance of normality was returning to most of the Highlands, with the *Squadrone* in the ascendant Rob Roy was not forgotten. Lieutenant General George Carpenter, who had replaced Cadogan as commander in chief in Scotland, assessed the situation in September 1716. There were still many former rebels who were uncertain of their safety and therefore had not returned to their homes. 'No man can depend on being safe; therefore they skulk about, and plunder the country in small partys.' To get them to settle down, they should be granted an amnesty. But there should be one exception to this leniency – Rob Roy should be excluded. 'As for Robroy, he is a great rogue, insignificant in himself, and [if] wee can gett his men from him is nott improbable but that Keppoch may be prevail'd on to catch him.'[9] MacDonald of Keppoch, who had not been attainted, was negotiating his submission to the government, and might agree to hunt Rob as the price of favour.

Great men sought to suspend their rivalry to cooperate in the hunt for Rob. Atholl was keen to demonstrate his loyalty by coordinating action with Montrose. In September he asked to meet Gorthie or Killearn, who were leading the search on Montrose's lands, and he commissioned his own chamberlain, Donald Stewart, to go into Balquhidder and obey any orders sent by Montrose.[10] Another of Atholl's men, who was unwise enough to claim that he could catch Rob, received not so much positive encouragement as a stark threat of the price of failure, being told 'that if he does not perform what he has undertaken he shal not continue longer in Atholl'.[11] Succeed, or be evicted. The new earl of Breadalbane was also active in the search. It was reported to him that Rob was keeping clear of inhabited ground on his estates, though he might be coming and going through the mountains.[12]

Before landlord cooperation could produce any result, the army took concerted action against Rob and the Lomond MacGregors. Late in September Montrose persuaded General Carpenter to agree that three parties of soldiers would march, from Finlarig, Stirling and Glasgow, their moves being timed so that they would converge on the MacGregors 'to surprize Robroy and his gang'. Rob had evidently returned to the Craigrostan area, and two detachments of soldiers would attack him and his men at dawn, while a third blocked a hill pass (perhaps the one leading to Balquhidder) which they might try to use to make an escape. 'There is a very great prospect of catching these rebell robbers' enthused the general. The operation, led by Major Green, was well planned, but it was ruined by a factor no amount of planning could have prevented – the weather. Torrential rain, it became clear in advance, would make the going difficult, and the commanders of the Stirling and Glasgow contingents therefore began their marches an hour or two earlier than ordered, showing sensible flexibility. But this was not enough. A tinkling little Highland burn that can normally be crossed with a stride can become a raging torrent in a few hours in a storm, and the troops found many virtually impassable. Green did well with his men from Glasgow to reach the MacGregor country just after dawn. The Stirling troops managed to arrive at about 8 a.m., but the Finlarig men did not get there until about 4 p.m. The three-pronged pre-dawn attack disintegrated in the downpour.

Surprise was lost, the 'rebels' had time to escape into the hills, and only fifteen prisoners were taken, two of them Lowlanders who had business dealings with the MacGregors. 'The major burnt Rob Roy's house and drove all their horses, cattle and sheep he could come att but some of these were so wild that he was obliged to let them go again'. As the troops retired, they came under fire from the rocks and cliffs for four miles, but its accuracy was poor. One grenadier was shot through the body but lived, another soldier was grazed on the head. Before he had left, Major Green had examined a site at Inversnaid at which it had recently been proposed that a barracks be built, 'and is fully satisfied that this is the only expedient that can secure the peace of that countrie and dislodge these ruffians from their strong holes'.[13] Green's expedition had been accompanied by James Graham of Kilmannan,[14] Montrose's factor, and he attempted to rally the soldiers' flagging morale by buying them eight pints of brandy before they retraced their marches.[15]

By this time the army's failure to catch Rob and other fugitives in the Highlands was leading to new strategies being assessed for restoring order. One, as Major Green indicated, was building permanently garrisoned barracks at strategic points. Rob's activities led to Inversnaid being the site most urgently considered. Another approach was the old 'use an ex-rebel to catch a rebel' theme, introduced by the suggestion that Keppoch might help. The next candidate for the job proposed himself. Gordon of Glenbucket had quickly changed himself from a Jacobite colonel into a man eager to make fulsome declarations of Hanoverian loyalty. In October 1716 he offered to join any attempt to take Rob. 'The station where Robroy keeps is att a great distance, butt Glenbuckett will assist in any method can be propos'd to apprehend that robber.'[16] It soon became clear, however, that Rob was not ready to await passively the further attentions of his many enemies. His response to the army raid on Inversnaid was the most provocative of his actions so far, and was aimed specifically against Montrose.

The timing of the army's raid on the Lomond MacGregors (late September 1716) may not just have been a matter of military convenience. The 29th was Michaelmas, when collection of rents was due to begin, and Montrose may have been anxious for a demonstration of authority to persuade as many of his reluctant Highland tenants as possible to pay – and indeed, to make it safe for his agents to collect the rents. Rob countered with a sensational demonstration of contempt for the duke's authority. On 20 November 1716 Montrose received a shame-faced letter from John Graham of Killearn, his factor and deputy sheriff of Stirlingshire. It opened 'I am obliged to give Your Grace the trouble of this [letter] by Rob Roy's command, being so unfortunate at present as to be his prisoner.' Killearn had been staying in a house at Chapelarroch, about six and a half miles north of Drymen, while collecting rents from Montrose's tenants. At about 10 p.m. Rob and his men had appeared out of the darkness and seized him. He would only be freed, Rob told him, on condition

- that Montrose cancelled all the debts that Rob owed him.
- that Montrose paid Rob 34,000 merks (about £1,890 sterling) to compensate for his losses at Auch and Craigrostan [Inversnaid].
- that Montrose give his word that he would never trouble or prosecute Rob Roy again.

Until Montrose agreed, Rob would carry Killearn, his accounts and bonds and the money he had collected, along with him. Killearn, anxious to show himself a responsible accountant even in the most difficult circumstances, calculated that the money Rob had seized amounted to the hefty sum of £3,227: 2: 8 Scots (about £275 sterling) – to the nearest computation he could manage. If forces were sent against Rob, Killearn added nervously, he had 'assurances of hard usage'.[17]

What was Rob playing at? He cannot possibly have believed that Montrose would agree to the terms he demanded, and even if he had done so, Rob's troubles would not have been over. He would have been free from debt to Montrose, but still attainted for high treason and in debt to others. Kidnapping a deputy sheriff would make escaping charges of treason even harder than it already was. Rob must have known this, and the kidnapping looks like an extravagant gesture of defiance on his part, and perhaps also an attempt to rebuild his credibility within the Highlands, after the burning of his houses at Auch and Inversnaid. And, of course, it was an attempt to humiliate Montrose personally, making him a laughing-stock as a great nobleman who could not protect his servants, get his rents paid, or control his estates.

It is possible that news of events in Edinburgh influenced the timing of the kidnapping of Killearn. Ever since 1712 legal proceedings had grumbled on in Edinburgh regarding Rob's debts and, above all, the legality of his disposition of Craigrostan to Glengyle and Bardowie. The argument that the 1711 disposition had been made as part of a plan to defraud creditors when he absconded the following year was evidently not in itself sufficient to 'reduce' it (have it declared invalid), so Montrose's lawyers had been diligently sifted through court records and had found evidence that there were already 'captions' outstanding against Rob at the time he had signed the disposition.[18] Disposing of his property when court orders were already in force against him for debt was illegal. Montrose's lawyers informed him of the welcome news that the court of session was going to reduce the disposition early in November 1716. Killearn was kidnapped two weeks later. Had Rob heard that he no longer had any chance of regaining his lands legally, and reacted furiously by organising the kidnapping? If so, the gesture was futile. On 27 December the court finally ruled (with some qualifications) 'That Rob Roy was in the terms of the act of parliament, by being under diligence and absconding, and so did reduce the disposition granted to Bardowie.'[19] There is of course irony in the situation. The decision affirmed that legally Craigrostan had belonged to Rob Roy, not to Glengyle and Bardowie, but this did not mean that Rob's creditors could immediately seek repayment from the estate, since in the interim Craigrostan had been forfeited to the crown. The creditors would have to start seeking payment all over again, this time from the government's forfeited estate commissioners.

Rob had perhaps calculated that the kidnapping of Killearn could not make his prospects any worse. If so, he was wrong. The uproar it caused gave Montrose ammunition for his attempt to persuade government that tracking down Rob Roy should be given high priority. He was not simply an outlaw or an insignificant rebel left over from the '15, but a man who had imprisoned an officer of the law, a deputy sheriff, thus treating the government with contempt. Montrose went straight to the top, immediately sending news of what had happened to one of the secretaries of state, Lord Townshend. The actions of Rob 'whom your Lordship has often heard named', struck at the honour of his majesty's government. He proceeded to remind Townshend of Rob's career – or his version of it. Rob, who had acted 'very foolishly as well as insolently' in offering to negotiate for Killearn's release, had put himself at the head of the MacGregors, 'a people who, in all ages, have distinguished themselves above others by robberies, depredations, and murders'. Ever since the 1688–89 revolution he had taken every opportunity of opposing the government. He was a robber pretending to act out of principal. Overcome by debt he had fled into the Highlands, and been protected by Breadalbane. His house at Auch being burnt, he had gone to Inveraray with about forty-five men, surrendered, sworn allegiance and been given protection. The theme of Rob surviving through Campbell support is being crafted into the narrative. When a friend of his had been captured, Rob had attacked and rescued him from some soldiers. Since the burning of his Craigrostan house, he had been robbing and plundering widely, preying on Montrose's tenants, and the duke was very concerned for the safety of Killearn who, being his servant, was very obnoxious to 'these barbarians'. Building a barracks was the only way to suppress them, concluded Montrose, and he had already put forward a scheme for this to General Carpenter.[20]

Montrose also related his tale of Rob's misdeeds to Carpenter himself, with emphasis on Finab's having given Rob a protection after his 'sham surrender', and claiming Rob had been kindly entertained at Inveraray for two or three days. The problem in capturing Rob lay partly in the fact that his was 'a rugged inaccessible countrey of about five or six miles in lenth, upon the side of Lochlomond, full of rocks and precipices'. Montrose added that Rob 'has his friends: but I hope the good time will come when all these dark misterys shall come to light'. Bringing down Rob, with luck, would also lead to the destruction of his 'friends' such as Argyll.[21] Montrose's henchman, Cockburn of Ormiston, also emphasised the Campbell dimension in the Rob Roy affair when writing to Townshend. He found it very odd, he remarked, that the independent companies could not stop his depredations. 'I have often heard it said Captain Campble of Ffannab would secure the country against this rober.'[22] This may seem an innocent comment, but the clear implication was that Finab as a Campbell could not be trusted.

Montrose was eager to exploit the kidnapping of Killearn to persuade government to follow his advice as to how to catch Rob, but one friend, George Baillie of Jerviswood, urged caution. If Montrose specified plans for action against Rob which then failed, he would be held responsible. Far better to demand action from government in general terms, and leave possible blame for failure to others. As for the independent companies not doing their duty, 'It's true this is hard,' but politically the time was not right for demanding their abolition.[23]

Meanwhile in London Montrose's ally, the duke of Roxburgh (who was about to become Scottish secretary), had got Townshend's agreement that Carpenter would be sent orders to do all he could to catch Rob, and that the general would send similar orders to Finab. 'I knew very well that this last would not signifie much, but I thought it not amiss to mention it, and indeed I believe it were best to say nothing of Rob Roy's manadgment since the rebellion broke out till the king comes. I believe few know more of it than I do myselfe but I do assure your grace I shall say nothing of it at this time.' Until the king arrived (from Hanover) 'I can say nothing to your grace about our great affair.'[24] The 'great affair' was clearly the destruction of Argyll. The *Squadrone* was keeping the secret of why it was so interested in Rob Roy, the fact that they believed he could provide evidence that Argyll was guilty of treason, by revealing that Rob had been 'managed' by the duke. This political bombshell was being prepared for dropping, but again the time was not yet ripe.

General Carpenter himself concluded, after the failure of Major Green's raid, that the best way of taking Rob Roy would be to bribe some of his followers 'otherwise he will always be too cunning and nimble for soldiers under armes'.[25] He had come to appreciate the limitations of regular troops in Highland terrain. Further offers of help, however, were available from gathering ex-rebel vultures. Ormiston was approached by the brother of Donald MacLean of Brolas, the tutor of MacLean (Sir John MacLean had died, and his successor was a minor). The tutor's brother would do all he could to capture Rob and release Killearn, acting with the help of MacDonald of Glencoe. In return he wanted some mark of favour for himself, and pardons for his brother the tutor[26] and Glencoe. Ormiston wrote immediately to Roxburgh, urging him to get in touch with the king in Hanover and General Cadogan to secure pardon at least for the tutor's brother 'if he bring in Rob Roye'.[27] Freeing the unfortunate Killearn was clearly a consideration secondary to the prize of capturing Rob Roy.

Killearn, however, was safe. Rob may have made big demands and uttered blood-curdling threats, but he was never a man to resort to cold-blooded violence. Quite possibly, he had not given much thought to what he was going to do with Killearn. As he was not to be killed, he was simply a nuisance to have to guard. Too amiable a man to act the villain for long, he let Killearn go, having held him for only six nights. His threats and the preposterous terms he had demanded from Montrose had been a sham from the start. His gesture made, his contempt for Montrose made clear, he freed Killearn. However letting his prisoner go did nothing to lessen the determination to catch him that the kidnapping had created. According to Killearn's own account of events, which he gave to Montrose, he had been kept in 'a very uneasy kind of restraint, being obleiged to change continually from place to place', and spending some time on an island in Loch Katrine. But then Rob had begun to think better of his actions, deciding 'that he would not mend his matter by retaineing Killearn his prisoner'. Rob kept the rent money Killearn had had, but gave him back his account books and other papers and bonds. He had no use for them himself – but it seems surprising that he did not keep them so as to inconvenience Montrose by disrupting his estate administration.[28]

Unique insights into the raid – and Rob Roy's recruiting methods – are provided by witness statements recorded during the trial of the only man ever charged of taking part in Killearn's kidnapping. James Graham, alias Gramoch Gregeroch, was tried before the justiciary court in Edinburgh in 1717. He admitted having been present at the kidnapping, armed with dirk and pistols, but claimed that he had been forced to take part in the raid. Defence witnesses testified that he had been having dinner in the house of one Alexander Graham (MacGregor) in Craigrostan (that 'nest of robbers') when Rob had appeared, and demanded that James join him. James had fled to the barnyard, but Rob had sent four men after him. They dragged him back. Rob, sword in one hand and pistol in the other, then threatened to shoot him in the head or 'cleave him to the teeth'. Not surprising, James went quietly. As he was led away, the kindly mistress of the household (presumably Alexander Graham's wife) followed to give him a supply of bread and cheese.

James was held overnight, then taken on the kidnapping raid. As a bystander, he noted details. Before Killearn's money chest was carried out to be loaded on horseback, he heard Rob say to Killearn, 'let the money be compte [counted], that it may not be said afterwards, I have taken away more money than I have done'. This was Rob, the man who believed his sins had been much exaggerated in the past. This time, though he was stealing, he wanted it to be recorded how much he stole. The forcing of the reluctant James to join in this criminal enterprise is ugly – but in the hierarchical society of the age it was typical of how men treated their underlings. Living in Craigrostan, James was, in Rob's eyes, his man, and had an obligation to serve him.

The Edinburgh jury decided that Gramoch was guilty of being present at the kidnapping, but accepted that he had been coerced. As in other cases concerning Rob and his family, the Scottish justice system was not as unrelentingly harsh and arbitrary as is sometimes thought. But the fact that for five months after the verdict Gramoch remained a prisoner in Edinburgh Tolbooth suggests that not all were happy with the result of the trial. Only after this period did Cockburn of Ormiston, as justice clerk, sign the decree 'assoiling' Gramoch.[29] Montrose's crony seemed reluctant to let free an associate of Rob Roy even though the jury had given its verdict.

By the time Killearn had been freed from his much shorter captivity, his case had been taken as near to the top of government as it could go in the king's absence. Townshend had recounted the crime of 'that notorious rogue Rob Roy', the kidnapping of Killearn, to the prince of Wales, 'who hes the utmost resentment of that insolent attempt of Rob Roy's'. The prince had decreed that it was 'highly for the honour of the government and for the interests of his majesty's subjects that all proper measures should be taken' to suppress Rob and his fellow rebels, and orders to this effect were dispatched to Carpenter.[30] Roxburgh too, in a letter to Cadogan, stressed the outstanding importance of Rob Roy. 'I must say to your lordship . . . that I know not any of the rebels in Scotland that it would be so much for his majesty's service, to have seiz'd as him: being satisfyed, that he can say a great deal, and in case he should say nothing I should still think it for his majesty's service to [pardon] those two mentioned in my lord justice clerk's letter [the MacLeans], in order to get so remarkable a robber as well as a rebel hanged.' Cadogan being a trusted political ally, Roxburgh mentions the hope that Rob would have sensitive intelligence to reveal – 'he can say a great deal'.[31] If caught, the alternatives to be laid before Rob were clear. Talk, or be hanged. Or quite possibly, as Rob must have known, talk and be hanged.

In Scotland General Carpenter dithered. Previous failures made him reluctant to commit regular troops again, so he expressed renewed faith in the best way to catch the 'arch rogue' being to send out parties from the independent companies, with regular troops quartered in towns and villages only in a supporting role. Or perhaps a proclamation could be issued offering reward and pardon to rebels who handed him over.[32] Carpenter talked with Finab, who promised (yet again) to take Rob, or at least drive him out of his homeland, and he was promised £50 sterling if he caught him.[33]

Rebellion and its aftermath had spread Rob's fame. But they cost him his houses and brought him attainder for treason. His attempted defiance in kidnapping Killearn was now bringing him the intensified wrath of government, and though he had escaped it in the short term it made his future prospects more hazardous than ever. One grain of comfort was that at least one of his opponents was personally scared of him. Ormiston, the justice clerk, was travelling north in December 1716, but decided he would avoid the Stirling road. Stirling might lie in the heart of the kingdom, but it was still reckoned that it could be in range of a raid by Rob, and given his 'kidnapping way' the justice clerk thought it best not to venture to use that route.[34] If Rob had had the audacity to imprison a deputy sheriff, a justice clerk might seem a tempting next step.

7

CLIMAX

Throughout 1716 the *Squadrone* had been increasing in power. Argyll had lost all his offices, not least because George I was on bad terms with his son, the prince of Wales, and was jealous of his growing popularity with the public. In part the king blamed Argyll's influence (as groom of the stole to the prince) for his family problem. After Argyll's fall purges began of officials and army officers who had supported him. But the duke was not a man who gave up easily. He sought power not through high political office for himself but through his influence over the votes of Scottish members of parliament and representative peers at Westminster. If he could deliver enough votes, the English ministers who dominated government would be quick buy his services as a political manager and abandon the *Squadrone*. Argyll's practice of opposing all government measures whenever excluded from power made him dangerous. In the early months of 1717 the government majority in House of Commons votes was very small, so though the *Squadrone* was for the moment winning the battle for power and office, Argyll was a force to be feared.[1] An outstanding example of 'Scotch pride and ambition', he fought 'to make himself absolutely a necessary man' to government.[2] Thus the *Squadrone* could not relax in its success. Bringing about the complete ruin of Argyll seemed more urgent than ever.

Obsession with catching Rob Roy intensified, and a few weeks between April and June 1717 saw the climax of the hunt for him come – and pass. That he lived to tell the tale (or some of it, as much as suited him) of the series of attempts to snare him in these weeks was remarkable, and for once his claims to occupy the moral high ground win some sympathy. Three powerful men sought to catch him by any means available. These men, the dukes of Montrose and Atholl and Justice Clerk Ormiston, Rob was to denounce as 'the triumvirate' engaged in a 'bloody conspiracy'.

Teasing out the meaning of a letter of 11 April 1717 from Montrose to Gorthie provides glimpses of the secret intrigues surrounding Rob. The results of Rob's recent 'management' made it plain, Montrose reflected, 'that he lys off haveing two strings to his bow, but in short the only true reason he can have for falling back is the traty [treaty] that for certain has been made with him of late'. Rob 'lying off' suggests that approaches to him had been made to do some sort of deal (on the lines of 'your safety in return for Argyll's head on a plate', no doubt) but that he was showing no interest in taking the bait. His stubbornness was attributed to his having another option open to him. The 'treaty' (a term used for negotiations as well as agreements) which was the second string to his bow presumably involved assurances Rob had received from Argyll. However, Montrose believed it should be possible to get Rob 'to see that it wold be more solidly his interest to fall on the method he was once in.' That 'method' that it was hoped Rob would accept, implies him making a deal with Montrose and the rest of the *Squadrone*. Saying that Rob had formerly been in 'that method' indicates that at some earlier point Rob had shown himself seriously interested in such a solution to his problems. Indeed, Montrose's letter goes on to indicate that Rob himself had taken the initiative in the matter – it would be of much use to government if Rob told the truth 'in the manner which he himself first proposed'. To try to win Rob back to such a scheme, it should be made clear to him that 'the utmost liberalety' of his present protectors – Argyll and his friends – would fall far short of what Montrose could do to make him 'easier in his circumstances'. There is more than a hint here that Montrose could get Rob pardoned for treason.

If that argument failed, Montrose suggested trying money. It would be a delicate issue to raise. Montrose clearly accepted here that Rob was a man of honour – in the sense that an offer of cash would be perceived as insulting unless carefully wrapped up in honeyed words and made to seem a side issue. One – nay two – thousand pounds sterling would be well spent in gaining Rob, Montrose calculated. Gorthie was to speak to Killearn on the subject, and see if a meeting could be arranged with Rob at which the conversation could 'be so contrived so as he should fully understand without speaking too plane [plain] that he should be made easie in that respect. I'm verie sensible that there's abundance of nicety in manageing a point of this kind'. An agreement reached by nods and winks and nudges would be far easier to accept than the stark truth that Rob was being pressurised to sell Argyll for cash and safety. Finally, Montrose pointed out that he was now giving Gorthie 'much more room to work upon than hitherto you have had,' another tantalising hint at earlier failed negotiations.[3]

Montrose was writing from London, where in-fighting among ministers was weakening the ministry and making it harder than ever to be certain of who was going to emerge with real power. To be able to produce Rob Roy and his hoped-for sensational revelations would have a major influence on the balance of power if it destroyed Argyll's hold on the votes of Scots MPs. Montrose's letter to Gorthie suggests he was desperate for quick action. When, just a few months before, Rob had suggested a deal when he kidnapped Killearn, the terms he had proposed had seemed outrageous. Now it seemed Montrose was ready to offer him practically anything – pardon, and enough money to make a new start. It was vital that Rob was convinced that he could only get such a settlement through Montrose. When Gorthie informed him that Rob believed that he might qualify for pardon under a proposed general indemnity, Montrose replied sharply that Rob must be told that he and his clan had no hope of benefiting from it. Further to persuade him that there was nothing to be gained from continued resistance, Rob was to be told of the scheme to build a barracks at Inversnaid to tame the surrounding country.[4]

Rob was now in a strange position, a rebel being hunted but a man also being courted with rival offers of protection and favour from the two dominant figures of Scottish politics, Montrose and Argyll. In terms of power to deliver reward, Montrose had most to offer. But politics was a fickle affair, and it would have been hard to be sure that Argyll would not replace Montrose in government favour in a few weeks or months. There were also considerations of trust. Argyll had proved reliable in the past, whereas Montrose had (in Rob's self-justifying account of his bankruptcy) betrayed and ruined him, and vindictively pursued him ever since. Moreover Rob's stand against him had severely damaged Montrose's reputation – and pride. Rob may well have doubted that he would ever forgive this.

The peak of the *Squadrone*'s attempt to gain Rob's testimony against Argyll by agreement rather than capture was now being reached. This came in a meeting that must have taken place in the first half of April 1717. New contacts had been made with Rob, and a meeting was arranged between him and the justice clerk at Cramond Brig, some miles west of Edinburgh on the road that led to

GLENGYLE HOUSE

Rob Roy is believed to have been born in an earlier house on this site. The house that Rob built for his nephew, Gregor MacGregor of Glengyle, was incorporated into the present structure. The water level of Loch Katrine (foreground) was raised in the nineteenth century: originally the house stood at the head of the loch, not at its side as now. *Copyright © David Stevenson*

OLD AUCHINTROIG HOUSE

This was where Rob Roy captured John MacLachlan in December 1715. Erected in 1702, it is the only building associated with Rob Roy to retain, more or less, its original external appearance. 2003. *Copyright © David Stevenson*

THE BRAES OF BALQUHIDDER

A view from the of the farm of Drumlich, where Rob Og murdered John MacLaren, looking eastwards down the glen towards Inverlochlarig, where Rob Roy died. March 2004
Copyright © David Stevenson

ROB ROY'S HOUSE AT COIRECHARNOCH

Though the surviving ruin is that of a later building, it is on the site of one of Rob Roy's houses.
View looking north across Glen Dochart. March 2004. *Copyright © David Stevenson*

ROB ROY'S GRAVE, BALQUHIDDER KIRKYARD

The bronze railings (erected in 1890) enclose three flat stones, centuries old by Rob's day, reused to
cover his remains, those of his wife Mary, and those of two of his sons, Coll and Rob Og. Queen
Victoria visited the grave in 1869. March 2004. *Copyright © David Stevenson*

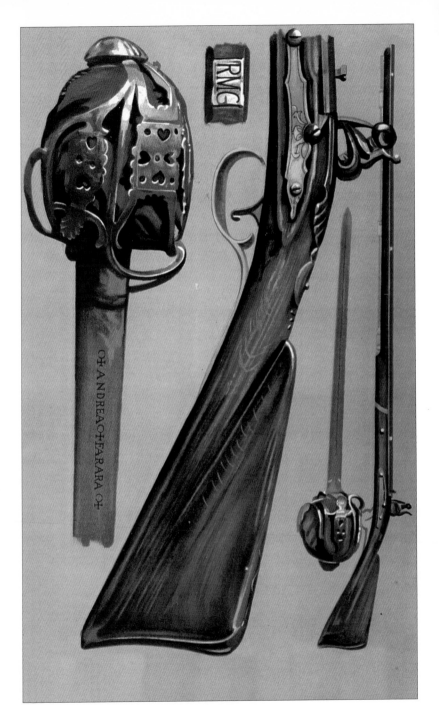

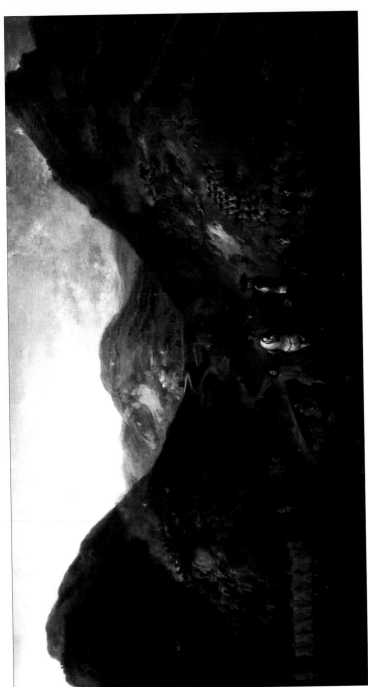

THE BATTLE OF GLENSHIEL

Painting by Peter Tillemans. It is often claimed that one of the figures depicted is Roy Roy, but this seems wishful thinking.

ROB ROY GOES OVER THE TOP
William Macready (1792–1873), 'the most romantic of actors', plays Rob Roy in 1848. The
extravagant figure in fantasy costume and weapons is supposed to depict Rob summoning his men
to battle during the 1715 Jacobite rising. A more irreverent interpretation would be that it looks
more as though he has been disconcerted by the swarm of midges rising up his kilt. Engraving by
J. Fairburn. *Copyright © Edinburgh University Library*

ROB ROY: A LEGEND STILL GROWING
In the mid nineteenth century an old ship's
figurehead depicting a Highlander was
whimsically erected on a ledge overlooking the
Leuchar Burn, in Peterculter, near Aberdeen. It
became identified with Rob Roy (or perhaps
had been from the first). Whenever one
wooden sculpture rots away it is replaced by a
new one, the version depicted here lasting from
1926 to 1991. The statue has begun to generate
its own legends, it now being claimed that Rob
once lept across the burn when it was in spate
from this rocky crag, to escape pursuit.
Copyright © Art Gallery & Museum Collection,
Aberdeen City Council

ROB ROY IN BRONZE
Statute by Benno Schotz, unveiled in Stirling
in 1975. The sculptor has taken account of the
tradition of Rob being able to tie his garters
without stooping. To avoid having to depict a
grotesque figure, he has opted for arms that are
unusually (but not ridiculously) long, combined
with unusually short legs. The result is a
stocky but striking figure.
Copyright © David Stevenson

Queensferry, the main crossing point of the Firth of Forth. Rob must have had guarantees for his safety at the meeting, and holding it at Cramond rather than Edinburgh no doubt allowed some of his men to check that no trap had been set to arrest him. Moreover, as a well frequented stopping place on a busy road, Cramond was a good spot for a secret meeting to take place unnoticed in the bustle.

Only Rob's account of what went on at this extraordinary conference between a notorious traitor and a senior law officer of the crown survives – or rather, it was the only account ever given, for Ormiston was to remain silent. Rob's narrative is highly emotional, and the allegation that he made in it is so extraordinary that, treated in isolation, it might be regarded as fantasy. But in the light of Montrose's letters, especially to Gorthie, it is entirely consistent with the duke's policy for dealing with Rob.

Ormiston, Rob stated, promised him pardon, in return for giving evidence – which Rob claimed would have had to have been false – as to Argyll's supposed treasonable contacts with Jacobites during the '15. The offer had first been made to him by Graham of Killearn, acting for Montrose. Though he had from the first regarded the proposed deal with the utmost horror, Rob related, he had agreed to the Cramond Brig meeting, where it had been repeated by Ormiston. Rob had left without giving an answer, anxious to escape from the treacherous justice clerk's clutches, but, for the moment, kept quiet about it.[5] There is every reason to believe that this was basically true. Montrose and Ormiston had proposed this squalid bargain. But two details of Rob's account may be questioned. Why, if Rob were fully resolved to have nothing to do with the deal from the start, did he take the risk of travelling to Cramond Brig? Perhaps he had hoped some deal he could accept as honourable could be worked out, but it is equally likely that he was intrigued. A trickster himself, he may have been tempted to delve further into the plot – and even somehow to benefit from gaining more knowledge of this high-level intrigue. The second detail of Rob's account of the Cramond meeting that may be queried is his statement that he was asked to provide false evidence. It seems unlikely that the cunning Ormiston, trained in the law, would have specifically asked for this even in a private meeting. What Rob probably meant was that Ormiston, convinced that Rob had accurate evidence that could convict Argyll of treason, demanded that he give such evidence, but Rob knew that he could not give such evidence without perjury. Yet Ormiston was a harsh, determined man, notoriously given to passionate rages, and, convinced that the conviction of Argyll would serve the ends of justice, he may have seemed to indicate that over-scrupulosity in witnesses was unwelcome.

The Cramond Brig meeting took place before 16 April 1717, for by that date the devious Ormiston had changed his tack, moving from one plan to another with remarkable speed.[6] He had failed to reach agreement with Rob, and the outlaw's good luck and wariness had meant that all attempts to capture him had failed. Rob no longer had any trust in him or in Montrose, having rejected their blandishments. There was no point in them trying any longer to lure Rob into a trap. Therefore someone Rob had more trust in should be persuaded to do the dirty work, and be promised a tempting reward for this service. Ormiston chose his target well, and summoned the duke of Atholl's legal agent in Edinburgh, John Douglas, to see him. Douglas was to write to the duke immediately. Atholl should arrange Rob's capture. If he did so, 'It would prove of singular use to your grace's interest and service, more as [than] he [Ormiston] can express att this time.'

Atholl was still trying to eradicate the stigma of having been unable to prevent three of his sons and many of his men joining the Jacobite rebels in the '15, which made him appear either weak in leadership, and therefore contemptible, or unwilling to prevent the actions of his men, and thus treacherous. Since the rebellion had been crushed, Atholl had been a political outcast, and his attempt to please the government by enforcing the 1715 act abolishing personal services had added to his humiliation at home. He had summoned his vassals to the head court of the regality of Atholl at Logierait to agree in future to make money payments to him in place of the traditional services. His vassals, who had so notably failed to obey him during the '15 rising, now turned out to be sticklers for tradition, and tried to insist on retaining their old services. They even talked of signing bonds to stand together against him, and drew up a document making rude comments about the failings of Atholl and his predecessors.[7] The maddened duke threatened to summon them before the House of Lords, and though the vassals in the end backed down the whole episode served to emphasise that he was despised on his own estates as well as at court. It was a hard fate for a sincere Hanoverian, and he was desperate to find some way of regaining credibility and resuming the places in society and politics that he believed were due to him through his blood and his wealth.

Now the devious Ormiston offered the duke a way of achieving this dream. If he managed to catch Rob Roy, when all others had failed, then he would have performed a major service to the government and would get his reward. Ormiston (as John Douglas related) gave advice on how to proceed. Atholl should get people 'of his [Rob's] own kidney to make proposals to him so he might surrender' to the duke. But Rob was to be 'managed' cautiously, and only limited promises for the future should be given to him. If he would not surrender 'your grace would pleas think of some sort of stratagem, whereby he might be seized; att any other rate.' Douglas urged Atholl to proceed with the scheme. 'I would engadge in it, becaus the fellow hes so often affronted [insulted] D[uke] Montrose in the like interprise.' Ormiston was working with Montrose, and therefore pointing out how pleased he would be if Rob's 'affronts' to him were revenged, but at the same time he was playing on ducal one-upmanship. For Atholl to succeed where Montrose had failed would be especially pleasing.

In passing on Ormiston's words to Atholl, John Douglas made no direct reference to the political urgency of capturing Rob, though he did mention the confusion in London, with some ministers being 'turned out' or resigning, rumours of replacements being appointed. In all, there was 'a dreadful jumble above'.[8]

Atholl leapt at the opportunity for redemption through Rob Roy, and on 3 June Rob became his prisoner. Rob was to claim that he had been betrayed. He had agreed to go to Atholl's mansion house in Dunkeld for talks, having had a promise of safe conduct made by Lord Edward Murray, Atholl's younger brother. But once in the house he had been treacherously seized. Atholl, on the other hand, claimed that Rob had surrendered voluntarily.

Which version of events was true? Had Rob voluntarily surrendered, or had he been double-crossed, promised safe conduct but then arrested? At first sight Rob's tale of betrayal looks the more plausible. Why would he have surrendered? Atholl's approach, offering to try to arrange a settlement for him, had doubtless been welcome, well worth investigating. But Rob, as the fact that he had remained free for so long indicates, was not naive. He would not simply have walked into Atholl's hands because he had offered to do him a good turn, without any guarantee of his safety. The sensible thing to have done would have been to have arranged to meet Atholl on neutral ground, to guard against any attempt at treachery. His meeting at Cramond Brig with Ormiston had been organised in this way, and so doubtless had his mysterious earlier meeting or meetings with Killearn. Yet Rob had agreed to leave himself defenceless by walking into Atholl's own house in Dunkeld. It is possible that Rob let his defences drop because he was exhausted and ill. He told Atholl that in the previous year he had never spent more than three nights in a row in the same house,[9] having to keep constantly on the move to keep ahead of the intensifying search for him, and it was to be reported a few days later that he was ill. 'I'm informed Rob lyes ill of an rose in his theigh, swelled so bigg, as he is not able to walk,' John Douglas wrote.[10] The 'rose' on Rob's leg probably indicates indicates that he was suffering from erysipelas or 'St Anthony's Fire',[11] known from the rash the infection caused as 'the rose'. The rash indicated the site of the initial infection, but the illness could develop into bleeding pimples and sores, and other symptoms could include high temperature, severe headaches and vomiting. Perhaps, sick, exhausted and desperate for rest, Rob had been too trusting of Atholl.

However, such an interpretation turns out to be too simple to fit all the evidence. It leaves three questions to be answered:

- Why, immediately after arresting Rob, did Atholl write to the king suggesting that he be freed?
- Why did Atholl not hand over his prisoner to the government, but instead send him to his own private prison in the Highlands?
- Why, having captured the most wanted man in the country, did Atholl not take adequate measures to guard him?

The answer seems to be that neither Rob nor Atholl told the whole truth about what took place in Dunkeld – though Atholl came closest. What happened, the evidence indicates, was neither unconditional surrender by Rob nor perfidious seizure of him by Atholl. Instead, there was collusion between the two men. A deal had been done. Rob would be made a prisoner, but on condition that he would be held by Atholl and not handed over to Montrose or the government. Atholl would then gain credit for having arrested him and (presumably, as Rob went along with the plan), arrange terms for a pardon for him. Rob had been 'arrested' and Atholl wanted full credit for this. It would not be a *Squadrone* success but his own, and to ensure this Rob would not be handed over to Ormiston and the legal system in Edinburgh. Instead Atholl bypassed them by writing directly to the king. Rob would be held as a prisoner, but so lightly guarded that if things went wrong he could easily disappear back into the hills. If the plan worked, Rob would gain a pardon and Atholl would be the hero of the hour. The *Squadrone*, which had urged him to catch Rob, was being double-crossed.

In this reconstruction of what was going on there is of course a degree of speculation. Much remains murky, and all parties involved were manoeuvring for personal advantage and prepared to betray each other whenever it proved expedient. Rob, it may be, saw submitting to a fairly open imprisonment as a way of gaining some desperately needed rest and recuperation, and probably he had no intention of betraying his dealings with Argyll.

Delight was the immediate response to Atholl's announcement that he was holding Rob prisoner. From Edinburgh Ormiston wrote 'I can't express the joye I was in' on hearing the news. 'I'm confident it shall be most agreeable news at court.'[12] But before his letters could even have reached court in London, victory turned into humiliation. Rob escaped. Atholl had sent him to the prison of his regality of Dunkeld, at Logierait about six miles to the north of Dunkeld. That this was folly on the part of Atholl was the reaction of the *Squadrone*. Instead of dispatching Rob south to Perth under a military escort, Atholl had moved him north, deeper into the Highlands, which would make it easier for him to escape to the safety of the hills or to be rescued by supporters. He had been sent to a private feudal prison, and such institutions were notorious for the ease with which prisoners escaped. Ormiston at once smelt danger, and pleaded with Atholl to send his prisoner to Edinburgh Castle. A strong detachment of soldiers would be sent from Perth to receive him, with orders to treat him 'civily' but guard him closely. Logierait was too far from any garrison to be safe, and 'he's [Rob's] in no smale danger if his old friends can possibly be masters of him, and I'm perswaded they will lay all irons in the fire to rescue him'.[13] Ormiston suggests not only that Rob might be freed by his old friends, supporters of Argyll, but that Rob's life might then be in danger from them. If it seemed that Rob might be doing a deal with Argyll's enemies, then from a Campbell point of view it might seem best that he was dead. John Douglas, Atholl's agent, was more specific, when he wrote backing up Ormiston's message. It was too risky, he told his master, to keep Rob at Logierait. It would be better if he were in some place where 'he is in no manner of hazard as to his life'. There was certain news of men, 'particularly Argyl's folks' planning to rescue Rob and 'they are resolvd att any raite [by any means] rather as [than] he should come in, to have him putt out of the way'.[14]

Montrose shared Ormiston's fears about Rob's safe-keeping. 'All I have to say att present about R.R. is I wish he was safe in Edinburgh Castle, for till he is once there I can't reckon we have him.' Prophetic words. Montrose wrote them on the evening of 12 June, but about 10 p.m. he received a letter from the justice clerk containing what Montrose described as 'the disagreeible news of R.R. haveing made his escape. I'm so much out of humor I'le say no more' was how he abruptly concluded his letter the next morning.[15] It may be assumed he had had a bad night, reflecting on how every attempt to catch Rob seemed to lead to disaster. Moreover, from the first it was realised by a wider public in Edinburgh that there was something funny about Rob's 'surrender'. It just didn't seem to add up. The 'gentleman' Atholl sent to Edinburgh to give Ormiston the bad news had talked about it to others on his journey. Crossing on 'the ferry' over the Firth of Forth between North and South Queensferry, he had spoken of how Rob had come to Atholl's house in Dunkeld. Rob had had 'six men with him, but put them off [sent them away] when he surrendered'. This confirms that Rob's imprisonment at Logierait was voluntary. He had told his own men to leave him with Atholl. 'Rob Roi surrendered to D[uke] Atholl but not meeting with such things as he expected has made his escape.' It was 'to be feared there is some mischief lirking under it', it was said.[16] Something was going on – though only Atholl and Rob himself knew quite what the agreement between them had been.

Atholl failed to heed the warnings about the folly of sending Rob to Logierait – because it were part of whatever plan he had afoot. On 6 June he intercepted a Captain Lloyd, who was hastening a military detachment sent from Perth to pick up the prisoner. The duke was furiously petulant. Rob was his prisoner. He had written to Roxburgh as secretary for Scotland to tell the king that he awaited his orders as to what to do with Rob, and he would not hand Rob over to the army until he had orders from court.[17] Atholl was determined to have as few intermediaries between himself and the crown as possible, lest his glory be shared by others. He immediately wrote to inform General Carpenter that he had refused to hand Rob over to Lloyd, but his plans were unravelling fast. As a great feudal lord, he had assumed that he could do what he liked in Atholl. It was his country. Some time before he had been described as being a very tall and awkward person 'of a very proud, fiery, partial disposition; does not want sense, but choaks himself with passion [anger]'.[18] Later, it was said that 'The pomp and state in which this noble person lives, is not to be imitated in Great Britain; for he is served like a prince, and maintains a greater equipage and retinue than five times his estate would support in another country.'[19] Over Rob Roy, the duke's sense of his own greatness had led him astray. He evidently had not thought it possible that the government would presume to send troops to confiscate his prized prisoner.

Pride, as the platitude says, comes before a fall. In this case it came remarkably quickly. An hour after dispatching his indignant letter to Carpenter, Atholl received disastrous news. Rob Roy had not waited to be either rescued or transferred to Perth. He had managed his own escape that morning. The duke hastily took up his pen again, and though less arrogant in tone than before he was not ready to concede that he had blundered. Rob's escape was not his fault, he wailed, but that of the government. Even if he had agreed to hand Rob over to Captain Lloyd, it would have been too late, for Rob had gone. It had been news of the sending of soldiers that had provoked Rob into escaping. As to the charge that would inevitably be made that Rob had not been properly guarded, 'I did think [it] was sufficient for one that had surrendered, for I think there can hardly be an instance of any that had done so that made his escape immediatly after'. This was self-justification, but it rings true. It seems very likely that Rob had indeed escaped because troops were coming for him. He had agreed to be Atholl's prisoner and Atholl had therefore taken no serious measures for his security. It had not occurred to the duke that his voluntary prisoner might escape – because it had not occurred to him that the government would would be so unmannerly as to try to seize his prisoner.

Atholl tried to redeem himself by ordering a large-scale manhunt. When Rob was recaptured, he would be handed over immediately to the garrison at Perth. The idea that Rob was his private prisoner, and that Atholl could use him to make some deal with the king, had had to be abandoned. A duke could not be expected to make an apology, but the angry Atholl went as far as expressing regret. 'I cannot express how vexed I am for this unlucky affaire' he muttered.[20]

The wrath of Ormiston was the first to reach poor Atholl. How could he have left Rob Roy at Logierait, in the heart of a Highland area where he had many friends? Neither Ormiston nor General

Carpenter would ever have believed he would do such a thing, for Ormiston 'was convinced those concerned for Rob Roy's being in custody would endeavour his rescue, so I am persuaded they would putt it out of reach either to sease him, or leave him in a capacity to surrender'[21] – another hint that it was feared Rob might now be in danger of capture by Argyll's men. Ormiston suggested that there might be more behind the escape than Atholl's carelessness, and others reached the obvious conclusion. Atholl and Rob had been in collusion in acting out a charade.

Most galling of all for Atholl must have been the congratulations he received from London on having arrested Rob, which only arrived after his prisoner had in fact escaped. Roxburgh's letter to Atholl on the matter is a remarkable testimony as to how important Rob had become in the political game. Atholl's news that Rob was imprisoned had reached Roxburgh at about 10 p.m. on 7 June. In spite of the time, Roxburgh had hastened to court and 'delivered your letter to the king, who I doe asure your grace is mightily well pleased with your care and diligence on this occasion, and of your great concern for his service, nor indeed was it possible for any one to have done a greter peice of service at this time'. King George had ordered Roxburgh to send immediately an 'express' post back to Atholl – and would have written himself had it not been so late. But the king could not 'approve of Rob Roy's being immediately set at liberty notwithstanding of what he proposes to doe, but will have him first caried to Edinburgh'.

The matter was dealt with in great secrecy. Atholl's letters to Roxburgh and the king with the news of Rob's arrest have not survived. This might be a matter of chance – loose 'state papers' often got lost. But it is telling that Roxburgh's reply to Atholl with the king's reactions to his news was not entered in Roxburgh's official register of out-going letters. Further, in the original letter, surviving in the Atholl archives, it is clear that the clerk to whom Roxburgh dictated it was not allowed to know who the letter was about. A blank was left for Rob Roy's name, which Roxburgh subsequently filled in himself.[22]

The *Squadrone* dream, of several years' standing, had for a moment seemed near success. Rob Roy had been caught. But then he had disappeared back into the Highlands, and the hunt had to be resumed. Back to square one. Atholl's Edinburgh agent, John Douglas, offered reassurance to his master from a peculiar angle.

He had not slept well since Rob's escape, but he had dreamed that Rob had broken his leg and been recaptured. This was surely a good omen. More practically, he had contacted Hamilton of Bardowie. In return for Bardowie's help, Douglas promised that Atholl would 'pardon the crime committed'. Indeed if Bardowie secured Rob and handed him over, Douglas promised that Atholl would easily settle all his differences with him.[23] The nature of Bardowie's 'crime', and how else he had offended Atholl, are not revealed. Other reports from Douglas followed, designed to make Atholl feel better about the disaster of the escape by raising his hopes that he could get hold of Rob again. Killearn had gone west to coordinate action, and Atholl's own zeal in the search 'putts it out of the power of enemies, from representing your grace with any sort of contrivane or connivance' in the escape. Indeed, Douglas in a cunning piece of sycophantic verbal manipulation of the truth, converted Rob's escape into 'that rascals retreat', at which he expressed glee. Atholl, it seems, had not so much let Rob escape as forced him into flight. Further good news was that Douglas had heard about 'the rose' in Rob's thigh that had incapacitated him, 'which I'm hopefull may produce the desired effects of my dream'. The dream about Rob's broken leg had not been wrong, just imprecise as to what was wrong with it.

The bad news was that Atholl's men had found out where Rob was laid up with his damaged leg – but then two of the men had sent intelligence to Rob and he had been able to escape. Moreover Douglas was now uncertain as to whether Bardowie would join in the search, and he doubted whether Grant of Pluscarden, whom Atholl had suggested could help, was trustworthy, for he was the brother of the laird of Grant and 'I know he is a strong friend of Roy's'. But Douglas tried to remain hopeful that Rob would be caught in the end, encouraging Atholl with the recollection that 'the king has never seen to be better pleased or satisfied with any service ever was done him, as with the account of your grace's letter, of his surrender'.[24] George I's reaction to Rob's escape he tactfully does not mention.

Atholl well knew that hopes of saving his reputation depended on swiftly recapturing Rob. On 8 June, using his powers as lord lieutenant and sheriff principal of Perthshire, he had issued orders to Donald Stewart, one of his baillies for the regality of Atholl, and three of his other leading estate officials to gather sixty or eighty 'of our men, out of our property' to be armed and sent in pursuit of Rob. They were to be 'indemnified of all blood shedding, slaughter, mutilations . . . whatever' committed in carrying out this task – though they were also enjoined to behave civilly and to take nothing (such as food and shelter) without paying.[25]

The pursuers got close, but not close enough. Donald Stewart was reported to have been ready to pounce on Rob on the morning of 13 June – but (as John Douglas had said) two of his own men betrayed the plan to the fugitive.[26] When, after ten days, nothing had been achieved by Atholl's men, he also employed (on the recommendation of his son, Lord James Murray) Alexander Stewart of Innerslanie, in Glen Tilt, 'to give me a handle to do for' Rob Roy. But Stewart was not even to tell his own family he was looking for Rob.[27] Atholl was coming, at last, to realise he could not even trust the men of Atholl whose allegiance he thought his by right.[28] On 24 June Douglas reinforced this unwelcome message. For once blunt, he told his master that, 'most of your men are his [Rob's] greatest ffreinds'. Moreover Bardowie had told Douglas that Atholl men would never take Rob, not because they could not be trusted, but because Rob had got into 'his lurking places', hideouts in places beyond Atholl's reach. But Douglas still managed a glint of optimism. He hoped to be able to contact Rob through Bardowie and Glengyle, and asked Atholl to commission him 'to concert all matters concerning him with any person (or if your grace thinks fitt to say Rob Roy)'.[29] A few days later Douglas himself and Alexander Murray, Atholl's secretary, were preparing to ride west themselves in search of Rob Roy or news of him. They were confident that their efforts to apprehend Rob would have a far better chance of success than Killearn's, for agreement with Killearn would mean him surrendering 'to Montrose, but if he do that I am much mistaken'.[30] Douglas and Murray, two men of the pen rather than the sword, experienced some difficulties in preparing for action. It was hard to hire horses, evidently because horses sent into the Highlands had a tendency not to be returned. On examining his neglected pistols, Douglas declared them unreliable: he needed a new pair.[31] Perhaps it is lucky their venture came to nothing, for they do not sound well qualified to face Rob Roy on his own ground.

Evading pursuit was difficult, but Rob's initial escape from Logierait had been simple. Stories circulated that he had got his guards drunk,[32] and it is likely enough that alcohol played a part in the affair. Some years later Rob's first biographer was to elaborate this theme, depicting Rob pretending to drink copious drams of whisky with his guards but cunningly pouring his drink into his vast red beard,

which absorbed it. Thus he remained sober.[33] The image of Rob and
his huge whisky-sodden beard may be entertaining, but it is not very
plausible. The most specific of the near-contemporary descriptions
of the escape depicts Rob 'taking the other [sic] dram heartily with
his guard; and when all were pretty hearty' through drink Rob said
that he wanted to send a servant with a letter to his wife, and that
he also needed to give the servant some verbal instructions. He was
allowed to go to the door with one guard, and entered into a deep
conversation with the servant, casually taking a few steps outside
the door. The guard, befuddled by drink saw nothing amiss. Rob's
wandering steps brought him close to where his horse was tethered –
and he suddenly mounted and rode off. The escape, it was noted was
mortifying to those who thought they had him safe as it delayed their
plans to bring charges against 'John Roy' – in other words, Argyll
('Red John of the Battles').[34] By another account, two servants rode
with him as he fled and they were able to escape in daylight through
Atholl's great estates because Rob 'gave out the duke of Atholl was
the best friend he had and that he was to make him his chamberlaine
till he gote him a better post'.[35] Perhaps Atholl had indeed made
some such promises to him in return for his cooperation. In a world
in which Breadalbane had made the outlawed Rob a baillie, anything
was possible.

Rob had escaped the army, but his efforts to arrange some deal
through Atholl which would keep him out of the hands of the
Squadrone had collapsed. There was no one left to turn to with
sufficient power to help him. Atholl had now joined Montrose in
the hunt for him, eager to redeem himself in government eyes. But
at least they wanted him alive, whereas Argyll's men might now be
prepared to assassinate him to keep him quiet.

As in the past Rob proved resourceful, and he made a bold decision
that may well have saved his life. He was surrounded by ruthless and
secret conspiracies, but there was one possible way out. It would
not solve all his problems, but it should at least reduce the pressure
on him. It was a very simple strategy. He would prick the bubble of
secrecy. He would make public what was happening, and, caught in
the bitter rivalries of great men, he would declare where he stood.
He would bid for renewed support from Argyll by publicising the
conspiracy against him. He would denounce the *Squadrone*, for he
saw it as his implacable enemy whatever he did. This might seem
dangerous, but once the plot was out and Rob had declared that he

was being pressured into giving false evidence, his value as a witness against Argyll would evaporate. Rob might still be hunted, but the intense political urgency would disappear.

It was a clear-headed, rational policy, but the man who made it was angry, and the wording of his 'Declaration to all true lovers of honour and honesty' that he circulated (dated Balquhidder 25 June 1717) is passionate in its bitterness and contempt for his enemies.[36] Honour and conscience, Rob began, had decided him to detect [expose] the assassins of his country and countrymen. He had been pressed to be 'the instrument of matchless villany' by giving false evidence against 'a person of distinction, whose greatest crime known to me was that he broke the party I was unfortunately of'. Clearly this is Argyll, whose 'crime' had been defeating the Jacobites. The proposal to give false evidence had first been made to Rob by Killearn, in the name of his master, Montrose, with life and fortune promised to Rob for his cooperation. Rob had greeted the proposal 'with the utmost horrour'. Then Lord Ormiston 'who trysted me to the bridge of Cramond, was no less sollicitous on the same subject, which I modestly shifted till I gott out of his clutches, fearing his justice would be no check on his tyranny'. Finally, completing 'the triumvirat in this bloody conspiracy', there was Atholl. He had 'coyduk'd [tricked] me into his conversation, immediately committed me to prison, which was contrary to the parole of honour given me by my Lord Edward in the duke's name and his own, who was privy to all that pass'd betwixt us. The reason why the promise was broke to me was, because I boldly refused to bear false witness against the duke of Argyle'. Here Roy is getting his own version of his relations with Atholl on record, evading the fact that he had evidently at first reached some agreement with him. Luckily providence 'had helped me to escape the barbarity of these monstrous proposals'. If he had not escaped 'my fate had certainly been most deplorable, for I would be undoubtedly [have been] committed to some stinking dungeon, where I must choose either to rot, dye, or be damn'd'. He would not, he continued, buy himself life, liberty and treasure if the price was perjury. The triumvirate would need to 'find out one of their own kidney' for their cruel and cowardly enterprise. He would not give full details of the foul plot against him, he declared, or of the way in which Montrose had persecuted him both before and after he had submitted to the government (by surrendering to Finab). In Rob's opinion, he and Montrose should be 'left alone to debate our own private quarrell'. He would soon show how little use Montrose was in serving 'either king or country'. On many occasions he had wanted to submit himself to the king's mercy, but Montrose and the others had prevented it.

Rob's declaration was short and explosive. In parts it seems a spontaneous outpouring of indignation, hatred and contempt, but it is likely that it was carefully crafted. Rob could doubtless have gone on for pages about his wrongs, but the declaration has been kept brief (about 480 words) and specific, which gives it impact. Facts are packed in, points carefully made, yet it brims over with tension and emotion. The message is clear: I would be valueless as a witness, I am committed once and for all to the duke of Argyll and will never trust or work with the dukes of Atholl and Montrose. A cautious man would have wrapped up these points in language which tried to avoid offence. That might have had the required result with less risk. But Rob chose to release some of his pent-up frustration and rage in a blast of defiance. A final piece of boldness (if the surviving copies of the declaration are to be trusted) comes in the signature – 'Rob Roy McGrigor'. Hardly wise, perhaps, and it might have been a good time to stress his adopted name of Campbell, but deeply satisfying.

Distribution of the declaration was limited. Rob had no access to a printing press. But what mattered was getting it to the right people, and a copy certainly reached Montrose. It had the desired effect. The politically-motivated search for Rob declined rapidly. Atholl and Montrose might still seek his arrest, to make him repent his scathing public insults, but both men must have been coming to the conclusion that pursuing him seemed a sure way to humiliation, and there was no pressing political incentive making catching him a priority. He had blown his possible unique importance as a witness.

Immediately before he issued his declaration, however, it had been decided to try to renew negotiations with him, and it was hoped that though he had escaped from Atholl the incident might have given him a fright, making him more willing than before to cooperate. Killearn wished to pursue such a policy, and Montrose wrote to Gorthie from London (18 June): 'I'm glad Killearn is to make furder tryall upon R.R. I must tell you that what you have done that way falls exactly in with what his Majesty suggested to my self t'other day. When talking of R.R.'s escape he said why should not Killearn try now to bring on again his correspondence with him, for that probablie he might now be more disposed to do it then formerly.'[37]

It was feared that Rob, in defiant mood after breaking free from *Squadrone* plots, would soon take his revenge on Montrose's property, and Killearn's correspondence at this time indicates that he was trying to take defensive precautions but encountering difficulties. He wanted to have ditches dug at Drymen to protect Buchanan Castle, but the Menteith tenant farmers he conscripted to do the digging proved uncooperative. They took the 'modern' attitude that they might pay rent for their land but were not bound to perform arbitrary feudal services for their lord. There were soldiers stationed in Drymen, but when Killearn turned to them they too decided that ditch digging was not their job. But they said they would do the work, Killearn wrote forlornly, if Montrose authorised him to pay them. Killearn begged for more troops to be sent immediately. Rob was reported to be willing to attack isolated parties of soldiers, and had now rallied in arms not only the MacGregors but many 'broken men'.[38] A few months before, on visiting the soldiers at Drymen, Gorthie had found them 'not easy in their quarters', for local people grumbled at having to quarter and supply them, and 'The gentlemen in the country don't like their company because it's disobleidgeing to Rob Roy.'[39] Keeping Rob happy seemed more important to people than obeying Montrose or the government.

Changes in government policy however, were already working to Killearn's advantage. There was a new determination to suppress the sort of Highland disorders which Rob had come to symbolise. Lawlessness had plagued many areas since the suppression of the '15, and the government had lost patience. It had been decided that the army would play a more active role than usual in peacetime law enforcement, and other less official action against troublemakers should be sanctioned. The first step taken seems to contradict the idea of a more aggressive Highland policy. The independent companies, supposed to be a Highland police force, were disbanded. This was a triumph for the *Squadrone*, which had persuaded George I that they were ineffective, corrupt and expensive. There was a good deal of truth in this, but the real motive was that the companies were failing to serve *Squadrone* interests, and the main target was Finab's company, notoriously controlled by Argyll. If there were to be effective military intervention in the Highlands, the worse than useless independent companies had to be swept away, and regular troops under central command employed in their place.

The new campaign was not focused on Rob Roy, but that

Inversnaid was chosen as the site for one of four Highland barracks which were to be built was due to his notoriety. Some time in mid 1717 a paper (probably drafted by Sir Patrick Strachan of Glenkindie) drew particular attention to raiding into Lowland areas between Dumbarton and Stirling. Glenkindie was at this time earning himself an evil reputation in Scotland. He had been captured by the Jacobites at Sheriffmuir but escaped while the rising was collapsing. Argyll had employed him to go to the Highlands 'to settle some garisons there and disarm all the rebells they could meet within [the district of] Mar'. After Argyll was replaced, General Cadogan had given Glenkindie a wider commission to arrest all the rebels he could, and he apprehended several 'gentlemen of distinction'. His zeal in tracking down rebels earned him hatred – and the loss of all his cattle in retaliatory raids – but brought him reward in the form of a knighthood and appointment as surveyor general to the commissioners for forfeited estates. In 1719 he was to become barrack master general of Scotland.[40] Given responsibility for taking possession of the estates of attainted Jacobites and arranging their sale, he had a strong vested interest in helping restore order in the Highlands – and one of the estates he was responsible for was, of course, Inversnaid (as the whole estate of Craigrostan was now generally called).

Glenkindie recommended that in the long term a fort or barracks be built at Inversnaid, but more immediate action was needed he argued 'to put a stop to the extraordinary depredations that have been committed within these last few days upon his grace the duke of Montrose's grounds and these of others and for preventing the ruin of those countreys which in all probability must happen before the barrack can be built unless some effectual remedy be now apply'd'. A hundred men should be stationed between Loch Katrine and Loch Lomond immediately, with thirty more at Kilmahog, near Callander.[41] By 25 June, the day that Rob issued his declaration in Balquhidder, news reached Edinburgh that orders had arrived for this to be done.[42]

On 5 July Brigadier George Preston (in command in Scotland) gave orders that a hundred men, under a captain and three other officers, were to march to Inversnaid.[43] Moreover the previous month, the king in council in London had given orders for building barracks in the Highlands, and Craigrostan/Inversnaid was to be given priority.[44] Rob's escape from the duke of Atholl had been a theatrical triumph, but the publicity surrounding it had finally persuaded a reluctant government of the need for a permanent military presence on his former lands.

It may well have been news of the approach of the troops ordered to Inversnaid by Brigadier Preston that led Rob to lead a raid on Buchanan Castle early on 19 July, one of his most famed exploits for its sheer cheekiness. His men broke into the park (enclosed cattle grazings) at Buchanan Castle and stole thirty-two of the duke's best cows. The monetary loss was secondary to the symbolic message. Rob was ready to strike at the castle which was, nominally at least, the centre of Montrose's little empire. Killearn as the duke's representative tried a traditional Highland way of raising men to resist, sending 'fiery crosses' through the area summoning men to assemble them to pursue the raiders. He ought to have known better. Montrose's tenants were mainly Lowland farmers, not willing to fight, and what Highlanders there were would be more likely to sympathise with Rob that fight him. Killearn had to report indignantly, 'as yet not one man has offered to stir'. As for arming the tenants of Menteith so they could resist raiders, as Montrose ordered, Killearn did not think it was a good idea. You could arm the tenants, but they still would not resist raiders. The MacGregors would simply take the weapons from them – indeed, there had already been some cases of this happening. Most landlords would have been happy to have had a peaceable peasantry. Montrose's were far too docile for his liking.

However, help was at hand, and on the same day as Rob's raid soldiers from Drymen led by Captain Brown, Killearn, and the few Menteith men whom he had managed to round up, marched in pursuit, determined to establish a garrison at Inversnaid as Brigadier Preston had ordered. If Rob's raid had been intended to divert them from their objective it failed to do so. Nor did the rumours he spread that he had recruited many of the broken men, and expected to be reinforced by many men from the independent companies, now they were being disbanded. Brown's force met no opposition until it approached Inversnaid. Then voices were heard shouting to them to hurry as Rob Roy 'was murdering some of the countreymen on the other syde' – doubtless an attempt to lead the soldiers into a trap. Brown advanced through boggy land as quickly as he could, while Killearn sent out two or three Menteith men who knew the country ahead as scouts – though they would only go after he threatened them. One of them strayed off to the right (east), and was captured by

Rob's men at Stronlachachar. Captain Brown meanwhile continued his advance towards Corriearklet. Twice Rob drew up his men to face him, but each time he withdrew at the last minute to avoid contact. By now it was so dark that only the heads of the Highlanders could be seen, silhouetted against the horizon as they retreated, and the pursuit was called off. The houses at Corriearklet were occupied by Brown's men, while Rob stayed in the hills all night. Estimates suggested he had about fifty men, while another thirty or forty were busy all night driving cattle away to safety. At daybreak Rob marched off, freeing his prisoners (he had rounded up about sixteen of the dispirited Menteith men) on their promising not to serve Killearn or to pursue him again.

The next day, 20 July, reinforcements led by John Graham of Drunkie and Patrick Graham arrived – with excuses (which Killearn did not believe) about why they had not been able to be present the previous day. It was not thought worthwhile to pursue the enemy as Rob's men could quickly disperse in the hills, and anyway, the objective of reaching Inversnaid had been achieved. The soldiers who were to be stationed there found whatever shelter they could. Killearn was more ambitious. He wanted to start work immediately on building the planned barracks. Official orders had not yet been given for this, but Killearn gave instructions that fifty of Montrose's men with spades, twenty-five horses and a week's provisions should assemble at Corriearklet in two days time, while other supplies were brought up Loch Lomond by boat. Killearn was full of enthusiasm, but there was a difficulty. He knew that the army's board of ordnance had prepared plans of the new barracks that were to be built in Scotland, but he didn't have a copy. Indeed he did not know quite where it was intended that the barracks should be built, which was a bit embarrassing. If only he could get the plan quickly, he urged, stone could be quarried, and lime and timber brought in, before the onset of winter.[45]

He need not have worried, for his scheme never got that far. As he could surely have predicted, Montrose's tenants refused to march deep into the Highlands to camp on Rob Roy's doorstep. Rob was prompt in sending out threats that he would burn the houses of anyone who cooperated with Killearn. The helpless factor, seething with rage at Inversnaid, sent out counter-threats. He would use the troops at his disposal to raid Montrose's tenants to raise enough money to pay others to do the digging at Inversnaid. Nonetheless, though the barracks itself was not begun, in time men from Montrose's estates built a hutted encampment for the Inversnaid troops – for which the duke charged the government nearly £350 sterling.[46]

Rob dared not attack the military detachment at Inversnaid, but doubled back with about forty men and raided Buchanan Castle again, this time concentrating on the Montrose estate girnals at Buchanan. Tenants paid much of their rent in grain or oatmeal which was stored in the girnals, and Rob now seized a large amount of meal – and even made the tenants carry it off for him. Reports located him on Buchanan Muir, planning to seize more cattle – or perhaps to intercept the supplies for barrack-building being brought up Loch Lomond. Again the frustrated Killearn begged for more troops, or 'that Ruffian will leave nothing. He is full of projects and very allart.' But he was not panicked into abandoning Inversnaid, as Rob must have hoped, and news that Montrose was returning from London to Edinburgh encouraged him. Surely he would be able to 'lett the tennents knou whither my lord duke or R Roy was their master'.[47]

Rob's raids on Buchanan Castle had been spectacular, and were to feature prominently in his legend. But there they appear as feats displaying Rob's power, whereas their real context was that they were desperate and unsuccessful attempts to stave off defeat. In spite of them, for the rest of his life an army garrison was to be stationed on 'his' land of Inversnaid. Yet, in a sense it is not altogether unreasonable to treat the raids as victories. They were successes in his long campaign to discredit Montrose personally. At the time those who wrote reporting his raids did not bother mentioning the establishment of the new garrison. Rob was the star performer, Montrose (even if he was really winning) the buffoon. It is hard not to sense elements of impudence and flair in Rob's tormenting of the duke. He had first plundered Montrose's cattle, then his corn. He still presented himself, with much success, not as a common thief but as a wronged man taking compensation in an orderly way. The raid on the girnals was no hit and run affair. Rob and his men came to them in broad daylight, and they took their time, as if they were there by right. He could risk this because he knew Killearn and the troops usually stationed in Drymen were safely out of the way at Inversnaid. Rob did not empty the girnals, or simply take all that could be carried. Instead (it was said, at least) he had sixteen bolls (one chalder) of meal carefully weighed out for him[48] – well over a ton. That was what he regarded as his due. To emphasise that he was justified in what he was doing, he even 'left a recept'[49] as if he had completed a routine business transaction. He was skilfully inflicting the maximum of humiliation on Montrose. The message seemed to be that he had more power over Montrose's estates, and more influence over his tenantry than the duke did. He could walk in and take the duke's grain with no fear of opposition, no need to hurry. He had even left a receipt as a kind of calling card. Rob, it has to be said, had style.

In July 1717 George I officially sanctioned the building of four barracks in the Highlands, and by October it was confirmed that one should be at 'the Ford of Innersnait to preserve a communication betwixt Loch Lomond and the river which falls into Loch Tay'. The smallest of the forts, it was to accommodate about a hundred men.[50] The barracks (the other three were at Bernera, Kilcumin – later Fort Augustus – and Ruthven in Badenoch) were to be built to a common basic design, but with some variation in size and detail. The locations of the barracks were based on strategic considerations. In Inversnaid's case, the argument was that it lay on the route from Dumbarton north up Loch Lomond, east to Loch Katrine, then by way of Balquhidder to Loch Tay, eventually linking up in Atholl with the main Perth to Inverness route. How important this Dumbarton to Atholl route was really considered to be is perhaps debatable. There is a strong suspicion that talk of overall Highland strategy is a rationalisation. The fort was really built because the duke of Montrose demanded it, to exclude Rob Roy from his homeland. In one sense it was a tribute to the duke's power. He was the only man to get a barracks built to advance his personal interests. But in another it was admission of failure. A great noble he might be, but instead of dealing himself with a problem on his doorstep he had had to turn to central government to do it for him.

Parliament voted the money to pay for the new buildings in March 1718, and work got underway on purchasing the ground at Inversnaid necessary to build on and provide an area of 400 feet around clear of buildings to give an open field of fire for muskets. James Smith, a prominent Scottish architect, was appointed 'surveyor and chief director for carrying on the barracks' in 'North Britain', with Major Thomas Gordon as his chief overseer at Inversnaid. Lieutenant John Dumaseque acted as his clerk of works and Lieutenant John Henry Bastide as draftsman.[51] Montrose wanted to be actively involved, but was rebuffed. The army's board of ordnance was in charge of the building programme, though 'old John Smith' did show Montrose the plans in London, and the board expressed its willingness to take advice as to the exact location of the fort. The plan was for a barracks capable of housing 100 men normally, and up to 150 in emergencies, though Montrose unsuccessfully pressed for a larger one, capable of accommodating 150 to 200 men, as being necessary to control the area. However, at least something was being done, and the duke had the satisfaction of learning that Inversnaid was to be the first barracks on which building started, and that it was planned for completion by the end of 1718.[52]

There was, however, a legal problem in that a small piece of the site was owned by a minor, and it was illegal for curators to sell land they were administering for a child. There was even talk of a special act of parliament being necessary to settle the problem. Smith was reluctant to start building, but at the end of May 1718 he was overruled. A military blind eye was to be turned on the legal technicality.[53] Building work began, and Dumaseque and Bastide produced 'A draught of Innersnait in the Highlands of North Britain' and another map showing the 'roads' (routes) linking it and other strategic centres – Ruthven in Badenoch, Kilcumin and Fort William.[54] Rob Roy's homeland was being pinned down by the stone of the barracks and recorded by the pen of the cartographer. It was no longer a place remote, almost unknown to Lowlanders, but a place defined and recorded with military precision.

Work on the barracks was, however, soon interrupted. Eight masons and quarriers were working on the site by August 1718. On the night of the 8th they were attacked by Highlanders, who seized them, stripped them of their clothes, and marched them back to the Lowlands, making them promise never to return. Clearly the locals, mainly MacGregors, were not going to have a garrison imposed on them without a fight. A political row immediately developed, concentrating not on the identity of the Highlanders involved but on the army's conduct – or lack of it. Some hundreds of yards away from the barracks and the masons' huts was the contingent of 100 soldiers in their temporary camp. They had done nothing to protect the masons, and there were strong suspicions of dereliction of duty. Why had the troops not intervened to save the workmen, Roxburgh demanded to know? His majesty was 'very ill pleased'. 'The king thinks it strange that the hutt for the workmen to lodge in should be built at such a distance as not to be under the protection of the troops,' said Montrose. The incident had made 'a great noise here [London]', and Montrose expressed himself 'extreamily disatisfied at the insolence' of the Highlanders involved.

The army's initial response was to claim that the workmen had not been driven out but had 'deserted' of their own accord. Not surprisingly this was not thought satisfactory, and orders were given for a close inquiry.[55] In fact an investigation into the workmen's actions had already been completed, though not by the army. Some of the fleeing masons and quarriers had returned to Edinburgh, and there they were rounded up by James Smith, the director of the barracks building programme. He brought them before justices of the peace to give sworn evidence. James Livingstone, mason, testified that at about 11 p.m. a man had knocked at the door of their hut, saying he was carrying letters to Captain Biggar, who commanded the detachment of soldiers nearby. Livingstone was the only man in the hut who was awake, so he had opened the door. Armed men then burst in, filling the building, and told the workers to prepare to leave. A thousand men were in arms, the raiders had claimed. Captain Biggar's soldiers were all dead, and the workers' hut was now to be burnt. The bewildered men were then marched sixteen or eighteen miles, being told they were going to be executed. But eventually they had been stripped of clothes and money, and made to swear never to return. Two other masons and two quarriers gave evidence confirming Livingstone's account.[56]

How the workmen had been expelled was now clear, but there remained the question of military inaction, and Captain James Biggar was court-martialled on 19 September 1718. His defence was unshakable. He had simply obeyed orders. His 100 men, drawn from Lord Shannon's regiment, had been quartered at Inversnaid and their orders had been that they were to arrest robbers, thieves and vagabonds, working on instructions from the civil authorities (justices of the peace and constables). He had never been ordered to protect the workmen, and his camp was located 550 yards away from the barracks. Not only was the barracks out of sight of the camp but it was separated from it by a river (the Snaid Burn) which was often impassable after heavy rain – as it had been on the night of 8 August. James Smith was also questioned, and he confirmed that he had never asked Biggar for protection for his workmen. Biggar was unanimously found not guilty.[57]

The incident was a humiliation for the authorities, and was no doubt much appreciated by Rob Roy. There is no mention of him in connection with the attack, but it was hard to believe he was far away. Like Rob's raids on Buchanan Castle, however, though spectacular the incident changed nothing. Work on the barracks continued, and it was completed in 1719.

8

DEFIANCE

John Graham of Drunkie had been linked to Rob Roy in earlier years in deals concerning loans and land. But on 20 July 1717 he had brought his men to support Killearn in establishing a permanent military presence at Inversnaid, and later in the year Killearn and Kilmannan employed him on Montrose's behalf as a pursuer of stolen cattle and catcher of thieves. Drunkie had had some success in his campaign, but the disbanding of Finab's independent company added to the problems he faced, for some of the former soldiers 'had taken up their old imployment of theeveing'. At one time Drunkie managed to lodge six thieves in Mugdock Castle, but Montrose's regality prison had proved as useless as Atholl's, for only one failed to escape and could be hanged. The other five 'joyned with their friends the McGregors commanded by Rob Roy and resolved to come upon Drunky in the night and murder himself and take all his cattell'. However, finding out that he had been warned and was prepared, they refrained from attacking his house and contented themselves with stealing most of his cattle and horses. Drunkie got together sixty men (including an officer and twenty soldiers, presumably from Inversnaid) and pursued them as far as Glenfalloch.[1]

As night fell on 28 January 1719 the soldiers and Drunkie's levy of Montrose's tenants quartered the glen with the soldiers in a house and Drunkie's men sleeping under whatever cover they could find. Nerves must have been on edge, because when they had arrived it had been reported that Rob Roy had 'that moment gone from thence' with nearly fifty well-armed men. Within half an hour several shots were heard from outside the house, and on opening the door it was found that the sentinel left outside had been shot. Rob's party shot several times into the house, then set upon Montrose's tenants, disarming them. One, it was said, was shot by Rob as he lay on his bed – though that does not accord with his usual avoidance of

161

unnecessary bloodshed. The soldiers, it seemed, had slammed the house door, keeping themselves safe and leaving the tenants to Rob's mercy.[2] According to Drunkie's own account, two of his men were killed.[3]

The attack on the soldiers strengthened Montrose's hand in his efforts to get government to renew action against Rob. The garrison at Inversnaid may have limited his activities in the barrack's immediate vicinity, but just a few miles away he had felt confident enough to take the offensive. On 12 February Montrose wrote to his faithful servant Gorthie, asking if he thought it would be a good idea to issue a proclamation promising anyone who brought in Rob Roy, dead or alive, a reward of say £200 or £300 sterling. He added cautiously 'you know this might have been done long ago but you know likewise why at that time it would not have been expedient: att present I think it would do well'.[4] Earlier Montrose had wanted Rob alive, to testify against Argyll. Rob's declaration in July 1717 that attempts had been made to make him perjure himself on the issue had largely destroyed his usefulness to Montrose, but perhaps the duke had still hoped that, in the twists of political fortune, Rob could at some time in the future still be useful as a witness against Argyll. By the beginning of 1719, however, events moved the political balance against Montrose. Argyll, denounced and out of favour since 1716, made a comeback as a royal favourite. On 6 February he became lord high steward. Two months more would see him created duke of Greenwich. The hope of acting in league with the king to destroy Argyll had vanished. This might have been good news for Rob – his former protector was back in favour. In fact it was very bad news indeed. From Montrose's point of view, he was now expendable. He had no longer even a pawn's part to play in a national political contest, he was simply a nuisance – a minor rebel and a thief. Whether he was taken dead or alive had become a matter of indifference.

Montrose's new suggestion was quickly put into practice. On 10 March the king issued a proclamation recounting Rob's attack on the soldiers in Glenfalloch. But, no doubt to the disappointment of Montrose, the proclamation called for Rob's apprehension and punishment, with no mention of 'dead or alive'. Perhaps, however, this is a verbal quibble: it may have been understood that handing over a body would count as apprehension. Whoever caught Rob would be paid £200 sterling, and would receive pardon if he was himself a rebel or an accomplice of Rob.[5]

Rob seems to have unconcerned that he had been honoured by being the subject of a royal proclamation. A letter of 2 April 1719 shows him living at Auch, which he refers to as his house and his home. Clearly the burning three years before had been a temporary setback. He talked of just having returned home, having been away in the north. He mentions having had a little scuffle with Glenfalloch's sons. 'I blesse God ffor it there was not a drop of my blood drawen' though one of his opponents was wounded. Were these the same Glenfalloch's 'bairns' whom Rob had recommended be bound to keep the peace in a dispute in 1711,[6] and who had drawn arms on Rob without provocation in a quarrel caused by drink in 1714?[7] Rob's letter moved on to money matters. He could not supply 100 cattle, as his unknown correspondent had asked, as the money would arrive too late for the current season. But perhaps some deal for forty or fifty could be arranged through Bardowie and Glengyle. Rob was back in business as a cattle merchant, and still doing deals with Hamilton of Bardowie – his largest creditor. But the legitimate businessman soon gave way in the letter to the rebel and bankrupt. There is an obscure reference to arms dealing. Rob mentions his debts to Bardowie and other creditors – and throws in a reference to that 'rebellious bugger the duke of Montrose . . . who is very far degenerate from his predecessors'. From the passionate Rob returned abruptly to the everyday. The 'picture' which his correspondent had written to him about had not arrived, but it would be 'very acceptable' to him. Alas it is not known what the picture Rob looked forward to depicted.[8] This is one of the very small number of letters that Rob signed 'Ro Roy' rather than his usual 'Ro Campbell'.

Rob's mood of defiance was perhaps fuelled by drink – and renewed hopes. On 16 April, two weeks after his reference to Montrose as a 'rebellious bugger', he penned a challenge to a duel to the duke that is worth quoting in full:

Rob Roy to ane high and mighty prince James duke of Montrose.
In charity to your grace's couradge and conduct, please know, the only way to retrive both is to treat Rob Roy like himself, in appointing your place and choice of arms, that at once you may extirpate your inveterate enemy, or put a period to your punny life in falling gloriously by his hands. That impertinent criticks or flatterers may not brand me for challenging a man that's repute of a poor dastardly soul, let such know I admit of the two great supporters of his character and the captain of his bands to joyne with him in the combate. Then

sure your grace wont have the impudence to clamour att court for multitudes to hunt me like a fox, under pretence that I am not to be found above ground. This saves your grace and the troops any further trouble of searching; that is, if your ambition of glory press you to embrace this unequald venture offrd of Roy's head. But if your grace's piety, prudence and cowardice, forbids hazarding of this gentlemanly expedient, then let your design of peace restore what you have robed from me by the tyranny of your present cituation, otherwise your overthrow as a man is determined; and advertise your friends never more to look for the frequent civility paid them, of sending them home without their arms [weapons] only. Even their former cravings wont purchase that favour; so your grace by this has peace in your offer, if the sound of war be frightful, and chuse you whilk [which], your good friend or mortal enemy.

The challenge to a duel is combined with insult. The two supporters of Montrose's character, and the captain of his bands, whom Rob offered to fight along with the duke, were, it may be guessed, Gorthie, Killearn and Drunkie. Rob's wild tirade, offering to fight four to one, has sometimes (astonishingly) been taken seriously, and it is certainly serious in its depth of emotion. But it was not a real challenge sent to the duke. It was a dream – come out and fight like a man, or give me justice – inspired by alcohol. He sent it to a friend, 'Mr Patrick Anderson at Hay', to amuse him. 'Receave the inclosed paper qn [when] you are takeing your botle: it will divert yourself and comrads. I got no news since I seed you only that wee had before about the Spaniards is like to continue.'[9]

The reference in the letter to Spaniards reveals why Rob was in such defiant and inebriated high spirits. Britain was now at war with Spain, and the Spanish were backing a new attempt to restore the Stuarts. A large Spanish army was to invade England, and a smaller force land in Scotland. Highland Jacobites were celebrating. For Rob, there was again a chance of a political revolution which would destroy his enemies. In his letter of 2 April (quoted above) Rob had reported that he had just returned from the north country. It seems quite possible that he had been to Stornoway in Lewis, or at least had gone north so as to be in touch with events there, for by 24 March the marquis of Tullibardine (Atholl's son) and two Spanish frigates carrying 300 Spanish soldiers had arrived in the Outer Isles.[10]

No wonder Rob was in an exultant mood. He could take the offensive, for rebellion had begun. He might be cattle trading in April 1719 but he was also cattle raiding. Montrose was in London, doing exactly as Rob had charged, clamouring at court for 'multitudes to hunt' him like a fox. The duke had received 'a long and full account of the insolence of Rob Roy and his followers, and of their exactions on the country,' particularly in the parishes of Buchanan, Drymen, Balfron, Luss and Kilmaronock, and part of the parish of Bonnill, developing blackmail, under the name of cess, into a regular local taxation. Most ploughlands were paying ten shilling in cess to Rob. Even Montrose, ready to think the worst of Rob, believed this story must be exaggerated. 'Surely this account must be magnified, for tho its agreed by all hands that the depredations and insolences from those vagabonds and robbers are great, yett had the exactions on those parishes been so regular sure I would have heard of it from you,' he wrote to Gorthie. But though Montrose doubted the truth of the allegations, he hastened to present them in full to the king. George I expressed the greatest horror at the abominations that were being committed, and asked what could be done. He accepted Montrose's latest suggestion, that one, two or three hundred of the 'best marching men' in the army in Scotland should be ordered to march through 'the whole Highlands to follow Rob Roy and his people from place to place, and in short to be ane awe and restraint upon the insolence of the Highlanders, while some other things, that I shan't mention at present, shall be done by the civill power in a legall way, to support the military. It's not to be thought that this party can apprehend Rob Roy, but as for certain they will oblidge him and his followers to leave their holes. Proper measures may be thought of at the same time to apprehend him by intelligence.' Static garrisons like Inversnaid could not subdue Rob, for he and his men seemed able to move past them at will. Now Montrose accepted that even his élite force of marching men would not actually catch him. For that, intelligence work would be needed. Sir Patrick Strachan of Glenkindie, that 'clever fellow well acquainted with the Highands', was to go to Scotland to organise the military operation.[11]

Montrose at first dismissed the rumours of Spanish invasion – 'we are in no manner of pain about them' – but those on the spot feared the worst, as they heard how Highlanders reacted to news of the landing in Lewis. Richard Struckburgh, commander of the garrison at Inversnaid (where the new barracks were approaching completion) reported on 21 April that he had been told that Lord Drummond, Tullibardine and Rob Roy were less than four miles away, with great numbers of men. They were raising more men, and intended to attack Inversnaid first. The garrison was very weak but Struckburgh promised he would defend his post 'as long as I have a man'. General Wightman, in command in Scotland, ordered reinforcements to Inversnaid, and the construction of ditches and palisades there.[12] The reports turned out to be alarmist, doubtless Jacobite propaganda intended to cause panic, and no attack came.

The Spanish in Lewis proved to be a damp squib. Tullibardine delayed on the island, not reaching the mainland, at Gairloch, until 4 April. When he attempted to sail further south, storms drove him back to Lewis. Loch Alsh in Kintail was eventually reached on 13 April. Campbell of Glendaruel had been sent out with letters to many Jacobite chiefs, and the responses from many were positive – but conditional. They were ready to rise, but only when they were certain that the main Spanish invasion force had landed in England. The results of the '15 rising had shown them that to rise on their own would be folly. Their caution was wise. The Spanish fleet, carrying 5,000 men, had sailed from Cadiz on 29 March but ran into massive storms that lasted forty-eight hours. Most of the ships were crippled, many only survived by throwing overboard their guns and the horses, arms and provisions intended for the invasion force. The ships straggled back to Spain, but the invasion plans had been shattered more effectively by the weather than they could have been by a naval battle.[14]

It took a long time for the news of this disaster to reach the Highlands, and meanwhile the Jacobite force dithered. The Earl Marischal wanted to march on Inverness immediately, with the help of 500 men that the earl of Seaforth said he could raise among the MacKenzies, but Tullibardine favoured waiting. Locheil and Clanranald arrived, ready to give support, but still the commanders argued. Tullibardine decided that everyone should board the frigates they had arrived on and return to Spain. On this the Earl Marischal immediately ordered the empty ships back to Spain, leaving the Spanish infantry on shore. The arrival of a British fleet made doubly sure that there would be no escape by sea – and brought disaster to the invaders because they had made their headquarters on the island castle of Eilean Donan. Under naval bombardment its Spanish garrison was forced to surrender, and most of the Jacobites' ammunition was captured. To crown their demoralisation, news now at last reached them that there was no longer any hope of a Spanish invasion of England.

In these circumstances it was inevitable that, in spite of the strength of Highland Jacobitism, recruits trickled rather than poured in. Among them was Rob Roy. One account refers to 'auxiliaries, such as Rob Roy, procured by my Lord [Tullibardine] himself for their pay',[14] as opposed to the regular clansmen, called out by their chiefs and provided for by them. Entries in Tullibardine's accounts give glimpses of Rob and his men:

15 May £3.3.0 [sterling] given to Rob to buy provisions
19 May £10.4.0 given to Rob for buying brandy, and the same amount to Glengyle
20 May 4 days' pay to 4 of Rob's men, 8/- in all
20 May £25.10.00 paid to Rob for buying cows
28 May £3.8.00 paid to Rob[15]

The small Spanish/Jacobite force had little choice but to await attack by the forces that the government had been given time to organise to march against them. Tullibardine took up a position in Glensheil, where the glen narrowed to a pass which could be dominated by gunfire from the hills. It was a good defensive position, and though Tullibardine's force totalled little over 1,000 men the advancing Hanoverian force under General Wightman had probably only a slight numerical advantage. But Wightman had the advantage of a battery of mortars, the Jacobites the disadvantages of low morale and poor training. When he attacked on 10 June the Jacobite right wing was pushed back, and then the left wing, commanded by Seaforth, came under attack. Reinforcements, including Rob Roy and his forty men, were sent, but the line had given way before they engaged battle, and Rob's men joined in the flight. Soon defeat was complete.[16]

Rob was present at two battles in his life, Sheriffmuir and Glensheil, but he and his men did not fire a shot in either. In neither case can he be blamed, however. At Sheriffmuir he arrived too late, at Glensheil he was held in reserve, and was thrown into a battle already lost. The makeup of his forty-man contingent is unknown, but they were probably a mixture of MacGregors and 'broken men' who for the moment accepted his leadership. As such, they may have been kept in reserve as they were not considered suitable as frontline troops. However, through not having been engaged in the fighting, Rob was able to keep some men together when the rest of the Highlanders fled to the hills and the Spanish surrendered. It was therefore Rob who on 11 June was ordered by Tullibardine to carry out the final act of the failed rebellion – blowing up the magazine to stop it falling into

Hanoverian hands, as a last show of defiance. Rob carried out orders, and while he was about it, 'looted' the abandoned baggage train.[17] In the circumstances, the word is over harsh, for the train was about to fall into enemy hands. Whatever he and his men took was being saved from their foes, and they would need whatever they could get to struggle home across the hills.

Tullibardine's defeat at Glensheil was welcome to government, but it made little impact. Once the feared Spanish invasion of England had evaporated what happened in the remote north-west of the Highlands was seen as merely a minor mopping-up operation. After the '15 there had been forfeitures of Jacobite estates, burning of houses, an attempt at disarming, and moves to build new barracks. No such action was taken after the '19. Indeed, it had been such a trifling affair that government probably took it as confirmation that complacency was justified. There no major political danger from the Highlands to be feared. Routine law and order enforcement, however, was a different matter. The search for Rob Roy continued, but the emphasis was on him as thief and raider, not as rebel.

Strachan of Glenkindie was now preparing to put into operation his plans for restoring order. Thieving and depredations in the Highlands were now (August 1719) at a level not reached since the 1688–89 Revolution, he reported. He did not mention that this was no doubt caused by the aftermath of the '19 rising, as frustrated Jacobites let off steam and those in flight from Glensheil sought to provide for themselves. Part of Glenkindie's political agenda now emerged. He was determined to 'disappoint the designs' of those who wanted independent companies restored. He planned instead to sign contracts with some Highland gentlemen – four or five would do – paying them to hunt down thieves. In many ways it was simply a revival and expansion of the old watch system. Instead of watches being employed and paid locally, the new contractors would cover large areas and be paid by central government. Only a minimum of military help would be required. These contractors, Glenkindie declared with foolish optimism, would immediately stop the trouble. The emphasis was at first to be on subduing Rob Roy. He was the symbol of Highland lawlessness – and dealing with him would please Montrose. 'I am convinced I shall make Montrose['s] country easie in a verie little time, besides I am in terms with one of the most capable men in the Highlands of Scotland whom I hope by time will shake hands with Robert Roy McGregor if he does not leave the kingdom.'

Who 'this gentleman' was who would track down Rob is unknown, but by 27 August Glenkindie had signed up two 'contractors', Coll MacDonald of Keppoch and Aeneas MacPherson of Killihuntly, to seize lawless men and present them before civil magistrates. A son of Cameron of Locheil had also agreed to sign on.[18] But little more is heard of the grand scheme. Glenkindie's 'gentleman' was not to get a chance to shake Rob by the hand. The scheme was a castle in the air, a dream he was incapable of implementing, but what finished it off may have been a quibble raised by Roxburgh as secretary for Scotland. Were the contracts that Glenkindie was having signed actually legal?[19] It is reassuring to know that even a leader of the *Squadrone* knew what a legal scruple was.

As to action on the ground, as opposed to planning, Drunkie was continuing to try to protect Montrose's estate. The Craigrostan thieves 'who are nou well known by their often comeing through the country' committed a great many thefts and depredations at harvest time in 1719, striking south into Strathendrick and the Campsie Hills. Normally raiders struck by night and withdrew at dawn. Now, it was reported, they spent the day openly in public ale houses, extorting what they liked from the country people. One man who refused to pay on demand had all nineteen of his cattle taken from him on 13 September, to help terrorise others into surrendering the few beasts demanded of them. Local landowners decided on action. Meeting at Drymen on 16 September 1719, they spent the night arguing. Some wanted Drunkie to take on responsibility for their lands as well as Montrose's. But others wanted a new 'watch' to be commanded by Glengyle 'by the assistance of Rob Roy his uncle'.[20] It was Rob who had influence among the thieves, being the greatest among them, so it made sense to revert to custom and buy his services, rebel or not. He might be pursuing a feud against Montrose, but he had no quarrel with the smaller landlords who supported this new watch. Provided they contributed to his upkeep, he was doubtless as happy to 'protect' them as to raid them. Montrose would have been horrified if he had heard of this. It indicated the complete failure of all the endless schemes that had been hatched over the years to catch his enemy.

If the government and great men like Montrose could not stop raiding, then lesser men were not concerned that Rob was an outlaw, an attainted rebel and (as a cattle raider) one of the main reasons for their losses. If doing a deal with him would stop raiding they would do it. It may be that in an ideal world, having Rob hanged would have been more to their taste, but no one, experience had shown, could do that.

Thus Drunkie's watch, supported by Killearn for Montrose, continued, but a new watch, led by Glengyle but evidently with Rob Roy as an honorary leader (a godfather), also emerged. There is little sign that either watch had a significant effect on the situation. In 1720 and the following few years, information about Rob Roy is sparse. Montrose, the justice clerk and their agents were no longer pursuing him as a matter of urgency, writing frequent letters about him. The charges of treason against Rob still stood, but there were a fair number of minor rebels lurking in the Highlands, and government had decided that it would be too much trouble to try to round them up as they posed no political danger. Jacobites might continue to dream, but the almost farcical collapse of the 1719 attempt was intensely demoralising for them. The Highland law 'problem' had reverted to being perceived as one of cattle-raiding, an internal law-enforcement problem which was a nuisance, even a disgrace, but not a threat to national security or of much interest to central government. Montrose had his Inversnaid barracks, but the hope that it would deter raiding had evaporated. Montrose grumbled at his continuing losses, but had the sense not to damage his reputation further by publicising the fact.

The government was not interested in attacks on civilians, so farmers and landlords on the fringes of the Highlands continued to suffer losses and to pay blackmail or watch money. But attacks on the military were a different matter, as shown by an incident early in 1720 which was the work of MacGregors.

A soldier of the garrison at Fort William had been murdered. A colleague, Alexander Greg, was accused of the crime, but there were not enough officers present to courtmartial him on the spot. Sergeant Daniel MacKay of the Royal Regiment of Fusiliers and a party of twelve men were therefore detailed as an escort to take the prisoner to Edinburgh to stand trial. MacKay's evidence detailed the long journey. He set out on 14 February. On the 16th as he entered Strathfillan he saw several armed men, but they fled. He and his men lodged that night in the house of one Malcolm MacGregor. He was away from home (innkeepers often seemed to be, when soldiers approached), but his wife, Isobel Aitkin, began to ask the prisoner questions. Mackay got worried, so he had the prisoner confined to a corner of the house, with two sentinels posted to see he did not speak to anyone. Tension declined, no doubt, but at about ten at night Isobel sent out two servants to try to find a woman who had stolen some clothes after staying the previous night – or so Isobel said. Sergeant Mackay was understandably suspicious, and his fears grew when he was told that one of the servants at the inn, James Graham, had previously spent fourteen or fifteen weeks in Edinburgh Tolbooth on suspicion of being a follower of Rob Roy. However, the night passed peacefully, and next day MacKay and his men marched on, and lodged for the next night at the Kirkton of Balquhidder – where again the innkeeper was away from home.

At about three in the morning a soldier had 'occasion to go to the door' and open it. He was immediately attacked by four armed men and wounded. Mackay got the door shut, and left four of his men to guard it, while the rest retired to a back room with the prisoner, but the attackers then fired in at the window of the back room, wounding four of the soldiers who exchanged fire with them. Mackay expected further attacks, but as day dawned the attackers melted away. Patrick Stewart, the inn-keeper, turned up at eight in the morning, 'and appeared to be in drink', which was looked on as suspicious.

. Mackay left hastily the next morning, and delivered his wounded men and his prisoner to Stirling, helped by horses provided by the duke of Atholl.[21] While Mackay was in Stirling, stories caught up with him as to the attack on him at Balquhidder. There had been about forty MacGregors surrounding the house, 'and that Robert Roye's pyper had been there the night before'. But the sergeant's account of events suggests that he did not realise why there had been so determined an attempt to free Alexander Greg. The name gives the clue. 'Greg' was a MacGregor. Seeing parties of red-coated Hanoverian soldiers passing Balquhidder on their way to and from Fort William was doubtless always resented, but it was accepted that nothing could be done about it. But to let a party carry a MacGregor off to almost certain execution was too much. An attempt had to be made to free a clansman.

It soon became clear that the attack had been on a smaller scale than the first exaggerated rumours had suggested – only about half a dozen men had been involved. But as an attack on soldiers in time of peace it was taken seriously, especially after one of the wounded soldiers died. News of the 'barbarous murder' at Kirkton of Balquhidder reached the royal court and caused anger. Investigation suggested that 'loose men that uses to frequent that country, but have no fixed residence' were responsible. The murder had taken place on the estate of the Jacobite Lord Drummond, who was in exile, but it bordered on Atholl's lands, so he was seen as the key figure in the hunt for the culprits. It was urged upon him that it would be very much in his interests to find them. After the debacle a few years before when Atholl had captured then lost Rob Roy, caution might have been expected, but he proved enthusiastic. However, he got nowhere, though much evidence was gathered. Patrick Stewart, the Balquhidder innkeeper, reported that on 18 February (the day after the attack) five armed men had appeared, two of them MacGregors. One of the men 'Hugh McIntyre, piper', played for half an hour while the two MacGregor colleagues challenged all present to say whether they believed that they had been guilty of the attack on the soldiers. Not surprisingly, no one took up the challenge. After this ritual intimidation of witnesses they swaggered off without, as Stewart sourly noted, paying for their drinks. Doubtless he had not liked to ask. Next day they appeared again at midnight and threatened to break down the door. He let them in and, drawing their swords and dirks, they asked for drink. He, not surprisingly, obliged, and eventually went back to bed, leaving them drinking.

Stewart's evidence and that of other witnesses provided Atholl with the names of men who 'no doubt were guilty' of that 'villaneouse action, the attack on the soldiers'.[22] But Atholl 'knowing' that and legal proof of guilt were different matters, and anyway, the supposedly guilty were safe in the hills, so he was not optimistic. Attempts at apprehending them were made. Keppoch and Killiehuntly were praised for their activities (indicating that Glenkindie's scheme for employing contractors to hunt wrongdoers was not quite dead), and Atholl received a pat on the head for his pains – his efforts would be mentioned at court. He tried to profit from the affair by suggesting that it was necessary that a barracks be built at Kirkton of Balquhidder, but this was ignored. There is a hint of trying to keep up with the noble Joneses here: Montrose had got a barracks (at Inversnaid) so Atholl wanted one too.

Even among the supposed forces of law and order some proved uncooperative, for Jacobite sympathies made them disinclined to bother much about the death of a Hanoverian soldier. Major William Jones, in command at Stirling, had tried to get the burgh magistrates to take depositions from the wounded soldiers, so their testimony would not be lost if they died. The magistrates proved obstructive.

The matter was nothing to do with the burgh of Stirling, and Jones had no commission to give them orders on the matter. When Atholl had tried to involve neighbouring landlords in the search, he found a similar lack of enthusiasm. John Campbell, writing as Breadalbane's agent, stated bluntly that for him to try to catch the guilty would damage the interests of his master's estates. It would raise the spleen of 'that desperat Clan' – the MacGregors – who would seek revenge. No steps would be taken, for fear of such reprisals.[23] Admittedly Breadalbane did propose to Atholl (23 April 1720) that they should consult together over joint action in the summer against stealing and thieving,[24] but it didn't work, and perhaps Breadalbane never intended it to, being merely a show of good intentions to keep the government happy. The two noble lords were soon back to the usual bickerings of neighbours.

The Balquhidder affair soon blew over. It was a time of riots in many Lowland burghs, and controlling them was a far more urgent matter for government than minor Highland incidents. All the incident reveals about Rob Roy is the name of a servant and that he had a piper – probably the Hugh MacIntyre mentioned as the piper at the inn. One could be an outlaw but still keep up a bit of style. But the references to Rob aroused no special interest, whereas a year or two before they would have been red rags to the *Squadrone* bull.

Meanwhile, the slow-grinding wheels of bureaucracy were at last settling the legal fate of Rob Roy's lands. The commissioners and trustees of forfeited estates in Scotland had been working to survey and value them, taking into account the submissions of creditors who had legitimate claims on them. The process was hugely complex, and Rob's estate of Inversnaid (or Craigrostan) received little attention, as it was by far the smallest to be forfeited. However, eventually it and a number of other estates were bought up by Robert Halket for the York Building Company, a London-based investment firm which had raised capital especially to finance this Scottish venture.[25] Montrose was a major investor in the company, and may have been the prime mover behind the idea of investing in Scottish land. But in August 1720 he wrote sadly to Gorthie that 'Our York Buildings is demolished for the present . . . I have lost above thirtie thousand pound which I promise you makes a considerable blank in my profits.' The 'South Sea Bubble' had seen a huge boom in speculative investment in the South Seas Scheme, but it had just collapsed, ruining many hundreds. In the disillusionment that followed the price of shares in many other companies, including the York Building Company, had also crumbled. Montrose went on to lament that he had also invested in the South Seas project. If only he had had the sense to sell his shares five or six weeks before he would, he lamented, he would 'have had ninety thousand clear gain in my pockett'.[26]

The York Company nonetheless managed to buy most of the forfeited estates it was interested in, but somehow Inversnaid was not sold to it. Therefore in September 1720 the forfeited estate commissioners published an *Abstract of the Rental of the Real Estate of Robert Campbell, commonly called Rob Roy*. The estate, the notice announced, was to be sold at public roup (auction) at Edinburgh on 13 October. The auction would be at 10 a.m., and would last half an hour, timed by an hour glass. The starting price for bidders was to be 'twenty years purchase', that is twenty times the net rent of the estate. A valuation allowed calculation of this. Rent due by tenants amounted to £56 sterling (£672 Scots) a year, but out of this £20 was payable to Colquhoun of Luss, the feudal superior, as feu duty, and £10 to the duke of Montrose as teind or tithe – a contribution to the salary of the parish minister. This reduced the net rent to £26, which would have made the starting price at the auction £520 sterling. In addition to the rent it was estimated that timber on the estate was worth £150 sterling.[27]

Inversnaid was just 'a trifling estate', in an area notorious for being difficult to control and blighted by having Rob Roy hanging around asserting that he still had the right to collect rent. Yet in the proportional terms of 'years purchase', it made a higher price than any other forfeited estate, selling for over thirty-one years purchase (£820 sterling), to Graham of Gorthie, acting for the duke of Montrose. Graham of Killearn, his factor, had already been acting as factor on Rob's former lands on behalf of the forfeited estate commissioners – though the rents he managed to collect for the moment stayed in Montrose's hands. Now work could begin on integrating the estate with the duke's other lands. That Montrose had been eager to obtain Inversnaid was easy to understand, for ownership of it would allow him to tighten his control of the area, and lording it over the estate would be a symbolic victory over Rob, his long-term tormentor. But there must have been other bidders to drive the price so high, though their identities remain unknown.[28]

Legal technicalities continued to plague the duke, even after the purchase of Inversnaid, for there was still the matter of how Rob's creditors (including Montrose himself!) were to be dealt with – they still had claims against the estate. But first the exchequer had to work out what it was owed by him for the rents Killearn had collected at Inversnaid in previous years. In June 1722 Montrose was pleased to hear from Gorthie that a commission of enquiry into his purchase of Rob's lands had been completed, though he urged Gorthie to concentrate on finding 'a method in time for preventing his [Rob's] being the uplifter of my rents as he once was.'[29]

Eventually the forfeited estate commissioners accepted as valid claims from fourteen creditors on Rob Roy's estate, totalling £2,376 sterling – and that was only the capital sum due, with no allowance for the compound interest that had accumulated over a decade.[30] Even so, it was about three times the £820 Inversnaid had been sold for, and even when accumulated rents (reclaimed from Montrose and Bardowie) were added, the total available to satisfy the creditors was only about £1,013. Creditors would, on these figures, only get about 42 per cent of their capital claims. Loss of a decade's interest made the settlement an even worse bargain for the creditors. In the end, they did slightly better than this. Montrose's own share of the money distributed by the commissioners was £120 15s 7d sterling, about 52 per cent of the £230 sum he had originally been owed. Graham of Gorthie got about £44, Hamilton of Bardowie about £417.[31]

Rob had claimed in 1711 that if his creditors took legal proceedings against him then this would reduce the proportion of their debts that could be repaid from his assets. Legal fees would mount on both sides. He could not have foreseen the scale of the conflict that would follow. Montrose's payment of £120 doubtless failed even to cover his legal fees, let alone the cost to his estates of Rob Roy's predatory activities, the loss of interest on his money for a decade and the incalculable cost to his reputation. And even the £120 he at last received, he must have reflected bitterly, was paid largely out of the money he himself had just paid to buy Inversnaid. In every sense, the fight with Rob had been a disaster. But for the duke it was a limited one. It was something that most of the time he could banish to the fringes of his life. It was an exasperation, a nuisance, but his financial losses had been minor in relation to his total income. His aristocratic lifestyle had continued without a tremor. By mid 1724 all creditors had been paid, and Montrose could take full possession of his new estate. He paid out nearly £960 sterling (this included interest since the sale had first been arranged) – and received back £120 as his share of the payments due to him as one of Rob's creditors.[32]

For Rob what he probably had regarded away back in 1712 as a matter of arranging matters with his creditors had got completely out of hand and destroyed his old life irrevocably. Moreover, the 'settlement' of his debts arranged by the forfeited estate commissioners in the 1724 was not a final settlement. In return for the payments from the forfeited estate commissioners, Rob's creditors had assigned their rights to pursue Rob for the rest of his debts to the commissioners.[33] Rob's creditors might have been 'all paid'[34] in that they had received a percentage payment from the commissioners, but claims outstanding still amounted to something like £1,500 sterling. Yet in reality Rob's debt problem was over. The forfeited estate commissioners were soon to be abolished and none of the creditors saw any point in throwing good money after bad in trying to hold Rob to account. Even if he could be caught, he had no significant assets to be seized. To Rob himself this made little difference in the short term. He might no longer be a debtor being actively pursued, but he remained a rebel.

Rob was probably living mainly in Balquhidder by this time, but a good deal of his attention was still stubbornly focused on 'his' lands of Inversnaid. Montrose had the advantage of the presence of a military garrison there to help impose his control over the area, and legal ownership was soon to follow, but this failed to stop Rob Roy collecting 'rents' from those he regarded as his tenants. In December 1720 Montrose wrote in fury that Killearn and the garrison should immediately go to Craigrostan, call the tenants together, make them pay their rents, and 'poind' all who failed to do so – that is, seize their goods to pay the debts. 'This may in appearance look hard but unless it be done I shall be sure to have Rob Roy to lift my rents every year and for certain with the good will of the tenants themselves. Whereas if the weight lye on their own purses, self interest will at last gett the better of their villanous inclinations . . . If this stress of double payment of rent should break them I am at no loss – an other sett of tennents will doe better.'

Tenants sympathetic to Rob were happily paying him rent, or so Montrose believed, then claiming that the fact that they had been forced to pay Rob meant they could not afford to pay Montrose rent as well. Rob might threaten to plunder them if they failed to pay him, but Montrose took this to be bluff: they 'may ask after Rob Roy for their relief [from paying two rents]: I beleive they won't be plundered hereafter'. If tenants decided to abandon their holdings 'I dare say I shall be better with a new colony.' Montrose clearly hoped that the Inversnaid garrison would overawe the tenants, but Killearn was warned that soldiers had no power to enforce civil law relating to rents. Regular courts must be held with Killearn as baillie and due legal process followed.[35] Montrose and Rob Roy might be the principal parties in the dispute, but it was the little men stuck in the middle, the tenants caught between the conflicting demands of the two, who suffered most.

On the wider scene, cattle raiding continued to be a nagging problem. In March 1721 it is entertaining to find Rob himself complaining of cattle being stolen from him.[36] Strachan of Glenkindie was entrusted with yet another scheme to solve the problem, whereby 300 men were to be stationed at ten different places in the Highlands to preserve the public peace – but all were in the eastern and northern Highlands, no threat to Rob.[37] Nonetheless, Rob was still under pressure at times. In October 1721 it was reported that he had 'taken possession of his old seat in Benbuy',[38] suggesting that retreat to this, the safest of his refuges, had been advisable. For once, Montrose was pleased by the reports of rent-collection at Michaelmas. 'I am glade of that success you have had in preventing R.R. from doeing the same thing this year that he did last. It's a most intolerable thing that one should be constantly plagued with that fellow; and that he should have it in his power to make reprisals, which I dare say he'd endeavour to doe by commanding some outrages or other unless you were very much on your guard.' Rob Roy might try to rob tenants under name of rent, but they now knew that if they let him they would pay dearly for it, as Montrose would insist on payment as well. They would have 'to pay twice, as those of Craigrostan have done'.[39]

Montrose's satisfaction did not last long. Rob was back 'collecting rent' within weeks. Everyone agreed, the duke complained, that it was a scandal and shame for any government to tolerate such behaviour, but it had gone on for many years and it was as far from finding a remedy as ever. Montrose had given up on the government. To make a fresh application for help would be 'making a noise without effect'. His rents were being plundered, he moaned from London. 'I run a risk of not only losing them this year but as often as this fellow pleases.' Troops should be demanded from the commander, Brigadier Preston – the static force at Inversnaid seemed to be proving useless. 'Its a generall maxim to make peace with ones sword in their hand.

Without troops I can expect no rent and to be obliged to have an escort to gather in ones money is a sharp prospect.'

Montrose was mellowing, tiring of the long struggle and considering making concessions. He wanted troops, but no longer saw their use as leading to Rob's destruction, but rather as a way of putting pressure on him to make peace. Troops should be stationed in Buchanan, he urged, until rent collection was completed. While they were there 'I think it may be proper not indeed to enter into any formall treaty with R.R. but to fall upon some proper wayes which can easilie be found out to let him know that if he'd live quietly and give no disturbance.' Montrose would no longer hunt him. Rob would, Montrose hopefully added, be ready to respond to such hints, 'for upon the whole he's no great gaine by his excursions, and if he beliv'd that he was not to be looked after [chased] or minded, I doe say he'd let [us] alone, for after all is it my business to play the Knight Erant?' If the government was too supine to uphold its own authority, it was not Montrose's duty to step in to do the job for it. The government had, in material terms, nothing to lose, whereas he had 'the stakes' – his rents – at risk.[40]

This was a major change of direction, and Montrose was trying to justify his climb-down to himself and others. He had decided that he would no longer regard Rob's defiance as shaming him. The shame was that of a government which was failing to maintain law and order. He tacitly accepted that in his obsessive attitude to the Rob Roy problem in the past there had been involved more than hard-headed estate management. He had allowed the feud to become personal, and had played Don Quixote, the knight errant determined to right wrongs and preserve honour at whatever cost. His sense of personal betrayal at Rob's original bankruptcy and his political ambition had led him into an unwise fixation on Rob.

Washing his hands of the responsibility for bringing Rob to justice was a personal decision of the chastened duke, but it also reflects a much wider, slower process. In the past feudal lords had accepted responsibility for law enforcement on their own lands and within their superiorities. They were part of government. Montrose had tried that approach, and it had failed. As an absentee landlord mainly concerned with collecting rent to support an extravagant lifestyle in London and Glasgow, and boost his political influence, his regional power had declined. He led the Graham kin, but what this meant in terms of loyalty and service was ebbing away fast. Increasingly he had turned to central government and the army for what his ancestors would have considered his own job. And, except at the height of *Squadrone* influence in government in 1717, government had proved to have its own agendas, and top priority was not given to restoring Montrose's personal reputation, battered by the humiliations Rob had inflicted on him. Once, the will of the head of a great earldom had virtually been the law, but the role of the barony, regality and stewardry courts of the feudal landowners in criminal law had declined – partly through the growth in power of central courts, but also because the feudal lords themselves neglected them. Enforcing criminal law at the local level was troublesome and expensive, so for the state increasingly to take over responsibility was acceptable. But when Montrose had looked to the central courts and national law, he found himself thwarted. The court of session had taken four long years to rule that Rob's disposition of his lands had been fraudulent. When he summoned the army to help him, he had found that officers would not do what he told them. They were sticklers for the distinction between military and civil law, and very correctly (except in times of actual rebellion, as in 1715 and 1719) were unwilling to become simply Montrose's agents in pursuit of his personal interests. Going through the procedures necessary for authorising military assistance in a civil dispute (over debt and rents, in this case) could be slow and inefficient. In an age in which courts and their officials were often corrupt and are accused of bias against the underdog, it is notable how often legal procedures seemed to help Rob rather than Montrose.

Frustrated, Montrose had decided in the case of Rob to step back from being a feudal law enforcer and act as a commercial landowner. Law enforcement was for the government, his interest was rent collection, and if maximising profit involved doing a deal with Rob, so be it.

Gorthie, ordered Montrose, was to be the one to ask Preston for troops, for the duke wanted to distance himself from the matter. He could easily get an order in London for troops to be supplied, he explained, but he didn't want to reveal that he couldn't defend himself from such an insignificant fellow as Rob without calling the army in. A suggestion that a detachment of dragoons be stationed in the stables of Buchanan Castle was rejected by the duke, as it would suggest humiliatingly that he could not protect his own home – which was too close to the truth to be acceptable.[41]

Rob had been downgraded in Montrose's new perception of the situation. His status had been high in 1717 when he could be of use in destroying Argyll, but now he was simply an annoying thief, and it was below the dignity of a duke to seem to be personally involved in action against him. Did Montrose reflect that he could have saved himself a vast amount of aggravation if he had taken the same stance in 1712? Anyway, he now wanted peace, though he had some doubts about how Rob would respond to his offer of a truce. 'I do belive that any advances made towards him would make him more saucie' so the business would have to be conducted in language of indirect suggestions and vague hints, rather than direct offers.[42] The impression must not to be given that the duke was in retreat and that Rob Roy had won.

No response from Rob Roy to suggestions of truce is known, and there were no extra troops drafted to put pressure on him. Nor was it clear that the main problem in the area was simply raiding by Rob. Glengyle (see previous chapter) had been hired to form a watch in 1719. This was re-formed in October 1721, when several landowners in Buchanan and Menteith signed a contract with Glengyle to pay him four shillings per pound (20 per cent) of the annual valuation of their estates for his watch. Very businesslike, as criminal rackets often are. The character of this one was revealed by the threats that landowners who failed to pay for his protection would be plundered, to demonstrate how badly they needed the protection they had been foolish enough not to pay for. In the case of one man who failed to pay up, his tenant's houses were raided on 21 November by eight armed men, and his clothes, money and other movable goods stolen and carried away to Glengyle to be shared out. In retaliation, Drunkie, leading his rival watch, raided Craigrostan, rounded up some cattle, and sent them to Mugdock.[43] In all this Rob Roy is not mentioned, but he had a close relationship with his nephew and it may be that the balance of leadership of active raiding – or watching, or protection racketeering or however it be defined – had passed from the older to the younger man.

However, though Rob was now in his fifties and perhaps less inclined than in the past to a physically active role, he still had a part to play in the family business. A recently discovered letter reveals his style. On 20 October 1724 Rob wrote to Alexander Buchanan of Dullater, near Kilsyth. 'I strenge very much [find it very strange]' that Buchanan's previous letter had not been 'ampleler' [more specific] as to a date for payment. 'If you have a mind that we will be concerne[d] with the keeping of the country', a meeting could be arranged with the tenants present. The letter is far from clear, and Rob signs himself 'your assured friend'. But the message seems to be, if you want your lands to be 'kept' (watched or protected), bring your tenants and we can arrange a deal.[44] Threat is implicit.

If Rob was less active in the Lomond area than previously, it may have been in part because he was concentrating his attention on Balquhidder. Having lost all hope of a settled life in Lomond, he was fighting to control land and maintain his influence in the Braes, the western glen of Balquhidder. Malcolm Murray (MacGregor) of Marchfield had in 1707 obtained from the duke of Atholl a feu of several farms in the area, among them Inverlochlarig Beg. Rob at some point obtained a lease of this farm as a tenant.[45] Marchfield subsequently sold the lands to John (Ian) Og Campbell (MacGregor),[46] who was active in acquiring lands in the area. Instability was being caused by the duke of Atholl granting a number of feus of lands in the area, sometimes to locals, sometimes to outsiders, and John Og Campbell seems to have been the main beneficiary. At the level of tenants a tendency towards subdivision of farms has been detected, while at that of owners (the feuars, with Atholl as their feudal superior) the move was towards consolidation into larger units.[47] Competition for land could be bitter, and Rob had to struggle for survival against John Og's drive for expansion. Rob had reputation and numbers of supporters on his side, but John had the financial resources.

A hostile account says John Og's ancestors 'were the most iniquitous characters the earth ever produced striving who would be the most wicked'. He called his new estate Glencarnaig, but when he 'came to take possession of the Braes of Balquhidder' he found he faced a problem, in the form of Rob Roy. Rob regarded the neighbourhood as, if not his family property in legal terms, his sphere of influence, and the men who lived in it as his men. He was not ready to let another MacGregor muscle in on the area without a fight, and the dispute soon became violent. It is alleged that 'Rob Roy MacGregor employed four of the MacGregors, some of his own low gang, to assassinate' Glencarnaig, but he 'being a cautious man and possessed of more country eloquence' –perhaps meaning cunning – escaped and, it is said, launched a rival, equally unsuccessful, attempt to have Rob killed.[48]

The chronology of the dispute is uncertain, but it may have begun with feus granted by Atholl in 1719. The marriage of Glencarnaig's daughter Margaret to Roy's son, Coll, in 1720[49] suggests an attempt to form an alliance. It failed, however, to end the rivalry of the two MacGregors. In August 1722 Glencarnaig gave orders for the uplifting (seizing) of the goods his tenants in the township of Inverlochlarig Easter, presumably in an attempt to enforce payment of rent he claimed. Two messengers and two sub-officers were sent to remove the goods, backed up by thirty armed men. But the tenants, 'a tribe of MacIntyres who had been there time unknown' had Rob Roy's support – his 'kindness'. Rob 'with his lads' set up an ambush and when Glencarnaig's men approached Rob captured the messengers, officers and three of the men, and the rest fled. The prisoners were released after twenty-four hours, on giving the customary oath never to return on the same business. Atholl's baillie in Balquhidder, Robert Stewart, seemed to think that Glencarnaig had been in the wrong in the dispute, and he was advised to submit himself to Atholl's mercy as feudal superior.[50]

This was just one incident in a long-running conflict. Rob 'kept them [the lands concerned] five years out of [Glencarnaig's] possession by open violence, and one way with another put him to an expense and loss above 30,000 merks', though Rob never had above a dozen men with him 'and those always of the tribe of which he was himself'.[51] In a court case years later Glencarnaig's son Robert, in giving evidence against two of Rob's sons, admitted that he bore them ill will 'because their father Rob Roy had grievously oppressed him and his family in relation to a feu which the deponent's father had purchased from the duke of Atholl out of which the deponent's father was kept for years by the said Rob Roy and was at length forced to give a tack [lease] to some of the said Rob Roy's friends of part of the said land to his great hurt.'[52]

Rob had established a secure foothold for his family in Balquhidder. Glencarnaig had tried to get rid of him, and failed. The duke of Atholl, Glencarnaig's feudal superior, seems not to have objected to having 'his' lands in Balquhidder harbour Rob, the man who had so famously humiliated him in 1717. Like Montrose, he had learnt the sense not to try to outwit his enemy.

Rob can have had little or no hope left of ever regaining Inversnaid and the lands he had once rented from Montrose, but he continued to make symbolic – and profitable – claims on them. In April 1723 Glengyle reported to Gorthie that 'my uncle Rob' had recently seized five bolls of corn from a tenant in Ardress, as he believed it to be his own. The tenant was desperate, for he held his land on the 'steel bow' system, which meant that his landlord had supplied the seed corn for sowing, and in return was paid a proportion of the harvest. He had received his seed corn for 1723 and it was time to sow, but Rob had stolen it. If he could not produce a crop, he would face starvation and eviction. Gorthie agreed to intervene and supply new seed corn – though the tenant would have to pay £14 Scots for it later.[53]

In comparison with the 1710s, Rob Roy's profile in the early 1720s is low. He is a nuisance to Montrose, and to Glencarnaig, but he is neither a threat nor of interest to politicians. Yet it was in these years that Rob became, briefly, the subject of media attention. Popular print and verse revealed how wide his fame had spread.

9

HIGHLAND ROGUE

Before the 1720s Rob's name had appeared only a few times in public print, whereas letters and other manuscript sources have hundreds of references to him. It would be possible to be misled into thinking that knowledge of his name was confined mainly to friends and relatives, to those he had business dealings with, and to those who sought to hunt him down. Then in the 1720s, when his most notorious misdeeds lay in the past, a scattering of references to him appear in print and manuscript verse which reveal him as a figure who was already on the way to becoming a legend, whose name was already rich in associations and worth evoking by journalists. Mention 'Rob Roy' and, it would appear, most people in Scotland would know who was meant. His name was 'weel kent' in popular broadside verses, but not as a central character. Rob himself, it seems, did not need to be explained to readers, but allusions to him were seen as useful in telling stories about others. The folk in whose company Rob is made to appear are notorious criminals. Horrible crimes and well-known outlaws were popular favourites (then as now), and though some criminals won sympathy and others disgust, they were often mixed together in the fascination with the underworld. Names of established criminal figures were added to irrelevant stories to try to boost some new criminal's claim to notoriety.

Rob appeared prominently in verses relating to the case of Nicol Muschet of Boghall (who was executed on 6 January 1721) and his associates. The case was a particularly nasty one, and therefore particularly attractive to the writers of broadsides (a forerunner of the tabloid press) and to their readers. Muschet had murdered his wife, Margaret Hall. After marrying her in September 1719 he had repented with remarkable speed, and in the year that followed he devised – or was persuaded to adopt – a variety of 'cunning plans' to free himself from her. First he thought simply of absconding, but his acquaintance James Campbell of Burnbank (or more correctly, formerly of Burnbank) undertook that, for £50 sterling, he would obtain a fraudulent divorce, some forged piece of paper which would persuade Margaret that she was no longer married. This came to nothing, so the inventive Burnbank (who was keeper of the ordnance stores in Edinburgh Castle) came up with a new idea. He was in debt to Muschet, and undertook, in return for Muschet not pressing him for repayment, to obtain two affidavits signed by witnesses as to Margaret's 'whorish practices', as evidence to support Muschet in seeking divorce.[1] Muschet then hid, after informing his wife he was going to London and would never see her again, hoping that her belief that she had been deserted would encourage her to indulge in such 'practices' for Burnbank to witness. His chosen hiding place, ironically, was the house of Alexander Pennecuik, one of the most copious writers of Edinburgh broadsides of the age.

This plan also failed, and there must be a strong suspicion that Burnbank was not trying very hard. From the start it seems likely that he had realised that Muschet was plain stupid, an easy dupe who would keep paying for daft plans. Having Margaret arrested for theft also proved a waste of time, as the prosecution failed. Muschet moved on to more direct plans to get rid of Margaret once and for all. Burnbank and one George Fachney, described in a broadside as 'professor of gaming, and one of the subalteren officers in Collonel Caldwell's new levied regiment of robbers',[2] undertook to murder poor Margaret. A grim comedy of errors – or more likely deliberate incompetence – followed. An attempt at poisoning failed. Two plans to drown her came to nothing. Ambushes designed to bludgeon her to death in the streets were thwarted, as there were always other people around at the critical moment. Eventually Muschet stirred himself to action, instead of relying on others. He stabbed poor Margaret and cut her throat. He was quickly arrested, and the squalid case briefly became a sensation.[3]

Three of the broadsides on the Muschet case mention Rob Roy, though two only in passing.

Rob Roy, Jardens, Baillies, and the Schaws,
Can truss a purse, and mock at human laws.[4]   *steal*

Here Rob has no distinctive character – he is lumped in with other criminals of ephemeral notoriety. Rob, it may be assumed, would have been infuriated to be thus represented as a cut-purse or common thief.

The second reference to Rob is rather more interesting. Campbell of Burnbank was sentenced to transportation to the West Indies for his criminal conspiracies with Muschet, and he is depicted as distributing his possessions before leaving.

> To Robin Roy my Highland Durk
> Wi' which I aft made bloody Wark.[5]

This is the earliest evidence that Rob Roy's abbreviation of Robert – Rob – has been identified with another – Robin. This change may mean no more than that the two-syllable 'Robin' suited the scansion of the verse better than the one-syllable 'Rob'. But it is more likely deliberate and marks the emergence of the association of Rob Roy with Robin Hood, both being seen as wronged men who had been driven into outlawry and were searching for justice, fighting against those in authority but sympathetic to the common people. However, that a bloody dirk is seen as a suitable legacy for Rob suggests that violence is also associated with his name.

A third broadside does not make the Rob/Robin connection but goes much further in establishing Rob as no ordinary criminal. George Fachney is on the run, and appeals for Rob's help.

A Lawland robber in distress,	
As by the following lines ye'll guess	
Sends his petition by express,	
'Tis his last shift	*expedient*
Unto your Highland mightiness,	
To lend a lift.	*give help*
I'm e'en as fou of grief and wae,	*even; full; woe*
As e'er ye was of usquabse;	*ever; whisky*
I ken nor what to do or say,	*know*
Tho' anes right stout:	
For if that you shou'd say me nay,	
My pipe's clean out.	*last hope's gone*

Being a Highlander, Rob is depicted as full of whisky – hardly tactful in the circumstances. Fachney goes on to explain his plight. The 'regiment' of robbers was collapsing, with

The maist feck in the en'my's hand,	*folk; enemy's*
and tried by law.	

Fachney hints that it was Rob's example that led him to become a robber:

You've thriv'n sae long at your bra' trade,	*brave*
And ay sae cannily you've sped:	
For a' fo'ks ken what life you've led,	
nae very leil,	*loyal*
That I turn'd fond, and unco' glad	*foolish*
to rob and steal.	

His leader, 'Colonel' Caldwell, is imprisoned in Edinburgh Tolbooth, and has given evidence against Fachney, who fears being hanged. Therefore he throws himself on Rob's mercy:

Now I'll be judged by you dear Rob,	
If I be taken by the mob,	
In hangie's halter I man bob,	*the hangman's; must*
A sair affront.	*sore*

So:

It's e'en to you, I'll make my main,	*appeal*
My heart's right sair.	*sore*

The baillies (magistrates) of Edinburgh were seeking the gang's blood:

But ye defy ay a your toes	*all on*
E'en gallant Grahmes and their Montrose	
Ye pit their hearts into their hose;	*socks*
And dings them a'.	
And when your claymore deals its blows,	
Ye scour awa'.	*run away*
It's true but that's a natter small,	
Ye've lost your fortune and your saul.	*soul*
Easy are ye if that be all;	
Ye're nae sair wrang'd	
But it wad e'en provok foks gall:	*even; bitterness*
For to be hang'd	
Na your estate ean neer be spent,	
For tho it's forfeit your content,	
And ilk a year ye draw the rent,	
Leaving a line.	

Rob is among the Highland hills with his blythe lads, so though he has lost his estate and his soul he is well off compared to Fachney, facing the hangman's noose. Moreover, whines the criminal, Rob had some compensation: he still collected 'rents' from Montrose's lands, 'leaving a line' (written receipt):

Now gallant Rob, 'tis in your power
Us from the gallows to secure,
Come down in this unlucky hour,
try to get back
The fame ye lost at Sheriffmir,
mind that's the knack,
Dear Rob . . .

More comic stuff – with another insult to Rob. Fachney is hoping
Rob will help him out but injudiciously recalls the allegations that
he had refused to fight at Sheriffmuir. There follows Rob Roy's
supposed answer to Fachney's supplication, and the complaints of
the caricature criminal gives way to the sterner tone of the famed
outlaw. Rob is blunt.

Your bold address I do reject,
Go villains and swing by the neck.

Rob has no sympathy for Fachney and his men. He might have
had, if they had fought lawyers, or quack doctors, or (rather oddly)
smugglers, but

. . . you are but punny rakes,
Riffling the honest pedlers packs,   *robbing*
Robbing from this and that poor sinner,
Who scarce know where to get their dinner
Go and be hang'd, you can't do better,
Take this for answer to your letter.[6]

The part Rob is thus made to play in Fachney's misfortunes is of
course totally fictitious, but it is highly valuable for what it tells us of
how people conceived of Rob Roy. Here, while he is still alive – and
indeed still an outlaw – are many central features of later stories about
him. Many points that might have otherwise been thought to be later
inventions are shown by this piece of doggerel verse to be of very
early date. Rob is perceived as being engaged in a vendetta against
Montrose, who had been responsible for the unjust loss of his lands.
His stealing he regards not as theft, but as collecting rent. Far from
seeking to hide his identity, as a thief would normally do, he provides
evidence of it by leaving receipts. He is a wronged but honourable
man fighting for his rights. He does not, like Fachney, prey on the
poor, and by implication he approves of those who rob the enemies of
the poor, though these enemies are described as crooked lawyers and
physicians, not the crooked aristocrats of Rob's real battles.

Again in 1724 Rob appeared in verse, and again in the context of the crimes of others. John Gordon of Glenbucket (who in 1716 had agreed to help in the hunt for Rob Roy) had turned some MacPherson tenants out of their lands in Badenoch. They took this badly, and a group of their sons went to persuade him to let the families keep their lands, and found him sitting on his bed as he was unwell. Negotiations went badly, and they drew their dirks and fell on him and, as he himself put it, 'Mangled him so unmercifully that he fell down as dead.' However, he is said to have had sufficient life in him to grab his sword and fight off his attackers. He took the hint, however, and lost interest in the Badenoch lands which were in dispute.[7]

The incident was taken as being yet another example of Highland barbarism, and Alexander Pennecuik immortalised the incident in his usual style of verse – though this piece did not make it into print.

> May that cursed clan up by the roots be plucked,
> Whose impious hands have killed the good Glenbucket.
> Villains far worse than infidel or Turk,
> To slash his body with your bloody durk -
> A fatal way to make his physic work!   *medicine*
> Rob Roy and you fight 'gainst the noblest names,
> The generous Gordons and the gallant Grahams.
> Perpetual clouds through your black clan shall reign,
> Traitors 'gainst God and rebels 'gainst your king,
> Until you feel the law's extremest rigour,
> And be extinguished, like the base Macgregor.[8]

Rob and the MacGregors might have had nothing to do with the MacPherson attack on Glenbucket, but his reputation was such that it had become almost obligatory to mention him when talking of violence in the Highlands

However, as well as being used as a sort of fashion accessory for other criminals, a manuscript account of some of the incidents of Rob's life was compiled. No copies of it survive, but it formed the basis of the first published biography of Rob, which appeared London in 1723. *The Highland Rogue* is, alas, inconsistent, badly written and fanciful, but once extravagant invention is stripped off it provides an outline of parts of Rob's life which is essentially accurate. Bad books can be influential, and the *Rogue* was to provide, directly or indirectly, the basis of 'biographies' of Rob until the later twentieth century. In the past authorship has often been attributed to Daniel

Defoe, but this rests on a misunderstanding of a comment by Sir Walter Scott. He stated that Defoe 'ought' to have written it, not meaning that he thought that Defoe had written it, but implying that if Defoe had written it, it would have had a lot more literary merit. The *Rogue*'s preface is signed 'E.B.' who has sometimes thought to have been Elias Brockett (1695–1735), author of a number of works on a variety of subjects but (deservedly) an obscure figure. However, it seems much more likely that E.B. was Edmund Burt. His famous *Letters from the North of Scotland* were not to be published until 1754, but they were written in the early 1720s, and as an official stationed in the Highlands he was in an ideal position to pick up tales about Rob Roy. If he was indeed the author it seems probable that his claim that the book was 'impartially digested from the memorandum of an authentick Scotch MSS' is an invention, the work being entirely his own.[9]

Popular lives of criminal 'heroes' had a big market in England, and the rambling title of *The Highland Rogue* seeks to locate Rob in that genre. He was 'elected captain of a formidable gang' famed for his 'exploits on the highway' – fitting him into the English category of Highwayman. There is sensationalism too, with a reference to 'the unequal'd villanies of the clan of the Mac-gregors for several years past'. In his preface, however, Burt makes high claims as to the authenticity of his work. He is not writing romance but 'real history' and 'nothing makes history more valuable than truth'. *Robinson Crusoe*, *Colonel Jack* and *Moll Flanders*, Defoe's successful novels are dismissed as not history. Brockett, by contrast, relies on his authentic manuscript, though making it clear that he is no mere copyist. The manuscript's style and disorder had been so 'insufferable that I could not preserve so much as one entire line'. But Brockett allowed himself one notable exception to his strict reliance on fact. He announced that he felt free to invent speeches. The great ancient historians had done this, so why shouldn't he? Fair enough.

An introduction on the MacGregors follows, with the usual comments on their violence, on Highlanders' obsession with clan and genealogy ('Tis hardly credible, how much vanity abounds among the vulgar inhabitants of the Highlands on account of their names'), on how in recent times they have become more peaceable than formerly – 'except now and then lifting (as they term'd it) a cow or a horse'.[10]

At last Rob Roy is reached – and the reader's confidence in the author's abilities as a historian is severely challenged. Rob was a man of prodigious strength and approaching 'a gigantic size'. He had a beard a foot long and his entire face and body were covered in red hair.[11] The description conjures up a vision of some semi-fabulous creature from the jungle, but after this Rob settles down to being human. It is as if the author suddenly realised that he had started in the wrong genre, and had hastily switched from 'wild man fables' to 'history'. Rob was a cattle grazier, 'a very diverting pleasant fellow in conversation', very strict in keeping his word, until he fell out with Montrose and was ruined. Taking refuge at Craigrostan guarded by 'stupendous high mountains, and rocks of a prodigious magnitude' he took to a life of banditry. But he was really quite a nice bandit, given to practical jokes, and ready to help the poor on occasion. He had taken part in the '15, but many suspected he 'had a much greater affection for the imagined spoil than his pretended prince', and in the end he achieved nothing but 'running away with the booty'.

Most of the main incidents of Rob's career are mentioned, such as his quarrel with Montrose, the kidnapping of Killearn, and his escape from Logierait, after which his captor (Atholl) became 'for a considerable time after, the common subject of lampoon'. He is described as acting as a judge, a reference to his appointment as a baillie by Breadalbane. This gives confidence that some of the incidents that cannot be independently documented may be based on fact. Some, which become standard in later accounts, are not in themselves unbelievable. Rob plays a joke on an 'officer' who comes to demand a payment due by him. He is treated in a friendly manner, but allowed to see what appears to be a hanged man (in fact a stuffed dummy). On enquiry, this is nonchalantly explained as the last man who tried to collect money from Rob, whereupon he flees in terror. Again, Rob provides money to a poor farmer to pay his rent, as Atholl is threatening to evict him. Once the rent is collected, Rob intervenes and steals it back. But other anecdotes stretch credulity. Rob kidnaps a gentleman, but finding he is in financial difficulties, gives him money and frees him. Rob make prisoner a drunken 'parson' (parish minister). Rob captures improbable numbers of prisoners whom he holds for ransom at Craigrostan. Rob makes an extraordinary number of escapes after being captured. Here invention runs wild.

The drunken minister story provides a lead-in for an odd theological insertion into the account of Rob's life, in which Brockett makes full use of the permission he has given himself to invent speeches. The minister, a Presbyterian and therefore a believer in predestination, denounces Rob for his sinful actions, Rob replies 'how often have I heard you teach that we are not free agents, but that all our actions were pre-ordained'. His kidnapping of the minister had happened, therefore it had been determined by God that it would happen before the creation of the world. How could Rob be blamed for what he did if it was pre-ordained? The concepts of duty and guilt were meaningless unless the individual had freedom of action. Thus, incongruously, Rob's life is made use of to illustrate the absurdity of Presbyterian theology and uphold free-will doctrines. The inclusion of this dispute on predestination in a biography of Rob Roy seems pointless. Its style and detail make it appear to be an insertion into the material derived from the 'Scotch MSS'. But the incident can be decoded through a clue in a letter which notes that a pamphlet recently published in London had attacked Sir Robert Walpole (the prime minister) and the earl of Islay (his chief adviser on Scottish affairs) 'under the simile of Rob Roy'.[12] This 'pamphlet' is evidently *The Highland Rogue*, and the stance taken by Rob in using religion to justify theft becomes a satirical attack on the notorious corruption of Walpole's government and on Islay. Rob Walpole is no better than Rob Roy, with word-play on the words 'rob' and 'robbery'. The biography of Rob has been published not just through its inherent interest but as a piece of political propaganda.

The Highland Rogue ends rather lamely. Having accumulated plunder, Rob had enough for the necessities of life and had no need to trouble his neighbours any more. Nothing remains to complete the history of Rob except 'the account of his death; which we have not yet receiv'd any certain advice of'. It is a bit careless of a biographer not to check whether his subject is alive or dead.

In trying to establish the facts of Rob's life, *The Highland Rogue* is of little value. Many of the 'facts' in it are true, but there are far more detailed and credible sources of information about them available elsewhere. However, as a source for what was being said about Rob in his own lifetime, the beginning of his legend, the book is useful. Rob is already a wronged man who stood up to great aristocrats and made them look foolish, a man who made daring escapes, who was generous to the poor, and played jokes. He was a good conversationalist and had charm. When a second edition, *The Highland Rogue, being a General History of the Highlanders*, appeared in 1743 the title included the statement that Rob had 'lived in the manner of the ancient Robin Hood of England'. Two legends were again entangled.

The 1720s saw Rob Roy emerge in print in both broadsides and a biography. He was also quite literally 'put on the map'. In 1725 Hermann Moll published a series of maps of Scotland. They were hardly up-to-date, being based on maps published in the 1650s – which in turn were based on the manuscript maps half a century older still. But Moll made some additions, and tried to make up for the embarrassment of the large blank areas on his maps in some parts of the Highlands by adding text, sometimes distinctly dubious. On his map of *The Shire of Lenox or Dunbarton* he inserted Inversnaid barracks (though the engraver unfortunately spelt it 'Innersnail'). Going further, Moll identified 'Rob Roy's Country'. Did Rob Roy ever know of this tribute to his fame? It is rare to become a cartographic feature in one's own lifetime, but clearly Moll thought it was the sort of thing that would interest users of his maps.

However, in a way typical of Rob's tendency to slip from the historical to the mythical, Moll has put Rob's 'country' in the wrong place, to the west instead of the east of Loch Lomond. Inversnaid is also misplaced. And the blank which represented the real Rob Roy country has been filled by a note claiming that Loch Lomond was famous for a floating island, fish without fins, and storms in calm weather. A fabulous place indeed for the legendary Rob Roy.[13]

10

JACOBITE REBEL TO HANOVERIAN SPY

In the years after the abortive rising of 1719 the government had been complacent about the Highlands. The episode had been regarded as showing that Highland Jacobitism was not a serious threat, and this proved a good excuse for doing what government was usually inclined to do about the Highlands – virtually nothing. But in 1724 Lord Lovat (Fraser of Beaufort had at last got his title officially recognised) submitted to George I a report on conditions in the Highlands, stressing high levels of disorder, connected primarily with cattle raiding and the raising of blackmail. This law and order problem, Lord Lovat stressed, was closely linked to the political one of the high level of active Jacobite sentiment among the clans – and especially among the more disorderly ones. After the suppression of the '15, and even after the further warning of the '19, effective action had not been taken. Attempts at disarming the clans had been undertaken half-heartedly and had mainly weakened the Hanoverian-inclined clans, which was absurd and dangerous.[1] The warning was well timed. There was peace abroad, and stability at home under the strong leadership of Sir Robert Walpole. There was no immediate hope of Jacobites obtaining help from abroad, and active Jacobite plotting was at a low ebb. In other words, there was an opportunity to take action without fear of provoking revolt.

George I therefore gave orders on 3 July 1724 to Major General George Wade to proceed to the Highlands and investigate the state of the country, especially as to 'depredations' and the allegations that pro-government clans had been disarmed but not Jacobite ones. He was also to make suggestions as to what should be done. Wade reported on 10 December. There were 22,000 men in the Highlands capable of bearing arms. Over half, 12,000, were ready, if encouraged by their chiefs, to make trouble or to rise in arms in favour of the Stuart Pretender. Cattle raiding was common and even when such 'banditti' were captured they were rarely prosecuted, as the legal processes were cumbersome and expensive, and those making charges feared having their houses burnt and their possessions destroyed or stolen in retaliation by clansmen of the accused. Sometimes offers of reward to informers led to the discovery of thieves and the restoration of stolen cattle, but clansmen had taken to swearing oaths on a dirk not to act as informers, on pain of death. As to action previously taken by the government, Wade told a sorry story of failure. The disarming act of 1716 had indeed failed. The independent companies had become corrupt. Officers were said to have defrauded the government by not keeping the numbers of men they were supposed to in arms, and they sometimes accepted payments to free prisoners instead of bringing them to justice. This was why King George had been entirely justified in disbanding the companies that had existed in 1719. Wade was being tactful, praising the king's judgement as a preliminary to suggesting that the decision to abolish the companies should be reversed. New companies of loyal Highlanders should be employed in 'preventing depredations, bringing criminals to justice' and 'hinder[ing] rebels and attainted persons' from living in the Highlands.[2]

Wade's report and recommendations – which included disarming, road building and forming six new independent companies – were approved, and he was appointed commander-in-chief in Scotland.[3] Instructions were issued to him on 1 June 1725, and these included a long overdue decision on what to do about those attainted for high treason during the '15 who were still in the Highlands. Many were willing to submit and agree to live peacefully, but there was no machinery for them to achieve this, so they had been forced to live lives of lawlessness. Wade was told on the one hand 'not to suffer persons who were attainted of high treason for the late unatural rebellion, to presume any longer to reside in the Highlands'. But if these people 'being convicted of their past folly and rashness, were willing and desireous to summit' to George I, then Wade was empowered to receive their offers of submission, and transmit them to the king.[4]

By this time, however, Scotland was not so peaceful as it had seemed a few months before. A new malt tax had brought the towns to the seething verge of riot, and in May 1725 a letter from an English army officer stationed there revealed a tense atmosphere. Captain John Crossley had recently travelled from Stirling to Elgin, and had found great hostility to the government. All Scots were bitterly opposed to the tax. But the Scots were also deeply divided among themselves. It would be difficult to disarm the Highlanders, and the Highlanders made 'the [neighbouring] Lowland gentlemen and farmers pay what is called black meal an annuall contribution'.

Crossley makes mention of Rob Roy's wife, who has remained totally invisible in surviving sources since her marriage over thirty years before. With most of her children now adult, she was playing an active role in the family business. 'Not long before I left Stirling,' the captain noted, 'the famous Rob Roy's wife went through the whole town and country thereabouts to those that held any land, acquainted them who she was and that she wanted such sums which they were obleiged to comply with, but this Rob Roy is a man of such honour that where he steels [steals] himself, those he protects from the insults of others, so that he is one of the most genteel rogues amongst them.'⁵ It was clearly a matter of routine. Landlords sent out their factors to collect rent, Rob sent out Mary MacGregor to collect blackmail – black rent. Crossley only commented because he was an outsider, and it seemed bizarre. But his brief remark reveals more. It is another indication of how Rob Roy was not regarded as a frightening gangster, but as a rogue – naughty, not nasty – a polite and affable bandit, who gave value for money.

Later in the century Ramsay of Ochtertyre also referred to Mary MacGregor as taking a high-profile role in Rob's blackmail business. Rob himself seldom appeared in the low country, obviously because he feared capture. Instead, 'he used to send his wife, or some female friend, to collect his dues; who came arrayed in laced riding cloths and accompanied by a couple of handsome fellows that ran before her. I have heard my grandmothers speak of those unwelcome visitants.'⁶ This a splendid image – Mary, as Rob's representative, dressed up to show she was a gentlewoman, mounted while her servants ran by her horse. She collected the protection money, while the servants provided the muscle which ensured payment and that she was treated with respect. Presumably, like Crossley's letter, this anecdote dates from the early 1720s, when Rob was still an outlaw but no longer being intensively hunted. It is worth noting that while Rob and his male associates would risk arrest by venturing into the Lowlands, his female agents were not troubled, even though they had strayed from their 'natural' domestic roles into involvement in men's business.

Captain John Crossley was right to fear trouble in Scotland. On his march to the Highlands late in June, General Wade had to divert forces to Glasgow to restore order in the aftermath of the fierce Shawfield riots against the malt tax. However, once in the Highlands he acted swiftly and effectively, showing how much could be done in a short space of time if circumstances were right and the will was there. Proclamations for surrendering arms were circulated, though licences to bear arms were to be available to drovers and to dealers in cattle and other merchandise. But Wade had more to offer than threats to the disobedient. Those who had been attainted for high treason during the '15 were offered pardons. All went surprisingly smoothly. Surrenders of arms were organised, and letters of submission begging Wade to obtain pardons from the king trickled in.

On 8 October 1725 at Finlarig there was a mass surrender of weapons by men from Breadalbane and Atholl, by McNabs, Menzies and Campbells, including 'Campbell alias Rob Roy'. Twenty guns, twenty-one broadswords, three targes, five dirks and one pistol were received 'From Robert Campbell alias McGregor commonly called Rob Roy'.[7] Very few of Atholl's men from Balquhidder, it was reported, had surrendered their arms 'except what the McGrigors brought who came in to the number of 40 each of them having a gun or a sword'. One of Rob Roy's sons led them, marching before them, 'and their pyper playing'. Rob was with them and after disarming in style he guided the English officer in charge, Colonel Peers ('a very civill gentleman') from Finlarig back to Callander.[8] The once dreaded Rob Roy was anxious to please.

On 19 October Rob followed up his disarming by making his formal submission to General Wade in Dunkeld.[9] Wade had devised a ritual for such occasions. The 'traitors' concerned appeared individually before him, then 'they laid down their swords on the ground, expressed their sorrow and concern for having made use of them in opposition to Your Majesty' and promised to live peacefully and dutifully for the rest of their lives. After this, they sent Wade formal letters of submission, to be laid before the king, who would decide whether they were worthy of pardon.[10] Such letters cannot be taken at face value. The fulsome declarations of loyalty, claims to have been misunderstood in the past and so on were just necessary ritual grovellings, and it is hard to know if there is much truth in them.

Rob's letter is an articulate exercise in the art of self-justification. Praising Wade's compassion, he asked to be excused for his importunity in trying to show himself not altogether unworthy of the mercy and favour Wade might obtain for him from the king. Nothing could excuse his crime of rebellion, but there were extenuating circumstances in his case. It had been his misfortune that when rebellion had broken out in 1715 he had been being pursued for alleged debt by Montrose. What he had really wanted to do was hasten to Stirling and enlist as a loyal soldier of King George. But had he done so he would have been in danger of being imprisoned for debt. The whole country being in arms, it had not been possible for him to remain neutral, so he had had no choice but to join the Pretender. This may stretch credulity, but the cheek of Rob's argument has to be admired. Forced to join the unnatural rebels, he went on, he had made sure he had never acted offensively against King George's troops – not quite true, but for once the well-known story of his failure to fight at Sheriffmuir would count in his favour. On all possible occasions, Rob continued, he had sent intelligence of the strength and actions of rebel forces to Argyll. As to his debt to Montrose (no longer said to be 'alleged' but accepted as real), that had now been settled. Rob ended with a repetition of his long-held wish to serve King George. One of his reasons for seeking pardon was so he could spend his life in serving a king whose goodness, justice and humanity were so obvious to all mankind.[11] Masterly, and with the implication 'I would never have been a rebel for ten years and caused so much trouble if it had not been that Montrose was oppressing me. It was all his fault.'

Face to face, Rob Roy made a good impression on Wade, and on 20 October the general singled him out for comment when writing to the secretary of state, the duke of Newcastle. 'I take the liberty to inform your grace that of the armes that was brought in to Bredalbin, the famous Rob Roy sent in a greater proportion and in a handsomer manner than his neighbours. I suppose this might be done with a view to pave the way for his submission to his majesty, which he came and made to me yesterday in this town. He assured me he never had the least thought of entring into the rebellion from any dislike he had to his majesty's government, or from any attachment to the Pretender, but to avoid the persecution of his enemy the duke of Montrose, with whom he said he had since accommodated matters, and satisfied all his demands. This appears the more probable from the civility with which he treated the king's soldiers, whenever he met with them straggling in the mountains, whom he never used to part with without drinking the health of King George. He has just now sent me his letter of submission.'[12]

Rob Roy's amazing gift of the gab had had its usual effect, and the picture of Rob wandering the hills offering lost soldiers a dram so they could toast the health of the Hanoverian king with him is delightful. But it is interesting that Wade does not record this as something Rob told him but as something he had heard from others, and it may well be that indeed he had indeed been amiable to stray soldiers who were no threat to him.

Rob's charm and readiness to submit were not the only thing that won him Wade's favour. Rob agreed to take up again the occupation of intelligence agent. Before he had betrayed Jacobites to Argyll, and now he would betray them to Wade. There was immediate work for him, for the general's suspicions had been aroused by news that a vessel with some gentlemen aboard was cruising in the Western Isles. Soon Wade could report 'Rob Roy tells me that two of those gentlemen landed on the coast about 5 or 6 weeks agoe and went to Glasgow. By their description he supposes one to be Cameron, and the other Foster, both of this country, and [he] believes they were sent upon the first notice they [the Jacobites] had of the Glasgow riot. He has promised me to find out who they are, and the busness they came upon, and to send me the account to Edinburgh.'[13] Rob, the notorious former rebel and outlaw, could be a very helpful fellow when it suited him. Wade sent his letter of submission to London on 27 October, and by 4 November the lords justices (in charge in London as King George I was in Hanover), had sent to their master asking for his assent to the pardon of 'the famous Rob Roy'. To 'save expence' it was decided to issue all the pardons that the king eventually granted to those who had submitted at the same time,[14] and this was done on 2 December 1725. Robert Campbell and ten others were no longer attainted rebels but free men.[15]

It was over. Rob Roy had been on the run for debt for thirteen years, for treason for ten. From his early forties to his mid-fifties he had been an outlaw. He had lost his land but hung on to life and liberty, and eventually emerged with sufficient resources to live, if not in great style. His presence in Balquhidder had become accepted. Atholl had decided in the end that having Rob hold land in his regality, rented from his vassals, was something that it was best to accept quietly.

Rob was now King George's man. The zeal he expressed to serve his majesty may have been exaggerated, but he was willing to trade intelligence for favour. His sons were to serve the Hanoverian cause more directly for, doubtless through a deal with General Wade, two of them were recruited into one of the new independent companies. One of those who heard of this bizarre twist connected to Rob Roy's submission was Alexander Pennecuik, the Edinburgh merchant and indefatigable satiric poet. He was inspired to produce a piece 'On Rob Roy's Pardon and Preferment. 1726', which has until now remained unpublished.[16]

> Welcom brave captain to your own banditti,
> Welcome as succour to a besieged citie.
> For service done at Sherriff-muir ingagement,
> Made captain of an independent regiament,
> Most just for it is known to every clan
> Rob Roy was ay ane independent man,
> Depended not on God nor king before,
> But only trusted to his own claymore.
> Long live the king in plenty peace and joy:
> Who makes a loyall lad of Robin Roy
> There is a near relation 'twixt the two
> One steals a crown the other steals a cow.
> Our king resembles now the king of heaven,
> By him the greatest sinners are forgiven,
> Like heaven he doth his clemency display,
> And to the hungary doth his gifts convey,
> Naked and empty sends the rich away.
> Now Robin neither rebell nor a thieff,
> Dare lift in View of gallows at the Creiff,
> Athol dispise and pis on poor Montrose.
> Success attend your fate you plundering Boy,
> Whilst gallant Grahams must bow to Robin Roy,
> Nobly goe on, more formidable grow,
> And join the half-starv'd Campbells of Lochhow.[17]

Rob had at last got his reward for his (supposed) service to the Hanoverians at Sheriffmuir – though he had in reality only got his sons enlisted in an independent company, not command of an independent 'regiment' for himself. Rob the cow-stealer was to serve King George the upstart crown-stealer, the poet jeers cynically. This highly seditious reference is sufficient to explain why Pennecuik's welcome to Rob Roy on his return to legality was not published. But he had got right what Rob had done to Montrose in the opinion of posterity. He had pissed on him.

Wade's activities in 1725 in securing at least partial disarming of the Highlands, forming new independent companies, and having rebels pardoned, had a notable effect in reducing cattle raiding and other lawlessness. His continuing involvement in the Highlands in the years that followed, building a new network of military roads, further emphasised government interest in creating a superstructure designed to control lawlessness and conspiracy. It was perhaps these changing circumstances that led to an alleged attempt by the Clan Gregor to change its status. The name and clan were still outlawed, and there seemed no hope of having the ban on them lifted. But they might be able to retain some identity by uniting with another clan. Meetings were held with the Grants at Blair Atholl, it is said, over fourteen successive days at the turn of the years 1725 to 1726. The MacGregors would unite with Grants, and take their name. But they would only do so if John Og Campbell (MacGregor) of Glencarnaig was recognised as chief of the new enlarged Clan Grant. On this point the talks broke down and the fact that the chief of the Grants (Sir James Grant of Grant) was not present 'hindered the agreement'.[18]

The story sounds absurd at first hearing. Why would the Grants, a major power in the eastern Highlands led by several powerful families of lairds, wish even to consider merging with the scattered MacGregors? Why would the (relatively) respectable and mainly Hanoverian Grants unite with the ill-famed Jacobite MacGregors? Moreover the only evidence of the incident is contained in a letter written in 1769. The author claimed to have been present at the meetings, but his account was written in support of the claim of Glencarnaig's grandson that he and his forebears had been recognised as chiefs of the MacGregors. The point of the story was to provide evidence supporting this fabrication, as it assumes that the MacGregors had accepted John Og as their chief in the 1720s.[19]

It is tempting therefore to dismiss the story of the proposed MacGregor–Grant negotiations as entirely fictitious. But it is possible that something lay behind the report. Wade's disarming and demoralisation of the Jacobites must have left the MacGregors with little hope that they would ever be allowed their original name back. They had adopted a number of different names, and while all might identify themselves as MacGregors under this guise, how long could this last, as different names tended to pull MacGregors into new loyalties (which, of course, was what government hoped would happen). The idea of all MacGregors taking the same name would give then some unity – even if that name were shared with another clan. There were, after all, other 'names' which included distinct identities under a single surname. The Clan Campbell was in a sense a single clan, but the Argyll and Breadalbane Campbells were recognised as distinct from each other. It made little sense anymore to talk of Clan Donald, when the MacDonalds were divided into the separate branches of Keppoch, Glengarry, Clanranald and so on.

Thus the idea of a 'MacGregor' branch of Clan Grant is not necessarily absurd. If the MacGregors (or some of them) were considering such a scheme, deciding that the linkage should be with the Grants made sense. A number of separate clans and names believed they were linked together by all being descended from an early Scottish king, Alpin. The Clan Alpin included, among others, MacKinnons, MacNabs, MacAulays, MacQuarries – and Grants and MacGregors. The concept of a common ancestor in King Alpin might usually have had no practical impact, but it does seem to have helped to produce longstanding effects on the relationship between the Grants and the MacGregors. Certainly Rob Roy had good friends among the Grants. When Atholl was desperately appealing for help in recapturing Rob Roy in 1717 he was warned that little could be expected from Grant of Pluscarden, as he was the chief of Grant's brother and 'I know he is a strong ffreind of Roy's'.[20] The chief was Alexander Grant, and he was to be succeeded in 1719 by his brother, James (formerly of Pluscarden), the chief at the time of the supposed 1725–26 negotiations. Patrick Grant of Rothiemurchus is said to have been 'known as "MacAlpine" because of his sympathy for the outlawed MacGregors.'[21] His younger brother, Colonel William Grant of Ballindalloch, was captain of one of the new independent companies raised by General Wade in 1725, and something of his relationship with Rob Roy is indicated by a letter Rob wrote to him on 26 May 1726. 'I cannot express myself how much we that are M'Grigors are oblidged to you. Yow are reckoned a great man in their books; but your last behaviour at Aberdeen will make them dore [adore] yow as one of their litle gods upon earth.' When news had spread of Ballindalloch's 'behaviour' the MacGregors 'cabal'd for twenty-four hours drinking your health and Captain Grant's. So, in short, I doe believe that their is none of your friends in this country but what would venter [venture] their lives for yow without asking questions.'[22]

This goes beyond the conventional flattery of the age, and suggests

JAMES GRAHAM, FIRST DUKE OF MONTROSE (1682–1742)
Portrait by Godfrey Kneller. Montrose became
Rob Roy's most implacable enemy after 1711.
Copyright © Collection of Lennoxlove House, Haddington

JOHN CAMPBELL, FIRST EARL OF BREADALBANE (*c.*1635–1717)
Portrait by Sir John Baptiste de Medina. For years Breadalbane was Rob Roy's main patron and
protector. *Copyright © Scottish National Portrait Gallery*

JOHN CAMPBELL, SECOND DUKE OF ARGYLL (1680–1743)
Portrait by William Aikman. Commander in Chief of the army in Scotland during the '15,
Argyll favoured Rob Roy in return for intelligence of Jacobite activities.
Copyright © Scottish National Portrait Gallery

THE PROSPECT OF FALKLAND FROM THE EAST

The partly ruined palace dominates the centre and right of the engraving. It was occupied for the Jacobites by MacGregor of Glengyle in January 1716, with Rob Roy as deputy governor. J. Slezer, *Theatrum Scotiae*, 1693. *Copyright © Trustees of the National Library of Scotland*

THE PROSPECT OF THE TOWN OF DUNKELD

The scene is dominated by the cathedral, left, and Dunkeld House, right. It was at Dunkeld House that Rob Roy 'surrendered' to the duke of Atholl in 1717. J. Slezer, *Theatrum Scotiae*, 1693. *Copyright © Trustees of the National Library of Scotland*

JOHN MURRAY, FIRST DUKE OF ATHOLL (1680–1724)
Portrait by T. Murray, 1705. Seen through the window is Dunkeld House,
where Rob Roy 'surrendered' to the duke in 1717.

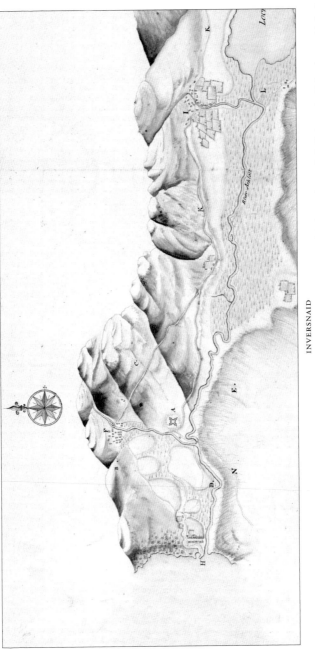

INVERSNAID

Depicted on a military map of 1718. H (far left) marks the harbour of Inversnaid. A (a little to the right) shows the newly built barracks. F (to the north) depicts the huts occupied by 100 soldiers while the barracks were being built. About 20 buildings are shown – not necessary the true number, but an indication that this, like other farms, formed a little 'township,' a group of houses of tenants and subtenants. I (centre) is Corriearklet, the farm where Rob Roy had been married. Corriearklet was situated to the north-west of Loch Arklet, though nowadays, due to the raising of the water level in the nineteenth century, it stands half way along the northern shore of the loch. J. Dumaresq and J.H. Bastide, A Draught of Innersnait in the Highlands of North Britain, 1718.

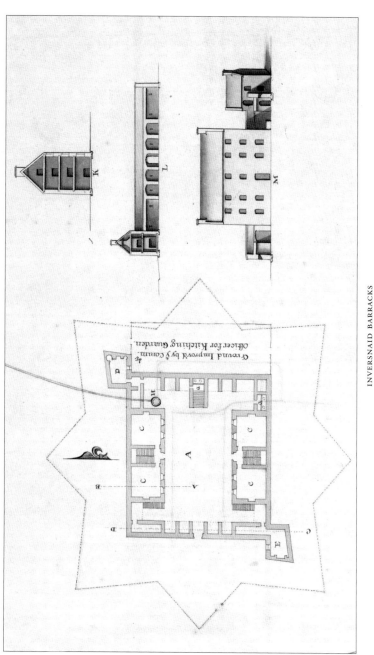

INVERSNAID BARRACKS

Plan and elevation by Andrew Jelfe. H marks the 'well,' a cistern carved out of the rock and supplied from a stream to the north which was diverted into it.

FIELD MARSHALL GEORGE WADE (1679–1748)
Portrait attributed to Johan van Diest. Rob Roy submitted to Wade in 1725 in return for a pardon from the king, and spied on Jacobite activities for him. Soldiers are shown toiling on one of Wade's many road-building projects, and behind them a road zigzags improbably up into the mountains. *Copyright © Scottish National Portrait Gallery*

By the King,

A PROCLAMATION

For the Discovering and Apprehending *Robert Campbel* alias *Mac-Gregor*, commonly called *Rob Roy*, for the several Crimes therein mentioned.

GEORGE R.

WHEREAS We have received Information, That upon the Eight and Twentieth Day of *January* last, a Party, consisting of an Officer and Twenty Men, marched in order to join another Party of the Tenants of the Duke of *Montrose*, that were following a Parcel of Cattle, that had been stolen from one *Drunkie*, a Tenant to the said Duke of *Montrose*; but it growing very dark the said Party were obliged to take Quarters at *Glanfallow*, in that Part of our united Kingdom of *Great Britain* called *Scotland*, where they were informed, that *Robert Campbel* alias *MacGregor*, commonly called *Rob Roy*, was ----- ment gone from thence with a strong Party, consisting of near Fifty Men well arme-- ----- the said Officer plac-- Three Sentinels upon the House as soon as he came there, no being ---ble to go further that Night, and that they had not been there above Half an Hour before they heard several Shots; Upon which they went out and found one of the Sentinels ----- led; That the said *Rob Roy*'s Party fired several Times into the House; but finding that to no Purpose, they followed the Party that belonged to the Duke of *Montrose*, and disarmed them all; and that the said *Rob Roy* shot one of the Men as he lay in his Bed: We, out of our Royal Inclination to Justice, and to the Intent that the said *Robert Camphel*, alias *MacGregor*, commonly called *Rob Roy*, may be apprehended and punished for his said Offences, in Contempt of Our Royal Authority, and to the Destruction of the Lives of Our Subjects, whereby all others may be deterr'd from committing the like Crimes, have thought fit, by the Advice of Our Privy Council, to issue this Our Royal Proclamation: And We are hereby graciously pleased to promise, That if any Person shall discover the said *Robert Camphel* alias *MacGregor*, commonly called *Rob Roy*, so as he be apprehended and brought to Justice for his said Offences, such Discoverer shall have and receive, as a Reward for such Discovery, the Sum of Two Hundred Pounds *Sterling*; Whereof our Commissioners for executing the Office of Treasurer of Our Exchequer, are hereby required to make Payment accordingly; and if any Person who is a Rebel or an Accomplice with he said *Rob Roy*, shall make such Discovery, as aforesaid, such Discoverer shall have and receive the said Reward of Two Hundred Pounds *Sterling*, and also Our Gracious Pardon for his said Offences. And We do hereby strictly Charge and Command all Our Justices of the Peace, and all other Our Officers, and all other Our loving Subjects, that they do use their utmost Diligence in their several Places and Capacities, to find out, discover and apprehend the said Offender in Order to his being brought to Justice. And We do hereby Command that this Our Proclamation be published in the usual Form, that none may pretend Ignorance: And We ordain these Presents to be printed, and Our Solicitor to dispatch Copies in the usual Manner.

Given at Our Court at St. James's *the* 10th *Day of* March 1719, *in the* 5th *Year of Our Reign.*

GOD save the King.

Printed by JAMES WATSON, One of His Majesty's Printers, 1719.

PROCLAMATION OFFERING A REWARD FOR THE ARREST OF ROB ROY
Issued in March 1719 after Rob attacked a party of soldiers in Glenfalloch
Copyright © National Archives of Scotland, SC54/15/1

ABSTRACT of the Rental of the real Estate of Robert Campbell, commonly called *Rob Roy*, lying in the Shire of ~~Dumbarton~~ *Stirling*

Ardess and the Ten pound Land of Craig-Roston.

~~Craig-Roston alias Invernenit.~~

	Sterling Money		
	L.	Sh.	D.
Payable in Money	56		

Annual Deductions.

	L.	s.	d.
Feu-Duty to the Laird of *Luss*,	20		
Teind or Tithe to the Duke of *Montrose*,	8	6	8
Total	28	6	8

Annual neat Produce

More to be Deducted of Teind or Tyth to the Duke of Montrose

Neat Produce £26 : :

£27 : 13 : 4
1 : 13 : 4

Woods valued at £150 : :

EDINBURGH, 16th SEPTEMBER 1720.

ARTICLES of the *Publick Sale and Roup* of the Estate of Robert Campbell, *commonly called* Rob Roy, *lying in the Shire of* ~~Dumbarton~~ *Stirling*

I. THAT the said Sale or Roup be at the Commissioners Office upon the 13th Day of *October* next, at Ten a Clock in the Forenoon, by an half Hour Glass, and the highest Bidder at the out-running of the Glass to be preferred to the Purchase.

II. The said Estate to be entered or set up at twenty Years Purchase.

III. The Purchaser's Entry be at the Term of *Martinmass* next, being the 11th of *November* 1720, and shall have Right to the Rents of the Cropt 1720.

IV. No Bidder shall offer less than 10 *l. Sterling* above the Sum offer'd immediatly before; and that each Bidder signs his Offer when he makes the same.

V. If any Question or Doubt arise amongst the Bidders, during the Sale, the Glass shall be stopt from running, till the Commissioners and Trustees shall consider and determine the Question in Dispute.

VI. For the further Satisfaction of the Buyer or Buyers, the Commissioners and Trustees will give to him a Note in Writing under their Hands and Seals, expressing the Particulars by him bought, and for what Estate and Interest therein, and the Price and Consideration thereof, and Time of such Sale and Contract.

VII. The Buyer or Buyers respectively, shall pay the Price agreed upon to his Majesty's Receiver-General for *Scotland*, or his Deputy, being the Receipt of Exchequer there, on, or before the 11th of *November* 1720; or at such further Time as shall be agreed upon between the said Commissioners and Trustees, and the Purchasers; with Interest from *Whitsunday*, being the 15th of *May* 1720.

VIII. The said Payment being certified to the said Commissioners and Trustees, they shall execute an Indenture or Contract of Bargain and Sale of the Estate so bought and paid for, as aforesaid, to every such Buyer or Buyers thereof, in Manner, and according to the Terms and Directions of the Act of Parliament, made in the Fourth Year of His Majesty's Reign, entituled, *An Act for vesting the forfeited Estates in Great Britain and Ireland in Trustees, to be sold for the Use of the Publick, &c.*

IX. If the Purchaser or Purchasers resectively, shall not pay the Sum or Sums of Money contracted for, within the Time or Times to be agreed upon, as aforesaid, he or they, shall forfeit one Fifth of the said Money contracted for, according to the said Act, and the Sale shall be void, and the said Commissioners and Trustees will thereafter proceed to a new Sale, as by the said Act is directed.

N. B. Every Bidder is to come prepared to give reasonable Satisfaction to the Commissioners and Trustees, of his being able to pay the Price he offers, or at least the Penalty, as is mentioned in the above Articles of Sale.

THE SALE OF ROB ROY'S LANDS

This is a proof copy (with manuscript corrections) of the announcement that his lands were to be sold by auction, 1720

Copyright © National Archives of Scotland, E636/7

THE
Highland ROGUE:
OR, THE
Memorable ACTIONS
Of the Celebrated
ROBERT MAC-GREGOR,
Commonly called
ROB-ROY.

CONTAINING

A genuine ACCOUNT of his Education, Grandeur, and sudden Misfortune; his commencing
ROBBER, and being elected Captain of a formidable Gang; his Exploits on the HIGHWAY,
breaking open Houses, taking Prisoners, commencing JUDGE, and levying Taxes; his Defence of
his manner of Living; his Dispute with a *Scotch*
Parson upon PREDESTINATION; his joining
with the Earl of *Marr* in the REBELLION;
his being decoy'd and imprison'd by the Duke of
----------, with the manner of his ESCAPE, &c.

INTRODUC'D

With a Relation of the unequal'd VILLANIES
of the CLAN of the MAC-GREGORS for several Years past.

THE WHOLE

Impartially digested from the Memorandums of an authentick
Scotch MS.

LONDON:

Printed for J. BILLINGSLEY *under the* Royal
Exchange; J. ROBERTS *in* Warwick-Lane;
A. DODD *without* Temple-Bar; *and* J. FOX *in*
Westminster-Hall. 1723. Price One Shilling.

ROB ROY: MISTAKEN IDENTITY

This is the earliest 'portrait' of Rob known to have been published, and appeared first in
K. Macleay, *Historical Memoirs of Rob Roy and the Clan Macgregor* (1818). The engraving
is in fact derived from a version of Richard Waitt's well-known portrait of Alasdair Grant,
known as the 'Clan Grant Champion'. *Copyright © St Andrews University Library*

ROB ROY: INTENSE AND BROODING

Another engraving derived ultimately from the 'Clan Grant Champion' portrait.

Portraits Illustrative of the Novels, Tales, and Romances of the Author of Waverley (1832)

LONG-ARMED ROB

An engraving also perhaps derived from a version of the 'Clan Grant Champion' portrait. The engraver has valiantly attempt to depict Rob with remarkably long arms, in accordance with the tradition that he could tie his garters below his knees without stooping. D. Stewart, *The Life and surprising exploits of Rob Roy Macgregor*.

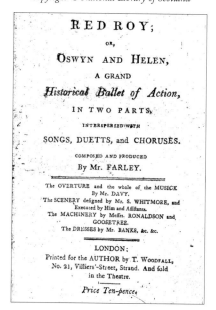

ROB ROY: CHEAP AND CHEERFUL

A woodcut on the title page of a chapbook of tales about Rob, produced cheaply for the mass market. *The Life and Exploits of Rob Roy, the Highland Freebooter* (Falkirk 1824)

Copyright © National Library of Scotland

RED ROY;

OR,

OSWYN AND HELEN,

A GRAND

Historical Ballet of Action,

IN TWO PARTS,

INTERSPERSED WITH

SONGS, DUETTS, and CHORUSES.

COMPOSED AND PRODUCED

By Mr. FARLEY.

The OVERTURE and the whole of the MUSICK
By Mr. DAVY.
The SCENERY designed by Mr. S. WHITMORE, and
Executed by Him and Assistants.
The MACHINERY by Messrs. RONALDSON and
GOOSETREE.
The DRESSES by Mr. BANKS, &c. &c.

LONDON:

Printed for the AUTHOR by T. WOODFALL,
No. 21, Villiers'-Street, Strand. And sold
in the Theatre.

Price Ten-pence.

RED ROY

Title page of the first known dramatic work based (extremely loosely) on the life of 'Robert Rouver MacGregor' known as 'Red Roy, the Robber,' performed in London in 1803

Copyright © British Library

ROB ROY TOPS THE BILL

Playbill for Isaac Pocock's play *Rob Roy MacGregor*, which was in production within weeks
of the publication of Sir Walter Scott's novel. Scott attended the first Edinburgh performance,
two days before the one advertised here (17 February 1819).

ROB ROY AT BAY

A still from the first feature film known to have been made in Scotland, in 1911.
John Clyde depicts a temporarily baffled hero, with fists clenched and expression defiant.

some major favour done not just to Rob but to the MacGregors in general by Ballindalloch, just months after the alleged Grant–MacGregor negotiations. It is therefore conceivable that some arrangement had indeed been discussed whereby the Grants would take the MacGregors under their wing as a sept of their clan, adopting the name Grant but retaining some identity. Yet the tale that the possibility of a MacGregor (Glencarnaig) becoming chief of an expanded Grant plan was discussed is not believable. It would have been so completely unacceptable to the Grants that it would not have been worth talking about.

If (and nothing can be proved) there were negotiations of some sort between the MacGregors and the Grants, Rob would have been an ideal negotiator, with his charisma, his existing friendship with the Grants, and his new-found (and distinctly part-time) identity as a servant of King George. What it was that Ballindalloch had done in 1726 that so pleased the MacGregors remains a mystery, but he was an excellently placed friend for Rob Roy. In the past he had profited from his connections with Finab's independent company. Now he had substituted Grant's. A passage in his letter to Grant about their Aberdeen meeting shows that Rob was already making himself useful. He had tracked down two of Breadalbane's tenants who had reset (received) cattle that bore the same brands as cattle stolen from Grant's country, and he had asked Breadalbane's chamberlain to investigate.

Rob's personality continued to impress. Lord Charles Murray (a brother of the first duke of Atholl) recounted a stranger's reaction to Rob in May 1726. A 'Mr Watson' was prejudiced against Rob, having heard of his misdeeds, and Murray was amused at his 'way of looking upon my introducing him to Rob Roy, whom he had a damnable ill opinion of, but I assure you now the derect contrary, for by God he's a jolly man, sais [says] he.'[23] Rob had retained the valuable knack of making friends out of enemies.

1726 was a peaceable year in the Highlands. Fury over the malt tax had waned, and Wade's military intervention was proving effective. In September Duncan Forbes of Culloden rejoiced that 'the last years madness is altogether cooled, and that the spirit of disaffection which formerly was very keen in this nighbourhood, has to my observation very much lost its edge. The Highlands are at present att rest, there is not the least complaint of robbery or depredations, and a great stick is become as fashionable an instrument in a Highlander's hand as a broad sword or pistols by his side, used formerly to be'.[24] Wade himself reported in April 1727 that the Highlands were 'in perfect peace'. The new independent companies were now all at their allotted stations.[25]

Under the surface, however, Jacobite plotting continued, and Rob Roy had a hand in it, in spite of his newly declared loyalty to King George. Late in 1726 he received a letter from a friend in Spain who was clearly a well-placed Jacobite exile who assumed that Rob was loyal to the cause. 'Dear Rob, At the writing of this I am drinking your health in good claret with extraordinary good company, and there is one of them who would be glad to see you.' In the allusive style of such conspiratorial letters, this means that an agent was being sent to Scotland and would contact Rob. The exile had written to Rob before, and promised to continue to serve his interests. 'I told you that our droving was going on extraordinary well. I have gotten you, with the assistance of some others of your friends here, to be one of our company's managers in the Highlands.' 'Droving' is the Jacobite plot in progress, the 'company' is the Jacobite cause. Rob is being promoted. But there is a warning. 'If you'l [you will] not manage to satisfaction, y'el [you will] not only ruin yourself, but also those who have acted for you.' Two gentlemen were being sent over 'from our company to your company' (from Spain to Scotland) and 'one of them is your own entire comrade, who has your instructions'. If Rob refuses to help the agents, 'my masters parks will be served without you'. Rob is being told that the Pretender can do without him: his 'pastures' (rewards) could be grazed by others instead of Rob. Finally, says the Spanish exile, 'be you sure to keep one thousand good noolt for me and I ashure you to take them off your hand on the first of August next'. The exile intended to be in Scotland by that date, and Rob would be rewarded with the price of a thousand cattle.[26]

Rob was in close touch with Campbell of Lochnell, who as captain of an independent company was keeping his hand on the Highland pulse, but he decided to remain silent for the moment as to the Jacobite plot. But he gave, perhaps deliberately, Lochnell one hint that he had knowledge of how events might develop. He told the captain that he was certain that Spain and Britain would soon be at war, and such a war lay at he heart of Jacobite plans, for it was believed that this would bring them Spanish help. That Highlanders were so keenly interested in war with Spain was something that Lochnell might have followed up, but he missed the point, and instead, as he thought there would be no war, he mocked Rob.

Rob was proved right. War began in February 1727 – and he immediately wrote to Lochnell from Balquhidder betraying the fact that he was in touch with Jacobites both in and travelling to Scotland. The timing of Rob's giving the government this intelligence suggests that he had been content to play a part in Jacobite conspiracy when it seemed fairly harmless. It kept him in touch, and helped him, like many others, to dream Jacobite dreams. But once Britain was at war with Spain the situation was entirely different. The sort of flirting with Jacobite exiles which government was usually prepared to turn a blind eye to would now be regarded as high treason; as conspiring with a foreign power in time of war. Rob was not ready to go back to a life on the run at the age of fifty-six and forfeit the pardon it had taken him so long to obtain.

Rob had three options. Firstly, he could have simply refused to take part in the Jacobite plot and simply remained silent about it. That, however, might have led to charges against him of failure to disclose information. Secondly, he could have just revealed what he knew. But Rob choose the third, the most duplicitous, option: he not only revealed the conspiracy but also eagerly volunteered to take the leading role in destroying it.

Two agents from the Pretender, Rob told Lochnell, had landed in England. One had travelled straight to the Highlands and Rob admitted meeting him and reading a letter he had brought to Rob from Spain – the letter discussed above (a copy of which he then sent to Lochnell) telling him that two more agents were to be dispatched. Rob had already received another letter, from 'a certain gentleman at London', asking him to supply intelligence to the government, and he was now prepared to do this. 'I am satisfied to go into any measures you please to propose to me only I may be safe, and not bring myself to any inconvenience thereby. If I'le engage in this affair, I'le go into it overhead and ears.'

First, 'I must go straight to the Highlands, and return again to meet the man that has stayed behind in England. He is ordered in his instructions to see me', and as he carried different instructions from those of the agent, Rob had already seen it was important to meet him. Next, money:

> If I were employed in this affair do you write to London for money:
> to defray the charges [expenses], for I am sure it will take a hundred

pounds sterling to do it. If I'le be concerned [employed] I will go through every inch of it. I could wish likewise to be so far ashured if I did the government good service in this affair, that I might promise to myself bread from them in the future, for I need not tell you my narrow circumstances occasioned by all the cross accidents and circumstances of my life.

'If I were encouraged to go in this affair, I'le engage under the penalty of loosing my life to get full intellegence of all the plots and projects they can contrive or imagine of landing in this nation, and likewise of any persons that will go into their measures,' by which Rob meant the two agents he was awaiting.[27]

Were a final nail was needed to seal the coffin of Rob Roy's reputation as Jacobite stalwart and man of honour, this letter is it. Desperation to serve and earn reward through betrayal is blatant. Being trusted as a Jacobite manager and being at the centre of a conspiracy had given him a valuable intelligence product to sell – and thus hopefully gain a secure financial future.

Further evidence of Jacobite plans was soon added to Rob Roy's – or possibly the source is still Rob himself, in anther guise. A letter to Lochnell 'from a Roman Catholick employed to procure intelligence' told of a Captain Sinclair of the Spanish navy, who was touring the western and northern coasts to find suitable landing places for an invasion by Spain. Four thousand men were to land in Scotland, eight thousand in England. The people of Breadalbane and 'a considerable body of Grahams' were ready to imprison Lochnell and his company as soon as they heard the Spanish fleet had sailed. Another agent, Captain Brown, had reached the Highlands from London.

General Wade acted swiftly, reinforcing garrisons and the independent companies. In addition, he resolved that it was

necessary to employ some proper person to observe the motions of Brown and Sinclair and to give an account of their proceedings. The person who seem'd to me the fittest for this purpose was R.R. who had then but very lately received his Majesty's pardon. He was an old acquaintance of Brown's, and believ'd by him to continue firm in the interests of the Pretender.

Rob was cautious, however, for he wanted there to be no doubt whatever that he had official permission to plot with Jacobites agents, and this was obtained from King George I himself. Rob's pay for his services was agreed at the £100 sterling he had requested.[28]

Rob was soon in the thick of the Jacobite plot. 'He gain'd such confidence with Brown as to be employ'd as his messenger with letters from him to some of the heads of clans.' Rob was submitting reports to Lochnell for transmission to Wade by March 1727, and by May he had met both Captain Sinclair and Brown and betrayed details of their activities. He travelled through the West Highlands delivering letters from Brown to chiefs it was hoped would agree to take part in a rebellion. Letters and copies of the instructions given to Rob by the conspirators, along with the names of the chiefs who had been approached and of Jacobites who had sheltered Brown, were all revealed by Rob, and he laid plans for Brown to be arrested at a time when he had letters from clan chiefs on him that would incriminate them.

Lochnell was at first suspicious that Rob 'might possibly be imposing on me' by providing fictitious information, but when Rob brought him the originals of papers, rather than just copies, he was persuaded that they were genuine, as they were 'wrote in a hand writing like a man of business, on gilt paper neatly folded'. They were too posh to be forgeries Rob had hastily concocted. He had, it seems, already been given £50 of the £100 promised, and Lochnell now gave him £25 more – and 'renew'd my assurances to him, that he will be put in a condition to live if he goes through with this service'.

There is no doubt that the information supplied by Rob was of great value to the government. In many ways it provided reassurance. While Brown had got in touch with a number of chiefs, they were mainly fairly minor figures. Brown made no contact, for example, with the men of Atholl, with the MacKenzies, the MacLeods, the Camerons or the Gordons, and few with the MacDonalds. Brown encouraged his contacts with assurances that the Pretender was well supplied with men, arms and money, but through Rob Roy's betrayal the army knew which Highlanders were actively 'disaffected' and which were not. The way in which the government's armed forces were distributed in Scotland was adjusted in the light of Rob's intelligence. The independent companies were placed where they seemed most likely to be needed – though not before some men were dismissed as their loyalty was suspected, and the rest took new oaths of allegiance to King George. Parties of soldiers were sent to the lands of suspect clans to carry out new searches for arms (only twenty muskets were discovered, hidden in a cave when Wade had been disarming the clans in 1725, and they were too rusty to have been used). Some of the suspect chiefs were interrogated, and rebuked by Wade for 'the folly and danger of listening to the ridiculous proposals of men whose fortunes were desperate [and] who had nothing to lose'.

By this time Jacobite dreams had again collapsed. The hoped-for Spanish invasion failed to materialise. Ironically, Brown become worried that Rob, his trusted friend, was in danger. There were stories circulating that orders had been given for his arrest. He should, therefore, make himself scarce. Brown urged: 'I wish you would take a trip to Arran to see your friend Bardowie.' John Hamilton of Bardowie, Rob's old cattle-trading partner and creditor, was by this time settled as the duke of Hamilton's baillie on the island of Arran. He was still regarded as Rob's friend, and as a man ready to give refuge to him when he believed him to be to be a Jacobite agent on the run. But Rob passed Brown's letter to General Wade, thus betraying Bardowie as well as everyone else. Rob might be very pleasant to meet, but as a friend he was not to be trusted.

Rob had betrayed a conspiracy which was going nowhere. Chiefs had, very sensibly, been unwilling to commit themselves in the absence of help from abroad, and Wade had warned them that he was watching every move they made (thanks to Rob's services). Brown and Captain Sinclair disappear back into the shadows of intrigue, though at least two Jacobites were arrested on Rob's evidence. James Stirling of Keir, fingered by Rob as one of the Pretender's leading agents in Scotland, was one of the very few men attainted for involvement in the '15 who had continued to live in Scotland and had refused the 1725 offer of pardon if he submitted. He had been left in peace, as no one had thought he was worth taking the trouble to arrest. But in August 1727, after Rob's intelligence had been received, he was seized on a charge of having let a messenger from the Pretender's court at Bologna stay in his house. He agreed to sue for a pardon and was freed in 1728.[29]

Keir may not have known who had betrayed him, but Rob's activities soon became known in Jacobite circles. A letter to Drummond of Balhaldie in February 1728 referred to 'honest John Fraser', who had been imprisoned for a time in Edinburgh Castle. 'For ought I can learn this piece of great service has been done by your friend R.R.'[30]

Allegations that in earlier years (1715–16) Rob had supplied intelligence to the enemies of the Stuart cause have in the past been explained away as not being betrayal but a sort of insurance, a leaking of unimportant information to secure himself from Hanoverian persecution. Such interpretations have been based on blind faith that treachery was not in his character. The evidence of his activities in 1727 shows how dangerous it is to indulge in special pleading. The main sources (cited above) that prove that he was a highly effective Hanoverian spy were published over a century ago, in a well-known collection of papers relating to the Jacobites. But those writing on Rob have somehow managed to overlook them. No one has wanted to accept that Rob played the role of double-agent with skill and enthusiasm. Yet academic historians *not* writing specifically on Rob Roy have had no difficulty in picking up the evidence of Rob's treachery, and have mentioned it in passing. Rob was letting 'Wade know what was going on' in return for cash payments.[31] Rob was Wade's 'super-grass'.[32] The Rev. John MacIntosh in the later nineteenth century was even more crushing about Rob. 'Now-a-days the man would be called among other things a thief and a police stooge prepared to sell anyone.[33] In 1715 his double-dealing in supplying evidence to the Hanoverians could be partly explained by the fact that he was a desperate man, on the run and under intense pressure. In 1727 he was a free man with a royal pardon in his pocket, selling intelligence simply for money.

Outwardly Rob looked a fine example of the reformed Highlander that official policy was seeking to create – once a rebel and cattle thief, now a government agent who contributed sons to serve the state in the independent companies. In June 1729 Rob delivered two 'very noted theives' to Graham of Killearn at Craigrostan, so he even cooperated with his old enemy, Montrose's agent, on land that had once been his own. Typically, however, when Killearn ordered the men to be sent to the regality prison at Mugdock, they were allowed to escape. Equally typically, Killearn was rather relieved. He could not have set a bad example by freeing them himself, but he had not wanted to go to the trouble of holding a trial.[34]

Rob the good subject doing his duty. It was too good to be true. Appearances soon proved deceptive. Rob, now approaching sixty, may no longer have been directly involved in the lifting of cattle, but as before his pardon he presided over a family enterprise. He and his sons were unable to resist the temptation and excitement – and financial gain – of the illicit. The conduct of his two sons who were soldiers in independent companies (Coll in Campbell of Lochnell's company, James in Campbell of Carrick's) is an excellent demonstration of the problem that in the Highlands it was often impossible to tell law enforcers and law breakers apart.[35]

Even while Wade was employing Rob as an agent in 1727 evidence was accumulating against him and his family. John Campbell of Achallader, acting for Lord Glenorchy, had persuaded 'McCalpan', a former servant of Rob, to inform against him. The triumphant Achallader set up a meeting in September 1729 with Lochnell and his two lieutenants, and confronted Rob with the evidence against him and his two sons Coll and James. MacCalpan described how he and another servant had been ordered by Coll (who was also present at this confrontation) to steal two oxen from MacLaren, a drover. The owner's marks, burnt on the horns, had then been erased, and the cattle incorporated in a small herd Rob was selling to Lord John Drummond.

Rob responded to interrogation with indignant denial. He had not sold any black cattle to Drummond or any of his family for seven years past – and, he asserted, if anyone could prove the contrary, then he would be content to be held guilty of all the charges made against him. McCalpan alleged that he had helped Rob's son James steal two horses from Glenorchy's lands. Rob again responded with righteous denial. His son James was the most honest man of his name, except one (the exception, no doubt, being Rob himself), and anyway when the horses had been stolen James had been stationed with his company in Stirling. Rob repeated his rhetorical challenge. If any of the points he had made in clearing himself and his sons of the charges against them could be disproved, he would admit all charges against him. If his evidence rebutting the charges proved true – and he was confident Lord Drummond and James's commanding officer, Campbell of Carrick, would support him – all charges against him should be dropped.

Rob's accusers tried again. Coll as well as James had been involved in dealing in stolen horses. Here the evidence proved overwhelming, and Rob adroitly changed tack. Stealing a few horses was merely 'the fooly of youth'. Boys will be boys, was his attitude, and it was not a matter to be taken seriously. Achallader was not so understanding. He wanted Rob and his two sons to be 'carryd in a string' (tied together) and sent to General Wade for severe punishment. But Lochnell evidently decided not to make too much of a fuss. The stealing of a few cows and horses, without violence, might be regrettable, but it was not worth upsetting the precarious order established in the region by making a great to-do about it. Rob was a valuable agent who might be lost if his sons were punished. The meeting ended inconclusively, with only Achallader determined to take matters further. He quickly discovered – as all those present at the meeting must have suspected – that Rob had been lying his head off while giving evidence. Drummond confirmed that he had bought cattle from Rob two years before – just at the time Coll was alleged to have stolen two from a drover. And Carrick confirmed from Stirling that the previous April, the time when James had been alleged to be involved in horse stealing, he had not been in Stirling – he had been away from his company for a month.[36]

The episode is classic Rob Roy – the fierce denials, the passionate indignation at his word being doubted, the torrent of plausible lies. His verbal assault on his sons' accusers was not only furious but skilful. He denied all that he knew could not be proved by witnesses present at the meeting, and minimised the significance of what could be proved. He was fighting to gain delay. In time witnesses would be found to expose his lies, but in the meantime Rob could slip away to meet General Wade, and he seems to have got his assurance that no further action would be taken. Rob was too important an intelligence asset to endanger through insistence on enforcing the law in a trivial matter. Achallader fumed. Cattle were stolen and nothing was done. Folk dared not complain of them being stolen, or even look for them 'least a worse thing befall them'. They were so used to being oppressed by thieves 'that they bear the yoke with ease'. General Wade should have Rob and his like transported to the colonies. If he sent 'these fformidable enemies to society to some distant world' this would win him the general praise in the present age 'as the roads will doe to futurity'. There is sour perspicacity here. Wade's Highland road-building programme was in its early stages, but already Achallader saw it would bring the general fame, though he resented the fact that it seemed to distract him from doing justice on cattle thieves. Meanwhile, Rob 'kept close in his den' until he was sure the fuss had died down.[37]

He was not, however, cowed. A report to Breadalbane in January 1730 laments that Rob Roy and his gang were beginning to infest the country.[38] But with his usual deftness, Rob yet again persuaded one nobleman to support him while he preyed on the estates of his neighbour. A very incoherent letter of August 1730 refers to the duke of Atholl as 'having much att heart the supporting of Rob Roy in his quarrel twixt him and the Broadalaben people'. Meetings were arranged, with Glengyle and Lord John Drummond involved in complex negotiations, but the outcome is unclear.[39] Scattered fragments of evidence point to continuing troubles in the years that followed. A 1731 letter to Atholl refers with frustrating imprecision to 'that affair of Rob Roy's'. 'There is no way of discovering a knave but by a knave. I am convinced Rob is heartie enough in it just now' – presumably meaning that Rob is heavily involved in knavery.[40] Donald Bayne MacNaughton, 'Rob Roy's man', spent a week in Breadalbane's prison in Killin in mid-1731, and Rob entered a protest about wrongful imprisonment.[41] In 1732 a son of Rob was imprisoned by Breadalbane's men.[42] In November of the same year a tenant who had taken over a farm that a kinsman of Rob's had wanted to lease had his two barns, full of corn and hay from the harvest, burnt down. Rob's son Ranald and others were suspected of the crime, and it was said that warnings had been given that any tenant other than Rob's choice that took the lease 'would incur Rob's displeasure'.[43]

It has been alleged that in 1732 Rob's sons James and Ranald went beyond matters of petty theft by playing a part in the kidnapping of Lady Grange. Lord Grange, a judge, was a brother of the Jacobite commander of the '15, the earl of Mar, but was himself a staunch Hanoverian – outwardly at least. He married Rachel Chiesley, a strange choice of partner as her father had murdered the president of the court of session. She evidently inherited his mental instability – or at least, she was determined and strong-minded. She was said to have been proud, violent and jealous, and wanted to live separately from her husband. Worse, she talked of denouncing him for treason, because of contacts he had with Jacobites. Lord Grange decided on a remedy occasionally employed to deal with women deemed impossible by their menfolk. She would be carried off to some remote spot and kept prisoner there. That Highland Jacobites were ready to cooperate in the plan gives some credibility to the claim that she knew more than was safe of their plottings. Lady Grange duly disappeared, and her husband declared that she had died. On her way to the West Highlands she was taken through Balquhidder, and spent a night there, her captors being a gang led by Walter Buchanan of Auchmar which included Rob Roy's sons James and Ranald. How far they took her on her journey is not known, but she ended up on St Kilda, the most remote of Scottish islands. On its rocky crags she was kept for seven years. Eventually she was allowed to move to Assynt, then to Skye, where she died in 1745 without ever seeing her native Lowlands again. The story of her fate did not emerge until many years after her death, and the part said to have been played in her imprisonment by Rob Roy's family remains unproved – there must be a suspicion that some writer has decided it would be neat to link up the notorious kidnapping with Rob's incorrigible family.[44]

In 1734 the indefatigable Achallader was still hunting for evidence against them. A breakthrough came when he captured Grigor Roy 'a famous rogue', who confessed that he had given two stolen cows to Rob's son James, and two to 'Rob Roy's clark'.[45] Bewilderment is in order. Why did Rob Roy have a clerk? Most of his business transactions were not of the kind that it was wise to commit to writing. There may be a clue to an answer in the letters written by Edmund Burt, an English official in the Highlands in the 1720s. Burt recorded much of the detail of ordinary life in the Highlands – though not always with full understanding and without bias. At one point he mentions the 'hanchman'. 'This officer, is a sort of secretary, and is to be ready, upon all occasions, to venture his life in defence of his master; at his haunch, (from whence his title is derived), and watches the conversation, to see if any one offends his patron.' Thus the hanchman – a variant of 'henchman' – was a personal attendant, and later Burt conflates him with a gillie.[46] A man's henchman/gillie presumably called a 'secretary' because he was a confidant who had knowledge of his master's personal affairs. A 'secretary' was a man who knew 'secrets'. This makes it plausible to argue that Achallader, translating henchman as secretary, has then modified it to clerk. Rob's henchman/clerk would have been an important figure in his little entourage, worthy of a gift of two stolen cows. Another 'official' alleged to have been in Rob's retinue was Alexander Stewart, 'the baillie'. He, it was said, was responsible for swearing men to secrecy when necessary as to Rob's movements or plans, thus justifying his legalistic designation. In the 1720s Edmund Burt described (as Wade did in his 1725 report) how cattle-raiders took oaths from their men never to inform on each other or take reward for recovering stolen cattle, the oaths being sealed by kissing a drawn dirk, the symbol of the fate that awaited a man who broke the oath. In addition, the baillie was responsible for taking oaths from prisoners that they would never pursue Rob again, as a condition of their release.[47]

Achallader, armed with Gregor Roy's evidence, was keen to prosecute

Rob's son James, but as before he met military opposition. Colonel Campbell – presumably Carrick, James's company commander – took custody of Gregor Roy, the thief and key witness to the fact that James was a receiver of stolen cattle, and then let him escape. He then declared that it would be impossible to prosecute James, a mere receiver, as the thief had not been prosecuted! But Achallader added darkly 'this I presume is nothing but a faint to screen James whose Christian profession of Popery is lyke to save him from the gallows'.[48] Rob Roy and his family, long reliant on the patronage of the Catholic Drummonds, had by this time converted to that religion, and the Drummonds were still powerful enough to protect their co-religionists. Like many Highlanders Rob was probably little interested in the squabbles of theologians over dogma and church government. In his childhood the church he had been brought up in was the Church of Scotland in one of its Episcopalian phases. In 1690 it had switched to Presbyterianism, which to Rob would have made little difference in practice but for the fact that it was fiercely hostile to the dethroned Stuarts. His sympathies therefore remained Episcopalian – though this would not have prevented him from continuing to accept the ministrations of nominally Presbyterian ministers. The same was probably true even after the family accepted Catholicism. Once the family, including (probably at the end of his life) Rob Roy himself, took the name Drummond, a natural next step was to conform to their patrons in religion.[49] Story names the priest who heard Rob Roy's first confession, at Drummond Castle, as Alexander Drummond – and makes much of how much Rob had to confess, and how delighted he was by his new church as it could absolve all his sins.[50] An anti-Catholic propaganda slant is thus given to the tale.

Catholic though he had now become, Rob had no hesitation in turning to an Episcopalian historian for a sympathetic account of Scotland's past – one which might not be Catholic in bias, but was certainly anti-Presbyterian and pro-Stuart. Bishop Robert Keith's *History of the Affairs of Church and State in Scotland from the beginning of the Reformation in the Reign of James V* was published in 1734, and listed among the subscribers were both MacGregor of Glengyle and 'Robert Macgregor, *alias* Rob Roy' – both men defiantly using the banned name MacGregor. Whether Rob was able to see his name in print as a sponsor of literature before he died is unknown, but it is a demonstration of how to the end he was a man who produced surprises. Finding him in the role of literary patron requires some adjustment of stereotypes of Rob the wild Highlander.

Rob's first and second sons, Coll and James, combined their posts as soldiers in independent companies with theft. His third and fourth, Ranald and Rob Og, thieved without the support of government salaries. One of their victims was Eupham Fergusson, a woman in her twenties who lived in Glenample. Two horses were stolen from her in 1733, and she soon found that it was well known that Ranald and Rob Og had lifted them. With bold determination she made her way to Rob Roy's house in Balquhidder, doubtless encouraged by knowledge that he was known, within limits, to be well disposed towards poor folk who sought his help. Ranald promised to pay her for the stolen animals, but then failed to do so – telling her to inform his father that he had paid her £19 Scots. Clearly Ranald was trying to bully her into saying the matter was settled, but she thought Rob would take her side. She told him what had happened, and he gave her fifteen shillings sterling, and later sent her ten more – a total of £15 Scots.[51] Here we have a tale of Rob the kindly bandit that must persuade the most sceptical of historians. It rests not on tales told much later of people unknown by name, but on the testimony of Eupham herself, given under oath in the justiciary court in Edinburgh. It is true that she was giving evidence for the prosecution in a case against Ranald – but she had no motive for inventing the information she gave about Rob's good deed.

In Rob's last years, the early 1730s, an old friend in exile recalled him with affection. William Drummond was of the Drummond of Perth kin, and (presumably through Catholic and Jacobite beliefs) he was serving as an officer in the Spanish army. Possibly it was he who had approached Rob in 1728 to act as a Jacobite 'manager'. In July 1730 he was in Barcelona, about to embark for Italy. That many of his men were fellow-Scots exiles seems implied by his comment in a letter to his brother and sister that 'there will goe many bonnets to the green'. Thinking of home, he added 'Pray let me know what become of Rob Roy my friend and Walter Macfarland, the true representative of the king of diamonds.' Walter MacFarlane of Arrochar was a noted antiquarian and genealogist; the king of diamonds was presumably code for the Pretender.[52]

Three years later, in October 1733, William Drummond again mentioned Rob Roy. He was stationed in Majorca, in a senior enough position to be commissioned to sort out the bad administration of the island. And he wanted, of all things, a piper. 'You may cause my father send to Rob Roy and offer him my humble services and tell him to get me a handsome fellow of a Highland piper and embark him in the first ship that comes to any port of the Mediterranean, bringing along with him his full accoutrements and flags with my lord duke of Perthe's armes with his armes compleat.' Drummond had, he explained, promised the viceroy of Catalonia that he would produce a Highland piper, and the viceroy was getting angry that one had not arrived yet. 'The fellow will make his fortune,' Drummond promised.[53] Did this strange commission ever reach Rob Roy? Was a piper with full regalia dispatched to strut and sweat in his plaid under the Mediterranean sun to amuse a bored Spanish grandee?

Rob had more pressing matters to deal with in his last years than reading histories or recruiting pipers. He was still locked in conflict over the occupation of land in the Braes of Balquhidder. His family was under pressure in the western Braes, where the Glencarnaig family was dominant. The Murrays of Atholl had little reason to favour Rob, and the violence with which Rob in the 1720s had tried to maintain his influence over lands claimed by Glencarnaig had gained him the enmity of that thriving family. Rob's two eldest sons had not found land in the disputed area, and had had to move to areas owned by the Drummonds of Perth to gain leases (Coll in the Kirkton of Balquhidder – it is said – and James in Glen Dochart). In 1732 Rob himself gained the lease of a holding in the Kirkton for his third son – but did so in a manner that led to a bitter feud in which his branch of the MacGregors was faced by the hostility of the other two most numerous names in the area, the MacLarens and the Stewarts.

A sister of Rob Roy's had married a MacLaren who held land in the Kirkton. Her husband died while their son John was still a child, and Rob Roy had been entrusted with the management of his affairs. Rob so managed matters that he and his third son Ranald emerged as the possessors of a lease of the land.[54] It had been arranged that Ranald would marry his cousin, Jean, a daughter of Glengyle,[55] so it was time for him to have a farm of his own. But the MacLarens regarded this as a betrayal of trust – Rob had used his control of young John's affairs to steal his lands. In fact by the date the lease was signed it seems clear that John was already an adult, for he was leasing land elsewhere in Balquhidder. It could be argued, therefore, that Rob's responsibility for protecting John MacLaren's interests had lapsed, and that there was no reason why he should not have used his friendship with the Drummonds to gain a lease of the lands. But the MacLarens had held the land for generations, and were not ready to give it up without a fight, maintaining that it was theirs by right and that Rob had swindled his nephew.

In one sense Rob's betrayal of his nephew paid off. His son Ranald was to retain his possession of the Kirkton land involved for over half a century. But the reactions of the MacLarens and others to what Rob had done were to make his last years a misery. Moreover, though Rob had the advantage of Drummond patronage and had taken that name, this alienated the Murrays of Atholl, while the family of Rob's rival, Glencarnaig, basked in Murray favour. Both Rob and Glencarnaig had become Campbells when the name MacGregor had been proscribed, but just as Rob's family eventually became Drummonds so Glencarnaig's became Murrays. It was as 'Robert Murray' that Glencarnaig's son Robert became baillie for the duke of Atholl in Balquhidder in 1731.[56]

By 1732, when he lost his holding in the Kirkton, John MacLaren had already gained leases of Wester Invernenty and Drumlich, a farm adjacent to Rob Roy's farm of Inverlochlarig Beg. These were lands over which Rob had formerly had influence, and it is possible that he regarded his out-manoeuvring his nephew in the Kirkton as a retaliation for perceived MacLaren aggression. That MacLaren was nicknamed 'Baron Stoibchon' (after Stob a' Choin, a mountain lying just south of Drumlich) may be an indication that he was recognised as a man of ambition. Rob had pulled a fast one on him in the Kirkton. MacLaren resolved to do the same to Rob.

The lease of Inverlochlarig Beg was due to expire at Martinmas 1732. Rob Roy was not offered a chance of renewing it. Instead a new lease was granted to John MacLaren. Considered in isolation from the personalities involved, such a change of tenant was not unusual. There was an existing tendency for farms in the area to be joined together, consolidated into larger units, and MacLaren already held neighbouring land. But in the circumstances it created a potentially explosive situation. The move to evict Rob Roy must have been authorised at a higher level, probably by Robert Murray younger of Glencarnaig as Atholl's baillie. But what John MacLaren really wanted was his old family holding in the Kirkton back, so he offered a compromise. If Rob and Ranald would surrender their tenancy there to him, then Rob could have the lease of Inverlochlarig Beg back. Conflict could be ended by an agreed exchange of territory. If this was not possible, Rob and his wife and youngest son, Rob Og, would be left landless.

The written evidence about the dispute, from which this account of it has been pieced together, only emerged after Rob's death,[57] and much remains obscure – especially what the relevant landlords thought of their tenants discussing an exchange of leases. Perhaps an exchange proved impossible to arrange, or perhaps Rob remained defiant. He remained in possession of Inverlochlarig Beg for the remaining two years of his life in defiance of MacLaren's lease, and sought to confirm his possession through resort to arms. Evidence of what happened is only preserved in tradition, and the accounts of events are often contradictory. However, the stories all have some points in common. Rob Roy fought a duel with a Stewart, and lost. Sir Walter Scott heard that the dispute was primarily over Wester Invernenty, which Rob claimed the MacGregors had a right to, and it is likely that the dispute was over more than just the right to Inverlochlarig Beg.

Rob gathered his MacGregor supporters near the Kirkton to settle the issue by force, but the MacLarens outnumbered him, for as well as having the support of Balquhidder Stewarts they had allies in the Stewarts of Appin. Two hundred Appin men were mustered. When the rival forces confronted each other Rob Roy backed down. He was old, and the number of men who had rallied to his call was inadequate for the task in hand. Indeed there had never really been a chance of a full-scale clan battle – the Highlands had not seen such a thing for over half a century – but rather a posturing display of rival forces, in which Rob was clearly the loser.

Rob's humiliation can be imagined. Eviction threatened. But he made a last gesture. He would fight a duel, with whoever his opponents chose to represent them. He must have known that he would lose, given his age, but physical risk was limited, as Highland duels were not 'to the death' but settled by the first drawing of blood. 'In fighting [a Highlander] think he wins the day that gives [inflicts] the first wound.'[58] For Rob a duel, even if lost, would preserve his honour. He would at least have fought for his cause, before limping off-stage. Alexander Stewart of Invernahyle, Stewart of Appin's brother-in-law, was chosen to fight Rob – or perhaps it was Appin himself. Even though Sir Walter Scott had got the story directly from

Invernahayle, by the time he recorded it he could not remember which man had fought.[59]

A different account is certain that it was Invernahayle who fought Rob. The young man, not surprisingly, prevailed over the ageing Rob, and the wound he inflicted 'caused Rob Roy's death'.[60] Yet another tale introduces a third candidate as having been Rob's opponent, claiming the duel resulted from a personal quarrel, not a land dispute. Charles Stewart of Ardsheal and David Stewart of Glenbuckie were travelling north, and stopped for the night at Kirkton of Balquhidder. Rob Roy came to the inn to pass the time with them. When they were 'warm with drink' and Rob 'had taken a hearty quantity of the whisky', he tactlessly remarked to Ardsheal that at the battle of Sheriffmuir the Stewarts of Appin had behaved badly 'It was shameful how you people fled.' He got a predictable response 'The people of Appin did better than you did that day. They went to the battle; but it was to the sheep-fold you went that day to sort your wethers.' A deep insult.

After a few more taunts by Rob – 'Well, Charles, although you are a big lump of a man, if you are not a better soldier than your father you are not much' – a duel was arranged for dawn. Rob cunningly took up position so his opponent would be looking into the rising sun. He did well at first, but then Ardsheal nicked Rob's ear. Rob's sword point 'took a trickle of blood' from Ardsheal's face, before Ardsheal's sword cut Rob 'under the chin and cut him to the throat and Rob conceded, sticking his sword in the ground'. Rob declared 'You have the maidenhead of my blood', to which Ardsheal replied that it was nothing he'd boast about, 'old fellow'. 'Too much whisky and unseemly language', Rob moralised about the incident. Very gentlemanly, Victorian style (at least in this translation from the Gaelic). Not long afterwards Rob died, after telling his sons not to blame Ardsheal for what had happened.[61] Yet another telling of the story has it that it was Rob (not his opponent) who suffered from having the sun in his eyes, as well as having the disadvantage of having stayed up all night drinking whereas his opponent had had a good night's sleep.[62]

How long there was between the duel and Rob's death, and whether the former contributed to the latter, is unknown. Certainly he was ill for some time before he died, for his widow was to note 'medicines and other necessaries during his sickness' among her expenses.[63] Later tales told of his being on his death-bed when an old enemy called to see him. Rob insisted on rising from his bed and being dressed and fully armed before he received his guest. If the visitor was, as is sometimes said, John MacLaren, then the atmosphere would have been tense, with the man wishing the patient well also being the man who was seeking to evict him from his farm.[64] Defiant gesture made, Rob died. A different deathbed scene is recounted in another anecdote. Rob was asked if he wanted extreme unction, the Catholic sacrament which involved a priest annointing the dying with oil. Rob 'said it was, he thought, a great waste of oil'.[65] Both versions are entertaining, but their veracity is doubtful.

Rob Roy died at Inverlochlarig Beg on 28 December 1734. For some this must have been good news, not least John Campbell of Achallader, Breadalbane's chamberlain, who had so often been infuriated by Rob's antics. He heard of Rob's death on 31 December and immediately dispatched an express messenger to Edinburgh with the news.[66] Perhaps this was how the *Caledonian Mercury* was able to carry an announcement of the death to a wider public on 9 January 1735. Rob Roy 'the famed Highland partizan' was dead.[67] In England, the *Gentleman's Magazine* also announced his death – though getting its date wrong. There he appeared as 'Rob Roy, the famous Scots Highlander'.[68] But though Rob's death was noted no account of its circumstances was given. Rob Roy was old news, a name from the past. The fact that he had died in his bed, however, aroused a wry comment:

> Keppoch, Rob Roy, and Daniel Murchisan,
> Cadets or servants to some chief of clan,
> From theft and robberies scarce did ever cease,
> Yet 'scaped the halter each, and died in peace.[69]

If custom was followed, Rob's death would have been the occasion for a 'lyke' or wake, with many gathering to pay their respects to his body. Music would play (though not the pipes) and people would dance 'as if at a wedding,' as a puzzled Englishman noted, with the widow leading the first dance. Much drink would be taken. Women would have performed the traditional keening – wailing or singing over the dead, perhaps with specialists from other parishes brought in to lead them. In the funeral procession women would again have cried their laments, 'and when they have done, the piper plays after the corps with his great pipe'. At the graveside, the women would have renewed their keening, then widened their mourning with a song for all their dead friends who lay in the graveyard.[70] Another account of Highland funerals (which also emphasises the 'fearfull owleing [howling] and scrieching and crying with very bitter lamentation' of the women) adds that there would be 'a compleat narration of the descent of the dead person, with the valourous acts of himself and his predecessors sung with tune in measure, continuall piping if the person was of any quality or professing arms'.[71]

As Rob's coffin was carried to the gave, according to Ramsay of Ochtertyre, the pipers played the tune, 'Chatill Mha Luille' that is 'In peace nor war shall thou ever return'. This can be identifies as 'MacCrimmon's Lament', still regarded as one of the greatest of pipe tunes. Words set to the tune have the haunting refrain

No more, no more, no more returning,
In peace nor in war is he returning;
Till dawns the great Day of Doom and burning,
MacCrimmon is home no more returning.[72]

A man is due respect at his funeral. Cold analysis long after the event may suggest that Rob Roy got a nobler send-off than he deserved, but to his friends and relatives MacCrimmon's powerful lament was fully appropriate for a man who had been much loved and admired, whatever his faults. He was surely not a man who needed to fear being sent to Hell at the Last Judgment. He would argue his case so convincingly, his charm and sincerity being deployed so persuasively, that Salvation would be his.

It was later said that Rob Roy's was the last funeral in Highland Perthshire at which a piper played, though this seems a bit too neatly symbolic of Rob's death marking the end of a cultural era to be literal truth.[73]

The burial took place in the kirkyard at Balquhidder. Later, three centuries-old engraved tombstones were reused to mark his grave and those of his wife and two of his sons. Much later still, a minister of uncharitable disposition was to remark, with humorous nastiness, on the appropriateness of this. Rob Roy had even stolen a tombstone for himself.[74]

In time, his native Gaelic tongue provided him with a long Gaelic epitaph, *Marbhrann do Rob Ruadh MacGriogair*. The conventions of the Gaelic epitaph, full of hyperbolic praise so unreal that it could, in translation, be misread by the modern ear as sarcastic rather than sincere, mean that it is of limited use to the historian. However, its description of Rob as a man familiar with two worlds, symbolised by their dress codes, is worth repeating. In plaid and sword he was a man of the Highlands, but he could also conform to Lowland ways, wearing a hat and fine cloak. The observation that 'You were not soft in the front of battle' is unfortunate, as he never fought in any battle. Perhaps the term could be extended to obscure skirmishes, but mention of his being backed by a thousand swords is poetic fantasy.[75] More prosaically, an inventory of Rob's goods at the time of his death reveals the stock of his little farm – thirteen cows, fourteen sheep, twenty-three goats, seven pigs, five horses (one of them blind), and a little corn and hay.[76] But of course his legacy was not to be his material goods, but his life and legend.

11
OUT OF ORDER

Nor have we attempted curiously to fix the dates of a series of exploits, when, for aught we know, the very substance of them may be the work of the imagination.[1]

Rob has died and been buried. But surely a lot has been left out in the account given of his life? Readers who have previously taken an interest in Rob Roy may be feeling bewildered, frustrated or cheated. Rob has been followed from birth to death, but many well-known incidents are missing.

The problem is that there are a huge number of stories about Rob Roy that only emerge long after his death and are not supported by any contemporary evidence. This is not to say that they are *all* fictitious, though certainly many of them are. But which are fictitious and which are not is often impossible to say. To complicate matters, such stories almost never supply dates as to when they are supposed to have happened, so it is impossible to fit them into a chronological framework of Rob's life. Rob was to achieve legendary, even heroic status, and heroes often become timeless. Dates and order of events become unimportant, and demands to know if they are factually true can seem irrelevant. Even if proved untrue in a literal sense, they still can have value simply as stories, or as indicators of Rob Roy's reputation. Nonetheless, an attempt to assess at least some of them as 'historical evidence' is worthwhile.

Some assessment can be made of credibility in terms of common sense and contexts. Overall the corpus of stories about Rob presents him as making an quite implausible number of daring escapes, and fighting an unbelievable number of duels. Sir Walter Scott fully recognised the problem two centuries ago. There were a great many anecdotes about Rob 'but they are generally speaking so improbable in themselves, and told with so many contradictions by the different narrators, that it is almost impossible to discover whereabouts truth lies in the mass of conflicting absurdities'.[2] These problems explain why this chapter is titled 'Out of Order'. This mix of tales, fantasies and glimmers of truth cannot be put in order, because it is usually uncertain whether they happened at all, and, if so, in what order.

Take one of the best-known tales, that of Rob's escape after his capture by his mortal enemy, the duke of Montrose. All precautions were being taken to prevent the escape of this notoriously slippery customer. He was disarmed, and mounted on horseback behind one of Montrose's men, to whom he was tied with a leather belt. But while being carried off to prison he persuaded the soldier to release the belt (or somehow cut it himself). When a river was being crossed at a ford, he slipped off the back of the horse into the river and escaped, swimming underwater but letting his plaid float off on the surface to provide a decoy for his pursuers to fire at. It's a good story, and it might at first seem plausible. Rob was a daring man, and proved impossible to capture and hold. His suborning of Montrose's man fits in nicely with other evidence that one of his main assets was his skill at wheedling and persuading. Moreover, Sir Walter Scott collected a version of the story from the grandson of the man who supposedly let Rob escape, James Stewart. When Stewart reached the river bank and Montrose realised that the prisoner had escaped, the duke hit him over the head with his heavy steel pistol, a blow from which Stewart never fully recovered.[3]

However, there are several insurmountable 'buts' about the story. Firstly, Montrose never took part personally 'on the ground' in a hunt for Rob Roy. He was far too great a man to get his hands dirty messing about riding round the Highlands trying to track Rob down. He gave orders to Graham of Gorthie, his chamberlain, who passed them on to Graham of Killearn, his factor, who in turn often gave instructions to underlings to get on with the job. The idea of the duke in person trying to catch the outlaw is flattering to Rob, but would have astonished both him and the duke. Secondly, as an objection to the story, sometimes placenames are mentioned in it. They locate Rob's capture in Balquhidder. But Balquhidder was deep in the duke of Atholl's regality of Atholl, and in Perthshire, of which Atholl was sheriff. The idea of Montrose, or even a posse of Montrose's men without the duke himself being present, marching into Atholl's jurisdiction, taking a prisoner and carrying him off, is beyond belief. Further, if the incident had taken place, there would have been a huge fuss, but there is no trace of it in contemporary evidence. Correspondence in the Montrose archives records in detail Rob's misdeeds, and attempts to capture him. It was at times a matter of high priority and urgency. Had Rob ever been captured by Montrose's men and then escaped there would have been a sudden spate of letters, first triumphant, then furious – as happened during Rob's one verifiable capture and escape, from the duke of Atholl in 1717. On what would have been a dramatic and controversial incident, the written record is utterly silent.

Other stories also make the same mistake of assuming that Rob's great enemies pursued him personally. The duke of Atholl captured him at Monachayle Tuarach deep in Balquhidder, but when the party was passing through a defile he escaped by throwing himself off his horse, and disappeared up a wooded hillside.[4] This sounds like a version of the 'escape into the river' story, with one duke substituted for another, escape by wood for escape by water. Alternatively, Atholl tried to seize Rob at his mother's funeral. Rob drew his sword, and the duke fired his pistol at him. Rob slipped and fell to the ground, and his sister (the 'Lady of Glenfalloch') thought he had been shot. She wrestled the duke to the ground – and would have strangled him if Rob had not pulled her off.[4] Such personal confrontations between Rob and his great opponents make better stories of derring-do than skirmishes with their servants. The only time during his hunted years that Rob came face to face with a hostile duke was at Dunkeld in 1717, when Rob came to Atholl's house – and even then the hostility was a matter of pretence.

Another type of tale makes Rob not only humiliate great men by escaping from capture, but threaten them face to face, forcing them to do his will. A MacGregor kinsman had been unjustly deprived of a tenancy on the Perth estate, so Rob burst into Drummond Castle and bullied the Lord Drummond into restoring the lease.[6] But an earlier variant of the story says that Rob beat up the factor to get the lease renewed.[7] Inflation may be suspected, a possible real confrontation with a factor turned into a face to face defying of his noble master. Another of these stories relates that Rob was on the run and he and his men built houses for themselves at the head of Loch Fyne. He then went nonchalantly to the duke of Argyll and told him of this as a *fait accompli*.[8] This obviously refers to the house the duke let Rob have at Benbuy in Glen Shira, but the incident has been turned from a favour by the duke into something Rob did through his own power and made the duke accept. Rather similar is the tale that Montrose tried to put pressure on Argyll to expel Rob from his territory. But Rob pointed out that though Argyll gave him lodging, he got his living (through raiding) from Montrose.[9] What Rob gets from the dukes he is taking for himself, and they have no control over it. The theme of the small man successfully defying the great has an appeal in any age.

Stories depicting Rob threatening or kidnapping lesser men have rather greater plausibility. He had after all carried off John MacLachlan in 1715, and kidnapped Killearn in 1716. In getting his levies of blackmail paid he must at times have had to lean hard on the reluctant. Rob, it is said, had a regular day at Doune for collecting blackmail. Henderson of Westerton refused to pay, and was carried off by Rob's men. But they had to stop for the night and he supplied them generously with liquor. After they were sound asleep he managed to make his escape.[10] Garden Castle (near Kippen) was occupied by Rob because Stirling of Garden had refused to pay blackmail. Rob seized a child from the nursery, ran to the top of a tower and threatened to throw the child over the battlements unless Garden paid up.[11] Yet again, Campbell of Aberuchil failed to pay until Rob broke into his castle and forced him to pay his due.[12] This last incident may echo the raids by Rob and his brother John on Aberuchil's lands in 1691, but it is hard not to feel that, as Rob's legend grew, anyone within the limits of his raiding wanted to have a family story about him. 'Heritage' of this sort became fashionable.

One of the most elaborate of these family traditions relates to the Aberdeen family of Gregory. Rob Roy was sent during the '15 rising to recruit men from among scattered descendants of the MacGregors in north east Scotland. In Aberdeen Rob met Dr James Gregory (who, as his name suggests, was descended from MacGregors), a physician who was later to become professor of medicine at King's College, Aberdeen. Rob took a fancy to Gregory's young son, also James, and offered to take him away to bring him up in the Highlands, but his father politely declined the offer as the boy was too young.[13] The story seems inherently unlikely – apart from anything else, Rob proposing to take a child into his care when recruiting for a rebellion would have been peculiar. Even to have bothered to drop in for a chat with Dr Gregory, an extremely distant kinsman, would have been surprising when recruiting was an urgent matter if the rebellion were to have credibility. Finally, it is impossible to fit a 1715 visit to Aberdeen in with Rob's known movements. The story also tells of a later encounter between Rob and Gregory, and it is known Rob visited Aberdeen in 1726. Possibly the two men did meet at some time, but the elaborations of the tales about them are embroidery.[14]

A tradition in the family of Nasmyth is simply bewildering, as it deals with a real event but involves in it someone who could not possibly have been present. The Edinburgh builder Michael Nasmyth, it is said, had a contract to build Inversnaid Barracks. He was present when Highlanders seized workmen there in 1718, and he had been dragged with them for miles through the snow. The ordeal had so damaged his health that he died eighteen months later. But the tale dates the incident at Inversnaid to 1703, fifteen years before it actually happened, and Nasmyth himself died in 1705. Possibly there is some confusion between Nasmyth and John Smith, the surveyor of barracks for Scotland in 1715, but the story is fiction – with the deep snow in August a bit of a giveaway.[15]

Other elements in tales can be related to known events, but join separate incidents together illogically. Rob's leadership of the 1691 heirship (raid) of Kippen may be doubtful, but at least it is a traceable event. But the stationing of militia volunteers from the western lowlands in Drymen and the surrounding area, which is narrated as being a response to his Kippen raid, is a reference to events a quarter of a century later, in December 1715 after Rob had led a Jacobite raid in the area. Rob's assumed leadership at Kippen reflects a wider trend to forget when Rob had been at the peak of his notoriety. The minister of Strathblane in the 1790s wrote of Rob's name 'being familiar to every inhabitant of this part of Scotland. The depredations which he and his descendants committed are still related with wonder'. Yet this did not prevent the minister from believing that Rob's heyday had been in the 1650s, well over half a century too early.[16] Another writer dated his downfall to 1688–89, rather than 1712.[17] Rob has begun to drift. It is the tales of his deeds and hardships that matter, not the specific historical contexts in which he acted.

Traditional accounts of Rob's misfortunes assume that the duke of Montrose took over Rob's lands in 1712. In fact, as has been shown, first they remained in the hands of those to whom Rob had disposed of them – Bardowie and Glengyle – and then they were forfeited to the crown. Only then did Montrose obtain them – by buying them. Montrose may have been able to seize Rob's goods on behalf of his creditors. But the story of the eviction of Rob's family from his house at Craigrostan by Montrose's men seems to be merely an extrapolation from the belief that the duke took possession of Rob's lands in 1712, rather than an actual description. Further elaboration leads to stories of his wife being badly treated at the time, or even raped. Walter Scott heard that she had been 'insulted in a manner which would have aroused a milder man than he to thoughts of unbounded vengeance'. As a novelist, he alluded to the supposed incident by having Helen (Scott did not even know the real name of Rob's wife, Mary) curse some soldiers, muttering that after what had been done to her, 'Ye have left me neither name nor fame – my mother's bones will shrink aside in the grave when mine are laid beside her'.[18] This coy allusion to rape, something unmentionable directly in a novel at the time, became the basis for outraged splutterings by later writers about atrocity and unimaginable barbarity – and somewhere along the line Killearn became the rapist. But the lurid incident is not credible. As Scott himself commented, it would have driven any husband to thoughts of 'unbounded vengeance'. Yet Rob showed no signs of such thoughts. He continued trying to negotiate a settlement with Montrose until the '15 rising. Subsequently he raided Montrose's property, but he never attempted any violence against the duke in person. The rape of his wife would surely have marked a turning point in Rob's dispute with Montrose, with an abrupt escalation of bitterness – yet no such change is detectable.[19] Rob never behaved like a man seeking to avenge the foul treatment of his wife.

Walter Scott had the advantage of talking directly in the early 1790s to a number of men who had met Rob Roy. But over a quarter of a century passed before he recorded what they had said, and he admitted that at times his memories of what he had been told were unclear. Add that to the fact that the old men he had talked to were already recalling incidents that had happened half a century or more before, and questions of accuracy become worrying. Eye-witness evidence, recorded after so long a period during which the vagaries of the human mind may unwittingly distort the truth, is not always the best evidence. Nonetheless it would be going too far to say that none of the tales reflect genuine experiences. Take the simple story told by a man 'half-frightened, half-bewildered' (presumably by age and vivid recollection) who recalled that when Rob had been working for his landlord in tracking some stolen cattle, he (aged fifteen) and his father had been sent with Rob Roy, so they could drive the cattle home once they were recovered. After the cattle had been found, the party had to spend the night on the hillside. It was frosty, but the Highlanders had their plaids to wrap themselves in. The two Lowlanders had no such protection, but a Highlander shared his plaid with the boy's father. He, however, was told by Rob to keep himself warm by walking about, watching over the cattle during the night. It was a clear, moonlit night and the wind got up. Once the Highlanders were asleep the shivering boy managed to untuck the end of one of their plaids and creep in under it, and slept. He feared trouble when he awoke, but escaped punishment. It is in a way a pointless little recollection (which annoyed Scott),[20] but this helps to give it credibility as account of an adventure that might well stick in a boy's mind.

A more elaborate first-hand account relating to cattle theft, however, raises problems. In about 1792 Walter Scott met the very elderly George Abercromby of Tullibody (born 1705), who had once met Rob. Tullibody told Scott that after he had first settled in Stirlingshire some of his cattle had been stolen, and he had gone to see Rob to negotiate their return and to arrange to pay him blackmail in the future. Rob had greeted him 'with much courtesy' in a cave and they had 'dined on collops cut from some of his [Abercromby's] own cattle, which he recognised the carcases of hanging by their heels from the rocky roof beyond'.[21] The basic story is not implausible – many over the years must have negotiated with Rob over stolen cattle and blackmail. But the presentation of the anecdote is a different matter. Abercromby had been a participant in the incident, but he was recounting it perhaps sixty years after it had taken place, and his account of a prized incident – 'I once met the famous Rob Roy, you know' – had easily (if unintentionally) become embellished over time. Moreover, what we have is not Abercromby's first-hand account, but Scott's version of it, and he was a man whose vivid imagination often compelled him to elaborate on simple tales. In this case, is the remarkably spacious cave a real setting, or Scott's romantic vision of a suitable setting for a famed bandit? Scott was writing a decade after creating his fictitious Rob Roy. And though it is true that there is a reference to how Highlanders in Lochaber would, after killing a cow, hang up the carcass and carve meat from it as needed,[22] killing a number of cattle and hanging them up at the same time, when they were not needed for immediate consumption, would have been folly. In response to tourist demand a 'Rob Roy's Cave' was identified on the shores of Loch Lomond, the best that could be offered was a mere heap of·rocks, not the grand cave of the story. It must be suspected that in recording Abercromby's tale Scott has fictionalised it, adding melodramatic touches. Stories grow in the telling.

Other tales derived from men who had known Rob also raise 'too good to be true' suspicions. Two are elaborate stories published by David Stewart of Garth in 1822. Like Walter Scott, he had talked to old men who had known and worked with Rob, so again the caution is necessary that there were long decades between the events the old men recalled and their telling of them, and then a long period between Stewart hearing them and publishing them. In one of Stewart's stories, Rob disguised as a beggar won the trust of a party of soldiers who were searching for him. He agreed to help them track down the outlaw, and led them to the house where he was staying. But when the soldiers rushed in to capture Rob, they were themselves seized by Rob's men lying in wait, and the true identity of the beggar was revealed. In Stewart's second tale, Rob's men were shadowing another party of soldiers, who were carrying off some prisoners. Rob dressed his men in goatskins, and routed the soldiers in a dawn attack, they being terrified by these savage, half-animal apparitions. Stewart wisely remarked that such tales 'perhaps, lost nothing in the telling'.[23] The stories may have had their distant origins in real events but acorns of reality have grown into luxurious oaks of fantasy, as listeners craved to hear stories of Rob and such demand was met with invention. Credulity could be remarkable. In 1809 Walter Scott met beside Loch Lomond 'an old follower of Rob Roy, who had been at many a spreagh (foray) with that redoubted freebooter, and shewd me all his holds [hiding places]'.[24] A sprightly old man indeed, for Rob had been dead for seventy-five years.

It seems to have been Scott who was the first to commit to print a description of Rob Roy having had such long arms that he could tie the garters of his stockings below his knee without stooping. The description has been repeated endlessly, but only a moment's thought is needed to realise that such a build would have amounted to deformity. By repute his hair had been 'dark red, thick, and frizzled, and curled short around the face', while his legs were described as like those of a Highland bull, 'hirsute with red hair, and evincing muscular strength similar to that animal'.[25] Could a man of so bizarre an appearance, with his anthropoid arms and animal legs, really have escaped capture so long? One commentator has attributed such descriptions to Scott being influenced by 'the new, and heterodox, scientific discourse of subhuman origins', and the 'Romantic vogue for the orang-utan'.[26] In fact, in manuscript rather than print, Dorothy Wordsworth had already heard the garters story in 1803. Perhaps she too had been attracted by the vogue for the orang-utan. Eighty years earlier still, the *Highland Rogue* had described Rob as huge and amazingly hairy, and that was long before orang-utans became fashionable. Moreover, for Gaelic speakers the saying *Tha gàrdean fada air*, 'he has long arms', was well known, and it was used to refer to a thief. Those who have stressed Rob's remarkable arms have been unknowingly calling him a thief.[27]

How is it that it has not been realised that the 'garters' anecdote is typical of the sort of rhetoric storytellers often employ, and is not meant to be taken literally? Saying a man is a strong as an ox is not intended to be fully believed.

Late eighteenth-century travellers mention the way in which Rob seemed 'to have resembled Robin Hood'.[28] He harried the oppressors of the poor[29] and he 'had his good qualities,' being a true friend to widows and orphans.[30] Scott believed from what he was told that Rob had been 'a kind and gentle robber' taking from rich, giving to the poor. Rob was benevolent and humane 'in his way.'[31] Plundering the rich was his greatest delight.[32] He gave a poor man money to pay his rent to Atholl, then after it had been collected by the factor, stole it from him – and gave it back to the poor man.[33] He kidnapped a gentleman but, finding he was in financial difficulties, gave him money and freed him.[34] One 'protector of the poor' tale is specific in detail if vague as to date. The minister of Balquhidder, Robison, was seeking an augmentation of stipend, which would have meant landowners having to pay more in teinds (tithes), which they would recover from their tenants. Rob 'advises' Robison not to proceed, to prevent the poor having to pay more – but he gave the minister a cow and a sheep each year as compensation for his lost augmentation. The tale is not entirely incredible, with Rob taking a leadership role in the community which would gain him prestige, and a James Robertson was minister of the parish (1710–23).[35] Local pressure on ministers not to seek augmentations was sometimes intense. Another account of the affair, however, gave the minister's name as Ferguson. Finlay Ferguson was indeed minister of Balquhidder (1723–72), but the doubt as to who the minister in the story was is disconcerting.

Another tale relating to some degree to real people and a real situation refers to the time at which Rob was guardian to his young nephew, James Graham of Glengyle. A 'man of rank' had a wadset, or mortgage, on the lands of Glengyle, whereby he could take possession if the money due were not paid. Rob had the money ready when redemption was due, but the lender claimed he had lost the bond whereby the money was due, so could not accept repayment.

Rob gathered men, captured him at Strathfillan, made him produce the bond – and once he had possession of it refused to pay the debt due on it.[36]

Though tales of Rob's prowess as a swordsman, of his bravery, his cunning and his charity, multiplied, other stories present him as a flawed hero. Two recorded by Scott come into this category. One time at Doune Rob offended James Edmondstone of Newton, who threatened to throw him into a bonfire and reminded him that he had broken Rob's rib in a previous encounter. If provoked again, Edmondstone would break his neck. Rob slunk off, and the incident damaged his reputation. Perhaps it did – but the story fits with his common reluctance to take part in brawls. On another occasion Henry Cunningham of Boquhan felt himself insulted by Rob, challenged him to a duel, and drove him from the field.[37] Not implausible in themselves as stories – but then it must have been fun to have stories about how your forebear not only met the great Rob Roy but had bested him.[38]

Some tales have Rob making an appearance in London, whereas there is no evidence he ever ventured even into England, let alone as far south as the capital. In the best-known story Argyll brought Rob to London and, without revealing his name, drew George I's attention to him. Only after Rob was safe back home does Argyll reveal that the striking figure the king had seen was the notorious outlaw. The most elaborate version of the tale turns it into an explanation of why Rob was pardoned. A Hungarian was making a living in London as a 'bully', challenging men to take him on in combat – 'to the death' sword fights. The bully had already had a successful career in Germany and France, and no one in London could beat him. But Argyll tells the king that his cowherd could defeat this foreign upstart. The king has him sent for, and when Rob appears (anonymously) he plays the part of an 'unpolished rustic', familiarly calling the king 'gudeman'. The king has him dressed in a suit of silk tartan, and he fights the Hungarian outside St James's Palace, eventually killing him. After he has returned home, Argyll tells the king that it had been the notorious Rob Roy who had fought so well, and the king pardons him.[39] Here, as in the tales that bring Rob and Montrose face to face, legend likes personal contacts between Rob and leading opponents.

In his lifetime Rob's reputation was known in England. His autobiography was published there, and he fought a mythical duel there. In later generations his name was to travel round the world.

12

THEIR FATHER'S SONS

Biographies do not usually include the lives of their subject's children. In Rob Roy's case, however, this seems appropriate, for in some ways his son's lives seem to work out themes from his own life, and the dramatic murder that first brought his sons to public attention was the violent conclusion to rivalry and hatred stirred up in Balquhidder by Rob's unscrupulous behaviour. A less logical but nonetheless compelling reason for looking at their lives is that two of them are full of dramatic incident that at times seems to put their father's life in the shade. Finally, I may plead the example set by Sir Walter Scott, who was unable to resist adding the story of the sons to that of the father.[1]

Rob Roy and his wife Mary may have had one daughter who survived to adulthood and married,[2] but her name is unknown. Genealogists tended to ignore daughters unless they made good marriages. Four sons also survived to adulthood,[3] and there are traces of a fifth, who died young. Dates of birth are commonly assigned to them, but what authority they are based on is unclear:

> Coll, born *c.*1704, died 1735.
> James Mor (Big) or Hamish, died in France 1754.
> Ranald or Ronald, born 1706?, died 1786?
> Robert or Rob Og (Young), occasionally referred to as Rob Roy, born 1717?, executed Edinburgh 1754.

James in later life is referred to as Rob's eldest son, but this probably means eldest surviving son, for tradition claims Coll as the eldest. To classify the four crudely, James was a schemer and plotter, whose ingenuity as a betrayer of those who trusted him made his father's ventures in such matters seem amateurish. Coll died young, the surest way of keeping an almost unblemished reputation. Ranald was the survivor, eventually adapting to changing times and living to old age. Rob Og was to begin his career with murder and end it on the gallows.

James and Coll were in their teens by the time their father became an outlaw, Rob Og was born when his father was already both outlaw and rebel. As with Rob Roy himself, it is not known where they got their schooling, but all were as at home in English as in their native Gaelic, their surviving letters being indistinguishable from those written by Lowlanders. From their father and his life they took a strong sense of their status. They were not ordinary folk but gentlemen, descended from past chiefs. His life demonstrated to them harsh truths about the struggle to survive and the necessity of unscrupulousness in pursuit of it. But it is impossible to discern any of the more amiable characteristics of the father in the sons.

Rob Roy died in December 1734. Rob Og was still living at home in Inverlochlarig Beg, but his three elder brothers had rented lands of their own. Ranald and (it is said) Coll had holdings in the Kirkton of Balquhidder, on leases from the Drummonds of Perth, while James held the farm of Coirechaoroch near Loch Dochart, some miles to the north, on the same estate. The Drummonds were to show friendship and support for Rob's family, though they were not ideal tenants. In 1733 James was about £530 Scots behind in rent payments, Coll about £130. Nonetheless, Ranald had been lent £200 to build himself a house, paying 25 merks additional rent a year as interest.[4]

Within a matter of months of Rob's death Coll also died.[5] Foremost in the minds of the three surviving sons, James, Ranald and Rob Og, was how to react to John MacLaren's attempt to outwit the MacGregors by taking over the lease of Inverlochlarig Beg, then offering it back to them in exchange for Ranald surrendering to MacLaren the tenancy of the disputed lands in the Kirkton of Balquhidder. There was much talk of the dispute in the community, and stories circulated of threats from the brothers about how they would like to get rid of the troublesome MacLaren – and they are plausible enough in the circumstances. It was the youngest of the three who acted. On 4 March 1736, fourteen months after Rob Roy's death, Rob Og approached John MacLaren at Drumlich, the westermost farm in Balquhidder. MacLaren was busy ploughing with two of his neighbours, and Rob shot him in the back, mortally wounding him, and then fled. John's kinsman, Donald MacLaren, drover in Invernenty, demanded that action be taken against him, but Rob's brothers James and Ranald sought to terrorise him into

not making a fuss by houghing over thirty of his stotts. Killing the
young bullocks on the spot would have been hard work, but a quick
hough, or slash at the back of their legs to cut tendons, was easy and
left the beasts so disabled that they would die anyway. Donald, in
case he failed to take the hint, was also threatened with death.

A search for the three brothers was organised, after some delays
due to fear and confusion. It was not until 13 March that a letter was
written to Atholl's factor, Alexander Murray, reporting 'the most
barbarous action'. All three MacGregor brothers and their adherents
were regarded as guilty, and Alexander Stewart of Invernahayle (who
organised the letter to Murray as he was in the area at the time)
urged that they all be seized and banished. Rob Og had threatened
that John was only the first of the MacLarens he intended to kill, and
people were afraid to venture outdoors without arms, and feared
for their cattle. Atholl, as feudal superior of Balquhidder, was urged
to restore order. 'These rogues must be extirpate off the face of the
earth', thundered Alexander Murray.[6]

Thereafter, things moved fast. On 15 March the *Caledonian
Mercury* offered a twenty-guinea reward, payable at Muirhead's
Coffee House in Edinburgh, for Rob's arrest, and gave a useful, if
not flattering, description of the fugitive. Rob Og was 'a tall lad,
aged about 20, thin, pale colour'd, squint eyed, brown hair, pock-
pitted, ill-legged, in-knee'd and broad footed'.[7] A few weeks later
the newspaper stated the reward for 'Rob Oig, of the tribe of Douil-
Cheir' had been raised to £50, and revealed that the money would
be paid by Stewart of Appin.[8] The Stewarts had supported John
MacLaren in the dispute over land which had led to the duel before
Rob Roy's death. Now his son had murdered MacLaren, and Appin
sought revenge.

James and Ranald were quickly arrested and sent to Perth on their
way to trial in Edinburgh.[9] After his father's humiliation over Rob
Roy's escape in 1717, the second duke of Atholl had the sense not
to trust to the security of his own prison at Logierait to hold Rob's
sons. But Rob Og made good his escape, and violence resulting from
the murder continued – 'The war in Ballquhidder is carried on with
vigour on both sydes' it was reported in May. Donald MacLaren's
house was set on fire, the noise of the fire alerting the inhabitants in
time for them to escape.'[10]

In the absence of Rob Og himself, it was decided to prosecute James
and Ranald and one Calum MacInleister. All three were charged

with conspiracy to murder John MacLaren, and James and Ranald
also faced charges of theft and of being of ill repute. Statements for
the prosecution and for the defence survive – giving, obviously, rather
different accounts of the events – as does the official record of court
proceedings, including statements by witnesses.[11] From these, the
crime can be reconstructed in some detail. The story of the dispute
over lands in the Kirkton of Balquhidder and Inverlochlarig Beg
was revealed, and the prosecution claimed that Rob's sons had been
heard making threats to MacLaren's life unless he gave up his claim
to the tenancy of Inverlochlarig Beg, and that James and Ranald had
persuaded Rob Og that he should do the killing. In the absence of
Rob Og the prosecution was concerned not with Rob's motivation
but with that of the elder brothers.

Little was said about James, who did not live in Balquhidder and
claimed not to have been there at the time of the murder,[12] but a case
was built against Ranald. It was argued he had paid his rent so badly
that he was about to be turned out of his Kirkton of Balquhidder
holding. He was therefore desperate to get Inverlochlarig Beg for
himself, and wanted MacLaren out of the way to open his way to
the farm. Ranald's defence was that he had paid his rent, had a long
lease, and his landlord had no intention of evicting him. He had,
therefore no personal motive for wishing MacLaren dead. Like his
brother James, he had a farm and security. It can be guessed where
this argument was leading. Only Rob Og was guilty, for he had most
to lose had MacLaren lived.

All in court accepted that Rob Og had been the firer of the shot
that had killed John MacLaren, and his elder brothers were ready to
argue that the murder had been planned and executed by Rob Og
alone. He, the youngest son, had still been living with his widowed
mother at Inverlochlarig Beg, and had hoped in time to take over the
lease of the farm. The grant of the lease to MacLaren threatened to
deprive him of what he saw as his rightful inheritance. In the offer of
a reward for Rob Og's capture his age had been given as about twenty,
but it seems that he was several years younger than this. Immediately
after the murder he had been described as 'not above fifteen years
old, but a mad rascal'.[13] At his trial at one point he was said to have
been about sixteen or seventeen years of age,[14] and Robert Murray
younger of Glencarnaig described him as 'a tender weakly lad'. He
believed 'Rob Oig to be of a mad quarrelsome disposition', and had
heard of 'severall mad pranks played by him' – once he had fired a

gun when in the presence of his mother and other members of his family, evidently just as a joke. Glencarnaig younger admitted he bore Rob Roy's family ill will, because of the long feud between his father and Rob, so his evidence might be dismissed as biased, but one piece of evidence he gave tended to exonerate Rob Og of one of the crimes attributed to him. He did not believe that Rob Og could have been responsible for the houghing of cattle after MacLaren's death. Some of the wounds were so long and deep that he did not think a boy of Rob Og's strength could have inflicted them.

The picture that emerges is of a boy rather than a man, of a boy regarded as weak and ungainly, and who doubtless was resentful of this. A boy known for foolish pranks, perhaps to draw attention to himself, perhaps a giving way to impulse. Humiliated by the forthcoming eviction of his mother and the loss of his own livelihood, he reacted with extreme violence of a sort that was bound to increase rather than solve his problems.

The detailed story of what happened on 4 March 1736 emerged in court. Rob Og had visited the house of one John Murray at Inverlochlarig Mor. There he had borrowed a gun, as he wanted to pass the time shooting birds. Calum MacInleister (MacGregor) agreed to go with him. He was a man well known for his medical expertise (he is called 'doctor in Stronvar' at one point) and was staying at Inverlochlarig Mor to treat Patrick Murray, who was dangerously ill from a bad leg. This contradicted the prosecution claim that the gun used in the murder had belonged to Rob Roy, and that Rob Og had had to send to get it, thus deliberately seeking out a weapon for criminal purposes. Rob Og and Calum passed Rob Og's brother Ranald, who was ploughing land at Inverlochlarig Beg to help his mother. Why Rob Og was not also helping his mother is not explained, but Calum stopped to talk to Ranald, while Rob moved on up the glen on his own. At Drumlich he encountered John MacLaren, Dugald Keir (MacGregor) who was a tenant on the farm, and a third (unidentified) man, who were also ploughing. Rob Og went up to them and, according to Dugald Keir, said that he wanted to see how the plough horses would react to the 'sight' of the gun. Given that nearly all the witnesses in the case gave their evidence in Gaelic that then had to be translated into English for the court, it seems likely that the 'sound' of the gun was what Rob Og actually meant. Was this intended as a threat, a warning that he intended to fire the gun – and that his enemy MacLaren was the obvious target?

To approach a man you were known to have a grudge against with a loaded gun in itself must have seemed threatening.

Certainly Dugald Keir thought the situation potentially dangerous, for he took the gun from Rob Og and emptied the powder out of the priming pan, so the gun could not be fired. He then gave it back to Rob. This may have contributed to what followed. Rob was not being treated as a man but as a child who could not be trusted with a loaded gun. He was not taken seriously – the gun was handed back to him once it was no longer ready to fire. That he had let the gun be taken from him meant that he had momentarily accepted being treated as a child, and he may well have felt angry and humiliated, determined to prove he was a man. And men often seek to prove themselves men by resorting to violence. The three men turned their backs on the boy (which again could be interpreted as disrespect) and returned to their ploughing. Then Dugald Keir heard a shot and saw MacLaren fall. Rob Og had reprimed his gun and fired. He immediately ran off, chased by Dugald, who caught up with him by 'the water' – the River Larig. 'And the said Rob did then say to the deponent, let John McLaren take that for endeavouring to remove my mother out of her possession.' He then drew a pistol and pointed it at Dugald, who backed off and let him go.

MacLaren had a gaping wound in the back of his thigh, caused by the scatter of small shot intended for shooting wildfowl. Calum MacInleister hurried to the scene, and sent for his surgical instruments, while the victim was carried to his house. But MacInlester's efforts to save his patient's life failed – and his reward for his efforts was to find himself in court on the charge of acting in conspiracy with Rob Roy's sons to kill MacLaren by mistreating his wound.[15]

In all probability, though Rob Og had harboured murderous thoughts about MacLaren, the murder was an impulsive, spur of the moment action. The opportunity had presented itself. He had happened on MacLaren while out hunting. Perhaps he had meant just to threaten him, and the contemptuous taking of his gun and removing of the priming powder had tipped him over the edge. Whatever, he fired and ran, doubtless not knowing how seriously his victim was wounded. He went home, to Inverlochlarig Beg. There Robert Murray younger of Glencarnaig, alerted to the shooting, found him, gun in hand. Rob Og repeated that he had acted because MacLaren was taking over his mother's farm. Weak and sickly though he was thought to be, Rob Og made good his escape – no doubt with the help of his brothers – and disappears from sight for eight years.

The trial of James and Ranald ended in August 1736 with their acquittal on both of the serious charges against them – of complicity with Rob Og in the murder of John MacLaren, and of theft. But they did not escape the verdict of being reputed thieves, and they were ordered to find surety of £200 sterling for their good behaviour in future, remaining in custody until this was arranged. Ten men, mainly named MacLaren, petitioned to be specifically included in the caution, to protect themselves, their lives and property. Not all were happy to see the brothers free.

The account of the murder given here rests essentially on the defence case, which the jury accepted. The prosecution had presented bits and pieces of evidence showing that the three brothers had made threats about MacLaren, but had not managed to show the existence of any specific plot that had led to his death. The defence on the other hand had produced a coherent narrative of events indicating that Rob Og had acted without premeditation, not as part of a conspiracy. Nonetheless, as sons of the notorious Rob Roy, it might be thought that James and Ranald were lucky to escape conviction from an Edinburgh jury. However, it emerges that in overcoming the accusations against them they had had powerful patronage. The duke of Atholl would have been happy to see them hanged, but James Drummond, the titular third duke of Perth (his title was only recognised by Jacobites), had paid for their defence. Their decision to adopt the name Drummond had turned out to be a good investment, and followed from the fact that both were tenants on his lands.

The young duke of Perth had spent most of his life in France, and 'it was one of the bad consequences of his [Jacobite] politics' that 'the people who then had his care persuaded him that the MacGregors were an oppressed people, principally on account of their attachment to the Stuart family, whose standard they would join with a numerous body as soon as he set it up'.[16] The duke's favour to Rob's sons extended to keeping them in his company after the trial, a move which horrified some of his own kin. When he visited James Drummond of Blairdrummond, James and Ranald followed him into the house. The enraged laird said he was proud to have the duke in his house, but the MacGregors were not welcome. They left, in 'high dudgeon'.[17]

The duke's commitment to the MacGregors was detailed in a letter from one of his advisors to Drummond of Balhaldie (the nominal MacGregor chief). The duke was resolved to 'treat [them] with as much kindness as any of his predecessors'. 'Kindness' implied an acceptance of kinship – artificial, but meaningful. Perth took responsibility for protecting the MacGregors – and obedience was expected from them in return. Of this kindness the duke 'has given a very remarkable instance in favouring Robroy's children who were like to suffer for a crime committed by a brother of theirs for which he was oblig'd to fly into foreign countrys to save his life, they having been accused as having been *arte et parte* in houghing Maclaran's cattle who was their brothers' accuser and pursuer for that murder'. Perth 'was at the charge of the process in defending them and got them acquitted at the bar they giving surety for their good behaviour for the future'. Therefore the duke 'expects as much freindship from that clan upon its being restored to its priviledges as any person can do, since he designs to follow his predeessors example and is ready to do them all the kindness lyes in his power'. But the duke made it clear that he would not keep Rob's sons in his service unless they did their duty. If any 'fails in that respect he hopes none of the clan will take it amiss that he discharge him'.

The duke was determined to rebuild his family's reputation and influence. In helping James and Ranald achieve acquittal, he had demonstrated his power, and his determination to protect those he regarded as his people. The example he followed was to be that of 'his predecessors whose virtues he intends to imitate as far as is possible for him to do, in protecting such as deserve well of him and who serve him faithfully in their respective stations under him'.[18] One of the earliest of all surviving references to Rob Roy, in 1689, had referred to him as living 'under the earle of Perth'.[19] Now, nearly half a century later, the Drummonds still regarded themselves as protectors of Rob's family.

Rob Og had said he had committed murder because his mother's farm was being taken from her, but it was taken anyway, and the widowed Mary MacGregor is said to have moved in with her son Ranald in the Kirkton. She outlived her husband by many years, for she is mentioned as still alive in 1754.[20] With one of her sons a fugitive and two under arrest she had presumably been evicted from Inverlochlarig Beg without further trouble.

In the years that followed James and Ranald continued to be tenant farmers – but also active in the raiding/blackmailing tradition.

A reference to a talk with a son of Rob Roy in 1741 is informative, though fiercely ironic. Nicol Graham of Gartmore was a Perthshire landlord whose estate lay uncomfortably close to the Highland line and who therefore was liable to raiding and watch/protection-type payments. The duke of Montrose had summoned a meeting to try to reach agreement about such matters, and Gartmore's response was bitterly sarcastic. 'But to be ernest in the affair, I don't think the country can put themselves under a better protection; to doe these fell[ow]s justice they are a very good sett of people, if you'l but use them with common civility. I saw a son of Rob Roy here t'other day. He told me, he came to tell me of the good success he had in gathering some seed corn among your tennentry here.' Rob's son rejoiced 'that about twenty five-years agoe people would have had the ill manners to have called this black-meal, but that now you are all good freinds together, for that he and his cusin [cousin – Glengyle] were to take equally betuixt them, [for] the keeping and protection of the country; that £40 sterling to each was the lest they could engage for. He is realy a very honest lad this, and a very fitt hand to be concerned, and I am of opinion that he and his freinds will not only be of great advantage to the country at present, but of great use to it in time to come',[21] concluded Gartmore angrily.

Gartmore's real message was something like 'these MacGregors are thriving on blackmail, taking seed corn as well as cattle, and yet it seems that paying them to form a watch is being considered. Instead of trying to get rid of this pernicious system it is becoming accepted as a normal part of life, and rather than regarding them as enemies we must pay up and pretend to be friends to avoid trouble'. Which son of Rob Gartmore had met is unknown, but the references to him and Glengyle as active in the blackmail business reflect reality. James and Ranald kept low profiles, unlike their father, pursuing the traditional trade on Lowlanders whom they regarded, in historical terms, as having once preyed on them.

The profile of the fugitive Rob Og was even lower. At some point he managed to escape to France. There in 1744 he joined the British army. Many regiments were stationed in the Low Countries, engaged in operations against the French in the War of the Austrian Succession and, as often before and since, the army was so desperate for recruits that it did not ask awkward question about the past. Rob enlisted in the North British Fusilier at Bruges.[22] There was a French plan in 1744 for the invasion of Britain with the support of the Jacobites to restore the Stuart dynasty, and it may be that Rob Og may have first hoped for employment in that venture, only turning to the British army when it was abandoned.

His career as a soldier of King George was short, however, for when the French defeated the British at the battle of Fontenoy in May 1745 Rob Og deserted. Quite possibly, he was captured and then easily persuaded to change sides by news that new plans for a Jacobite rising in Scotland were well advanced. In July 1745 Prince Charles Edward, in Jacobite eyes the prince of Wales, landed in the Western Isles with a few followers, and once it became clear that the rebellion he had begun had some potential the French belatedly set about providing some help for it. Lord John Drummond (the brother of the titular duke of Perth) had been commanding a Jacobite regiment in the French army, the Escossais Royale, and he was commissioned to gather Irish and Scots units in the army to join Prince Charles.[23] Rob Og was to be with this Drummond force when it landed in Scotland in November 1745.[24]

Rob's brother James Mor was already active – both for and against the Jacobite cause. By one account he still held the lease of a farm in 1744 from the duke of Perth, who was at the centre of Jacobite activity within Scotland,[25] and it is said that he was sufficiently trusted by the duke for him to flee to James's farm for safety when he feared arrest in 1744.[26] But Perth's conduct was straining his followers' loyalties. In 1741–45 he had imposed large rises in rent on his tenants, without investigating whether they would be able to bear the increased burdens. Some tenants refused the new leases, others only agreed to accept them if concessions were made by Perth, who then offered some rebates. After the '45 had failed, even the government officials sent in to run the Perth estate accepted that some of the duke's new rents were unrealistically high.[27] With hindsight it seems pretty clear that what Perth was doing was not taking a new interest in estate management, but raising a fighting fund for the Jacobite cause. There was, however, the risk that he would alienate tenants by raising rents – and yet he would need their support in the event of a rising. James Mor was certainly alienated, for he gave up his tenancy on the Drummond estate. In his eyes, he had been virtually evicted by extortionate rent demands. His long-term master and protector had it seemed betrayed him, and the fickle James was ready to turn Hanoverian spy to seek revenge.

In April 1745, James Mor – 'one Mr Drummond' – approached

Lieutenant General Joshua Guest, and the solicitor general, Robert Dundas, claiming he had evidence of correspondence between a Highlander and the Pretender's son, Prince Charles, about an invasion of Britain. But he wanted promise of reward for his services, and demanded that Lieutenant James Campbell of Lord John Murray's Regiment (The Black Watch) be given leave to accompany him to the Highlands, presumably to gather evidence. Though by this time it was well known that Prince Charles was planning a landing in Scotland that year, official interest in what James might reveal focused at first on intelligence concerning the recruiting of Highlanders into Lord John Drummond's French regiment. With his close connections with the Drummonds, James seemed to be ideally placed as an agent, so he was offered hopes of reward, and the king agreed that Lieutenant Campbell should be granted leave. James, however, was not satisfied with whatever offers were made to him, and he did not become a government agent until some months later. He was subsequently to claim that he had all along been working in the Jacobites' interests, seeking to infiltrate the regime, but if he had intended that, surely he would have accepted whatever offer the government made to him. In reality he was ready to sell himself to the Hanoverians – but only if he got a good enough offer. It was not a matter of which side he supported, but which side he calculated would do most for his advancement.

By the summer rumours of an impending Jacobite rising had intensified, and Robert Craigie, the lord advocate, made a new attempt to recruit James. 'As I know the man I will use all my endeavours to bring him to meet with me privately' and 'induce him to speak out all that he knows'. A raid on Drummond Castle intended to arrest Perth failed in July, so James's value as a spy close to the Drummonds was increased.

James Mor and Craigie met in Edinburgh on 2 August, and James was able to lull any suspicions of his motives by showing that he had good reasons for wanting to betray Perth, his former master. A few months before he had ceased to be a tenant of the duke, and he implied he had been evicted, being forced to move to Corriearklet in his father's homeland. He represented himself as a man of some significance, chief of the MacGregors and others who had followed his father. 'The clan of which he is reckoned the chief is dispersed through the Duke of Perth's estate.'[28] Who better to spy on the duke than a former tenant with a grievance?

Craigie was pleased to have recruited James, but unease lingered. 'I know this man to be a brave sensible fellow.' But 'he is of the temper of most of his countrymen [Highlanders]. They want to be paid for their work' and James was demanding rewards. Moreover 'the known character of his clan and ffamily are sufficient to caution against trusting him too far'. Still, on balance 'I think he is worth purchasing considering his enterprizeing genius and his connections', though 'at this juncture' care should be taken to avoid him having the power to damage government interests.[29]

James's main ambition, he revealed, was to be given a commission as an officer in the Black Watch. He said this was necessary so that it would be clear that he was a Hanoverian, and therefore could not be accused of being a spy or an informer, though as the lord advocate pointed out this was contradictory. If James became an officer in the British army he would not have much access to Jacobite secrets. Nonetheless, Craigie favoured granting James Mor a commission, as an ensign or lieutenant in the Black Watch. The marquis of Tweeddale as secretary of state, agreed. He recommended that James, 'a sensible fellow', be commissioned.[30]

However by this time James was involved in changing horses in midstream. Perhaps his flare of resentment at having lost his farm on the Perth estate had faded, or more likely he suddenly came to believe that Jacobitism might not be a lost cause. It might offer him a better future. The much talked of rising that had been expected in 1744 had failed to materialise, and perhaps James had expected that the landing of Prince Charles anticipated for 1745 would turn out to be another such pipedream. But while he was negotiating with Craigie news arrived that the prince had actually landed. James Mor may have found it necessary to adjust his loyalties.

That James had been in contact with the government was known in Jacobite circles, though it was believed that the government had approached him rather than *vice versa*. Quite possibly James himself had revealed his Hanoverian contacts, as part of some intricate double-dealing seeking to sell himself to the highest bidder. He was regarded by the Jacobites as 'far from inclined to accept' the considerable offers he received from the authorities, but 'yett would not seem entirely [to] refuse, but chose rather to appear their freind, whereby to gett into their confidence'.[31]

The Jacobites rose to the bait. James's contacts with the lord advocate could be used to feed false intelligence to the government.

Though it was known that Prince Charles had landed, reports were confused about his movements in the western Highlands. James could be used to conceal them further. Promised reward, James 'far from being unsusceptable of flattery, irregardless of his own private interest' agreed to be recruited, though it sounds as though at this stage the Jacobites thought he was a fool. It was important to feed false intelligence to the government, 'to blind them as much as possible', and for this purpose 'no body was found so fitt' as James Mor.[32]

Amidst fast-changing events a bolder scheme was soon hatched, which assigned to James Mor a key role in getting the rising off to a good start. While the Jacobite clans of the west were gathering in arms, he would lead a pre-emptive strike on the army garrisons of the Great Glen. First, in his guise of a Hanoverian agent, he would get orders from the government for the commanding officers of Fort William and Kilcumin (Fort Augustus) to give him command of raiding parties of soldiers. He would then use them to sally out and seize Cameron of Locheil, MacDonald of Glengarry and other chiefs in the area before their men were in arms. In reality, however, James would act as a double agent. He would ensure that the parties of soldiers were so large that they weakened the garrisons sufficiently for the Jacobites forces to attack and capture the forts. Even if the assault on the forts failed, they would take prisoner all the soldiers in James's parties.[33]

James was intelligent enough as an agent to mix truth and sensible advice with his fictions. 'Now it's the time for sleeping dogs to awak' he told Craigie. Jacobites regarded the government as supine, and this encouraged them to rebel. Absolutely true – but also intended to prepare the way for revealing 'his' scheme to capture Jacobite chiefs. First tell the lord advocate he must act – then reveal a scheme for immediate action. Given the right authorisation and support, he announced, he believed he would be able to arrest the main Jacobite chiefs at a meeting that was being planned. To do this, he would need the names of all those the government 'corresponded with in the Highlands', so 'that I may be supported be them from time to time as my need requires'. Moreover, he must have clear orders from the army commander, Sir John Cope, to the governors of Fort William and Kilcumin requiring them to supply as many men as James required, day or night, for him to use to arrest the chiefs.

It is astonishing that James's cover was not blown at this point.

What he was asking for was the name of all those in the Highlands who were cooperating with the government, and permission to lead troops from the two main garrisons in the north into a Jacobite-dominated countryside. Yet so desperate were Craigie and Cope for intelligence and for some way of nipping rebellion in the bud that he got at least some of what he wanted. In spite of lingering suspicions orders were sent to the governor of Kilcumin to work with him on any scheme which seemed to have a good chance of success and was consistent with the safety of the troops involved. James departed north again 'in quest of intelligence and new adventures' as Craigie put it. The lawyer seemed quite excited by these dramatic activities, and he was being astonishingly naive in his dealings with James. Perhaps the judgement is justified that Craigie's 'career is chiefly remarkable as the most conspicuous instance, at the bar of Scotland, of a high position in the service of the state being attained by constant plodding and the judicious use of moderate talents.'[34]

James hastened to Cameron of Locheil's house to put the Jacobite variant of his plan into action, but found he was too late. The forts he had hoped could be seized had just been reinforced, and skirmishing with the Jacobites had begun.[35] Undeterred, he hastened back to Edinburgh, and on 24 August entertained Craigie with more confused reports of the situation. Only later was it suspected that he had taken the opportunity to arrange with a Jacobite printer in Edinburgh for the production of copies of proclamations by Prince Charles.[36]

By this time government control of the Highlands was collapsing. General Cope had moved north with whatever forces were available, hoping to reach Kilcumin, but the gathering Jacobite forces, greatly out-numbering him, occupied the Corrieyairack Pass. Cope felt it was impossible to advance further, and exaggerated reports of the enemy's strength undermined whatever confidence the government forces had. One contribution to this propaganda was made by James Mor, in a letter of 29 August to Craigie which informed him that the Jacobites commanded the Corrieyairack, which was true, but then added falsely that troops and cannon were being landed on the west coast, including Lord Drummond's French regiment.

James now tried a new ploy. He claimed that he was on the run, the Jacobites having evidently found out he was a spy. He was in danger from Jacobite 'flying parties' sent out to recruit men and track down enemies. If he was caught 'I am sure they'll use all severity possible against me.' He begged, therefore, that General Guest would send orders that the garrison of Inversnaid admit him and protect him. Then (transforming himself from refugee into military commander) he would protect the barracks from any flying parties, provided ammunition was sent. The answer to James's urgent letter was to be sent to his house at Corriearklet.[37]

The idea of handing Inversnaid over to a son of Rob Roy was absurd. James surely realised this and was working on the principle that anything was worth trying. He probably received no reply to his letter, and did not wait for one, for within a few days James Mor, his brother Ranald and Glengyle, had seized and burnt Inversnaid barracks, taking eighty-nine prisoners.[38] It must have been a congenial way for James to publicly announce his 'conversion' to Jacobitism. As Rob's son and heir he had destroyed the barracks that had symbolised and enforced his father's loss of his former lands.

The two brothers were (along with Rob Og) active in the campaign that followed, serving in a regiment of MacGregors led by Rob Roy's nephew Glengyle.[39] There was an unfortunate complication in that 'Old Glengyle had frequently been mad and bound for moneths together within these few years', as Robert Craigie reported after examining the chief's son.[40] Glengyle was, however, evidently enjoying a lucid interval in August 1745, and simply assumed he would be colonel of the MacGregor regiment. By one account Robert Murray younger of Glencarnaig, the other contender for the position, decided that in order to prevent disunity it was best not to challenge a man who 'was sometimes stark mad', accepting that Glengyle 'was a good man when himself'.[41] Thus the regiment had a commander who was 'seldom to be depended upon, being frequently delerious'.[42]

Cope, fearing that he would be trapped in the north by a Jacobite move southwards, quickly evacuated his forces by sea, only to be routed by Prince Charles's army at Prestonpans on 21 September 1745. James Mor and Ranald shared in the victory, though James's leg was broken and he had to be carried off in a litter. He withdrew to Inversnaid, which he later claimed to have defended against repeated attacks. His wound had sufficiently healed for him to rejoin the Jacobite army before the battle of Culloden in April 1746 and thus he shared with Ranald (and probably Rob Og) in the disastrous defeat that ended the rising – and James was again wounded.[43] At least, that was his own later account of events, but he was an accomplished liar.

In August 1746 there was a report that 'the famous Robert Roy

MacGrigar's' three sons were in the Inversnaid area. They had all been officers in the rebellion and 'keep some armed men, oppressing and plundering the neighbours' which would continue until troops were sent in.[44] Soon, however, they were forced into flight. The brothers were not prosecuted in the aftermath of the rising, but James Mor and Ranald, having property in Scotland, suffered in the campaign of brutal reprisals. 'The whole of the Braes of Balquhidder was burned and spoiled the year after forty-five; no man can describe the cruelty of the savage soldiers', it was said later.[45] Robert Murray of Glencarnaig's mansion house and all the houses on his estate were burnt. The loss was measured in 'couples', or the sets of roof beams. Three hundred and sixty-four couples were destroyed, and the crofts of Inverlochlarig Mor and Beg, the latter of course having been Rob Roy's last home.[46] The losses of Rob's sons were much smaller – but were all they had. James had 'all his goods . . . plundered, burnt or confiscated'.[47] Ranald's house in the Kirkton of Balquhidder was burnt and his cattle taken. But he proved lucky. It emerged that the commission to troops to burn and loot rebel property had expired the day before his farm was attacked, and he obtained an order that full compensation should be paid to him. Whether it was ever paid is a different matter, and he had the further problem that he leased his land from the Drummonds of Perth, whose estates were now forfeited to the crown. However, he managed to get the forfeited estates commissioners to accept his tenancy in 1747, producing in support of his claim to the land the lease the Drummonds had given his father and himself in 1732,[48] the root cause of John MacLaren's murder.

Ranald coped with the aftermath of the '45 by keeping his head down. The more active James Mor continued to play with fire. Having first served then betrayed the Hanoverians in 1745, he made new approaches to them after the defeat of the rising. The side that was winning was always the best side to be on. However, though he obtained a protection from the lord justice clerk, Andrew Fletcher, in 1747,[49] it seems he received little encouragement – having no substantial intelligence to sell.

It looked for a time as though Rob Og might settle down. At some point (presumably after the '45) he married a daughter of Graham of Drunkie, his father's old enemy. But she soon died, and in 1749–50 he was responsible for the pregnancies of two Balquhidder girls.[50] Perhaps the consequent complications persuaded him to marry again, but his primary motive was evidently the acquisition of money rather than the avoidance of sin. The way he went about finding a new wife proved disastrous for all concerned. 'Taking' rather than winning a wife or negotiating a marriage was not unknown (as Lord Lovat's case half a century before had shown), but it was a practice that was fast dying out. Just as it has been said that Rob Roy was an anachronism in leading the life of a Highland cateran or cattle-lifter in an age when this was coming to be seen as bizarre, so his son Rob Og was behind the times. He was to gain a wife by force, though the evidence strongly suggests that the driving power behind what happened was his brother James, that veteran plotter.

As usual in such cases of forced marriage the victim was an heiress, though in this case on a modest scale, as befitted Rob Og's status. His choice, or target, was one Jean Key or Kay.[51] There had been some contact between her family and Rob Og's, for she recalled having seen James in her father's house. Her father's death had left her as his heiress to a landholding he possessed in Edinbellie, some miles west of Drymen. She married one John Wright, but he died (October 1750), leaving her a widow at the age of nineteen. Her inheritance from her father and her husband was said to have been worth 18,000 to 20,000 merks, about £1,000 sterling, not a vast sum but very tempting to desperate men. Jean was later to say bitterly that she wished she had never had a groat.

About six weeks after her husband's death Rob Og sent a message asking to see her. She refused, and though alarmed she believed 'that these M'Gregors were so much subdued now, that it was impossible they should attempt anything by force'. She was wrong. Rob Og, with his brothers James and Ranald and other armed men, arrived at her house after dark on 8 December. A witness told how the gang wore 'big or Jocky coats', which concealed swords and pistols, and how they spoke much 'in the Irish language' among themselves, a tongue incomprehensible to those in the Kay household. The men forced their way into the house and Jean was hastily hidden in a large meal girnal. When the intruders (switching to English) began issuing dire threats of the consequences of her not being produced, Jean's mother, Janet Mitchell, made her come out. Faced with the demand that she marry Rob Og, she asked for time to think – her husband had only recently died. James replied bluntly that it would not matter if he had died the previous day, his brother Rob Og 'wanted [lacked] a fortune, and had come there to push for one'.

Overawed by being told that Glengyle was waiting on the moor outside with a hundred armed men, ready to come to the raiders' aid if necessary, no one was ready to risk intervening when the girl was seized, carried out screaming, and mounted on a horse behind Rob Og. She threw herself off, badly spraining her side, but was pulled up and laid across a horse in front of the rider, though she was later allowed to sit up. At Rowardennan, on the bonny bonny banks of Loch Lomond, she was forcibly married to Rob Og, while James held onto her, by a man brought from Glasgow 'whom they called Smith, a priest, a little fair man'.[52] Jean's aunt, who was allowed to see her a day or two later, testified graphically that Jean's arm was as blue with bruises as if it had been dipped in a vat of dye from elbow to shoulder, she had been held so tightly. After the ceremony light refreshments were served, and in the afternoon Jean was forcibly bedded. The couple then got up to join the company for the evening.

This account was to be that later brought forward by the prosecution case, though some defence witnesses were to assert that Jean had courted Rob Og secretly, and that she arranged for him to carry her off because she knew her mother would oppose the match. She had married voluntarily, and had not been stripped to be bedded but had undressed herself. On grounds of weight of evidence and simple plausibility, the prosecution case is by far the stronger, but after the event there was some ambiguity in Jean's behaviour. What had happened to her had happened to others, and usually the women concerned accepted their lot. Jean had been kidnapped by armed men and forcibly married but, shocked and confused, she may at times have fatalistically accepted her new husband, while at others she determinedly rejected him. If she got the marriage denounced as invalid, then Rob Og's bedding her was rape – or, if she was held to have consented – fornication. In either case her reputation would be ruined. Moreover rejecting a determined MacGregor 'husband' thus leaving him open to prosecution would be unlikely to improve her life expectancy. As to the MacGregor brothers, they knew the project was risky, but assumed that Jean would eventually accept her fate. All would be well.

From Rowardennan Jean was taken by boat up Loch Lomond to Glenfalloch, and then to James Mor's house in Glen Dochart.[53] If she refused to accept the marriage, she was threatened, she would be carried off to France. From the point of view of her captors, things were going wrong. Jean was not cooperating. Moved to Killin, she was put under pressure to sign a deed of 'factory', a power of attorney that would allow others to act in her name in financial matters. She pretended that she was unable to write, but when James found that she could, he drafted a letter to Rob Og which he then made her copy, back-dated to before her abduction. In this, she asked Rob to carry her off.[54] In another move which showed their anxiety, her captors took Jean to Ranald's house at Kirkton of Balquhidder. There, boldly attempting to show that nothing untoward was going on, Rob Og went to church with her – and both of them assured the minister, Finlay Ferguson, that they were married (even though the performance of the marriage had been irregular, as it had been carried out by a Catholic priest, the marriage was valid if Jean consented to it). A week in 'Arkrostan' (Craigrostan?) followed. Negotiations with friends of her family took place, but were inconclusive, not least because Jean's captors would not let her act freely because they could not rely on her to say the marriage was voluntary. Jean's own attitude was evidently wavering, a longing to be free of the MacGregors being modified by constant threats from them, by James's dominating personality, and by fear of a future with her reputation destroyed. Eventually James decided on bold action. He would go to Edinburgh with Jean. Perhaps it was regarded as unsafe for Rob Og to venture there, as he might be arrested and charged with his murder of John MacLaren many years before, but it is equally possible that only James was daring enough to confront courts of law to try to get his brother's marriage accepted.

Action in Edinburgh was needed because Jean's mother and uncle had presented a petition to the court of session asking for a 'factor' to be given power of attorney to control her property, so her income could be used to take action to get her freed and her abductors punished. The petition had been accepted, so James had to take legal counter-measures if he were to have any hope of gaining control of Jean's estate. Jean herself, wavering and confused, seemed at this point to have been stoically ready to accept her fate, reconciling herself to having Rob Og as her husband. Therefore twice, in February and March 1751, James and Jean presented before judges of the court of session 'bills of suspension', requesting that control of Jean's estate should be returned to her from the court-appointed factor.

Jean declared herself content to accept her marriage, but the judges were suspicious. They refused the bills and 'sequestered' her, sending her to a safe house where she was guarded and her family given access to her, so she could be free from what was clearly believed to be the malign influence of the MacGregors. Once back with her family Jean denied consent to the marriage, and soon gave evidence against her abductors. She had only supported the bills of suspension, she said, through dire threats of the consequences to herself and her relatives if she had refused. At one point James had tried a different tactic, falling on his knees before her and begging her not to ruin him, his wife and his seven children. Finally, before seeing the judges Jean said she had been made to swallow something 'that had confused her'. Elsewhere in the evidence there is an allegation that at times during her 'marriage' to Rob Og she was drugged, which might help explain her inconsistent behaviour. Jean may have exaggerated, but now (pressurised by her family) she was certain that she wanted a Lowland and not a Highland future. James emerges as a master manipulator, with an array of persuasive techniques from bullying to pleading in his repertoire, but once Jean was out of his control he was powerless.

Jean was free, and had given evidence against her abductors, but she remained the loser. When released from sequestration she was too terrified of MacGregor revenge to return to her home in the country. She went to Glasgow and died there a few months later from smallpox.[55]

Moves to prosecute her abductors had already begun. 'Robert Roy MacGregor alias Campbell alias Drummond alias Oig', his brothers James and Ranald, and five other men were cited to appear before the court of justiciary on 20 May 1751. On their failure to appear they were declared fugitives.[56] Sentences of fugitation were issued against them, declaring them outlaws as fugitives from justice, but only three of them were ever tried – those who could be arrested. One of them was Duncan Campbell or Drummond in Strathtyre. But there was a legal technicality to be overcome before he could be tried – a matter of nomenclature. He and others had been cited to stand trial under the name MacGregor, the lawyers concerned having forgotten that the name was banned by law (though it could be cited as an alias). Duncan insisted that his name was Drummond – not surprisingly, as accepting that his name was MacGregor would in itself have laid him open to serious punishment under the 1693 proscription act. The prosecution saw the impossibility of proceeding against someone whose name was not legally usable. The case against Duncan MacGregor was therefore abandoned – but he was immediately committed to prison again as Duncan Drummond.

James had fled from Edinburgh after Jean Key was arrested, but was hunted down and captured at about the beginning of November. He was found, 'imagining himself safe in Argyllshire where he had settled in a remote corner', by soldiers of Pultney's regiment stationed in Fort William. Taken to Fort William, James Mor reverted to form, and offered information on Jacobite activities. Lieutenant Colonel Crawfurd, in command at the fort, was suspicious, for he knew about James's change of sides at the beginning of the '45. Yet James was, like his father, extraordinarily persuasive. He had been forced to join the rebels in 1745, he said; he regretted the past and wished to atone for it. He wanted to be useful, and he had a wife and eight children to provide for (one more than the seven he had talked to Jean Key of at the beginning of the year). Crawfurd was sensible enough to recognise that James was acting out of 'the fright he is now in' at being arrested, as he had thought the government couldn't catch him, but he believed that 'this should make him loyal' at least 'for some time'. James would be of 'infinite use' and was 'sensible and clever'. He should, Crawford recommended, be freed and employed as a secret agent.

On 19 November 1751 Lieutenant General Churchill wrote to the secretary of state, the duke of Newcastle, about the offers of service by James, 'eldest son to the famous Rob Roy, who your Grace has probably heard of'. He was a fellow of the most infamous character 'but does not want parts [abilities]'. As Jean Key was conveniently dead there was little chance, so Churchill believed, of sufficient evidence being produced to bring James to trial over his part in the affair, thus he would in all probability be freed anyway, meaning that there could be no objection to the army running him as a secret agent. Can James's own wheedling voice be heard behind this dubious legal argument?[57]

Newcastle agreed that James should be run as an agent, but Henry Erskine (the justice clerk) intervened. It needed to be remembered, he argued, that James had offered to supply intelligence both before and after the '45 rising 'and then returned to the rebel herd with a sneer'. James was 'an abandoned arch rogue', and Erskine was 'intirely satisfied in his own breast' that he could not be trusted.[58] Moreover, he believed that the conviction of James over his involvement in the Jean Key abduction could be achieved.

General Churchill and Crawford had meanwhile developed elaborate plans for setting up James as an agent. If the army simply freed James, it would look suspicious, destroying his credibility with the Jacobites. He would have to 'escape' and this could be done most plausibly while he was being moved to Edinburgh. But planning this would take some time, so to provide an excuse for James not being marched south immediately he was to be instructed to fall seriously ill.

The plan soon fell apart. So many knew that some plot was afoot that it became clear that a stage-managed escape would lack credibility, and though James was talking copiously Churchill soon realised that nothing he said could be trusted. He was therefore moved to Edinburgh, without including an escape option in his travel arrangements.[59] Then, for a few months, everyone seemed to lose interest in him. However, in June 1752 the earl of Holdernesse (secretary of state) intervened. What prompted his sudden interest in the case is unknown, but he complained of delays and demanded that the legal authorities in Scotland proceed immediately with the prosecution of James Mor. The lawyers hastened to obey, and James was tried in July, though Jean's family was reluctant to be involved through, it was thought, fear of MacGregor retaliation if he was convicted.[60]

The prisoner was unanimously found guilty of abduction. But though the jury accepted that Jean had not consented to what had happened to her, it considered it an alleviation of the offence that she had afterwards accepted the marriage. The charges of forcible marriage and rape were therefore dismissed as not proven. The court then rose, intending to sentence James the next day, 6 August. But a complication arose. Some of the jury had gone home immediately after the verdict, but a majority of them had gathered and discussed the case further among themselves. They concluded that the jury in delivering its verdict had failed to make its meaning clear. Mentioning 'alleviation' and only convicting James of abduction had been intended to exempt James from capital punishment, but it seemed the judges had not realised this. They therefore drew up a declaration to the court explaining the point.

The jury had given its verdict and this had been recorded. For a number of jurors meeting afterwards (possibly over drink) to have then decided to add a rider to the verdict the whole jury had given was highly irregular. Yet the court decided that the jurors' declaration must be taken into account, and that both sides in the case should make further submissions. Sentencing was therefore delayed. As the court 'term' was ending for the summer vacation, the delay was to be a long one, until 20 November.

James had gained a breathing space, but cannot have been optimistic about his future. William Grant, the lord advocate, still expected a sentence of death to be passed.[61] However, a new potential lifeline soon appeared for James, indicating that he might be more useful alive than dead by involving him in a case politically far more significant than his own.

In May 1752, just before James's trial, Colin Campbell of Glenure had been murdered in Appin in the west Highlands. Glenure had been factor on one of the many Jacobite estates forfeited after the '45, that of Stewart of Ardsheal, and he was shot when on his way to evict some tenants. James Stewart in Aucharn (or 'of the Glens') was arrested and prosecuted as an accessory to the crime, though it was widely believed that Allan Breck [Pox-marked] Stewart had actually fired the shot that killed Glenure.[62] An intense manhunt (later to be fictionalised in Robert Louis Stevenson's *Kidnapped*) began, since the authorities regarded Glenure's death as rebellion rather than simple murder, and they were determined to stamp out all signs of resistance to the post-'45 regime in the Highlands. The Campbells were particularly zealous in seeking to avenge Glenure's death.

At this point it became known that James Stewart had visited the imprisoned James Mor in Edinburgh Tolbooth a few weeks before the Appin murder. James claimed that Stewart had been vitriolic in denouncing Glenure, the hated factor, and that he had sought to involve James Mor in a plot to murder him. James was to give Stewart a letter to Rob Og, his brother, urging him to do all he could to help Stewart to murder Glenure. In return, James was to get a lease of land on very favourable terms. Rob was to be given money so he could go to France, where the exiled Stewart of Ardsheal would either get him a commission in the French army or a pension.

This story was probably revealed by James Mor himself to Duncan Campbell of Barcaldine (a half brother of the murdered Campbell of Glenure), whom he had been appealing to before his trial for money to pay his lawyers. Barcaldine now urged that James should receive a pardon in exchange for testifying against James Stewart at his trial. A recommendation that a pardon be granted was sent to London but it was rejected. James 'has been instrumental in and privy to several atrocious crimes'. Justice should be done 'to the utmost extent of that justice he shall appear to have deserved', it was ruled. In any case, the king was in Hanover, so a pardon could not be obtained for James Mor until after the trial of James Stewart had taken place, too late for James's pardon-bought evidence to be useful.[63]

James Mor was cited to the trial of James Stewart in Inveraray as a witness, but remained a prisoner in Edinburgh. Stewart was convicted and hanged without any need of his evidence. Was the evidence he had been ready to give in return for a pardon the truth? Or was it yet another example of James Mor's quick and fertile invention at work? It is impossible to be sure, but it is notable that James Stewart implicitly accepted (in his speech on the scaffold) that he had visited James Mor in prison, though he denied that there had been any murder plot.[64] James Mor's story is not unbelievable. The Stewarts had been desperate to get rid of Glenure, and who better to turn to for help than the two most notorious of the wild MacGregors, James Mor and Rob Og? After all, the latter had long before proved himself ready to shoot a man in the back.

All else having failed, the thoughts of James Mor and his friends turned to escape from prison, as the date set for sentencing him edged nearer. An anonymous letter had claimed that his followers would raid Edinburgh Tolbooth to free him, so he had been transferred to Edinburgh Castle for greater security. In reality the move probably made escape easier than it would otherwise have been, for it gave James far more privacy than was available in the overcrowded tolbooth. Between six and seven on the evening of 17 November, when it was pitch dark, James made his escape. He had been visited by one of his daughters and two of his younger children. She helped disguise him as an old cobbler, and then staged a mock quarrel with him about poor workmanship. He simply walked out of the castle past the guards, carrying old shoes and muttering about being ill treated, and disappeared. When it was realised what had happened there was official fury. All the sentries on duty were arrested and, eventually, brought to trial. Richard Coren, the lieutenant governor of the castle, was lucky to escape – he accepted responsibility, but explained that he had been extremely ill at the time and incapable of seeing the orders he gave executed. He had failed to give orders that James Mor should not receive visitors – but then no one had ordered him to give such orders. Inevitably, there were allegations of an army conspiracy to let James escape so that he could then be used as an agent, but the true explanation seems to be much more mundane – sloppiness and neglect of duty by sentries. In spite of an intense search James was not recaptured, though it was rumoured that he was in the Craigrostan–Balquhidder area.[65]

Frustrated, the authorities hastened to the trial of the one remaining suspect who was still in jail, Duncan Drummond (MacGregor). He was tried in January 1753, and unanimously acquitted.[66]

Only when Rob Og was eventually caught did the luck of the prosecution change. Rob had initially fled to France, hoping for support from the exiled Stuarts. One of those he approached was John Gordon, the principal of the Scottish College in Paris. He had been forced to leave his country because of his services to the Jacobites in the '45, Rob Og explained. His 'lawfull marriege' to Jean Key was being used as a pretext to persecute him. But he had stayed in Scotland until the folly of his brother James had forced him to flee abroad. James's escape from prison had led to such an intense hunt for fugitives that it had become no longer safe to stay in the country. Through his 'having been imprudent enough to make his escape out of the castle of Edinburgh though he was not in any danger as my law[y]er affirmed' Rob Og had lost all chance of remaining at liberty. 'His evasion I say has oblig'd me to get out of the way likwise.'

Instead of sympathy for a brother fearing a death sentence, there was petulance at the inconvenience caused by his escaping. On first reaching France, Rob explained to Principal Gordon, he had attached himself to a Scots regiment in the French army, but the pay was 'not suffiient to sustain me in the caracter of a gentleman here'. Rob Og had failed to secure himself the means to support the status of a gentleman by seizing Jean Key, and now hoped to get it by being put on the 'list of gratifications' which named those receiving allowances from the Stuarts.[67] Rob's pleas failed – there were too many exiles with claims on Stuart gratitude for all to be supported, and though Rob may have fought valiantly in the '45, the blots of the murder of John MacLaren and the abduction of Jean Key were ineradicably on his record. Disastrously, he decided to return to Scotland. In May 1753 he was reported as being back in Balquhidder, 'in good plight, well mounted'. To account for this it was said that 'it looks as if he had been plying on the Highway in England', though this allegation that he had been guilty of highway robbery on his jouney home is doubtless mere prejudice.[68]

Soon after his detection Rob Og was arrested, at a fair in Gartmore, by soldiers from the barracks built at Inversnaid to curb his father.[69] General Churchill was delighted. 'The taking Rob Roy [Rob Og] gives me great pleasure and will give great satisfaction above. He . . . has been guilty of many enormous crimes of which, murder rape and desertion only compose a part.'[70] But Rob's trial was delayed through legal bungling and uncertainty. First the indictments served against him, for the murder of John MacLaren in 1736 and the abduction of Jean Key in 1750, were rejected on a legal technicality, and then there was long debate about the puzzling verdict in the trial of his brother James in 1752, which was somehow held to be relevant to his case. Not until January 1754 did he stand trial before the court of justiciary. By custom, all the evidence had to be heard and the jury pronounce its verdict at a single sitting. This began on the 27th at six or seven in the morning. Evidence was heard until three o'clock the following morning, and the jury pronounced its verdict at 10 a. m. on the 28th, after a marathon sitting of well over twenty-four hours. The exhausted jurors found him guilty, and he was sentenced to death.[71]

On the scaffold on 16 February 1754, 'very genteely dressed', Rob Og 'read for a considerable time' from a work by the Catholic divine, John Gother – perhaps, appropriately, from *Instructions and Devotions for the Afflicted and Sick, with some help for Prisoners, such especially as are to be tried for Life* (London, 1725). He then (though Gother had advised against scaffold speeches) 'declared he died an unworthy member of the Church of Rome' (a judgement with which it is hard to disagree), and accepted guilt for the violence used in abducting Jean Key. He attributing his downfall to the fact that, two or three years before, he had been guilty of 'swerving' from his Catholic faith.[72] His body was carried back to Balquhidder for burial.

James Mor, meanwhile, had resurfaced. After walking out of Edinburgh Castle he had fled, by way of the Isle of Man and Ireland (where he claimed to have discovered that there were thousands of MacGregors under other names), to France. There, like Rob Og, he mixed with Jacobite exiles and sought money from them. Some of his hopes rested on William Drummond of Balhaldie, who had been secretary to Prince Charles, and James expressed devotion to him as chief of the MacGregors. His carefully edited accounts of his past – his loyal service in the '45 which had led to his being driven into exile, the fact that he was the son of 'Rob Roy MacGregor who had distinguished himself' in the 1715 rising – brought him a grant of 300 livres from the Stuarts, though this was probably never paid, and he did not get a pension. Lord Strathallan was partly convinced by the propaganda: 'James Drummond, son of the late Rob Roy was employed in the prince regent's [Prince Charles's] affairs by James, duke of Perth, before his royal highness's arrival in Scotland, and he behaved with great bravery in several battles in which he received many dangerous wounds.' But even the sympathetic Strathallan felt it necessary to add that 'I would be sorry to answer for him, as he has but an indifferent character as to real honesty.'[73] Many suspected (not surprisingly) that he was a British spy, his escape from Edinburgh Castle having been contrived to give him credibility.

Disappointed at his reception by the Jacobites, James Mor turned to a new survival scheme, suggested to him by Duncan Campbell of Barcaldine. He was still determined that the second suspect for the murder of Campbell of Glenure, Allan Breck, should join James Stewart on the gallows. James Mor, he proposed, should arrange for Allan to be kidnapped in France and delivered to England.[74] If James did this, he could expect a pardon for his crimes. James took up the challenge. He and Allan moved in the same Jacobite exile circles in France so befriending him as a prelude to betraying him would not be difficult, and as a bonus if James delivered Allan Breck he could expect the rewards offered for his capture, £300 sterling, as well as a pardon.

James Mor's plan for the kidnapping involved an international clan mafia of men willing to serve. There were living in Holland some dependable 'English Campbells'. James would lure Allan Breck to Holland, and there the Campbells would seize him and carry him off to Britain. Entering with enthusiasm into the secret agent role, James suggested setting up a secure method of identification whereby he and the 'English Campbells' could identify each other. Barcaldine should impress a wax seal on a card, then tear it in half through the seal, and send half to the Campbells, half to James himself. Having matched the two halves, James would hand over Allan to the justice he himself had managed to escape. A thoroughly nasty scheme, but James stressed that he was not just thinking of himself. In escaping from Edinburgh Castle he had left his poor wife and children to rely on charity from friends, and she had then been big with child. There was also his brother Rob, then facing trial. Could the earl of Breadalbane be persuaded to intervene for him, and get him banished instead of executed?[75] Why James should expect the 3rd earl of Breadalbane to favour him is unknown, but the earl's response to later approaches indicates distaste and lack of personal acquaintance with James – the earl had been told 'he is a very worthless and a false artful fellow', which, sadly, was a sound assessment.[76]

The abduction in Holland plan for dealing with Allan Breck came to nothing, so James Mor substituted a plan to kidnap him in France and deliver him to Dover. But 'the very night I intended to have carried him away', Allan had suspected some treachery and fled – and took some of James's clothes and four of his snuff boxes with him, as the frustrated kidnapper complained. Or was this another invention, designed to show that he was trying hard to serve the British regime? Certainly he did gain some credibility, and he sought to exploit this by approaching the duke of Albemarle (the British ambassador in Paris). Albemarle had been commander-in-chief in Scotland in 1747, and remembered James then being granted a pass to protect him. James now pleaded with him for a new pass to go to London in safety to negotiate with government ministers, hinting that he had important Jacobite secrets to reveal. In return he wanted a pardon and a job – and with luck a pardon for his brother Rob Og as well. Part of his motivation, he declared was concern for his family – no doubt genuine, though his claim that he now had fourteen children suggests an almost miraculous increase in family size in a matter of months. The more desperate James became, the more children he had.[77]

As a master of betrayal James Mor feared being betrayed. He therefore insisted that his safe-conduct to travel to England must be granted under 'George's own sign manual' or signature. He might be setting off to negotiate terms with His Majesty King George II's government, but James is here writing of the matter to a Jacobite, so is careful not to call him king.[78] The protection was eventually granted, dated 3 November 1753 and guaranteed that all proceedings against James would be suspended while he was in Britain, until he was ordered to leave.[79]

A letter of the same date from James to a friend in Scotland again reveals that his treachery was not aimed solely at personal advantage. 'You may judge that any man who left his wife and family in such a despicable condition would venture on a great many hazards to contribute to their relief without which I can have no happiness.'[80] An honourable motive for dishonourable conduct.

Soon James was in London, being interrogated and 'revealing' a Jacobite plot, entirely of his own invention, for thousands of Irish

Jacobites (including, presumably, the MacGregors he had found there) to descend on Scotland. With his usual bluster he had a plan to thwart the 'plot'. Two warships should be sent to the Irish coast, and the Black Watch should be stationed in northern Ireland. A hint that 'his pocket is quite run out' brought him a little money, but permission to return to Scotland was refused. He undertook a mission to Calais, outwardly as a Jacobite, and met exiled leaders – or so he claimed when, back in London on 23 November, he revealed the discussions he was supposed to have had with them. When secretary of state Holderness consulted Albemarle, however, the duke replied that 'I would not have your lordship give much credit to Macgregor'. There were 'many falsehoods' in what he said and he was 'a most notorious scoundrel'.[81] James no longer had any credibility. He had nothing important to tell, and there was no sense of crisis to frighten the government into believing whatever intelligence it could get. Europe was at peace, and there were no powers ready to support a Jacobite cause that was seen as having finally failed. As one of James's friends put it, in the circumstances there could be no plots that were not 'chimeras and the raveings of drunken fools'.[82] Or, in James's case, the inventions of men at the end of their tethers.

Nonetheless, James was – or said he was – offered a government job, though first he would have to go to Scotland and be sentenced for the abduction of Jean Key, to satisfy public opinion. That he would go free, he was told, would be arranged in advance. James refused the job, claiming pompously that it was unsuitable for a gentleman and that he would do nothing to disgrace his family. As with Rob Og, the obsession with the idea of gentility haunted the family. The status of gentleman remained unbesmirched by murder, kidnapping and treachery, but could be undermined by accepting the wrong job – even if that job were needed to be able to live in the style of a gentleman. However, James's refusal to agree a settlement with the government may have been influenced by more than social niceties. How could he be confident that he really would walk from the court of justiciary a free man? He of all people knew that it was best to trust no one in the murky world of espionage. While he was in London news arrived from Edinburgh of his brother Rob Og's execution, to drive home that however ramshackle the judicial system was, it could sometimes bite. Moreover, as James complained, at his death Rob had undermined the family reputation in government eyes. The problem was not that he had been executed as a convicted criminal, but that he had declared that he died a Catholic. 'It's certain my brother dieing openly Roman Catholick hurt me much and gave the ministry a very bad impression.'

The irony is obvious. A year before Rob Og had blamed James Mor for causing inconvenience by escaping from prison. Now James Mor rebuked Rob Og for being a nuisance by dying the wrong way. Their callous self-centredness is stunning.

Quite probably the government offered James nothing, his story of a job turned down being intended to win him credit with the Jacobites. Betraying the identities of men in the Isle of Man who had helped him in his escape from Scotland was scraping the bottom of the bucket of intelligence, and was certainly not enough to buy him a pardon. On being questioned about his tall stories, James lapsed into a long illness – possibly genuine. In April 1754 he was given three days to leave the country, the duke of Newcastle dismissing him as 'so vile a fellow'.[83] James Mor slunk back to France, where he claimed he had betrayed no one. But it was too late for him to regain any plausibility. News of his London visit leaked out, or was deliberately leaked to discredit him, and the British press reported that he had made very important disclosures to the government.[84] These reports were widely believed by Jacobites at home and abroad, and threats were made to James's life as he was assumed to be a British agent.

In the last months of James's life he attempted yet again the impossible task of rebuilding his reputation so the Stuarts would agree to support him. It was not just his only hope but that of his family. A letter (July 1754) from one of his daughters, Malie (Mailidh, Molly) depicted its plight. Her mother was living 'in a most destetude manner' with one of Malie's brothers, but he had 'no kindness to her' and she was miserable. Malie was desperate to hear from her father 'if you got any gratification' (pension from the Stuarts) but added sadly 'yet every body hear thinks you'll never get any'. She did not believe stories of her father's treachery. He would never be undutiful to the royal family, and as for her, if she had twenty lives she would give them for the old dynasty. Malie clung to her Catholic faith to avoid despair, but the letter becomes incoherent, distraught. She had not enough faith to believe she would ever see her father again. Enemies lurked everywhere and it was impossible to tell who one's friends were.[85] James had the consolation of knowing that one person in the world still loved and believed in him. The troubles of his family were much on his mind, but whether he had the insight to see that it had been his own actions that had brought disaster to it cannot be known.

James Mor's last known letter was to Balhaldie, his chief. He asked for the loan of 'your pips and all the other little trinkims belonging to it' (bagpipes and accessories). 'I would put them in order, and play some melancholy tunes.'[86] James died shortly afterwards, in October 1754 in Paris of a 'high fever'.[87] Melancholy tunes would certainly have been a suitable end to the melancholy story of his life of betrayals.

Back in Scotland, however, General Humphrey Bland was so unwilling to trust anything related to James Mor that he refused to believe he was dead. He had been seen back in the Highlands, he claimed, having faked the news of his own death so he could return home safely. He must be hunted down because 'he has a fruitful invention at forging lies' and might claim (again) to be a Jacobite agent.[88] But nothing more is heard of this. James, it turned out, could at last be trusted. He was dead.

Now only one of the four sons of Rob Roy survived. Ranald had escaped arrest for involvement in the Jean Key affair, probably by lying low in Balquhidder. He kept in touch with his brother James up to the latter's death,[89] but he had learnt his lesson, and became an exemplary tenant of the annexed estate commissioners. He was mentioned in a report in the mid 1750s as keeping a public house and distilling aquavitae (whisky), and was praised as the only man in the barony of Balquhidder to use lime to fertilise his land, reaping fine crops as a result.[90]

In 1760 he petitioned for more land, presenting himself as a model improving tenant. He possessed a quarter of the Kirkton and the mill, and had built himself a good house of stone and lime, two storeys high. He had kept the mill in good repair, and enclosed the mill lands. But he was unable to enclose and improve the rest of his arable land as it was divided into strips intermingled with those of other tenants, according to traditional practice. Nonetheless, by use of lime he had greatly increased his crops, and at the last harvest his crop had been as great as that of the other three quarters of the Kirkton put together. His neighbours could hardly keep themselves, far less afford to make improvements. He therefore wanted his lease extended to cover the whole of the Kirkton.[91] Campbell of Barcaldine, the factor for the Perth estates, supported Ranald's petition. As a farmer he set a 'laudable example'.

The two other Kirkton tenants, Duncan Stewart and Robert MacLaren had 'neither ability nor inclination' to follow his example, claimed Ranald. Stewart was always in arrears with his rents; MacLaren was a poor man who would willingly give up his land if he were otherwise provided for. Ranald got his lease for the whole of the Kirkton. The fate of the evicted Duncan Stewart was, according to his son, harsh. He was an old man who had possessed his land for about fifty years. On having to leave it he 'was obliged to betake himself and his numerous family to live in a sheep's sheal whereby the poor old infirm man contracted cold and sickness, whereof he died within or about twelve moneths thereafter.'[92]

However, Ranald's past threatened to catch up with him, for his application for the lease drew attention to him. In the course of investigating his suitability as a tenant, the estate commissioners stumbled on the fact that he was officially an outlaw. In May 1751 he and his brothers had been declared fugitives from justice and 'put to the horn' over the kidnapping of Jean Key. Ranald hastened to petition the justiciary court. He had only failed to appear for trial because he was scared of his brothers, and he had lived peaceably for the past decade.[93] The petition was granted, the legal proceedings still technically in progress against him were 'relaxed', or abandoned. That hurdle overcome, Ranald revealed further ambitions, in 1762–3. He wanted to drain land, alter the course of a burn, and set up a lint mill. His neighbours complained that these activities would involve encroaching on their lands, and the fact that he was also suspected of informing the estate commissioners of their misdeeds added to tensions.[94]

Ranald was still a tenant in the Kirkton when he died in about 1786. His father's astute, if disreputable, move in installing him as a tenant in place of poor John MacLaren, murdered half a century before, had paid off. For eighteenth-century believers in imposing civilisation, progress and improvement on the Highlands, Ranald's life displayed an encouraging pattern. From wild son of the most notorious of all wild Highlanders, he had turned to seeking land and wealth not by force but through hard work and improvement.

He had accepted that the place of the Highlands in Britain had been transformed. Repression after the '45 had finally broken the clan system. Internally, Highland society had been demilitarised. Jacobitism was dead – so dead as a real force that it was possible for some Hanoverians to begin to regard it in a nostalgic, sentimental way, seeing the old Highland society and culture that was being destroyed not as barbarism and threat but as exotic and romantic. Better still, as positively useful. The military zeal of the old Highlands had been diverted into the service of the British Empire. The heroic deeds of Highland regiments became famous. The Stuarts had dreamed of making Highlanders the bulwark of their regime, but it was the Hanoverians who had finally done it. So tamed were the Highlands that in 1775 the act proscribing the name MacGregor was repealed.[95]

A generation later, the Clan Gregor acquired a chief. Drummond of Balhaldie, elected chief in 1714, had died in 1749, and though the title had (in the eyes of James Mor and others) descended to his son, in effect this was meaningless – and indeed it had long been more fantasy rather than reality. But in the 1790s one of the most successful MacGregors of the age, Sir John Murray of Lanrick, claimed recognition of his status as chief. He was a grandson of John Campbell of Glencarnaig, Rob Roy's old adversary back in the 1720s, who it was now claimed had been chief of the clan. This was nonsense, but the books were cooked to the satisfaction of the court of the Lord Lyon, which recognised Murray's hereditary right to the chieftaincy. The MacGregors were a clan again – but only because what was called clanship no longer had anything to do with power or land or putting loyalty above the law. A hollow victory perhaps, but a meaningful one to those who called themselves MacGregor.

Rob Roy, who had avoided violence wherever possible, perhaps surprisingly inspired no popular ballads. But Rob Og, guilty of murder and rape, did.[96] In what may be regarded as the earliest of the many surviving versions of the ballad, Rob Og is correctly named as the protagonist, but in the other versions the name Rob Roy is substituted, and indeed even during his lifetime Rob Og had sometimes been called Rob Roy. The notorious father's name was so well known that it was applied to the notorious son. Yet later in the ballad Rob Roy is mentioned not as the protagonist but as the protagonist's father. Identities are being confused and merged. This change could only be made because the ballad at first was handed down orally. Its text was not set rigidly for all time by the fixity of print. Place names, personal names and other details vary from version to version, according to the whims of the singer or the preferences of the audience.

The piece deals with the abduction of Jean Key. Francis Child, the great ballad collector, published twelve versions of the piece, and eleven have 'Rob Roy' as the hero and open with a stanza such as:

> Rob Roy's frae the Hielands cam
> Unto the Lawland border,
> And he has stown a ladie fair,   *stolen*
> To haud his house in order.   *keep*

But the twelfth version (here argued to be the oldest) begins:

> From Drunkie in the Highlands,
> With four and twenty men,
> Rob Oig is cam, lady fair
> To carry from the plain.

Drunkie was the home of Rob Og's first wife's family. Eleven versions deal with the forced marriage and bedding that follow in terms like:

> Six held her up afore the priest
> Four laid her in a bed, O;
> Maist mournfully she wept and cried
> Whan she by him was laid, O.

They then move on to other matters. But the Robin Og version is harsher and dwells on the episode, with two additional stanzas in which she resists and laments:

> But ere she lost her maidenhead
> She fought with him till day.

This Rob Og version, which gets the name of the hero right, and is starker in its violence, is surely the closer to the ballad's origins than the eleven others – even if, as the 'heroine' was a widow, the maidenhead is a literary fancy.

In eleven versions, though the hero is called Rob Roy, he boasts of the prowess of the real Rob Roy, his father, sometimes depicted as still alive, sometimes as dead.

> Rob Roy he was my father called,
> MacGregor was his name, lady;
> A' the country, far and near,
> Have heard MacGregor's fame, lady.

> He was a hedge about his friends,
> A heckle to his foes, lady;   *person who gives a beating*
> If any man him did gainsay,
> He felt his deadly blowes, lady.

In the Robin Og version, however, Rob Roy is merely mentioned in passing, without praise. Thus the later versions cash in on the evocative resonances of the Rob Roy name by making this the name of the central character, as well as the name of his father, whose fame is emphasised.

Rob Og's misdeeds had inspired a ballad, but his father's reputation soon swamped his. Rob Og's name was forgotten, for public opinion preferred a ballad about his father – even if it told of disreputable behaviour.

13

LIFE AFTER DEATH

Even before his dramatic downfall in 1712, the name 'Rob Roy' had been well enough known for letter writers – even men who did not known him personally – to know who he was by reference simply to his first name and sobriquet. His reputation was then that of businessman, one of the most influential men among the (in legal terms, non-existent) MacGregors, and a man well liked in the Highlands. His sensational bankruptcy in 1712 spread his fame much more widely than before, and then in 1715–16 notoriety as a rebel of dubious loyalties was added. There followed the few years in which he tormented Montrose and was hunted with zeal.

These were the years that brought him a long-lasting reputation as a little man who was unjustly oppressed by the great but who fought back valiantly and even wittily. He was a criminal, but a sympathetic one. His quarrel was with vicious and arrogant nobles, and when he humiliated them it was hard not to admire him. Growing interest in him was reflected in the 1720s, with the Edinburgh broadsheets mentioning him and the *Highland Rogue* being published. But even before his death interest was dwindling, to judge from written sources – manuscript and print. His most entertaining exploits lay in the past, his misdeeds were low-key and only had local impact. His death was worth a mention in magazines, but no more. In the decades that followed he was widely remembered in the Highlands in oral tradition, but there is no indication that he would ever achieve the national status that he was later to acquire. The trials of his sons in 1736 and 1752–54 brought his name back to public attention. A mutiny in the Black Watch in 1743 stirred up interest in Highland lawlessness, and this inspired a second edition of the *Highland Rogue*.[1] A history of the regiment, also inspired by the mutiny, explained that 'A clan is pretty much the same thing with what the Tartars call a hord, and that is very nearly what we understand by the word tribe, that is a small body of men under the absolute command of a chief.' Indeed the Highlanders were so warlike that regular troops were no match for them. As proof of this fact 'the exploits of the famous Robert MacGregor, alias Campbell, commonly called Rob Roy, *id est* [that is] Red Robin from the colour of his hair, which are very well known' were cited. He had 'rendered manifest' Highland prowess, and 'after a series of treasons and robberies, it had been found expedient to grant him [Rob] a pardon, purely to prevent him doing further mischief'.[2]

The great upheaval of the '45 threatened to swamp the memory of Rob Roy under waves of fresh stories of valour and oppression. Yet in the rising's aftermath the author (Graham of Gartmore) of a 1747 paper on how to tame the Highlands presented Rob as an outstanding example of the Highland 'problem'. 'This man, who was a person of sagacity, and neither wanted strategem nor address, having abandoned himself to all licentiousness, sett himself att the head of all the loose vagrant and desperate people of that clan at the west end of Perth and Stirling shires, and infested those whole countrys with thefts, robberys, and depredations.' Few within his reach – a night's journey – escaped without paying 'both a heavy and shamefull tax of blackmaill'.[3]

John Ramsay of Ochtertyre gave a fuller account. Rob was 'a gentleman by birth, in a clan where every man, however poor, finds no difficulty in making out a long and honourable pedigree', a repetition of the common sneer at the obsession of Highlanders with genealogy. Rob, 'a man of insinuation and strong mother-wit' was much favoured by Montrose before their quarrel. 'It matters little which of the parties was right or wrong in this transaction, but Rob thought himself oppressed, and regarded his title to his lands as indefeasible. Being now desperate, he carried on a sort of predatory war against the duke, his tenants and friends,' and was protected by Argyll. Breadalbane's role in harbouring Rob has already dropped out of sight. Ochtertyre provided, from what he had heard, some embellishment to events. When he kidnapped Killearn Rob had forced the factor to carry him (a big man) across the burns, which were in spate. A nice symbolic touch. The man who had been acting as agent for Rob's great enemy now had to act as his gillie. When Rob raided Montrose's girnals he forced the tenants to use their horses to carry the grain – but gave them food and drink, and left receipts. 'This extraordinary man, for the age and country in which he lived, seems to have formed himself on the model of former times, when such characters were common. He even affected somewhat of the state of a chieftain, which he could the better do that there was no longer a laird of Macgregor to head the clan.' Rob had been at the battle of Sheriffmuir 'but on that occasion he is said to have acted more cautiously than became a hero – being, indeed, never distinguished for personal courage, though the course of his life surely required it'. Through his depredations and blackmail Rob 'contrived in the Braes of Balquhidder [to live a] merry if not a creditable life, in great fulness, than which nothing could be more acceptable to his myrmidons [followers], who had all their several parts assigned them. At length, to the great reproach of government, he died in his bed at his house in Balquhidder, having a little before become Roman Catholic, partly to quiet his conscience, and partly to make his court to the family of Perth, from whom he expected great favours to his son and kinsmen'. Ochtertyre was clearly intrigued by Rob, the felon who believed he was a gentleman of honour and a patriot (he was opposed to the union with England), the man who was a thief but also a thief-hunter.[4] But he still thought it a pity that he had not been hanged. He might have been a pleasant person, but justice ought to have been done.

Ochtertyre died in 1814, though his comments on Rob had probably been written several decades earlier. They were not published until 1888, but it seems that Sir Walter Scott knew of his manuscript or had talked with him about Rob, for a number of the points Scott made in the introduction that he added to his novel *Rob Roy* in 1829 seem to derive from Ochtertyre's work. Scott, like Ochtertyre, presents Rob as an anachronism, a type of man common in earlier ages but out of place in his own, and emphasised that Rob's deeds were all the more remarkable for being performed so close to settled centres of law and civilisation.

In the mid-eighteenth century memories of Rob were mainly stored in popular tradition, but in the wider world changes in sensibilities and in attitudes to the Highlands and their people led to new perceptions of him. Old Highland ways, once seen as threatening, came to be regarded with misty nostalgia. As all around the world, once native peoples and cultures had been subdued and gainfully employed in a new order, sadness for their passing became fashionable. Also altering were the perceptions of the Highlands as terrain. What in past generations had been horrible barren wastes of moor, rock and water came to be seen as possessing grandeur, the wildness of untamed nature. The Highlands became a place to visit rather than to avoid. As tourism developed, many accounts of visits to the Highlands came to mention Rob Roy in passing. Alexander Campbell heard of Rob as collecting Montrose's rents and using them for 'the maintenance of the widow and the orphan'. But just as this exaggerated his charitableness, the story that he had kept Killearn a prisoner on bread and water for several weeks exaggerated his severity.[5] Perhaps, it may be suspected, the distorting curse of the tourist industry was already setting in, the tourist guide pressurised into inventiveness so as to have a good repertoire of tales of local heroes for the entertainment of gullible customers.

Soon after Campbell's tour, Romantic poets arrived in formidable force, in the persons of William Wordsworth, his sister Dorothy, and Samuel Taylor Coleridge, who toured the area in 1803. When they stayed on the shores of Loch Katrine, 'We mentioned Rob Roy,' Dorothy records (indicating that the party had arrived already primed to expect tales of him) 'and the eyes of all glistened; even the lady of the house, who was very diffident, and no great talker, exclaimed, "He was a good man, Rob Roy!"' Dorothy was told how 'Having an arm much longer than other men, he had a greater command with his sword. As a proof of the length of his arm, they told us that he could garter his tartan stockings below the knee without stooping, and added a dozen different stories of single combats, all in perfect good-humour, merely to prove his prowess. I daresay they had stories of this kind which would hardly have been exhausted in the long evenings of a whole December week, Rob Roy being as famous here as ever Robin Hood was in the forests of Sherwood; *he* also robbing from the rich, giving to the poor, and defending them from oppression.'[6] Dorothy Wordsworth's account reveals the development of the myth of Rob as a great fighter of duels (often fought just for fun), suggesting a much more dashing figure than the cautious avoider of violence that had been the true Rob.

William Wordsworth visited Rob Roy's grave and was moved by it (after a few years' thought) to verse, opening jauntily:

A famous man is Robin Hood,
The English ballad-singer's joy.
And Scotland boasts of one as good,
She has her own Rob Roy![7]

Like Dorothy, William could not resist celebrating Rob's 'wondrous length and strength of arm'. The poem then turns to musing on Rob as a man of principle, of moral creed. Books and laws did not enlighten but complicated life, and Rob emerges as a man taught a primitive morality by nature.

> Since, then, the rule of right is plain,
> And longest life is but a day,
> To have my ends, maintain my rights;
> I'll take the shortest way.
> . . . . they should take, who have the power,
> And they should keep who can.

This is 'the good old rule'. Right has, surprisingly, become might. The 'wild chieftain of a savage clan' is a lover of 'the *liberty* of man', but this is seen as consistent with the use of force to assert his own authority. The two were reconciled in the poet's mind, it seems, by seeing Rob as asserting his own liberty so he could use it to assert the liberty of others. Wordsworth is envisioning Rob's role as it might have been had he lived in a later age, that of the French Revolution. In rebelling against feudal oppressors he stood for the liberties of man. More than that, he gave (or would have given) example and leadership. In revolutionary France Napoleon was now in power – not as a despot but as an enforcer of the liberties of man on Europe. In revising his poem, Wordsworth added a stanza dreaming of Rob as Britain's saviour:

> And, if the word had been fulfilled,
> As *might* have been, then, thought of joy!
> France would have had her present boast,
> And we our own Rob Roy!

For Wordsworth, in one perspective Rob had lived too late, in an age when alien law and authority was being imposed on the Highlands, and he had had to take to the sword to defend his natural rights. But from another angle Rob had lived too early. If he had lived in the age of the French Revolution, the age of 'us who now behold the light', he would have fought for that great cause, his activities not being confined to a few obscure Highland glens. Rob has been startlingly updated, from failed Jacobite to frustrated Jacobin – but with a touch of the noble savage thrown in.[8] It is a bizarre vision, Rob Roy as a village Napoleon.

Embarrassingly, it turned out that Wordsworth had been worshipping at the wrong grave. Like his sister and Coleridge, he had been assured by local people that the grave was at Glengyle, whereas of course Rob had been buried in Balquhidder.[9] The poet refused to be discomfited when this was pointed out to him. His poetical inspiration was valid, because he had *thought* it was Rob's grave. But it is a cautionary tale. Old stories about Rob are not to be trusted just because they are told by local folk.

Before Wordsworth's poem was published, Rob Roy made his first known appearance on the stage, in a theatre in London. In 1803 the Little Theatre in the Haymarket produced *Red Roy; or, Oswyn and Helen*, written by Charles Farley with music by John Davy, and the piece was revived in South Shields and Durham in 1809–10. A brief summary of Rob's life was prefixed to the text – though his deeds are attributed to the years around 1600, over a century too early – recording how 'Red Roy, the Robber, (from his complexion and the fiery colour of his beard) was a noted Robber'. With a desperate gang he had infested the Highlands, committing daring outrages against Montrose and hoarding his loot in a cave. The play itself is a melodrama telling how Rob falls for the fair Helen and kidnaps her. His wife first tries to kill her rival, but then helps her escape. Rob recaptures her, but is pursued. He takes the girl to the top of 'a very high rock' and threatens to hurl her into the torrent that rushes below. Finally Rob is shot and wounded, and he himself falls to meet his fate in the torrent.[10] Thus, though the fame of Rob Roy is exploited, he is depicted as a conventional villain, with no redeeming features. The theme of abduction of a woman in the play may suggest that the ballad tradition of confusion between Rob Roy and his son Robin Og is present. *Red Roy* contains the first mention of a 'Helen' in connection with Rob, and perhaps it was here that Sir Walter Scott found the name he gave Rob's wife in his novel.

Tourists were taking an increasing interest in the Trossachs (strictly the area between Loch Archay and Loch Katherine, but by extension coming to include the surrounding mountains and the area Lomond area between Loch Katrine and Loch Lomond). They came to enjoy the scenery, the geology, and the evocation of mythical pasts. Walter Scott gave a huge boost to the trade by locating his bestselling poem *The Lady of the Lake* (1810) around Loch Katrine – to the fury of a Loch Lomond guide who wished he could drown Scott for having diverted attention to a rival loch.[11] Scott had been fascinated by the area and its past, and by Rob Roy himself, for over twenty years – he dated the collection of several of his anecdotes about Rob Roy to 1787 and 1792. His continuing interest in Rob emerges now and then in his letters in the years that followed. Scott's gullibility – or willingness to suspend disbelief when tempted – led him to be successful in acquiring relics of the hero. In 1712 he bought Rob's gun (a firelock musket). It had the letters 'R.M.C.' engraved on it, standing for Robert MacGregor Campbell, so its provenance was clear.[12] Did it ever occur to Scott that this was a bit too good to be true? Eventually Scott blithely added to the gun Rob Roy's 'skene dhu' (knife), dirk, sword, purse and sporran – and for good measure a brooch that had belonged to his wife.[13]

Once Scott turned his talents from poetry to historical fiction he can hardly have failed to have considered Rob Roy as a potential character, but it was not until the fifth in his series of novels that his interest in Rob emerged. Starting with *Waverley* Scott's novels were a great success, and important in marketing the series were inscrutable titles, like *Old Mortality* and *The Black Dwarf*, combined with a carefully cultivated secrecy as to authorship. His fifth novel was planned as a tale of family feud and Jacobite conspiracy, with the leading character an Englishman, Francis Osbaldistone. The plot exposes Osbaldistone to both Lowland (Glasgow) and Highland life and society, both of them new and strange to him, allowing Scott to comment on the differences between them. The Highland scenes are dominated by Rob Roy, hunted but resourceful, elusive, and influential. He is prepared to be violent, but is predominantly the beneficent manipulator who ultimately prevails and ensures that plots against Osbaldistone are thwarted.

In Scott's mind Rob represents a backward society, fascinating, in some ways attractive, but basically doomed, and rightly so. The new, commercial, 'civilised' world is supplanting it. What makes Rob an excellent illustration of the contrast between old and new is that, from Scott's perspective, Rob had lived so recently, and operated in such proximity to Lowland centres of commerce that the two worlds could be starkly juxtaposed. Rob is a man of honour, but his world, as seen through the narrative eye of Osbaldistone, is typified by 'dirt, violence, ignorance, and squalor'.[14] It is destined to disappear, like the societies of 'natives' everywhere, but it has a colour, an exoticness that makes its passing the cause of some regret. Thus Scott's picture is, on the whole, hard-headed. Those who rode to profit on the back of the *Rob Roy* boom that he began, however, were to have little time for Scott's socio-economic ponderings, and so concentrated on the heroic, the comic and the sentimental. And, perhaps above all they adopted Scott's visual image of Rob: exceeding hairy and long armed.

In spite of his fascination with Rob Roy, Scott seems to have decided that his life and legend were too insubstantial to bear the burden of being the main subject of a novel – and perhaps he thought them of too limited an appeal to sustain the interest of his English and Lowland Scots readers. He therefore used Rob *in* a novel rather than write one *about* him. Rob is in danger of being reduced to being a sort of exotic novelty turn, a caricature noble savage. Perhaps that is too harsh. His appearances in the book may be occasional, but they are dramatic and influential. He appears mysteriously at critical moments to influence events, and tellingly illustrates the contrast between Scotland's two cultures.

Scott at first had no title for the new novel he was writing, and it was his publisher Archibald Constable who suggested the title *Rob Roy*, perhaps fearing that Scott would lumber him with an indigestible *Osbaldistone*. As Scott later admitted, Constable's 'sagacity and experience foresaw the germ of popularity'[15] which the title *Rob Roy* offered. But at first he was taken aback by the idea: 'Nay, never let me have to write up to a name . . . You well know I have generally adopted a title that told nothing.'[16] This, perhaps, was Constable's point. *Rob Roy* as a title would prime the market in advance, referring to a figure already well known and regarded as intriguing. Scott allowed himself to be persuaded, and committed himself to the title as a useful marketing device.

By the autumn of 1717 the title of the eagerly-awaited new novel by the 'author of Waverley' was being publicised. 'The whole world is now anxiously expecting the appearance of *Rob Roy*', announced *Blackwood's Magazine*, so it was happy to present some account of Rob 'drawn up by a gentleman long resident in that quarter of the Highlands where many of Rob's exploits were performed. All anecdotes are traditional, believed authentic'. The gentleman would provide a narrative of the facts 'on which the "Mighty Unknown" has doubtless erected a glorious superstructure'. For four months (October to December 1817) the magazine produced a 'Memoir of Rob Roy Macgregor, and some Branches of his Family', retelling many stories of Rob and his sons.[17] The author called himself 'Dicaledon' ('of Scotland'), a pseudonym of Kenneth Macleay, a Glasgow physician, and his articles served as a pre-publication publicity campaign for the novel, arousing interest in Rob.

In December 1817, as the last 'Dicaledon' article appeared, Scott sent off the corrected proofs of *Rob Roy*, with the light-hearted message:

> With great joy
> I send you Roy
> 'Twas a tough job
> But we're done with Rob.

The book was published on the last day of 1817 (though it is dated 1818), and Constable daringly had 10,000 copies printed. His optimism was justified, for a second impression of 3,000 was needed a fortnight later[18] and several further reprints followed in quick succession.

From the first *Rob Roy* was hugely successful, and others immediately began to seek to profit both directly from the fictional version of Rob Roy created by Scott and more widely from the high profile the name now had. Within weeks of publication of the novel, four plays loosely based on it had appeared.[19] *Rob Roy* in Edinburgh was followed in London by the rather oddly titled *Rob Roy; the Traveller's Portmanteau* ('historical melodrama'), Isaac Pocock's *Rob Roy MacGregor; or, Auld Lang Syne* ('musical drama'), and *Rob Roy: the Gregarach* ('romantic drama'). John Davy, veteran of the *Red Rob* play of fifteen years before, composed the music for Pocock's piece (much of it taken from old Scots songs), and it appeared in many theatres in the decades that followed. On 15 February 1819 Scott saw it at the Theatre Royal in Edinburgh, and when King George IV, swathed in tartan and stage-managed by Scott, visited Edinburgh in 1822 a royal command performance was held.[20]

Pocock's drama followed Scott's plot fairly closely, though the real crowd-puller was not the earnest Englishman Francis Osbaldistone or the wild and brooding Rob Roy, but the comic adventures of Deacon Nicol Jarvie. Other playwrights while plundering Pocock for material, strayed far from their source.[21] All that was needed to justify the name of 'Rob Roy' for a theatrical piece seems to have been an outlaw (often, but not always, with a Highland setting and flashes of tartan) and a lot of songs. The first of a number of fully operatic versions appeared in 1831,[22] and it was soon joined by several Rob Roy overtures (the best-known being that by Berlioz).

But the operas made even less attempt than many of the plays to follow Scott's version of Rob Roy, let alone to take an interest in the real man that lay behind that image. Rob Roy became a name recognised throughout Europe and beyond, evoking courage, adventure, romance, a character exotic and intriguing.

Publishers as well as theatres cashed in on the boom Scott had created. Kenneth MacLeay revised his *Blackwood's Magazine* articles and had them published in book form as *Historical Memoirs of Rob Roy and Clan Macgregor, including Original Notices of Lady Grange* (Glasgow, 1819), contained the first of several supposed 'original' portraits of Rob. The lower end of the market was served by chapbooks – short works printed on cheap paper and sold by travelling salesmen. Works like *The Life and Surprising Exploits of Rob Roy Macgregor* and *The Life and Exploits of Rob Roy, the Highland Freebooter* (Falkirk, 1824) appeared in a number of editions[23] with overlapping titles and contents, drawing heavily on Scott and MacLeay. *The Trials of James, Duncan and Robert McGregor* (Edinburgh, 1818) transcribed the records of the trials of Rob's sons James and Robin Og in 1752–54, a valuable but neglected source for the history of the family.

Printed ballads, pirated from theatrical productions, catered for those who wished to sing about Rob Roy for themselves. Lifted from Pocock's play was:

A famous man was Robin Hood,
The English ballad-singer's joy,
But Scotland had a chief as good,
She had, she has, her bold Rob Roy.
        Chorus. A famous man, &c.

A dauntless heart McGregor shews,
And wondrous length and strength of arm;
He long has quell'd his Highland foes,
And kept his friends from harm.
        Chorus. A famous man, &c.

But Pocock was in no position to complain of plagiarism, as he in turn had plagiarised from Wordsworth's poem on Rob Roy's grave.[24] Also taken from Pocock and printed as a ballad was his closing chorus:

Pardon now the bold outlaw
Rob Roy MacGregor, O,

> Grant him mercy, gentles a',
>> Rob Roy MacGregor, O,
>
> Let your hands and hearts agree,
> Set the Highland laddie free,
> Make us sing wi' muckle glee,
>> Rob Roy MacGregor, O.[25]

Rob had now become identified with the 'Highland Laddie,' the allegorical figure of Jacobite lore who denoted the Stuart pretender to the throne. Another popular piece, in a similar rollicking style was:

> Have you seen the mighty man,
> Rob Roy M'Gregor, O,
> Chieftain of the Gregor Clan,
> Rob Roy M'Gregor, O,
> Shrouded in immortal fame
> He forsook his native hame
> To the Lawland Glens he came,
>> Rob Roy M'Gregor, O.

But it turns out that this Rob had gone to the Lowlands in predatory search of a 'bonnie lass', reviving the old ballad confusion of Rob Roy with his son Rob Og.[26]

A few ventured to mock:

Ode to the Great Unknown

> I like long-arm'd Rob Roy. – His very charms
> Fashion'd him for renown! – In sad sincerity,
> The man that robs or writes must have long arms,
> If he's to hand his deeds down to posterity![27]

Moreover, especially in the 1870s and 1880s, there was a fashion for staging burlesque versions of Rob Roy's story, with such mocking titles as *Robbing Roy, or, Scotched and Kilt* (1879) 'kilt' representing a Scots pronunciation of 'killed'.[28] Too much romance and sentimentality had led to a healthy reaction. For most poets, however, earnest reverence continued to be appropriate. The story that when Rob was told on his deathbed that an enemy was coming to visit him he had insisted on being fully dressed and armed to receive him, inspired the American William Hosmer to the *Death of Rob Roy*:

> With heather pillowing his head
> The dying outlaw lay.[29]

That Rob had submitted and was not an outlaw to the end of his life was something that some legend-makers were reluctant to admit. William Thornbury set his *An Adventure of Rob Roy* not in a world Rob himself would have recognised but in what is presumably intended to be the time of the harsh repression of Jacobitism after Culloden. Hanoverian soldiers are leaving a trail of smoking straths and bloodstained villages behind them, killing children in their beds. A party of them enter a Highland Inn. Rob is present, and denounces their conduct. The soldiers present arms, evidently intending a massacre.

> The Highlandman laughed loud and long,
> Then kicked the benches over,
> Danced three steps of a Highland reel,
> And cried, 'I'm Rob the Rover!'[30]

He then killed some of the soldiers with his broadsword and forced the rest to flee. This, perhaps, deserves the much-contested prize for the most ludicrous caricature of Rob Roy ever produced. In comparison J.B. Blackie's *Rob Roy's Cave*, though plodding, comes as a relief.

> Here lodged Rob Roy; proud kings have palaces,
> And foxes holes, and sheep the sheltering fold;
> Fish own the pools, and birds the plumy trees;
> And stout Rob Roy possessed this granite hold.
> . . .
> When kings were weak, lords false, and lawyers knaves,
> Rob Roy saved honest men from being slaves.[31]

How he did this is not made clear.

Rob Roy's post-Scott status thus produced hosts of poetic, dramatic and musical representations. Visual images were also required and, as already noted, one was first supplied in Kenneth MacLeay's *Historical Memoirs* of 1818. It is taken from an 'original portrait' – but unfortunately it was not actually a portrait of Rob. At some point in the development of the Rob Roy legend his name had become attached to the most famous full-length oil painting of a Highland fighting men dating from the early eighteenth century, which depicted a striking figure, with sword threateningly held aloft. It was so popular that several copies of it were made. It is now known to be Richard Waitt's 1714 depiction of Alasdair Grant, known as the 'champion' of Clan Grant, but Maclean assumed it to be Rob Roy, and made a drawing based on it, which was then engraved and published in his book. But Rob has been cut down to size. The engraving is half rather than full length, and Rob has been deprived both sword and targe. Interpreting expression in portraits is subjective, but this Rob looks a little apprehensive as he looks out at the viewer. Another version from the same original, published a few years later, puts a bit more spirit into the man. It is still half-length, but the eyes seem both piercing and brooding, his moustache instead of drooping bristles fiercely.[32]

Macleay simply assumed that the Grant champion portrait was Rob Roy. John Sobieski Stolberg Stuart (otherwise John Hay) sought to argue the point. A self-proclaimed illegitimate grandson of Bonnie Prince Charlie, and undoubted king of tartanomania, he identified no fewer than five portraits of Rob, all in fact those of the Grant champion. His argument proving that the picture must be of Rob was, however, absurd – it *must* depict Rob Roy, he asserted, because no other Highlander at the time had been famous enough to arouse such interest.[33]

Rob also acquired a tartan. By one account the simple black and red check which aquired this name got its name from it being used in a theatrical production about Rob in Glasgow in 1818,[34] and an 1818 list of tartans in production includes the Rob Roy. But a sample of the tartan labelled as being Rob Roy's was submitted to the Highland Society of London in 1815–16 by Sir John MacGregor Murray of MacGregor, and the existence of a 'black and red' tartan was listed in 1794. As far back as the 1740s a portrait of the earl of Wemyss shows him wearing such a tartan. What seems to have happened is that a genuinely old tartan at some point was given Rob's name to help market it, probably during the vogue for all things Highland that led, from the 1790s, to the systematic listing of tartans (many of them just invented) and attaching traditional names to them.[35]

Statues of Rob Roy came later than printed images.The first known was a distinctly improvised figure created in the 1850s by adapting a figurehead salvaged from an Aberdeen whaling ship. Taken to Peterculter, the figurehead was provided with two logs for legs, lead boots and a canvas kilt, and it was then erected high on the rocks overlooking the Leuchars Burn. 'The Mannie on the Rock' became a local favourite, and whenever it rots away it is replaced by a new wooden statue: the fourth was erected in 1991. According to story, the statue stands where it does to commemorate a great leap Rob once made over the Leuchars Burn when it was in spate,[36] perhaps when pursued. But it is hard not to believe that the story is a recent invention, made up to explain why Peterculter has this odd statue.

A more professional work was produced by Thomas Stuart Burnett in the 1880s, towering seven feet tall. It was bought by John Aird (rich industrialist and Conservative MP) and installed in his house in London. Later, like Rob himself, it fell on hard times, but was eventually rescued from a scrapyard, repatriated to Scotland – and sold at auction for £44,050 in 2002.[37] A century later a descendant of Rob commissioned a new statue, which was unveiled in Stirling in 1975. The sculptor, Benno Schotz (then Queen's Sculptor in Ordinary for Scotland) tried hard to make his work conform to the old 'could tie his garters without stooping' stereotype of Rob. Realising that making length of arms do all the work would produce an unbelievably grotesque figure, Schotz gave Rob unusually (but not incredibly) long arms combined with notably short legs, so he could perform the garters trick. The result is a striking but stocky figure.[38]

The twentieth century produced a new medium to promote Rob Roy. His name formed the title of the first feature film ever made in Scotland, starring John Clyde, in 1911. The film itself is lost, but stills from it depict a fierce and hairy Rob. 'The sensation of the cinemagraphic World,' an advertisement proclaimed, 'a great and ambitious work that will stir the heart of every Scotchman throughout the world.'[39] Gaumont's *An Adventure of Rob Roy* appeared the same year, and an American *Rob Roy* in 1913. In 1922 there was another Gaumont version, with epic fight scenes boosted by a large contingent from the Argyll and Sutherland Highlanders. The real Rob, usually so careful to avoid violence, would have been appalled, but crowds had to be turned away from overflowing cinemas. 1953 saw a Disney version, 'Rob Roy, the Highland Rogue', drawing from one critic the comment that the acting was so wooden that it might as well have been a cartoon. Then in 1995 came *Rob Roy* starring Liam Neeson, 'the first truly believable representation with which Scots can feel comfortable and even justifiably proud of that period of Scottish history'.[40] 'Truly believable' only to those who know little or nothing of Rob Roy, and why Scots should be proud of a period in which (as depicted in the film) a nice guy like Rob is persecuted by nasty aristocratic baddies is not explained. Candles attract moths. Celebrity names all too often attract drivel.

The posthumous world of Rob Roy had been a fairly narrow one until 1817. He was a figure about whom many stories were told, in Scotland and to some extent (as the Wordsworths' 1803 visit to his homeland indicates) in England. After 1817 he quickly became an international presence, as a romantic, suffering hero and an archetypical Scottish image, at home and abroad. The 'market' for Rob Roy and the 'Rob Roy Country' took off, and today his name has become central to the tourist economy of the Trossachs, an area which seems to expand constantly as more and more places seek to insert themselves under its tourist-attracting wings. Dorothy Wordsworth saw the beginning of the process when she returned to the area in 1822. Things had much changed since 1803. She had then been one of a small group of friends travelling on their own through country that seldom saw strangers. Their tour had been something of an adventure. In 1822 there was already something of the 'package holiday' about her visit. She and her companions had visited 'Rob Roy's Cave' in 1803, guided by a 'little Highland woman' who spoke no English.[41] But in 1822 Dorothy came with a boat-load of tourists, accompanied by a piper clad in tartan. 'Our Highland musician tunes his pipes as we approach Rob Roy's caves. The grandeur of nature strangely mixed with stage effects; but it is good acting.' 'Touristification' had set in, and all the passengers piled out of the boat and pushed their way through the rocks said to have been Rob's hiding place. They were there, they told Dorothy, because Sir Walter Scott has made the place so much talked about. 'Coming out all they can say is "Well! there is nothing to be seen; but it is worth while, if only to say that one has been there."'[42] The 'been there, seen that' mentality was already well established.

Before Scott Rob Roy had often been 'labelled' by referring to Robin Hood, to indicate what type of outlaw he was. After the novel was published, other men began to be 'labelled' by reference to Rob himself. A Welsh counterpart was the first to appear, in *The Life, Exploits, and Death of Twm John Catty, the celebrated Welch Rob Roy, and his beautiful bride Elinor, Lady of Llandisent, etc.* (c. 1830). An Englishman followed, in *Memoirs of a Smuggler . . . containing the principal events in the life of John Ratterbury of Beer . . . commonly called the Rob Roy of the west* (1837). The idea then spread across the Atlantic, with the *Autobiography of Samuel S. Hildebrand, the renowned 'Missouri Bushwhacker' . . . and unconquerable Rob Roy of America* (1870), and *The Hunted Outlaw, or, Donald Morrison, the Canadian Rob Roy* (Montreal, 1889).

Rob Roy had become a name for the romantically heroic, the

outlaw you wanted to evoke sympathy for by suggesting that he was more victim than criminal. He became so many things at the whim of those who endlessly recreated him that the original vanished. In the tales of Robin Hood, originating many centuries before those of Rob Roy, the individual whose activities had given rise to tales has been lost completely. It is not possible to say whether he was yeoman or nobleman, or what century he lived in – or even to be sure there ever was such an individual.[43] In various semi-fictional guises Rob has travelled some way down the same road. But the relative recentness of the age in which he lived meant Rob never lost touch with reality entirely, for it was an age of record-keeping and letter-writing. Thus it is possible to rescue Rob from myth and return him to his own time and place and individuality.

Sir Walter Scott, who had done so much to turn Rob into a fictional character in 1817, twelve years later did more than anyone else before the twentieth century to seek to identify and study Rob as a historical character. It has been suggested that Scott did this because he felt some guilt at having fictionalised Rob for commercial ends. He had agreed to a book title to please the marketing men, and in a sense sold Rob short. Rob had suffered the humiliation of not being the main character in the book that bore his name.[44] He might be presented as 'heroic' but the character people remembered the book for was Nicol Jarvie.[45]

Whatever his motives, when Scott was preparing the 'Magnum Opus' edition of his works in 1829 he added to *Rob Roy* over a hundred pages of introduction devoted to anecdotes, letters and other documents about the 'real' Rob Roy. The historian is grateful, but it has been argued that in literary terms the addition is a miscalculation. The new introduction may be intended to justify the use of Rob's name as the title of the book, but it means that the reader, having been primed by this mass of detailed introductory material on Rob, is likely to be bewildered and disappointed by finding that the novel itself appears, for a great many pages, to have nothing whatever to do with Rob Roy. Scott, however, could now feel he had done Rob justice at last, and he took pride in the fact that he had partly redeemed the MacGregors from the evil reputation given to them by their oppressors. 'I was the first literary man of modern days who chose the oppressed clan as subjects of pity and sympathy.'[46]

Scott thus tried to rescue the historical Rob Roy from the fiction of his novel, and to place him in the wider context of his clan history of being oppressed and hunted. Rob becomes, rather unworthily, a symbol for all the injustice MacGregors had suffered at the hands of their neighbours and government. Eric Hobsbawm provided a different context for Rob in his study of *Bandits*. The fact that Hobsbawm did not include Rob's life in his study makes it all the more striking that Rob fits remarkably closely with one of the types of bandits he identifies – the 'noble robber' or good bandit, a category typified by Robin Hood. These are men driven out of their established place in society by injustice and persecution. They fight back, with the aim of regaining their rightful position within society. In doing so, they rely on popular sympathy and support. No one will betray them, so they become invulnerable, indeed in some cultures almost magically invisible. In their role as outlaws they prey on rich oppressors to pursue their personal quarrels, and they become identified with generosity to the poor – by giving them charitable help or intimidating their oppressors. To be cynical, it could be said that these bandits needed to ensure that they retained the sympathy or active support of the people if they were to escape those hunting them, so helping the poor was partly self-interest. But there is more than this involved. Having found out, by their own outlawry, how corrupt or malign those in power are, they genuinely develop a feeling of sympathy for and identification with others who are suffering hardship and oppression. In keeping with this, they are not gratuitously violent.

The 'noble robber' has been forced into outlawry – it is not a career choice. His ambition is to have wrongs righted and return to his true place in society. His perceived enemy usually is not distant king or government but some local oppressor, and the hope is often to penetrate somehow beyond that malign influence, contact true, legitimate authority,[47] and be pardoned once it is recognised that the outlaw has been unjustly treated and deserves reward or employment as compensation. In the case of Rob Roy, the malign oppressor that stands between the outlaw and justice is Montrose. At times Rob flirted with the Stuart claimants to the throne as the legitimate, just authority that would save him, but eventually he settled for George I, explaining that he had been loyal all along. Pardon was duly rewarded with employment – as a spy. Rob does not get all his perceived wrongs righted – and does not entirely abandon his law-breaking lifestyle – but partial reconciliation has been reached. In a sense he triumphed, simply by surviving. He had seen off Montrose, getting a pardon directly from the king.

Through north and south America, through western, central and eastern Europe Hobsbawm traced noble robbers who in some degree in life, and to a much greater degree in legend, parallel Rob Roy. The attraction of the story of the man wronged who fights back, defies the powers that be, and survives, is transcultural. Robbing from the great and giving to the needy has a universal appeal. Even those who normally support law and order and disapprove of the criminal can feel currents of sympathy – and identification. Most people feel at one time or another that they have grievances that they have put up with out of fear of the consequences of protesting, but have felt shamed by their passivity. By identifying with a Rob Roy one can dream of how bravely defiant one might have been oneself. The power asserted by defying law does not corrupt but is used to good ends, until it can almost seem that the Robin Hood/Rob Roy figure has been outlawed because he helps the poor. The care for the deserving outweighs the crime of law-breaking. Just one example of how universal some of these 'noble bandit' stories can be involves the motif of 'bandit gives poor person money to pay a debt, then steals it back from the collector'. It is told of Rob Roy, but also of Jesse James in the Wild West, and an Argentinean bandit of the 1930s. Bandits could be (or be believed to be) redistributors of wealth in the community.[48]

Rob Roy, then, can be seen as a stereotypical noble bandit, though he was not to know that a marxist historian centuries later was to create this category. In some ways, many of the things he did were what came naturally – as to other noble bandits – in his circumstances. He had not intended to become an outlaw, but once he did he could only justify what had happened, both to himself and others, by protesting his innocence, adopting an outraged self-righteousness and, as the bitterness of the feud with Montrose deepened, demonising him as the noble enemy who oppressed the poor. The story becomes one of good versus evil, with good heroically making a fool of the forces of evil.

14

MAN *VERSUS* MYTH

Now, the question of Rob Roy's loyalty must be faced some time or another, and it must be admitted quite frankly that he was not over-scrupulous nor truthful, and the long and the short of it is that it is wiser not to look for public school ideas in a Highland cateran[1]

Such brisk common sense is refreshing, but rare.

In this book the story of Rob Roy's life has been told, and his reputation in the centuries after his death has been examined. It has become clear that the man of the legend differs greatly from the man who actually lived, yet it is striking how much of the legend came into being in Rob's own lifetime. Moreover, much of the interpretation the legend provides of his own actions and those of others was created by Rob himself. His explanation of his downfall and his life as an outlaw won him a popular regard that he has never lost. He was a master at bypassing difficult questions and convincingly presenting his own version of events. In person and on paper he was outstanding at making people believe him and sympathise with him – not least because they liked him. Even those who disapproved of his actions tended to be won over when they met him.

This charisma, the ability he had of gaining people's liking and trust, was doubtless central to his business success. It was also absolutely crucial to his survival in his long years of outlawry. But it may be that this charisma gave him an over-confidence that contributed to his downfall, by inspiring in him an unrealistic belief that he would always be able to manipulate events and people to his own advantage. In 1711–12 he clearly faced a severe financial crisis. Perhaps, at that point, it would have been possible to negotiate a settlement with his creditors, though that would have been humiliating, the loss of his reputation for trustworthiness, and quite possibly the loss of his land. Rob would have been negotiating from a position of weakness. Boldly – or recklessly – Rob decided to create a strong negotiating position for himself. He would put his lands out of the reach of his creditors, he would continue to raise money from them, which he knew he could not repay, and then abscond to safety under Breadalbane's protection. His creditors could take legal action against him, but it would prove impossible to enforce the law, and eventually they would see sense and agree to negotiate with him. In the interim, Rob could busy himself creating his own legend, of an honest man unjustly hounded by the great. In reality, he was an accomplished conman carrying out a well-planned fraud.

In financial terms, the creditors would probably have been wise to go along with Rob's scheme, bitter as that would have been. They might well have got a better deal from him in 1712 than the one they eventually had to accept from the Forfeited Estate Commissioners over a decade later.

Rob's calculations were based on the assumption that all his creditors would be motivated primarily by wanting their money (or as much of it as possible) back. They might denounce Rob for his fraud, but it would be level-headed financial interest that would guide their actions. Fatally, one man turned out to be more interested in revenge for the insult of being defrauded than in his money. The amount Rob owed the duke of Montrose was, in terms of the duke's total wealth, trifling. But his reaction was not based on that loss. He was one of the greatest men in Scotland, of ancient noble blood and the highest rank of the nobility. He had come to trust Rob Roy and done business with him. He had helped him. He had taken this man from an outlawed clan notorious (in the perception of others) for violence, theft and perfidy, under his wing. In all probability Montrose, like most other people, had liked Rob and found him entertaining company. So far as was possible in view of the huge gulf in social status between them, Montrose probably felt friendship.

Then he had been betrayed. Rob had made a fool of him, deceived him, betrayed his trust. This was not just a simple case of a bad debt for his estate officials to sort out. It was a personal matter. Rob must be brought to justice as a matter of honour, in this instance infinitely more important than money. Thus Rob found himself not just an everyday bankrupt but the target of determination to obtain retribution by one of the greatest landowners in the country, a man who was also one of its most powerful politicians. Rob was publicly denounced and Montrose put himself at the head of the cause of his creditors, and sought vengeance. Rob's hopes of compromise were doomed.

Indeed, he was trapped. He can never have calculated on such intransigence and aggression from a creditor. Thus ironically Rob was in a sense correct in claiming that his troubles stemmed from persecution by Montrose. If the duke had not made such a fuss, Rob in all probability could have done deals with his creditors and escaped fairly lightly in spite of the blatant fraud he had committed. But Rob's insinuations that the quarrel had somehow been initiated by Montrose was false. The duke had reacted to gross betrayal.

But if Rob was trapped, so too, it turned out, was the duke. It may well be that he regretted his initial over-reaction to being duped by Rob, once his rage had died down. He found himself in a situation in which Rob, under the protection of Breadalbane, could move pretty freely in much of the Highlands, continue to trade, even act as a judge. Montrose, for all his might, could do nothing about it, and the fact that he could not catch Rob was a humiliation. The outlaw's fame began to spread, and the theme of a little man successfully defying malicious oppression by a great one (Rob's own version of events) proved very appealing. Even Montrose's colleagues in the nobility must have found it hard to suppress a chortle at his discomfiture. But for Montrose to back down and give up the obsessive quest for Rob was unthinkable. It would be a further embarrassment, an acceptance of failure. He would lose face.

Rob had not the power to end the confrontation, and Montrose could not bring himself to end it. The resulting stalemate might have continued indefinitely, but the coming of the Jacobite rising of 1715 made that impossible. In Rob Roy's cleverly manipulated rendering of events, even the fact that he ended up on the losing side in the rising was Montrose's fault. Had Rob ventured into the Lowlands to join the Hanoverian army, the devilish Montrose would have had him arrested. True enough, no doubt, but it is pretty hard to believe that Rob ever had any inclination to join the Hanoverian forces. Rob was, however, truthful in claiming that the situation in the Highlands made it impossible for him to remain neutral. In civil war many are forced into taking sides who would prefer to remain aloof. In Rob's case there were the additional problems that had he failed to join the Jacobites he would have lost credibility with his own clansmen, and much of the sympathy for him that existed in the Highlands. Worst of all, perhaps, Breadalbane's friendship would have been replaced with enmity. That might well have proved fatal.

Rob had to declare himself a Jacobite, and there can be no doubt that his underlying sympathies lay with the Stuart cause. His public drinking of Jacobite toasts in 1714–15 came before rebellion had begun, and thus before it became necessary to declare his commitment to the cause. To his innate feelings there may well have been added, in driving Rob into active Jacobitism, growing desperation about ever making peace with Montrose. Personal victory might be achieved by destroying Montrose as part of the wider Jacobite destruction of the Hanoverians.

Rebellion was obviously a risk, but there seemed no alternative. However, risk management could be undertaken to increase the odds of survival whatever the outcome of the revolt. Here again Rob relied on the friendship of great men. He was on good terms with the Campbells of Argyll – and the appointment of the duke of Argyll as the Hanoverian army commander must have given a major boost to Rob's morale. The Jacobite officer would double up as a Hanoverian spy.

A foot on either side of a fence is an uncomfortable stance, difficult to maintain for long. The Jacobites were aware even before the rising began of Rob's treachery. It may seem surprising that this did not lead to his being denounced, but a great many people, Hanoverian as well as Jacobite, were being careful to hedge their bets, to try to ensure that even if the side they fought for lost they and their families would not face complete ruin. Moreover Rob Roy's was a well-known and respected name among the MacGregors, and probably he would be able to persuade more to rise in arms than any other man of his clan. He was a useful man to have outwardly on your side – even if he was not to be trusted. As has been suggested earlier, it is tempting to see the uses made of Rob by the Jacobites during the rising as revealing a policy of keeping him away from the main Jacobite army, and from its councils of war in Perth. He was employed, but kept on the fringes, so the intelligence he might be able to betray would be low level. He was on the expedition to Inveraray, but he was not summoned to join the army when it advanced towards Sheriffmuir. He was then sent on a recruiting expedition to the west, and immediately after that sent to Fife on an expedition that seemed pretty pointless. Perhaps it was partly the MacGregors in general that were being held at arms length like this, as even fellow Highlanders tended to regard them as wild and ill-disciplined, but suspicion of untrustworthiness was centred on Rob Roy.

The Jacobites were duly defeated, and Rob was then pursued as a rebel attainted for treason as well as an outlawed debtor. He continued the raiding of Montrose's lands which he had begun in the guise of being a Jacobite army officer, thus moving from the passive defiance of the duke he had shown in 1712–15 (by staying beyond his reach) to aggression and provocation. He may have calculated that, in time, this might pressurise Montrose into settling with him. But in the immediate aftermath of the '15 Rob's main thought may have simply been that his new boldness could not make things worse – and, of course, he may have been driven by economic necessity into raiding. He could no longer make a peaceful living in the safety of Breadalbane.

The intense pursuit of Rob Roy in 1716–17 was, ironically, only marginally about him being a rebel or a raider of Montrose's lands. Its essence lay in the belief that Rob could ensure the conviction of the duke of Argyll of treason for his secret contacts with Jacobites. Rob had embroiled himself in the shadowy world of intelligence during the rising and now paid the price. In the end, he did not betray Argyll as Montrose demanded. The reasons for this were doubtless mixed. Montrose might be able to get Rob a pardon, but was an unscrupulous and ruthless man. Could Rob trust him? Further, Rob doubtless detested Montrose. He believed passionately in his own story that Montrose was unjustly persecuting him, conveniently forgetting that the first betrayal had been his own. Argyll, though powerless to do much to help Rob at this time, had shown friendship – and to agree to bear witness against him would of course alienate the one member of the nobility who was not already hostile to him. It might indeed lead to Rob being assassinated. All these were considerations of self-interest, but doubtless in Rob's decision to throw in his lot with Argyll in Scotland's political squabbles there were more intangible factors involved. Though Rob had notably proved in the eyes of many by his conduct that he was not 'a man of honour', he nonetheless had his own sense of honour. There were certain things he could not do without destroying this self-defined sense of his own honour. Central among them may well have been betraying Argyll or submitting to Montrose.

Rob escaped the traps closing around him in July 1717 by issuing his declaration from Balquhidder denouncing Montrose, Atholl and their minions for their plotting. The power of secrets is destroyed by making them public. The politically-driven hunt for him was wound down. Pursuing him became mainly motivated by Montrose's determination to protect his own property, though the fact that Rob was officially still a rebel allowed him to get military aid, in the form of the establishment of the garrison at Inversnaid. Montrose finally succeeded in expelling Rob and taking over his Inversnaid estate – though raiding from further a field continued. Montrose continued to complain, but was tiring of the fight, reconciled to not catching Rob. Over ten years all attempts had proved counter-productive. Perhaps he persuaded himself that it was after all beneath the dignity of a man of his exalted status to take an interest in pursuing a fairly insignificant outlaw.

At this time, in the early 1720s, Rob Roy briefly attracted the attention of the print media, a demonstration of how widespread his image of himself as the oppressed ordinary man had become. But interest faded. He might still be on the run, but nobody was taking much trouble to run after him. He was no longer newsworthy. His capture, to Montrose and government, would have been welcome, but as another cattle-raider mopped up, not an occasion for special rejoicing. His lands had been sold and his creditors accepted that there was no point in pursuing him any further. Rob himself was ageing, and probably more interested in holding on to land in Balquhidder than in twisting Montrose's tail. The years which were to form the basis of so many tales about Rob were over. No resolution of the conflict between him and Montrose had been reached, but there was tacit acceptance that it was best to take it no further. In 1725 a new Highland policy gave Rob Roy the opportunity to beg King George I for a pardon, and he took it. It was no doubt humiliating, but it must have been balm to Rob's wounds that he was able (in his letter begging for a pardon) to get away with blaming his unfortunate treason in 1715 on Montrose. The duke was no longer at the centre of politics, and no one thought it worth consulting him about pardoning the treason of a man who placed responsibility for the offence on him. Rob might have submitted to the king, but he never submitted to Montrose.

Pardon brought Rob new opportunities for employment, and betrayal of men who trusted him, as a government spy. Perhaps he didn't like it, perhaps he was hard up, but he did the work. Yet his reputation as a good man was so well established that this was ignored by the growing legend. In wider perceptions he remained the basically honest man who had been unfairly treated and had stood up for himself manfully, year after year, humiliating great and arrogant oppressors. He was likable and popular, and had conformed to the well-established Robin Hood motif by sympathising with and helping the poor. Above all, perhaps, he had proved himself a survivor. He gave hope to others by achieving things which seemed impossible. He had come out in the end, honour intact (if you didn't look too closely) and still defiant. He might have lost his lands, but he had retained his reputation and retained the dignity of farming his own land until his death – though it was a close-run thing, with the threat of eviction hanging over him on his deathbed.

At some points in the course of writing this book the author has been concerned that he might seem to be acting not just as judge, but as police investigator, prosecution and jury as well. This has been impossible to avoid if a new, realistic picture of the historical Rob Roy is to be drawn. And historians are like policemen and prosecutors. They collect and assess evidence, and (ideally) argue for conclusions based on it. In the instance of Rob Roy the case for the defence has been repeated endlessly in the past, based on a desire to provide satisfying stories and maintain a heroic myth. Any attempt to provide balance which changes this image will be bound to seem at first sight to be biased in favour of the prosecution. There is no way of presenting a Rob Roy based on evidence rather than wish-fulfilment that does not admit that he was a man who carefully planned to defraud those he owed money to, and that he gave and sold intelligence about Jacobites to their enemies. Any assessment of the man which does not accept the reality of these events is make-believe. One can summon up some empathy with the fraud. The pressure of financial failure is a pretty common cause of crime, as those caught in a net of debt struggle desperately to free themselves, and often end up making things worse. But it is hard to say anything to alleviate the contempt aroused by his betrayal of his Jacobite associates.

That is a verdict on Rob's 'crimes'. But obviously there is more to a man than a judicial assessment of his offences. Isolated faults do not – or do not necessarily – determine assessment of a whole life or personality. From Rob's own perspective, sincerely believed in, and that of those who sympathised with him and helped develop his legend, his actions as an outlaw were justified (apart from his treachery to fellow Jacobites, which, being unforgivable, is ignored). Rob had indeed been oppressed and persecuted by Montrose (let's not mention again the fact that this was a reaction to Rob defrauding him). Rob was a little man harassed by the great and arrogant dukes of Montrose and Atholl, and bravely defied them (edit out the fact that he only survived through the help of other great men – Breadalbane and Argyll – and not on his own). He stood for honour (well, he believed he maintained his honour) and self-respect. He didn't steal but collected what was his by right. He had no taste for violence. And, by scorning the great (those he wasn't grovelling to at the time) almost by default Rob was on the side of the poor.

In the battle for 'hearts and minds' Rob Roy was the victor in his struggle with Montrose. He emerged with a reputation which led (with a bit of help from Sir Walter Scott) to his becoming a national hero. And he successfully branded Montrose for posterity with a sinister caricature image of aristocratic oppression, the perfect foil to contrast with Rob's own good qualities. Montrose may be denounced in the Rob Roy stories, but he is a vital part of them. Every hero needs a villain to battle against. It was Montrose who made Rob famous. Who would have heard of Rob today if Montrose had not been intransigent over Rob's debt to him? Generals need wars if they are to become famous, Rob needed (though he did not seek) the challenge of Montrose in order to rise from obscurity. Moreover, if not quite the caricature villain of legend, Montrose certainly displayed an unprincipled ruthlessness when he thought catching Rob might help him to political power by destroying his rival Argyll. He, Atholl and Cockburn of Ormiston did, as Rob indicated, form a triumvirate of men prepared to do almost anything to achieve their ends.

Looking at Rob not in isolation but alongside such 'respectable' villains in the 'establishment' is greatly to his advantage, as is considering him in a much wider context of his contemporaries. It is a dispiriting thought that in this book it is hard to identify anyone who is likely to impress the reader favourably with his principles or character. Rob lived in an age steeped in double-dealing and corruption. That he betrayed fellow Jacobites must be set alongside the fact that many of them were prepared to help hunt him down if there was money in it. Men might be Hanoverians or Jacobites, Whigs or Tories, but most were above all interested in their own and their families' fortunes, and were prepared to be ruthless and unscrupulous pursuing them. And such qualities were not regarded as entirely bad. There could be respect, even admiration, for the man who got the better of others by trickery, theft and double dealing (unless you were a victim). These were important survival skills. Cunning, cheating and twisting, if successful, might bring approval. In Rob Roy's case such qualities were exercised by a man with great personal charm who avoided gratuitous violence, treated those who were not his enemies well and created a legend of a wronged little man fighting back, maintaining honour and seeking justice. Rob had a touch of that indefinable gift, star quality. Cattle raiding might be a common sort of activity, but Rob at times brought to it wit and style, in the ways in which he taunted Montrose. All this won Rob popularity. It might be accepted that he was a criminal, but there was a belief that this was somehow 'not his fault'. He was a 'rogue' or 'rascal' (in the milder usages of these words), whose exploits might well bring a smile to the face, not a villain whose actions aroused horror.

Above all Rob's story appealed because he was a survivor, a man whose cunning, resourcefulness and determination led to his remaining free in spite of the odds. Neither Montrose nor Atholl nor the army could hunt him down. In the end, he could claim victory. His enemies gave up the hunt. He died in his bed, a free man.

That is the perspective posterity has adopted. But another perspective is possible, depicting Rob as a loser. By ill fortune or ill management, his business failed. He lost his lands, and spent over a decade of his life on the run, often in great danger. In material terms he died in much poorer circumstances than those he had been born into. The prospect of eviction haunted his last years. He might have escaped the law, but seen in this way his life displays not inspiring triumph for a little man fighting injustice but, on the contrary, providence punishing a criminal. He might have escaped the sentence of a court of law, but he suffered greatly as the result of his disastrous fraud of 1711–12. He betrayed his fellow rebels in 1715, but gained nothing, for he was attainted for high treason by the Hanoverians he had sold himself to. Rob's crimes ruined his life. Conventional morality is satisfied.

That would of course be harsh and narrow-minded as an overall conclusion of a man who was so well liked, and whose suffering when being hunted were most intense not when the pursuit was fuelled by desire to enforce the law of the land, but by the totally unscrupulous political machinations of men of high rank and office who saw him simply as an expendable pawn to be used to further their ambitions.

Will the new perspectives on Rob presented above, by a historian trying to stick to the rules of his craft in assessing evidence, undermine and eventually supplant the popular image of the man?

Not a hope. To some the 'real' Rob Roy may seem more attractive than the invented one. He is a believable, complex human being living and acting in a specific historical context, rather than a cardboard cut-out hero. But the attraction of the mythical Rob Roy rests on a different level and appeals to much wider tastes. He is a hero, someone to look up to and admire, an inspiring example of injustice being defied, wrongs being righted. A figure whose life, with its many daring escapes and gripping duels, is far more exciting and inspiring than that of the original man. This mythic Rob won't die. Apart from anything else, he is a major tourist asset. He must live on so money can be made out of him.

Perhaps all the historian can hope for is that it be accepted that there are two Rob Roys. One lived and breathed. The other is a good story, a lively tale set in the past. Both may be accepted as 'valid', but they serve different needs and interests. The 'factual' man and the 'creative' fiction can live alongside each other. But it is important to recognise that they are not the same man.

ABBREVIATIONS

A & T	J.G.S. Murray, *Chronicles of the Atholl and Tullibardine Families* (5 vols., 1908)
Atholl Mss	Stewart-Murray of Atholl papers, Blair Castle (catalogued in NRAS survey 234)
BL	British Library, London
CB	G.E. C[okayne], *The Complete Baronetage* (6 vols., Exeter, 1900–9)
CC	Commissary Court Records, NAS
CH	Church Records, NAS
CS	Court of Session Record, NAS
Clan Gregor	A.G.M. MacGregor, *History of Clan Gregor* (2 vols., 1898–1901). An online electronic edition has been published by www.clangregor.org with an introduction by Peter Laurie (2002)
CP	G.E. C[okayne], *The Complete Peerage* (new edn., 14 vols., London, 1910–98)
DI	Diligence Records, NAS
MacGregor Cartulary	Compiled by the Rev. W. MacGregor Stirling, 2 vols., 1822, in Stirling Council Archives, MacGregor of MacGregor Mss, PD60/812, 813
Macleay, 'Memoirs'	Dicaledon [K. Macleay], 'Memoir of Rob Roy Macgregor, and Some Branches of his Family', *Blackwood's Magazine*, ii (Oct–Dec 1817), 74–80, 149–55, 288–95. Reprinted in K. Macleay, *Historical Memoirs of Rob Roy and the Clan Macgregor, including Original Notices of Lady Grange. With an Introductory Sketch . . . on the Condition of the Highlands prior to the year 1745* (Glasgow, 1818)
DNB	*Dictionary of National Biography*

Douglas, *Baronage*	R. Douglas, *Baronage of Scotland* (Edinburgh, 1798)
Fasti	*Fasti Ecclesiastiae Scoticanae* (9 vols., Edinburgh, 1915–81)
E	Exchequer Records (including Forfeited Estates), NAS
GD	Gifts and Deposits, NAS
GD18	Clerk of Penicuik Mss, NAS
GD26	Leven and Melville Muniments, NAS
GD27	Kennedy of Dalquharran Papers, NAS
GD50	John MacGregor Collection, NAS
GD87	Mackay of Bighouse Mss, NAS
GD103	Society of Antiquaries of Scotland, NAS
GD112	Breadalbane Mss, NAS
GD124	Mar and Kellie Mss, NAS
GD160	Drummond Castle Mss, NAS
GD161	Buchanan of Leny Mss, NAS
GD170	Campbell of Barcaldine Mss, NAS
GD220	Montrose Mss, NAS
GD248	Seafield Muniments Mss, NAS
Highland Rogue	E.B., *The Highland Rogue: or, the Memorable Actions of the Celebrated Robert Mac-Gregor, commonly called Rob Roy* (London, 1723)
HMC	Historical Manuscripts Commission
HMC 10	HMC 10, *Tenth Report, Appendix i* (1885)
HMC *Atholl*	HMC 26, *Twelth Report, Appendix viii* (duke of Atholl and earl of Home) (1891)
HMC *Lords*	HMC 17, *House of Lords*, new series (12 vols., 1887–1977)
HMC *Montrose*	HMC 2, *Third Report* (including duke of Montrose) (1872)
HMC *Portland*	HMC 29, *Duke of Portland* (10 vols., 1891–1931)
HMC *Stuart*	HMC 56, *Stuart Mss* (7 vols., 1902–23)
HMC *Townshend*	HMC19, *Townshend* (1887)
HMC *Various*	HMC 55, *Various Collections* (7 vols., 1901–13)
Hutcheson, *Rob Roy*	A.M. Hutcheson, *Rob Roy MacGregor*, Part i, *His Family and Background*; Part ii, *His Life and Character*, Occasional Papers of the Clan Gregor Society, nos. 4 & 5 (Alloa, 1996–99)
JC	Justiciary Court Records, NAS

Lenman, *Risings*	B. Lenman, *The Jacobite Risings in Britain, 1689–1746* (London, 1980)
Murray, *Rob Roy*	W.H. Murray, *Rob Roy Macgregor: His Life and Times* (Glasgow, 1984)
NAS	National Archives of Scotland (formerly Scottish Record Office)
NLS	National Library of Scotland
NRAS	National Register of Archives of Scotland
PRO	Public Record Office, London
PRO, SP54	State Papers, Scotland, 1707–1781. Photostat copies at NAS, RH2/4/299–389. The papers are listed in *Descriptive List of Secretaries of State: State Papers Scotland, Series Two (1688–1782)*, (List & Index Society, vols. 262–4, 1995–96)
PRO, SP55	State Papers, Scotland, 1713–42. Photostat copies at NAS, RH2/4/390–99
RD	Register of Deeds, NAS
Riley, *Ministers*	P.W.J. Riley, *The English Ministers and Scotland, 1707–1727* (London, 1964)
RRR	*The Real Rob Roy: A Guide to the Sources in the Scottish Record Office* (Edinburgh, 1995)
RS	Register of Sasines, NAS
Scott, *Rob Roy*	Sir Walter Scott, *Rob Roy* (1817; cited from the Edinburgh, Waverley edn, 1901. The long Historical Introduction to the novel was not added by Scott until the 1829 edition.)
SH	Sheriff Court Records, NAS
SHS	Scottish History Society
SP	J.B. Paul (ed.), *The Scottish Peerage* (6 vols., Edinburgh, 1900–99)
RPCS	*Register of the Privy Council of Scotland* (38 vols., 1887–70)
Stewarts of the South	*The Stewarts of the South, their Branches and* the http://www.heartlander.scotland.net/ heritage stewarts-of the-south.htm [genealogy, written *c*. 1815–20]
Trials	*The Trials of James, Duncan, and Robert M'Gregor, Three Sons of the Celebrated Rob Roy, before the High Court of Justiciary, in the years 1752, 1753, and 1754. To which is prefixed a Memoir relating to the Highlands, with Anecdotes of Rob Roy and his family* (Edinburgh, 1818) [the title is in error in attributing to Rob Roy a son called Duncan]

Wodrow, *Correspondence*   R. Wodrow, *The Correspondence of the Rev. Robert Wodrow*, ed. T. M'Crie (3 vols., Wodrow Society, 1841–2)

NOTES

1. The Obscurity of Childhood

1 M. Hunter (ed.), 'A Collection of Highland Rites and Customes', *The Occult Laboratory. Magic, Science and Second Sight in the Late Seventeenth Century*, (Woodbridge, 2001), 69. Another edition of the *Collection* was edited by J.L. Campbell (Cambridge, 1975).

2 'Collection', 69.

3 The site now lies to the side of the loch, as raising the water level of the loch in the nineteenth century increased its length.

4 In 1678 Rob's sister Susanna was also baptised at Buchanan, confirming the family preference for the church there. Typescript account of Rob Roy, GD50/184/84/2Lb.

5 Murray, *Rob Roy*, 1.

6 F.M. MacNeill, *The Silver Bough* (4 vols., Glasgow, 1957–64), i, 39–45.

7 'Collection', 69–70.

8 For such random usage of epithets see R.A. Dodgshon, 'Pretense of Blude' and 'Place of thair Dwelling', in the *Nature of Highland Clans, 1500–1745. Scottish Society, 1500–1800*, ed. R.A. Houston and I.D. Whyte (Cambridge, 1989), 178.

9 Report by James Fraser, 1702, *The Occult Laboratory*, 213.

10 E. Burt, *Letters from a Gentleman in the Highlands of Scotland*, ed. R. Jamieson (5th edn, 2 vols., London, 1818), i, 216.

11 D. Hume, *Commentaries on the Law of Scotland, respecting the Description and Punishment of Crimes*, ed. B.R. Bell (2 vols., Edinburgh, 1986 – facsimile of 4th edn, 1844), ii, 551.

12 E. Grant, *Memoirs of a Highland Lady*, ed. A. Tod (Edinburgh, 1992), i, 245. Elizabeth Grant, writing in the 1850s, added 'It has been the fashion of late to father all moss trooping [cattle raiding] throughout the Highlands on Rob Roy.'

13 See A.I. Macinnes, *Clanship, Commerce and the House of Stuart, 1603–1788* (East Linton, 1996), chapter 1, for analysis of many features of Highland society.

14 F.D. Dow, *Cromwellian Scotland* (Edinburgh, 1979), 144.

15 C.H. Firth (ed.), *Scotland and the Protectorate*, (SHS, 1899), xxxvii.

16 *Clan Gregor*, ii, 143; *RPCS 1669–72*, 74.

17 *RPCS, 1678–80*, 43; *RPCS, 1681–2*, 82.

18 Atholl Mss, box 42/II/(1)/2, 3.

19 *RPCS 1683–4*, 550.

20 *Clan Gregor*, ii, 276; Murray, *Rob Roy*, 121.

21 Three sisters of Rob Roy can be named. Margaret is said to have married John Leckie of Croy Leckie, (H. Howlett, *Highland Rogue* (Edinburgh,

1950), 51, in 1677), the year before her sister Susanna, was baptised. Another sister, evidently Sarah, married Alexander, second son of the MacDonald chief killed in the massacre of Glencoe (*Papers Illustrative of the Political Conditions in the Highlands of Scotland, from the Year MDCLXXXIX to MDCXCVI* (Maitland Club 1845), 105&n; GD50/184/84/4E). That a sister of Rob's married Campbell of Glenfalloch (as stories tell) has been shown to be genealogically impossible, (GD50/184/84/4E).

22 J. Ramsay of Ochtertyre, *Scotland and Scotsmen in the Eighteenth Century*, ed. A. Allardyce (2 vols., Edinburgh, 1888), ii, 490.

2. Cattle Trader, Cattle Raider

1   *Clan Gregor*, ii, 191; Murray, *Rob Roy*, 88.
2   J. Philip, *The Grameid* (SHS, 1888),136.
3   See note 20 below.
4   The account of the raid is based on a declaration given by Cardross's tenants on 6 Sept., GD26/8/38, cited P. Hopkins, *Glencoe and the end of the Highland War* (1986), 190.
5   *RPCS 1689*, 7, 614; *RPCS, 1690*, 138; *Clan Gregor*, ii, 258.
6   W.L. Melville (ed.), *Leven and Melville Papers*, (Bannatyne Club, 1843), 369.
7   E.W.M. Balfour-Melville (ed.), *An Account of the Proceedings of the Estates in Scotland, 1689–90*, (SHS, 1954–5), ii, 86.
8   *Calendar of State Papers, Domestic, 1689–90* (1896), 457. The phrase was used elsewhere of Highlanders by Lowland Scots speakers, eg., 'Angus McDonald alias the young halked stirk', *RPCS, 1669–72*, 75. My thanks to Harry D. Watson on this matter. Another Highland reiver active in the late seventeenth century who was known as 'Halket Stirk' was Donald MacDonald, see P. Hopkins, *Glencoe and the End of the Highland War* (Edinburgh, 1986), 29, 37n49, where his name is translated as 'Spotted Bullock'.
9   *An Account of the Proceedings of the Estates in Scotland, 1689–90*, ii, 102–3.
10 *RPCS 1690*, 3, 39; *Leven and Melville Papers*, 394–5.
11 H. Howlett, *Highland Constable. The Life and Times of Rob Roy MacGregor* (Edinburgh, 1950), 26n.
12 Argyll Muniments, Inveraray, cited in NRAS survey no. 1209, p. 45, as being in bundle 109.
13 *APS*, ix, 464–5.
14 *RPCS 1690*, 580; Hopkins, *Glencoe*, 268.
15 *RPCS 1691*, 99–100, 124–5.
16 *RPCS 1691*, 347.
17 *Statistical Account of Scotland* (Edinburgh, 1791–99), xviii, 332.
18 See for example *Clan Gregor*, ii, 274–5; W. Nimmo, *History of Stirlingshire* (2 vols., 1880), i, 139; Murray, *Rob Roy*, 108–11. Howlett, *Highland Constable*, 26, is an exception, pointing out that there is no evidence of Rob's involvement in the Kippen raid.
19 *A Proclamation, anent the Resetters of the Clan, and Name of Greigour or McGreigour* (Edinburgh, 1691).
20 The evidence that Rob swore the oath consists of an entry in what was evidently a register recording swearings of the oath of allegiance. Rob's name appears along with that of two of his cousins and five of his 'servitors'.

A photograph of the (undated) entry is at NLS, Ms Acc 10742, no.24, though the ms source has not been identified.

21 *RPCS, 1691*, 536–8, 540–1.

22 *RPCS, 1691*, 615–16.

23 Atholl Mss, box 29/6/33, 36, 51.

24 *RPCS 1691*, 573, 592.

25 *Papers Illustrative of the Political Conditions in the Highlands of Scotland, from the year MDCLXXXIX to MDCXCVI* (Maitland Club 1845), 105&n.

26 T. Thomson & C. Innes (ed.), *Acts of the Parliament of Scotland*, (12 vols., 1844–75), v, 44–5; ix, 324–5.

27 B. Lenman, *Jacobite Risings*, 139.

28 Full text in *Clan Gregor*, ii, 204–5, 257–8; D. Hume, *Commentaries on the Law of Scotland, respecting the Description and Punishment of Crimes*, ed. B.R. Bell (2 vols., Edinburgh, 1986 – facsimile of 4th edn, 1844), ii, 546–7.

29 NAS, RS59/8, f.247v–248r; *RRR*, 26. *Clan Gregor*, ii, 206 cites this document, but overlooks the word 'quondam' which indicated that John was deceased.

30 *Clan Gregor*, ii, 206.

31 *Clan Gregor*, ii, 169, 187–8.

32 *Clan Gregor*, ii, 170, 200.

33 GD112/39/166/10.

34 *Clan Gregor*, ii, 205–6, 264.

35 NAS, RS59/8, f.247v–248r; *RRR*, 4, 26; Murray, *Rob Roy*,120. Craigrostan was a £10 land 'of old extent', Inversnaid a £3 land within it.

36 GD112/39/167/5.

37 *Clan Gregor*, ii, 170, 200.

38 *A. & T.*, i, 351–4; Atholl Mss, box 42/2/18–19.

39 See Atholl Mss, box 45/7/129.

40 Atholl Mss, box 29/7/121, 124.

41 NAS, PC1/53, pp.110–12, 119.

42 Murray, *Rob Roy*, 114.

43 *Clan Gregor*, ii, 263. See also a memo of the 1720s in GD220/6/501/2 in which Montrose's agents discuss whether Montrose's attempts to gain possession of Inversnaid might be thwarted by a possible claim to the land by Dougal Graham under the 1695 wadset.

44 Howlett, *Highland Constable*.

45 J. Macky, *Memoirs of the Secret Services* (Roxburghe Club, [1895], reprinted from the London 1733 edn), 121.

46 GD170/646/1, Campbell of Barcaldine Papers. A NAS catalogue identified the author of these letters as 'Robert Campbell officer to the laird of Lochinell', simply because there is a letter to this man in the collection (GD170/646/5). But there is no evidence to support this identification. This has delayed identification of the real author as Rob Roy.

47 'A Collection of Highland Rites and Customes,' *The Occult Laboratory. Magic, Science and Second Sight in the Late Seventeenth-Century*, ed. M. Hunter (Woodbridge, 2001). Another edition of the *Collection* was edited by J.L. Campbell (Cambridge, 1975).

48 GD170/646/2/1.

49 GD170/646/3. It is not until this 1696 letter that Rob's links with Barbreck are mentioned, but I have assumed that they underlay his close links with Barcaldine in later years.

50 GD 170/646/2/2. The note is not signed, but is almost certainly by Rob.

51 *Clan Gregor*, ii, 276; Murray, *Rob Roy*, 121. *A. & T.*, i, app. xliv-xlv.

52 Atholl Mss, box 29/7/147.

53 *A & T*, i, appendix, xliv-xlv; *Clan Gregor*, ii, 276–7. Murray, *Rob Roy*, 121–2, is wrong in stating that the submission was signed at Blair Atholl.

54 In December 1695 a Robert MacGregor was a prisoner in Glasgow, and was ordered to be sent to Flanders – where he would have been enlisted in the army, *Clan Gregor*, ii, 207. The prisoner has repeatedly been asserted to have been Rob Roy, but there is no evidence whatever to support this, and it involves the argument that he must have escaped before deportation. Moreover Rob Roy was firmly established as 'Robert Campbell' by this time, not MacGregor.

55 L. Leneman, *Living in Atholl, 1685–1785* (Edinburgh, 1986), 147–8, 151, 167, 187.

56 GD112/39/176/10, 12.

57 T.C. Smout, *Nature contested. Environmental history in Scotland and northern England since 1600* (Edinburgh, 2000), 67–8.

58 P. Hopkins, *Glencoe and the End of the Highland War* (Edinburgh, 1986), 456.

59 *RRR*, 25

60 GD170/646/4. The seal used by Rob on the letter depicts a mermaid with her normal attributes, a mirror and comb. A mermaid in Loch Voil in Balquhidder reappears in stories of the origins of the Maclarens (neighbours of the MacGregors), who included one on their coat of arms. A Gaelic poem of this period refers to a game in which men swapped dirks at random, R. Black, *An Lasir* (2001), 268–9.

61 The charter of confirmation of Craigrostan to Rob was not issued until 1706, and not till then did he formerly take sasine of the land. *Clan Gregor*, ii, 199; 209–10; GD161, box 4, miscellany 1, nos.55–8.

62 21 Nov 1712, in E636/7.

63 GD220/6/1790/5.

64 GD220/6/297/2.

65 *Clan Gregor*, ii, 479–81.

66 *A & T*, v, app. lxxxii; J. Stewart, *Settlements of Western Perthshire* (Edinburgh 1990), 86.

67 G. Hamilton, *A History of the House of Hamilton* (Edinburgh, 1933), 100. Nimmo, *History of Stirlingshire* (2 vols., 1880), 137, wrongly dates the marriage 1703.

68 GD161, box 2, Bardowie Writs, no.70.

69 GD220/6/795–8.

70 Most documents connecting Rob Roy and 'Bardowie' do not specify 'younger'. But the father, born 1645, was an old man, and may have handed over business matters to his son and heir. This was a quite common practice, and in such cases 'younger' was often dropped in describing the heir, as he was now effective laird.

71 W. Macfarlane, *Geographical Collections*, ed. A. Mitchell, i (SHS, 1906), 337, 138. The description is by Alexander Graham of Duchray.

72 C. Nairne, *The Trossachs and the Rob Roy Country* (Edinburgh, 1961), 30.

73 W. Fraser, *The Red Book of Menteith* (2 vols., 1880), ii, 446–7; GD112/78/1; *RRR*, 8.

74 'A Collection of Highland Rites and Customes', *The Occult Laboratory*.

Magic, Science and Second Sight in the Late Seventeenth-Century, ed. M. Hunter (Woodbridge, 2001), 56.

75 R. McOwan, 'Rob Roy lived here', *Scots Magazine*, 136, no.4 (Jan 1992), 351.

76 N. Tranter, *The Heartland* (London, 1971), 124.

77 A. Campbell, *A Journey from Edinburgh through parts of North Britain* (2 vols, Edinburgh, 1802), i, 122. There were two settlements called Portnellan, one lying on Montrose's lands, one in Strathgartney, which belonged to the Drummonds of Perth (eg., GD160/103/2, GD160/212/20). Which one Rob's house was in is not clear.

78 *RRR*, 10.

79 *RRR*, 4, 21.

80 Moray Mss, Darnaway Castle, box 8, nos. 1026, 1027, summarised in NRAS 0217, inventory, iv, 103–4. Lieutenant William Holborn was in 1709 appointed major of an independent company garrisoning Stirling Castle, C. Dalton (ed.), *English Army Lists and Commission Registers, 1661–1714*, (6 vols., 1892–1904), v, 228, vi, 219; C. Dalton, *The Army of George I* (2 vols., London, 1910), i, 236.

81 'Arichiebeg', GD220/6/1605/13.

82 Murray, *Rob Roy*, 147, 268; *RRR*, 4, 21–2.

83 GD220/6/1605/28.

84 RS10/4/1, 136v–137; *RRR*, 4, 27.

85 GD112/41/3, p. 167. Tradition claims that Rob Roy had a house in Coirechaoroch, W.A. Gillies, *In Famed Breadalbane*, (Perth, 1938), 390. Ordnance Survey maps show the supposed site of Rob's house, and one of Rob's letters (1711) was written from there, GD112/39/257/5.

86 *RRR*, 18, 26–7.

87 GD220/5/58/1; GD220/6/700/25.

88 NLS Ms 1314, Delvine papers, ff.1, 2.

89 Perth and Kinross Council Archives, B59/26/11/1/17. In the bond Rob is referred to, unusually, as 'in Glengoill'.

90 Ronald I.M. Black, *An Lasair: Anthology of 18th Century Gaelic Verse* (Edinburgh, 2001), 147.

91 HMC *Portland*, iv, 276–7.

92 James Ferguson, *Robert Ferguson the Plotter* (Edinburgh, 1887), 343–59.

93 *A. & T.*, ii, 22; *Clan Gregor*, ii. 278–9.

94 Atholl Mss, box 45/4/6.

95 Atholl Mss, box 45/4/87; *A. & T.*, ii, 24; *Clan Gregor*, ii, 278.

96 *A. & T.*, ii, 26; HMC *Atholl*, 61–2; *Clan Gregor*, ii, 278.

97 NLS, Ms 1640, Ochtertyre Papers, vol. vi, Government, Clanship, Law, f.261v. I am most grateful to Angus Stewart, QC, for drawing my attention the fact that this manuscript contained material not printed in J. Ramsay of Ochtertyre, *Scotland and Scotsmen in the Eighteenth Century*, ed. A. Allardyce (2 vols., Edinburgh, 1888).

98 J.S. Gibson, *Playing the Scottish Card. The Franco–Jacobite Invasion of 1708* (Edinburgh, 1988), 144–5.

99 Lenman, *Jacobite Risings*, 90.

100 GD112/39/216/16, 23; HMC *Lords*, viii, 131–2, 135–6, 161–2, 166–7, 172, 197–200, 202.

101 GD112/39/216/23; GD112/39/217/33.

102 Atholl Mss, box 50/1/6.

103 P.H. Brown (ed.), *Letters Relating to Scotland in the Reign of Queen Anne*, (SHS, 1915), 109, 141.
104 Lenman, *Jacobite Risings*, 91–3.
105 GD26/9/450, letter book.
106 GD220/5/251.

3. Downfall

1   'Note of captions produced against Rob Roy', in GD220/6/1790/6.
2   *RRR*, 2.
3   NLS, Ms 1314, f.3.
4   W. Fraser, *The Red Book of Menteith* (2 vols., Edinburgh, 1880), ii, 448.
5   GD112/39/257/2, 5.
6   RS10/4/1, 136v–137.
7   RS3/101, f.429v–432r.
8   GD220/5/1720/3a,b.
9   *RRR*, 2, 22.
10 HMC *Montrose*, 381.
11 *RRR*, 10; GD220/5/813/13; GD 220/5/1887/1.
12 'Note of captions produced against Rob Roy', in GD220/6/1790/6. See also NAS, E.636/6.
13 GD220/6/1790/6.
14 *RRR*, 10; GD220/5/1710/17.
15 NAS, RS3/101, f.429v–432r.
16 GD220/5/1707/16.
17 Atholl Mss, box 45/10/67.
18 *RRR*, 11; GD220/5/1707/16–17a.
19 GD220/5/1707/17b.
20 Contemporaries refer to the advertisement about Rob appearing in 'the gazette'. There were two papers with this name at the time, *The Evening-Post, or, the New Edinburgh Gazette* and *The Scots Post-Man, or, The Edinburgh Gazette*, so I presume the advertisement appeared in one of them, though I have not seen copies of the relevant issues. Scott, *Rob Roy*, i, cxiv, erroneously stated the advertisement appeared in the *Edinburgh Evening Courant*, no. 1058, but no such paper existed in 1712. I assume he meant *The Scots Courant*, where it did appear in no. 1058.
21 Atholl Mss, box 45/10/67; *Clan Gregor*, ii, 280. Extracts in *A. & T.*, ii, 138–9.
22 GD220/5/771.
23 The earliest reference to this 'MacDonald' that I know occurs in 1800, where he appears as Rob Roy's defaulting partner – T. Garnett, *Observations on a Tour through the Highlands* (2 vols., London, 1800), i, 63.
24 Hutcheson, *Rob Roy*, ii, 53, 95.
25 *SP*, vi, 261–4.
26 Riley, *Ministers*, 262.
27 J. Macky, *Memoirs of the Secret Services* (Roxburghe Club, 1895), 118.
28 G. Lockhart, 'Scotland's Ruine'. *Lockhart of Carnwath's Memoirs of the Union*, ed. D. Szechi (Aberdeen, 1995), 93.
29 M. Young (ed.), *The Parliaments of Scotland. Burgh and Shire Commissioners*, (2 vols., Edinburgh, 1992), i, 292–3; *SP*, vi, 262.
30 J. Ramsay of Ochtertyre, *Scotland and Scotsmen in the Eighteenth Century*, ed. A. Allardyce (2 vols., Edinburgh, 1888), ii, 295–8.

31 Advocates' Library, Session Papers, Arniston Collection, *Graham of Gorthie v Campbell of Glendaruel*, four papers dated 11 and 15 Dec 1712. I'm most grateful to Angus Stewart, QC, for this reference. RD4/110, f.593; GD220/5/1707/16, 17a, 18.

32 *History of Parliament. The Commons, 1715–54*, ed. R. Sedgwick (3 vols., London, 1970), ii, 75–6.

33 Summary in GD220/6/1790/6.

34 Summary of Rob's letter in GD220/1790/6.

35 GD220/6/1790/1–3.

36 GD220/5/1710/22.

37 GD220/6/1790/1, 2, 3; GD220/5/1710/22.

38 *RRR*, 2.

39 *RRR*, 2.

40 E606/5, p.31.

41 RD2/101, registered 19 June 1712; *RRR*, 2.

42 Information from Domhnall Uilleam Stiubhart.

43 GD112/39/267/2.

44 GD112/39/267/2.

45 GD112/2/117/4/63; GD112/39/286/27; *RRR*, 8.

46 GD112/39/268/21.

47 GD112/39/286/27.

48 GD220/5/290/5.

49 GD170/631/14. Murray, *Rob Roy*, 160 and map, erroneously locates Auch in Glen Dochart, though Howlett had got it right, *Highland Constable*, map.

50 Atholl Mss, Box 45/11/11; *A&T*, ii, 151–2; *Clan Gregor*, ii, 280–1.

51 GD220/5/297.

52 GD220/5/966, 967.

53 He is said to have moved from home to land ten to twelve miles away that he had leased, and I take this to mean to Auch, HMC *Montrose*, 381.

54 GD220/5/1888/1,2.

55 For an account of the rents of Craigrostan collected by Bardowie in 1713–17 see GD220/6/297/6.

56 GD220/6/1790/5.

57 GD112/39/269/21.

58 This is a transcript by John MacGregor in GD50/184/84/4E. No source is cited.

59 T. M'Crie (ed.), *Correspondence of the Rev. Robert Wodrow*, (Wodrow Society, 1842–3), i, 547n. The published text refers to the deceased as 'Locheil,' but Dr Louise Yeoman kindly confirmed for me that the original, NLS, Ms Wodrow, Lett. Qu. VIII, f.3, reads 'Lochnell'. *SP*, ii, 202; 'Notices relative to Rob Roy', *Analecta Scotica*, ed. J. Maidment (1st series, Edinburgh, 1834), i, 14.

60 NLS, Ms 4002, ff.190–1.

61 NAS, RH9/2/57. Extract in W.A. Gillies, *In Famed Breadalbane* (Perth, 1938), 179–81.

62 GD112/39/271/7.

63 GD112/10/1/3/11.

64 GD112/15/150/310.

65 GD112/10/1/3/12.

66 GD220/5/286/4; HMC *Montrose*, 381.

4. *Chiefs, Pensions and Politicians*

1   See W. Ferguson, *Scotland. 1689 to the Present* (Edinburgh, 1968), 62.
2   Riley, *Ministers*, 159–71.
3   On 16 March 1708 the House of Commons discussed plans for hindering the clans of Scotland 'from being at the directions of their Heads in case of any rising or rebellion', HMC 7, 8th Report, part 2, *Manchester Mss*, 97, cited in Riley, *Ministers*, 103.
4   HMC *Portland*, x, 338.
5   Allan Cameron is often called 'Captain', indicating that he had military experience. He may well have been the lieutenant of that name who is recorded serving in one of the independent companies in 1703 and 1712, K.M. Murray, *A Military History of Perthshire* (Perth 1908), 45, 46.
6   HMC *Portland*, x, 367–74.
7   It is notable that John and Allan Cameron and Balhaldie (their brother-in-law) had all been leading members of the masonic Lodge of Dunblane at an earlier date (1696), indicating that their friendship was long-lasting, D. Stevenson, *The First Freemasons: Scotland's Early Lodges and their Members* (Aberdeen, 1988; Edinburgh, 2001), 207–08, where 'Allan' Cameron's name is wrongly given as 'Alexander'.
8   HMC *Portland*, x, 410.
9   HMC *Portland*, v, 121–122.
10 HMC *Portland*, v, 216–17.
11 GD112/39/260/5; P. Rae, *History of the Rebellion rais'd against His Majesty King George I* (2nd edn, London, 1746), 408; *Clan Gregor*, ii, 268–9.
12 HMC *Portland*, v, 220.
13 HMC *Portland*, x, 313.
14 Domhnall Uilleam Stiubhart has pointed out to me a Gaelic poem which mocks Appin for his pretensions by having his 'relative' (fellow Stewart) Queen Anne speak to him 'like an old homely Gaelic cailleach'. 'Poems from the Maclagan Mss', *Transactions of the Gaelic Society of Inverness*, xxii (1897–8), 173–5.
15 HMC *Portland*, v, 341, x, 414–15, 435–7.
16 *Clan Gregor*, ii, 269; Rae, *History of the Rebellion*, 408–9.
17 The Jacobite duke of Berwick made the connection with the Cameron crest, and seems to suggest that 'Sword in Hand' was a code name for Allan Cameron in particular, HMC *Stuart*, i, 350.
18 HMC *Portland*, v, 314.
19 HMC *Portland*, v, 340.
20 HMC *Portland*, v, 461.
21 W. Cobbett (ed.), *Parliamentary History of England*, (12 vols., London, 1806–12), vi, 1339–40.
22 NLS, Ms 3186, Balhaldie Papers, ff.41–42.
23 NLS, Ms 3186, Balhaldie Papers, ff.53–54.
24 NLS, Ms 3186, Balhaldie Papers. ff.55–56.
25 HMC *Portland*, x, 437.
26 W. Buchanan of Auchmar, *A Brief Enquiry into the Genealogy and Present State of Ancient Scottish Surnames* (Glasgow, 1723), 88. For another reference to mention of Glengyle's claim to the chieftaincy see E. Burt, *Letters from a Gentleman in the Highlands of Scotland*, ed. R. Jamieson (5th edn, 2 vols., London, 1818), ii, 348n. In 1754, it was said that at the Jacobite court in exile some believed Glengyle rather than Balhaldie's son was the chief of the MacGregors, *Clan Gregor*, ii, 445. But Glengyle himself

rejected suggestions that he was chief, declaring his loyalty to Balhaldie, *Clan Gregor*, ii, 444. Buchanan's *Brief Enquiry* was part of his *A Historical and Genealogical Essay upon the Family and Surname of Buchanan. To which is added a Brief Enquiry into the Genealogy and Present State of Ancient Scotish Surnames, and more particularly of the Highland Clans* (Glasgow 1723), with a separate pagination. The list of subscribers to the book includes many names which appear in this present book – Finab, Glengyle, Gorthie, Killearn, James Grant of that Ilk and his son Humphrey, Haldane of Gleneagles, MacLauchlan of Auchintroig, James Grahame of Corriearklet and others.

27 *Clan Gregor*, ii, 269–73, 354. According to one account, Rob Roy had agreed not to complicate matters by putting forward a claim to the chieftaincy on his own behalf – in return for a payment of 2,000 marks. See Rev William MacGregor, typescript 'History of the Clan Gregor', at GD50/102/2/2/219. In *Clan Gregor*, ii, 273 it is stated that the bond electing Balhaldie was kept 'a profound secret' from MacGregors not involved, but in reality Balhaldie openly acted as chief during the Jacobite rising the following year.

28 'The earl of Mar's Legacies to Scotland', ed. S. Erskine, in *Wariston's Diary and other Papers* (SHS, 1896), 199–200, 210, 216.

29 HMC *Portland*, v, 499.

30 HMC *Montrose*, 378.

31 PRO, SP55/3, 46–7.

32 HMC *Montrose*, 375.

33 GD220/5/482/1/1; *RRR*, 12. Cited B. Lenman, *The Jacobite Clans of the Great Glen 1650–1784* (London, 1984), 78.

34 GD220/5/472/2.

35 GD220/5/506/1; HMC *Montrose*, 378.

36 *A. & T.*, 2.176–7, Atholl Mss, box, 45/12/15; GD220/5/454/21; HMC *Montrose*, 373.

37 *A. & T.*, 2, 117–8; *Clan Gregor*, ii, 281.

38 GD220/6/1789/5.

39 GD220/5/556/1; HMC *Montrose*, 377.

40 GD220/5/814/2.

41 GD220/5/814/6.

42 GD220/5/454/48.

43 Montrose resigned office in August 1715.

44 GD220/5/556/2. Murray, *Rob Roy*, 169, arbitrarily dismisses the 'rumour' that Rob was distrusted as 'nonsense'. For other references to the story that Montrose had been dismissed from office see PRO, SP54/7/32, 33.

5. Rebel

1 PRO, SP54/7/11.

2 J.H. Burton, *History of Scotland* (2nd edn, 8 vols., Edinburgh, 1873), viii, 254.

3 G. Charles, *History of the Transactions in Scotland, in the Years 1715–16, and 1745–6* (2 vols., Stirling and Leith, 1817), i, 86–7; Burton, viii, 254–55.

4 The address is cited in a review of the *Culloden Papers* in the *Quarterly Review*, xiv (1815–16), 314–15. It is said that it was delivered to Argyll, who failed to deliver it to the king. Certainly he would have been unwise to associate himself with an address from so many men he knew were in reality disloyal.

5   1, Geo I, c.20; J. Cay & O. Ruffhead (eds.), *Statutes at Large*, (9 vols., London, 1758–73), iv, 95–6.

6   Burton, *History*, viii, 266–7; W. Ferguson, *Scotland. 1689 to the present* (Edinburgh, 1968), 66–7.

7   *The Annals of King George, Year the Second* (London, 1717), 35–6.

8   1 Geo. I, c.54; *Statutes at Large*, iv, 128–30.

9   PRO, SP54/9/21. Islay does not specifically refer to the acts but it seems clear that the 'notion' he refers to is the policies they set out.

10 GD220/5/816/2.

11 PRO, SP54/7/23.

12 C. Petrie, *The Jacobite Movement. The First Phase, 1688–1716* (London, 1948), 175 remarked of Mar and the '15 that never had the wrong man appeared in the wrong place at the wrong time so completely.

13 Lenman, *Risings*, 134.

14 PRO, SP54/7/32, 33.

15 PRO, SP54/7/11, 19.

16 J. Houston, *Works* (Edinburgh, 1753), 88.

17 PRO, SP54/8/89.

18 PRO, SP54/8/80.

19 Wodrow, *Correspondence*, ii, 76.

20 GD220/5/816/15.

21 GD220/5/816/13; PRO, SP54/8/116.

22 GD220/5/816/15.

23 NLS Ms, Wodrow Letters, Qu, x, f.44r (no 28).

24 PRO, SP54/9/2C.

25 NLS Ms, Wodrow Letters, Qu, x, f.50r (no. 33).

26 *Clan Gregor*, ii, 284–5; J. Dennistoun (ed.), *The Loch-Lomond Expedition* (Glasgow, 1715; reprinted, Glasgow, 1834).

27 *The Loch-Lomond Expedition*, 3.

28 G. Charles, *History of the Transactions in Scotland, in the years 1715–16, and 1745–6* (2 vols., Stirling and Leith, 1817), i, 313–15. This obscure work has generally been ignored by historians, but it gives details of the 1715 around Inveraray and south of Loch Lomond which I have accepted as reliable, drawn from some sources now unknown.

29 P. Rae, *History of the Rebellion raid's against His Majesty King George I* (2nd edn, London, 1746), 429; *Clan Gregor*, ii, 288. Some time in October Gordon, Rob Roy and others sent a message to 'Fonnab and the rest of the gentrie in Inveraray', presumably urging them to join the Jacobite cause, GD112/15/152.

30 *Collection of Original Letters and Authentick Papers, relating to the Rebellion, 1715* (Edinburgh, 1730), 58; *Clan Gregor*, ii, 289.

31 *Collection of Original Letters*, 52.

32 *Collection of Original Letters*, 72.

33 J. Anderson, *Papers of John Anderson Reprinted from the Dumbarton Herald* (1914), quoted in J. Baynes, *The Jacobite Rising of 1715* (London, 1970), 60; PRO, SP54/9/74, 80.

34 *Clan Gregor*, ii, 289–90.

35 *Collection of Original Letters*, 84–5.

36 PRO, SP54/9/80.

37 Baynes, *Jacobite Rising*, 61–2; G. Charles, *History of the Transactions in Scotland, in the years 1715–16, and 1745–46* (2 vols., Stirling and Leith, 1817), i, 317–19.

38 HMC *Townshend*, 164.

39 PRO, SP54/9/80.
40 Baynes, *Jacobite Rising*, 71.
41 P. Rae, *History of the Rebellion*, 466; 290.
42 J. Sinclair, Master of Sinclair, *Memoirs of the Insurrection in Scotland in 1715*, ed. J. Macknight (Abbotsford Club 1858), 209.
43 Baynes, *Jacobite Rising*, 139–54.
44 Baynes, *Jacobite Rising*, 134, 138.
45 R. Patten, *History of the Late Rebellion* (London, 1717), 213, quoted in *The Jacobites and the Union*, ed. C.S. Terry (Cambridge, 1922), 135n.
46 J. Hogg, *Jacobite Relics* (2 vols., Paisley 1874 edn), ii, 4.
47 *A Dialogue betwixt William Lich-Landle, and Thomas Clean-Cogue, who were feeding their Sheep on the Ochel-Hills, upon the 13th of November 1715* [1715].
48 R. Campbell, *The Life of the Most Illustrious Prince John, Duke of Argyle and Greenwich* (London, 1745), 205.
49 NLS Map Room, Ms 1649 Z.03/45a, b, c.
50 Colm Ó Baoill (ed.), *Bàrdachd Shilis na Ceapaich. Poems and Songs of Sileas Macdonald*, (1972), 27–43.
51 Ibid., 33.
52 NLS Map Room, Ms 1649 Z.03/45a, b, c.
53 *Clan Gregor*, ii, 378.
54 W. Mackay, 'The Camerons in the rising of 1715', *Transactions of the Gaelic Society of Inverness*, xxvi (1904–07), 74. The paper is reprinted in Mackay's *Sidelights on Highland History* (Inverness, 1925), 347–77.
55 The fullest and best analysis of Sheriffmuir is in Baynes, *Jacobite Rising*, 137–54, though he believed that Rob had been to the east rather than the west of the battle.
56 Atholl Mss, box 45/12/97.
57 PRO, SP54/10/74B.
58 Rob's letter is in the Argyll manuscripts at Inveraray Castle, which at present are not accessible. The text is printed in Murray, *Rob Roy*, 192–93.
59 Murray, *Rob Roy*, 192, 193.
60 PRO, SP54/7/19.
61 *Old Auchintroig, Buchlyvie, Stirlingshire. Part 1, Archaeological and Architectural Investigations* (2002), report commissioned by the National Trust for Scotland, i, 27–8.
62 GD220/6/1790/8; NLS Ms, Wodrow Letters, Qu, x, f.195 (no. 157).
63 G. Charles, *History of the Transactions in Scotland, in the years 1715–16, and 1745–6* (2 vols., Stirling and Leith, 1817), i, 288–91; GD220/5/817/30.
64 W. Ferguson, *Scotland. 1689 to the Present* (Edinburgh, 1968), 67.
65 GD220/529/4, 6; HMC 3rd Report, *Montrose* 378; NLS Ms, Wodrow Letters, Qu, x, f.198 (no. 159); NLS Ms 874, Abbotsford, f.462 (newspaper cutting reprinting Glasgow newspaper reports of 1715–16); Smith, *Strathendrick*, 74.
66 GD220/5/817/30, 32; GD220/5/529/8
67 GD220/5/817/33; NLS, Ms Wodrow Letters, Qu, x, f. 208v (no. 168).
68 GD220/5/817/33.
69 D. Stevenson, 'Scotland's Leather Guns', *History Scotland*, ii, no.6 (2002), 11–18.
70 GD220/5/817/33.
71 NLS, Ms Wodrow Letters, Qu, x, f.203r (no. 162).
72 GD220/5/817/30.
73 Atholl MSS, 45/12/97.

74 A.I. Macinnes, *Clanship, Commerce and the House of Stuart, 1603–1788* (East Linton, 1996), 164.

75 PRO, SP54/11/16, 19.

76 T. M'Crie (ed.), *Correspondence of the Rev. Robert Wodrow* (Wodrow Society, 1842–3), ii, 116–17; *Clan Gregor*, ii, 116–17.

77 PRO, SP54/11/19, 47.

78 PRO, SP54/11/47.

79 *Clan Gregor*, ii, 290–1. In the surviving copy of the orders, both the instructions to move to Doune and those to move to Dundee are contained in a single order by Mar dated 27 January, even though they are contradictory. Either the copy has conflated two separate orders or, possibly, the collapse of the Jacobites was proceeding so quickly that the orders were changed half way through writing, and the fact that the superseded part had not been deleted was not noticed.

80 *Correspondence of the Rev. Robert Wodrow*, ii, 118.

81 PRO, SP54/11/18.

82 *News Letters of 1715–16*, ed. A.F. Steuart (London, 1910), 97–8.

83 *Correspondence of the Rev. Robert Wodrow*, ii, 135.

84 PRO, SP54/11/121.

85 H. Tayler, 'John, Duke of Argyll and Greenwich', *Scottish Historical Review*, xxiv (1947), 64–74

86 *Clan Gregor*, ii, 289.

87 *Clan Gregor*, ii, 292.

88 A complication soon arose over the act forfeiting rebel estates. It was claimed that the liferents of the estates concerned had already been forfeited under the 1715 act as the owners had failed to appear in Edinburgh as ordered, so the new forfeited estate commissioners could have no claim to them until their owners died! PRO, SP54/12/220A, 220B. The matter was settled in favour of the new commissioners.

6. Burning Houses

1   SC54 /23/53/16.

2   GD220/5/973; Murray, *Rob Roy*, 200–1. *Clan* Gregor, ii, 314–15 erroneously states that the house that was burnt was Monachayle Turach in Balquhidder.

3   GD112/39/273/6; GD220/5/820/26;

4   GD220/5/820/26.

5   Atholl MSS, Box 45/12/124.

6   GD112/39/281/9. For Rob's house in Glen Shira, see *Argyll, an Inventory of the Monuments*, vol. vii, *Mid Argyll and Cowal. Medieval and Ancient Monuments* (Royal Commission for the Ancient and Historical Monuments of Scotland, 1992), 563 and *New Statistical Account of Scotland*, vii, 26. The present Beinn-Bhuidhe House lies two and a half miles down the Glen from the supposed Rob Roy's house. A story about Rob being involved in a fight about rights at a funeral associates Rob with Glen Shira as early as 1714, but this hardly counts as hard evidence, P. MacIntyre *The Barons of Phantilands; or the MaCorquodales and their Story*, 31–34.

7   Murray, *Rob Roy*, 200–01.

8   GD220/5/821/12; PRO, SP57/29, pp. 327–30, 39–42.

9   PRO, SP54/12/179.

10 GD220/5/729.

11 Atholl Mss, 45/13/177; *A. & T.*, ii, 273.

12 GD112/39/275/22.

13   PRO, SP54/12/188, 205A, 205B, 208. Murray, *Rob Roy*, 205, 270 and Howlett, *Highland Constable*, 202 cite a printed report of the raid from the *Flying Post* of 18 Oct 1716.
14   James of Kilmannan was presumably the son, or at least the heir, of Archibald, the deceased MacGregor chief.
15   GD220/6/716/2. It is always assumed that the house burnt was at Inversnaid, though the sources do not mention its location.
16   PRO, SP54/12/226A.
17   PRO, SP54/12/261B. This is a copy of Killearn's letter of 19 November.
18   GD220/5/1720/1; noted Hutcheson, *Rob Roy*, ii, 55, 96.
19   GD2205/1720/ 3a, b.
20   HMC *Montrose*, 382; [Evidently PRO, SP54/12/261A].
21   HMC *Montrose*, 382–83, says this letter was sent to Townshend but it was addressed to Carpenter.
22   HMC *Montrose*, 382 [evidently PRO, SP54/12/269, dated 28 Nov].
23   GD220/5/701/3. Brief summary in HMC *Montrose*, 369.
24   GD220/5/687/6.
25   HMC *Montrose*, 383; *RRR*, 14.
26   I am grateful to Major Nicholas MacLean Bristol for identifying the tutor for me.
27   BL, Add Ms 61632, Blenheim Papers, Add 1711r-v.
28   GD27/6/7/32; PRO, SP54/12/269. An island near Stronlachacher is known as the Factor's Island, being said to have been the site of Killearn's imprisonment.
29   *Information for Sir David Dalrymple of Hailes, His Majesty's Advocate, Pursuer . . ., against James Graham alias Gramoch Gregeroch, Panel* (1717), copy at NAS, GD1/61/35; NAS, JC3/8, pp. 49–53, 69–76, 105, 234.
30   GD220/5/690/2; summary HMC *Montrose*, 383–4; PRO, SP55/6, pp.45–6.
31   BL, Add MS, 61632, Blenheim Papers, f.168.
32   HMC *Montrose*, 383; GD220/5/689/6.
33   HMC *Montrose*, 383; GD220/5/689/7, 12.
34   HMC, *Montrose*, 375. The subject of the letter is given in HMC as the justice general, but this makes no sense as that office was held by the earl of Islay, a man Rob would have no reason to harm. I have therefore assumed the justice clerk is meant. The original of the letter has not been traced in GD220.

7. Climax

1   Riley, *Ministers*, 263–77.
2   J. Houston, *Works* (Edinburgh, 1753), 90–1.
3   GD220/5/822/16.
4   GD220/5/822/18.
5   HMC *Montrose*, 384; *Clan Gregor*, ii, 320–21.
6   Murray, *Rob Roy*, 201–2, dates the meeting a year earlier, Apr 1716, but provides no evidence or argument to support this dating.
7   L. Leneman, *Living in Atholl* (Edinburgh, 1986), 47.
8   Atholl Mss, box 45/13/85.
9   *A. & T.*, ii, 267–8; HMC *Atholl*, 71; *Clan Gregor* i, 317; Atholl Mss, box 45/13/115.
10   *A&T*, 2, 273; Clan Gregor, ii, 320 – summaries of Atholl Mss, 45/13/146.
11   Murray, *Rob Roy*, 230.
12   Atholl Mss, Box 45/13/116.

13   *A. & T.*, 2, 268; *Clan Gregor*, ii, 317; Atholl Mss, box 45/13/118.
14   Atholl Mss, 45/13/122; *A. & T.*, ii, 269; *Clan Gregor* ii, 317.
15   GD220/5/823/2.
16   'Notices relative to Rob Roy', *Analecta Scotica*, ed. J. Maidment (1st series, Edinburgh, 1834), i, 14.
17   *A. & T.*, ii, 269; *Clan Gregor* ii, 317; Atholl Mss, box 45/13/121.
18   J. Macky, *Memoirs of the Secret Services* (Roxburghe Club, [1895], from the London 1733 edn), 115.
19   Daniel Defoe, quoted in Lenman, *Jacobite Risings*, 140.
20   *A. & T.*, ii, 269–70; *Clan Gregor* ii, 318.; Atholl Mss, box 45/13/126.
21   Atholl Mss, box 45/13/132.
22   Atholl Mss, box 45/13/125.
23   Atholl Mss, box 45/13/135.
24   Atholl Mss, box 45/13/140, 146.
25   GD220/5/729/3.
26   *A. & T.*, ii, 273; *Clan Gregor*, ii, 320; Atholl Mss, 45/13/146.
27   *A. & T.*, ii, 272; *Clan Gregor*, ii, 319–20; Atholl Mss, box 45/13/141.
28   *A. & T.*, ii, 272; *Clan Gregor*, ii, 319–20; Atholl Mss, box 45/13/141.
29   Atholl Mss, box 45/13/150.
30   Atholl Mss, box 45/13/156, 157.
31   Atholl Mss, box 45/13/157.
32   GD112/39/275/15–16.
33   *Highland Rogue*, 50–55.
34   'Contemporary Account of the Escape of Rob Roy', *Archaeologica Scotica*, iii (1833), ed. Sir Walter Scott, 296–97
35   GD112/39/275/15.
36   GD220/6/1783/11, transcribed in HMC *Montrose*, 384. A second copy of the declaration, in 'Rob Roy', ed. C.D. Lamont, *Notes and Queries*, 2nd series, vi (1858), 495, differs in a few verbal details.
37   GD220/5/823/4.
38   GD220/5/976/1.
39   GD220/5/1931/3–4.
40   J. Allardyce, *The Strachans of Glenkindie* (Aberdeen, 1899), 26–69, 40–42; Dalton, *The Army of George I* (2 vols., 1910), i, 347.
41   PRO, SP55/8, 31–33.
42   GD220/5/1721/7.
43   PRO, SP54/13/140.
44   GD220/5/823/5, 6.
45   GD220/5/976/4.
46   PRO, SP54/13/140.
47   GD220/5/976/2.
48   W.A. Gillies, *In famed Breadalbane* (Perth, 1938), 182.
49   GD112/39/275/19.
50   PRO, SP55/7, 70.
51   *Inventory of the Ancient and Historical Monuments of Stirlingshire* (Royal Commission on the Ancient and Historical Monuments of Scotland, 2 vols., 1963), 273–75.
52   GD220/5/824/19, 25.
53   PRO, SP55/9, 4–7.
54   NLS, Ms 1648, Z.3/13, 15, 17.
55   PRO, SP55/8, 100–2, 104–7; GD220/5/825/35.
56   PRO, SP55/8, 106–7.
57   PRO, SP58/8, 110–13.

8. Defiance

1 'Memorial for [by] Jo Grahame of Drunky', 17 Apr 1722, NAS, GD220/6/1790/9.
2 NRA, SC54/15/1. This printed version of the proclamation against Rob has some words lost through tears, but these can be supplied from the ms version at PRO, SP55/8, 167–9. A facsimile of the printed version appears on the front cover of *RRR*.
3 GD220/6/1790/9.
4 GD220/5/828/15.
5 See note 1 above.
6 GD112/39/257/2, 5.
7 GD112/39/271/7.
8 NLS, MS8454, ff.198–89. This is a negative photocopy of the original letter, and is hard to decipher. The original is in the Mitchell Library, Glasgow, Brisbane papers, papers box 19, bundle xxxiv.
9 NLS, MS 901, ff.141–2, 'Facsimile of the hand-writing of Rob Roy. From the original in the possession of Mr David Haig of the Advocates Library.' It should be said that the reading 'botle' in Rob's letter to Hay is not 100 per cent certain – though it is hard to come up with any plausible alternative. The seal on the letter depicts a stag, with initials that appear to be 'A.Mᶜ.'
10 W.K. Dickson (ed.), *The Jacobite Attempt of 1719*, (SHS, 1895), xliv.
11 GD220/5/829/6.
12 PRO, SP55/8, 193.
13 *Jacobite Attempt*, xxxvii-xli, xliv-xlv.
14 HMC *Various*, v, 241–2.
15 Atholl Mss, 45/15/27; HMC *10th Report*, 124–25; *A. & T.*, ii, appendix, cxiv, cxvi. Some details of precise dates of payments vary between different versions of the accounts.
16 *Jacobite Attempt*, xlix-liii; C.S. Terry (ed.), *The Jacobites and the Union*, (Cambridge, 1922), 248.
17 HMC *Portland*, v, 586; HMC *Various*, v, 241–72.
18 PRO, SP55/8, 257, 259–62.
19 PRO, SP55/8, 266.
20 'Memorial for [by] Jo Grahame of Drunky', 17 Apr 1722, GD220/6/1790/9.
21 *A. & T.*, ii, 307–9; Atholl Mss, 45/16/10, 15.
22 *A. & T.*, ii, 309, 312, 305–06
23 Atholl Mss, 45/16/35.
24 Atholl Mss, 45/16/ 47.
25 D. Murray, *The York Buildings Company. A Chapter in Scottish History* (Glasgow, 1883), 24. Craigrostan is not mentioned in a bundle of 'Papers relating to the purchase of estates made by the York Building Soc.', at E607/10.
26 GD220/5/834/10.
27 NAS, E607/3. The abstract is dated 15 Sept, though what appears to be a proof of it is dated 16 Sept. A copy of this 16 Sept version is corrected in ms – mistakenly transferring Craigrostan from Dunbartonshire to Stirlingshire (E636/7, reproduced in facsimile on the back cover of *RRR*). A corrected version of this is at NLS, Ry. 1. 1. 136 (26).
28 GD220/6/1019/15; *A Further Report Humbly offer'd by the Commissioners of the Forfeited Estates, who acted in Scotland. Presented to the Honourable House of Commons; Wednesday, 18th day of January 1720 [1721]* (London, 1724), 2.

29 GD220/5/841/1.

30 E636/1–11.

31 E.606/5, p. 31. J.R.N. MacPhail (ed.), *Papers from the Collections of Sir William Fraser* (SHS, 1924), 271–3.

32 GD220/5/1733/9; GD220/6/1023/34, 35.

33 *Papers from the Collections of Sir William Fraser*, 271–3.

34 GD220/5/1733/9; *RRR*, 16.

35 GD220/5/834/25.

36 GD112/39/275/22

37 PRO, WO 4/23, ff.180r, 209r-v.

38 GD112/39/281/9.

39 GD220/5/537/10.

40 GD220/5/837/11.

41 GD220/5/837/15.

42 GD220/5/837/20.

43 GD220/6/1790/9.

44 Transcript (by Dr B.L.H. Horn) and facsimile in Lyon and Turnbull auctioneers, Edinburgh, sale catalogue for 23 Sept 2000, p.12.

45 MacGregor Cartulary, ii, 699.

46 Genealogical tables in Howlett, *Highland Constable* and Murray, *Rob Roy* make Malcolm Murray and John Campbell brothers, but this was not the case. John Campbell of Glencarnaig is often called 'Murray' in later sources, but it was evidently his son Robert who changed his name from Campbell to Murray, to please the duke of Atholl. To add to possible confusion, John was also sometimes known as 'of Coiletter' or Kelleter, from lands he held (or had once held) in Glenfalloch.

47 J. Stewart, *Settlements of Western Perthshire. Land and Society North of the Highland Line* (Edinburgh, 1990), 82, 88.

48 *Stewarts of the South*, 46–47, 50.

49 *Clan Gregor*, ii, 490–91.

50 Atholl Mss, box 46/2/227, partly transcribed in *A & T*, ii, 344–5; *Stewarts of the South*, 50.

51 R. Douglas, *The Baronage of Scotland* (Edinburgh, 1798), 304–6. Robert Douglas had died in 1770, and the article on the MacGregors which was added later has been succinctly described as 'piece of sustained fiction marred only by the occasional intrusion of fact' (Martin MacGregor, quoted in the introduction to the electronic edition of *Clan Gregor*). It was written by Duncan Murray, of the Glencarnaig family, and thus its bias against Rob Roy and the family of Glengyle is easily explicable

52 NAS, JC7/21, 3 Aug 1736. See also *Burke's Peerage and Baronetage*, 106th edn. (2 vols., 1999).

53 GD220/5/1005/3.

9. *Highland Rogue*

1 23 March 1721. *Information for James Campbel of Burnbank, Pannel, against His Majesty's Advocate* (Copy in NLS).

2 [Alexander Pennecuik], *Huy and Cry for apprehending George Fachney, Professor of Gaming, and one of the Subalteren Officers in Collonel Caldwell's new levied Regiment of Robbers. By John Dalgleish, Lockman of Edinburgh*, copy at NLS S.302. b. 2. (71).

3 W. Roughead, 'Nicol Muschet', *Juridical Review*, xxix (1917), 18–43.

4 [A. Pennecuik?] *Burnbank and George Fachney's Last Shift: or, a Strange*

Plot at a Dead Slift, copy at NLS, S. 302. b. 2(72) endorsed 'This came out 23 Feb. 1722'.

5 *Burnbank's Farewell to Edinburgh* [1722]. That there was a real-life connection between Rob Roy and Campbell of Burnbank seems simple coincidence, unknown to broadside writers. In 1708 James Campbell of Burnbank had contracted to sell Rob Roy eight chalders of meal annually for seven years. Both men had then been respectable figures, small landowners. But Burnbank had already been in financial difficulties, and begging for military employment.477 In 1711 to 1712 he sold his lands though he continued to use the designation of 'Burnbank', *Real Rob Roy*, 4; NAS, GD124/15/727, 814. Confusingly, the new owner of Burnbank, a younger son of the 9th earl of Argyll, was also a James Campbell, and he has sometimes been confused with the criminal Burnbank. See 'Papers relative to the abduction of Miss Wharton by the Hon. James Campbell of Burnbank', in *Argyle Papers*, ed. J. Maidment (Edinburgh, 1834).

6 *The Supplication and Lamentation of George Fachney, an Officer in Caldwell's Regiment of Robbers, to Rob Roy in the Highlands, with Rob Roy's Answer* [1722]. The only known copy of this printed broadside is in the Huntington Library, San Marino, California, to which I am much obliged for a photocopy.

7 W.D. Simpson (ed.), *The Book of Glenbuchat*, (Third Spalding Club, 1941), 74–5; PRO, SP54/19/44C.

8 A.H. Millar, *History of Rob Roy* (1883), 266.

9 The identification of E.B. with Burt is the inspiration of Domhnall Uilleam Stiubhart.

10 *Highland Rogue*, xiii, xiv.

11 Hypertrichosis (abnormal hairiness) is a known disorder, but if Rob suffered from it surely some other contemporary would have mentioned it.

12 Atholl Mss, NRAS, 234/46/8/15.

13 H. Moll, *A Set of Thirty-Six New and Correct Maps of Scotland divided into its Shires* (London, 1725). The three wonders of Loch Lomond also feature in the *Highland Rogue*.

10. *Jacobite Rebel to Hanoverian Spy*

1 E. Burt, *Letters from a Gentleman in the Highlands of Scotland*, ed. R. Jamieson (5th edn, 2 vols., London, 1818), ii, 254–67.

2 J.B. Salmond, *Wade in Scotland* (Edinburgh, 1938), 42–9.

3 Salmond, *Wade*, 49–50, 52–3.

4 Burt, *Letters*, ii, 291–2.

5 PRO, SP54/15/17; Murray, *Rob Roy*, 252.

6 NLS, Ms 1640, Ochtertyre Papers, vol. vi, Government, Clanship, Law, f.259r.

7 BL, King's Mss, 102, ff.16r, 22r-v.

8 GD112/39/285/5; W.A. Gillies, *In famed Breadalbane* (Perth, 1938), 182.

9 PRO, SP54/16/52, f.233.

10 Burt, *Letters*, ii, 313–14.

11 Burt, *Letters*, ii, 338–70; *Clan Gregor*, ii, 334–35.

12 PRO, SP54/16/52.

13 PRO, SP54/16/52, 74.

14 PRO, SP54/16/59, 67.

15 PRO, SP 35/60/6, listed in *State Papers Domestic George I (SP35)* (List & Index Society vol. 165, 1980), 39. A bizarre piece of journalistic invention

in a London newspaper portrays Rob and the other ten Scots as having
been held in Newgate in London before being carried to Gravesend to be
transported to Barbados, but their pardon then arriving before they were
shipped, A.G.F. Griffiths, *The Chronicles of Newgate* (2 vols., London,
1884), i, 226. Griffith quotes from the *Weekly Journal*, 24 Jan 1727, but I
assume this is error for Jan 1725/6, the garbled report of the pardons thus
appearing a few weeks, rather than over a year, after the event. Murray, *Rob
Roy*, 253, gives credence to the report (which he cites as having appeared in
the non-existent *Edinburgh Weekly Journal*).

16 The manuscript survives in a collection of printed broadsides, at NLS, Ry. II.
a. 21(85). The hand and paper suggest a date considerably later than 1726.
The ms is endorsed 'Dr Pennycock', but the poet Dr Alexander Pennecuik
had died in 1722, so the reference must be to his nephew and namesake.

17 Loch Awe, reputedly the original home of the Campbells.

18 Stirling Council Archives, PD60, MacGregor of MacGregor Mss, letter of
1769 in bundle 885, and MacGregor Cartulary, ii, p.726.

19 Eventually he succeeded, and the modern chiefs of Clan Gregor are
descended from him.

20 Atholl Mss, box 45/13/146, summarised in *Clan Gregor*, ii, 320 and *AT.&T.*,
ii, 273.

21 H.D. MacWilliam, *A Black Watch Episode of 1731* (Edinburgh, 1908),
12.

22 W. Fraser, *The Chiefs of Grant* (3 vols., Edinburgh, 1883), ii, 531–32. The
original is in the Grant of Ballindalloch Mss, in bundle no. 847 (see NRAS
0771).

23 NRAS 182/1/9.

24 PRO, SP54/17/51.

25 HMC *Townshend*, 199.

26 This letter, and the one about to be discussed, is at Raynam Park, Norfolk,
in the papers of Lord Townshend (secretary of state). Both are copies, not
originals. I am most grateful to Susanna Wade Martins for drawing these
two important letters to my attention. S.W. Martins, *'Turnip' Townshend.
Statesman and Farmer* (North Walsham, 1990), 74–5.

27 Martins, *'Turnip' Townshend*, 72–4.

28 J. Allardyce (ed.), *Historical Papers relating to the Jacobite Period, 1699–
1750*, (2 vols., New Spalding Club, 1895–6), i, 151–53.

29 W. Fraser, *The Stirlings of Keir* (Edinburgh, 1858), 71, citing Wodrow,
Analecta, iii, 436; PRO, SP54/19/137.

30 NLS, Ms3186, f.153.

31 R. Mitchison, 'The Government and the Highlands, 1707–1745', *Scotland
in the Age of Improvement. Essays in Scottish History in the Eighteenth 29*,
ed. N.T. Phillipson & R. Mitchison (Edinburgh, 1970), 35.

32 A.I. Macinnes, *Clanship, Commerce and the House of Stuart*, (East Linton,
1996), 197.

33 J. MacIntosh, *The Dewar Manuscripts, i, Scottish West Highland Folk
Tales, collected originally in Gaelic by John Dewar* (Glasgow, 1964), 324.

34 GD220/5/1103/13.

35 J. Prebble, *Mutiny. Highland Regiments in Revolt* (Harmondsworth, 1977),
31, wrote that the independent companies pursued the MacGregors and
other outlaws 'as if they were wolves, extracting joyous payment for old
grievances'. That Finab's company had once protected Rob Roy, and that
his sons had now been recruited into others, makes a nonsense of this.

36 GD112/39/290/19.

37 GD112/39/290/19.
38 GD112/39/291/1.
39 GD220/5/1152/3.
40 Atholl Mss, box 46/6/22.
41 GD112/15/213/18.
42 GD112/15/232/1, 28.
43 GD220/5/1223/9.
44 *DNB*; Houston, *Rob Roy*, ii, 112, 114–15.
45 GDI12/39/295/2.
46 E. Burt, *Letters from a Gentleman in the Highlands of Scotland*, ed. R. Jamieson (5th edn, 2 vols., London, 1818), ii, 60.
47 'The baillie' is said to have been with Rob Roy when he kidnapped Graham of Killearn in 1716, D. Stewart of Garth, *Sketches of the Character, Manners, and Present State of the Highlands* (2nd edn, 2 vols.,Edinburgh, 1822), ii, xiii, xiv, xvii.
48 GD112/39/295/3.
49 At the time of his death Rob's son Coll was owed a small sum of money by Mary MacGregor, relict of Robert Drummond alias Roy, NAS, CC6/5/24, 18 Dec 1735 and 5 Nov 1736. I assume these were Coll's parents, and thus that Rob Roy was using the name Drummond as his sons did.
50 For Father Alexander Drummond see B.M. Halloran, *The Scots College, Paris, 1603–1792* (Edinburgh, 1997), 20, 70, 139, 211.
51 NAS, JC7/21, 3 Aug 1736.
52 GD160/569/1.
53 GD160/569/2.
54 *Clan Gregor*, ii, 337. The lease, for nineteen years, backdated the change in tenancy to Whitsunday 1731, presumably the date an earlier lease to the MacIntryres had expired. The new lease was for nineteen years, and granted possession of a quarter of the Kirkton lands and a half of the mill, GD50/184/84/4N.
55 Murray, *Rob Roy*, 255; *Clan Gregor*, ii, 337.
56 Stirling Council Archives, PD60, MacGregor of MacGregor Mss, in bundle 49.
57 See Chapter 12.
58 M. Hunter (ed.), 'A Collection of Highland Rites and Customes', *The Occult Laboratory: Magic, Science and Second Sight in the Late Seventeenth-Century*, (Woodbridge, 2001), 61.
59 Scott, *Rob Roy*, i, lxxxii-lxxxiv. Another version of the duel story also got the lands in dispute wrong. It claimed that Rob was trying to take over a lease from John MacLaren, and that the farm at the centre of the dispute was Monachayle Tuarach. John Mackenzie, in *The Dear Manuscripts, i, Scottish West Highland Folk Tales, collected originally in Gaelic by John Dear* (Glasgow, 1964), 324.
60 *The Dewar Manuscripts*, 324. See also M. MacLaren, *The MacLarens. A History of Clan Labhran* (Stirling, 1960), 68–9.
61 *The Dewar Manuscripts*, 162–5, 325.
62 NLS, Ms 4002, ff.192–3.
63 Murray, *Rob Roy*, 260.
64 Scott, *Rob Roy*, i, lxxxv; Murray, *Rob Roy*, 258–59.
65 NLS, Ms 1640, Ochtertyre Papers, vol. vi, Government, Clanship, Law, f.258v.
66 GD112/29/73/23.
67 *Clan Gregor*, ii, 335.

68 *Gentleman's Magazine*, v (1735), Jan issue, 51, reprinted in *Notes and Queries*, 2nd series, v (Jan-June 1858), 272.

69 R. Chambers, *Domestic Annals of Scotland* (3 vols., Edinburgh, 1859–61), iii, 470, quoting a 1737 ms poem on Wade's roads in Scotland.

70 'A Collection of Highland Rites and Customes', 71; Burt, *Letters from a Gentleman in the Highlands of Scotland*, ii, 107–8; T. Garnett, *Observations on a Tour through the Highlands* (2 vols., London, 1800), i, 119–20. One traveller heard that the 'festivities' at likewakes sometimes led to conceptions, thus more than making up (in population terms) for the death of the individual who was being commemorated. In his allusive language, wakes led to 'such gambols and frolicks among the younger part, that the loss which occasioned them is often more than supplied by the consequences of that night'. T. Pennant, *A Tour in Scotland, 1769; and a Tour in Scotland and Voyage to the Hebrides, 1772* (3 vols., 1776), i, 112. The claim that 'multitudes' attended Rob's burial from a vast area of the Highlands (Murray, *Rob Roy*, 259, 261) seems to be simply invention, though doubtless the death of so notable a figure attracted a good turnout.

71 Report by James Fraser, 1702, *The Occult Laboratory*, 213.

72 NLS, Ms 1640, Ochtertyre Papers, vol. vi, Government, Clanship, Law, f.258v. The Clan Stewart gets double credit for its help here. Angus Stewart, QC, pointed me towards the Ochtertyre Ms, while Domhnall Uilleam Stiùbhart identified the tune referred to. The tune and words of the lament are often dated 1745–6, but it's use at Rob's funeral shows that it was earlier. In truth, there is no evidence of it's precise origins, though that it was composed by a MacCrimmon for a MacCrimmon need not be doubted.

73 D. Stewart, *Sketches of the Character, Manners, and Present State of the Highlands*, ii, xiii. Stewart of Ardvorlich was said to have attended the funeral, a representative of the clan whose duellist may have hastened Rob's death. Rob's rest in his grave has been disturbed on more than one occasion. As late as the 1830s, it was reported, other MacGregors were buried under 'his' stone, and in 1841 it was found that the stone had been removed and the ground dug to a depth of three or four feet, presumably in search of relics, *The Times*, 17 September 1841, reprinted from the *Stirling Chronicle*.

74 The Rev. John MacIntosh, in *The Dewar Manuscripts*, 324.

75 R.I.M. Black, *An Lasair: Anthology of 18th Century Gaelic Verse* (Edinburgh, 2001), 144–9.

76 Murray, *Rob Roy*, 261.

11. *Out of Order*

1 *The trials of James, Duncan, and Robert M'Gregor, three sons of the celebrated Rob Roy, before the High Court of Justiciary, in the years 1752, 1753, and 1754. To which is prefixed a Memoir relating to the Highlands, with Anecdotes of Rob Roy and his Family* (Edinburgh, 1818), cxxviii.

2 *Trials*, lxvi-lxvii.

3 Scott, *Rob Roy*, i, lxxvii-lxxix.

4 Dicaledon, 'Memoir of Rob Roy Macgregor, and some branches of his family', *Blackwood's Magazine*, ii (Oct–Dec 1817), 78.

5 Dicaledon, 'Memoirs', 152. If a sister of Rob's was married to Campbell of Glenfalloch this might have explained why Rob showed restraint when involved in several scuffles with Glenfalloch's sons; they were his nephews. Elsewhere tradition recalls 'the Lady of Glenfalloch' as unjustly demanding

an extra stone of cheese in rent from a tenant, whereupon the sons of the two protagonists fought a duel, *Clan Gregor*, ii, 261.

6   Dicaledon, 'Memoirs', 150.

7   *Ascanius, or the Young Adventurer . . . to which is subjoined Memoirs relating to the Highlands, with Anecdotes of Rob Roy and his Family* (Aberdeen, 1843), 208.

8   Dicaledon, 'Memoirs', 153.

9   T. Garnett, *Observations on a Tour through the Highlands* (2 vols., London, 1800), i, 64.

10 A.H. Millar, *History of Rob Roy* (1883), app. i-ii.

11 Dicaledon, 'Memoirs', 152.

12 Dicaledon, 'Memoirs', 80.

13 Scott, *Rob Roy*, i, xviii-lxii, Murray, *Rob Roy*, 173 states that the young James (who also became professor of medicine at King's) told Sir Walter Scott this story. But the younger Gregory was dead (1755) long before Scott was born (1771).

14 Scott, *Rob Roy*, lvii-lxii.

15 S. Smiles (ed.), *James Nasmyth, Engineer, an Autobiography*, (London, 1833), 11-12; R. Chambers, *Domestic Annals of Scotland*, (3 Vols., Edinburgh, 1861), iii, 374n; J.C.B. Cooksey, *Alexander Nasmyth, FRSA, 1758-1840* (Whitingehame House 1991), 1.

16 Sir John Sinclair (ed.), *The Statistical Account of Scotland* (21 vols., 1791-99), xviii, 581-82.

17 D. Stewart, *The Life and surprising Exploits of Rob Roy Macgregor* (Newcastle, [post-1817]).

18 Scott, *Rob Roy*, ii, chap. 30.

19 Hutcheson, *Rob Roy* ii, 59, 97, 103, also notes that Rob's conduct was incompatible with his wife's having been raped.

20 Scott, *Rob Roy*, i, lxxiii-lxxvii. Scott used this as a framework for a scene in his novel.

21 J.G. Lockhart, *Life of Sir Walter Scott* (10 vols., Edinburgh, 1903), i, 240; Scott, *Rob Roy*, i, 170-73, 316-17.

22 M. Hunter (ed.), 'A Collection of Highland Rites and Customes', *The Occult Laboratory. Magic, Science and Second Sight in the Late Seventeenth-Century*, (Woodbridge, 2001), 58.

23 D. Stewart of Garth, *Sketches of the Character, Manners, and Present State of the Highlands* (2nd edn, 2 vols., Edinburgh, 1822), ii, xvi-xvii.

24 H.J.C.Grierson (ed.), *The Letters of Sir Walter Scott* (12 vols., London, 1932-7), ii, 235.

25 Scott, *Rob Roy*, i, xlvi-xlvii. The reference in D. Stewart, *The Life and Surprising Exploits of Rob Roy Macgregor* (Newcastle, n.d.) to Rob's long arms might seem to precede Scott's, as many library catalogues date this chapbook to about 1801. In fact it clearly postdates the 1829 edition of Scott's novel, as it contains quotations from its historical introduction.

26 W. Scott, *Rob Roy*, ed. I. Duncan (Oxford, 1988), xxiv-v.

27 D. Wordsworth, *Recollections of a Tour made in Scotland A.D. 1803*, ed. J.C. Shairp (Edinburgh, 1894), 93.

28 T. Garnett, *Observations*, i, 61.

29 Alex Campbell, *A Journey from Edinburgh through Parts of North Britain* (2 vols., Edinburgh, 1802), i, 225.

30 Thomas Pennant, quoted in Campbell, *Tour*, i, 225.

31 Scott, *Rob Roy*, i, xlvii-xlviii.

32 *Highland Rogue*, 55–9; Dicaledon, 149, 150.
33 Garnett, *Observations*, i, 65.
34 *Highland Rogue*, 23–28.
35 Scott, *Rob Roy*, i, lxxiii.
36 *Ascanius, or the Young Adventurer*, 207.
37 Scott, *Rob Roy*, i, li-liii.
38 As well a being a great swordsman, Rob has been hailed as a notable exponent of Scottish backhold wrestling, one of the 'highly developed survival skills' he and the MacGregors were expert in, W. Baxter, 'Scottish Backhold Wrestling and Rob Roy', *The Scottish Banner*, June 1999. As in this type of contest 'the wrestlers grip each other around the waist at the back, the right hand goes under the opponent's left arm and the chin rests on the opposite right shoulder' in a real conflict (without a remarkably cooperative enemy) this would not be a survival skill but an invitation to a quick death – a sword or dirk under the ribs when you flung your arms open to hug your opponent.
39 NLS Ms 874, Abbotsford, ff. 455–6.

12. *Their Father's Sons*

1 Scott, *Rob Roy*, i, lxxxvii-cxii
2 In a letter of 1753 Rob's son James Mor mentions 'my brother in law Nicol', *The Trial of James Stuart (The Appin Murder)*, ed. D.N. Mackay (London, 1907), 364. James probably refers to the husband of his sister, but the term 'brother-in-law' was occasionally used of the husband of one's wife's sister.
3 Though Rob is not known to have had any illegitimate children, traces survive of what has been coyly referred to as 'certain social irregularities'. Before the first page of the earliest surviving register of baptisms for Balquhidder (1691) there is a very badly damaged page which lists couples guilty of, or accused of, fornication. Still visible now are the words 'Rob Roy McGrigor wt [with] Janet Dow McGrigor'. The rest of the entry is illegible (General Register Office for Scotland, OPR 331). But in the 1880s it was transcribed as stating that Janet was 'his servant in Crigans', and that Rob was also charged along with 'a daughter of Donald Roy Ferguson in Balquhidde', *Social Life in Scotland*, ed. C. Rogers (Grampian Club, 1884–86), iii, 400. No date can be attached to these references, but the surviving Balquhidder kirk session minutes, covering 1710 to 1736 (NAS, CH2/469/1, 2), do not mention any case being brought against Rob.
4 E777/68, pp.224, 246. Another source places James at Invervonchoill Beg, a few miles to the west of Coirechaoroch, at this time, GD50/184/84/21; E. Beveridge, *The 'Abers' and 'Invers' of Scotland* (Edinburgh, 1923), 119.
5 NAS, CC6/5/24, 18 Dec 1735 and 5 Nov 1736.
6 A. & T., ii, 415–17.
7 *Caledonian Mercury*, 15 Mar 1736 (no. 2488, p. 17063).
8 *Caledonian Mercury*, 22 Apr 1736 (no. 2505, pp. 17131–2), cited E. Beauchamp, *Braes o' Balquhidder. An Historical Guide to the District* (4th edn., 1993), 83.
9 A. & T., ii, 416–17.
10 In GD170/797/44.
11 *Information for His Majesty's Advocate ... against James and Ronald Drummonds alias Macgregors, sons to the deceast Rob Roy alias Campbell MacGregor, and Callum Macinlester alias MacGregor, Pannels* (Edinburgh

1736); *Information for James Drummond and Ronald Drummond, and Callum M'Inlester, alias Macgreigors, Pannels, against His Majesty's Advocate* (Edinburgh 1736); NAS, JC7/20, 21, 26 July – 4 Aug 1736.

12 GD50/184/84/2I, p.7.

13 *A. & T.*, ii, 417.

14 *Information for His Majesty's Advocate*, 1–2.

15 Scott, *Rob Roy*, i, liii-iv relates a story of a staunch follower of Rob Roy called 'Macanaleister, or Fletcher' who once saved Rob's life, but this may be a confused reference to the Calum who appears in Rob Og's life at this point. The MacInlesters were regarded, like the MacGregors, as one of the clans forming the Clan Alpin, Douglas, *Baronage*, 506.

16 J. Ramsay of Ochtertyre, *Scotland and Scotsmen in the Eighteenth Century*, ed. A. Allardyce (2 vols., Edinburgh, 1888), ii, 493–4.

17 NLS, Ms 1640, Ochtertyre Papers, vol. vi, Government, Clanship, Law, f.260r.

18 NLS, MS 3186, MacGregor or Drummond of Balhaldie Mss, ff. 237–8.

19 See Chapter 2 above.

20 W.B. Cook (ed.), *Local Notes and Queries from the Stirling Observer*, (1883), 227 (as cited in GD50/184/84/4N); *Clan Gregor*, ii, 442.

21 GD220/5/1532.

22 Later the 21st Regiment of Foot. It is sometimes said Rob Og joined the Black Watch, but this is contradicted by his cousin Glengyle younger, PRO, SP54/25/36B, and by Lieutenant General Charles Churchill, NLS, Ms 309, p.228.

23 A. Livingstone, W.H. Aikman & B.S. Hart (eds.), *No Quarter Given. The Muster Roll of Prince Charles Edward Stuart's Army, 1745–6*, (3rd edn, Glasgow, 2001), 88.

24 NLS, Ms NLS, Ms 309. p.228.

25 Murray, John, *Memorials of John Murray of Broughton*, ed. R.F. Bell (SHS, 1898), 68. Murray says the farm was on 'Loch Tron', eight miles from Drummond. The only loch that seems to fit is Loch Turret, north-west of Crieff. It has been said that in 1738 James had moved to the farm of 'Tyranioch', but it has not been identified, GD50/184/84/21.

26 Murray, *Memorials*, 159.

27 V. Wills (ed.), *Reports on the Annexed Estates, 1755–69* (Edinburgh, 1973), 23.

28 PRO, SP 54/25/19B, 41A,41B. Corriearklet is my interpretation of 'in Corrocklat' in Buchanan parish (NLS, Ms 7068, ff.10–11) and 'at Corrieclat' (PRO, SP 54/25/97B).

29 PRO, SP54/25/65.

30 [G. Omond], 'Some Passages in the Life of Hamish MacGregor', *MacMillan's Magazine*, lxii (1890), 47–51; PRO, SP54/25/41C, 47A, 52A, 53, 63B, 55.

31 Murray, *Memorials*, 159.

32 Murray, *Memorials*, 159–60.

33 Murray, *Memorials*, 161. James later claimed that it was the influence of the duke of Perth and a 'strategem' of Buchanan of Arnprior that had made him join the Jacobites, PRO, SP 54/41/48B. Murray gives the name as 'Arran' but Arnprior is meant.

34 G. Omond, *The Lord Advocates of Scotland* (2 vols., Edinburgh, 1883–1914), ii, 27.

35 Murray, *Memorials*, 167–8.

36 Omond, 'Some Passages', 49–51; PRO, SP 54/25/97A, 97B.

37 NLS, Ms 3036, ff.150–2.

38 *Clan Gregor*, ii, 335–6; Omond, 'Some Passages', 50. The 89 prisoners probably included the 40 captured captured by Glengyle when they were at work mending roads for the duke of Argyll, R. Forbes, *The Lyon in Mourning*, ed. H.Paton (3 vols., SHS, 1895–6), i, 194.

39 Sir Walter Scott, in his *Tales of a Grandfather*, stated that five (rather than three) sons of Rob Roy fought for the Jacobites in the '45. This was cited in *Muster Roll of Prince Charles Edward Stuart's Army, 1745–6*, ed. A. Livingstone, W.H. Aikman & B.S. Hart (Aberdeen, 1984), 167. But the 3rd edition, oddly titled *No Quarter Given* (Glasgow, 2001) omits the citation. It lists James Mor and Ranald as captains in the duke of Perth's regiment, and also, along with Rob Og, in the MacGregor regiment. The two regiments were so closely linked it is sometimes hard to distinguish them, 66, 174, 175.

40 PRO, SP54/25/36A.

41 *Clan Gregor*, ii, 369.

42 Murray, *Memorials*, 444.

43 *Clan Gregor*, ii, 436.

44 C.S. Terry (ed.), *The Albemarle Papers* (2 vols., New Spaldimg Club, 1902), i, 27.

45 *Stewarts of the South*, p.47.

46 *Clan Gregor*, ii, 494.

47 *Clan Gregor*, ii, 436.

48 *Clan Gregor*, ii, 337.

49 PRO, SP 54/41/48A, 52; *Clan Gregor*, ii, 440; D. Murray Rose, *Historical Notes; or Essays on the '15 and the '45* (Edinburgh, 1897), 172; Omond, 'Some Passages', 51.

50 The resultant babies were baptised in Balquhidder 20 July 1750 and 7 May 1751.

51 For the abduction of Jean Key and the trials that followed see *The trials of James, Duncan, and Robert M'Gregor, three sons of the celebrated Rob Roy, before the high court of justiciary, in the years 1752, 1753, and 1754. To which is prefixed a memoir relating to the Highlands, with anecdotes of Rob Roy and his family* (Edinburgh, 1818); *Unto the Honourable, the Lords of Council and Session, the Petition of Janet Mitchell, Relict of the deeeast [sic] James Kay Portioner of Edinbelly, and Thomas Kay Tenant in Boquhan, brother to the said James Kay* (12 Febuary 1751, GD15/796); *Scots Magazine*, xiii (1751), 260, xiv (1752), 345–61, 556–7.

52 This was probably Bishop Alexander Smith, J. Darragh, *The Catholic Hierarchy of Scotland. A Biographical List, 1653–1985* (Glasgow, 1986), 10,125. Smith was doubtless the priest being hunted as a 'popish bishop' and a 'trafficking priest' in 1751, PRO, SP 54/41/50, 52.

53 In *Trials*, 212, James is referred to as living in 'Invervorich'.

54 Rob Og had this forged letter addressed to him as tacksman (leaseholder) of 'Bailliefurl' (*Trials*, 231) but its location has not been identified.

55 NLS, Ms 308, pp.66–67.

56 NAS, JC18/9, Register of Criminal Letters, 1751–80, pp.1–16.

57 PRO, SP 54/41/48A, 48B.

58 For correspondence about the capture of James and the discussions over his future, see PRO, SP 54/41/48A, B, 50, 52; NLS, Ms 308, pp.66–7, 69–70, 73, 75–6, 78, 82–3.

59 PRO, SP54/41/50, 52, 53.

60 PRO, SP54/42/15, 16A, 20.

61 PRO, SP 54/42/28E.

62 See J. Fergusson, 'The Appin Murder Case', *The White Hind and other Discoveries* (London, 1963), 133–79.

63 D.N. Mackay (ed.), *The Trial of James Stuart (The Appin Murder)*, (London, 1907), 347–49; GD87/1/47, quoted in R. Gibson, 'The Appin Murder', *History Scotland*, iii, no. 1 (2003), 15; PRO, SP54/42/28E, 29A, 29B, 31, 32A; NLS, Ms 295, ff.60–1, 67. *See also* A. Stewart, 'The Last Chief: Dougal Stewart of Appin (died 1764),' *SHR*, lxxvi (1997), 213.

64 Gibson, 'The Appin Murder', 13.

65 PRO, SP54/42/37, 38, 42A, 42B, 46A, 46B; NLS, Ms 309, pp. 43–50; I.T. Rae, 'Edinburgh Castle, 1751–3', *Book of the Old Edinburgh Club*, xxxii (1966), 83–4.

66 PRO, SP54/42,42A, 46B; SP54/43/3.

67 NLS, Ms 3187, ff.157–8.

68 *The Trial of James Stewart*, 361; GD87/1/58, quoted in Gibson, 'The Appin Murder', 15.

69 *Scots Magazine*, xv, May 1753, 261.

70 NLS, Ms 309, pp. 227, 228.

71 *Scots Magazine*, xv (1753), 362, 580, 626–7.

72 Murray, *Clan Gregor*, ii, 425–33; *Trials*, p. 156–207.

73 Omond, 'Some Passages', 50–1. James Mor's fantasies of thousands of MacGregors and other Jacobites in Ireland ready to invade mainland Britain gave hope to Balhaldie and other naïve Jacobites leading them to renewed futile plottings. D. Zimmerman, *The Jacobite Movement in Scotland and in Exile, 1746–59* (Basingstoke, 2003), 108–9, 114.

74 Omond, 'Some Passages', 53.

75 *The Trial of James Stuart*, 364–5.

76 *The Trial of James Stuart*, 362. See also GD87/1/64 and 66 for attempts by James Mor to get help from Breadalbane.

77 *Clan Gregor*, ii, 440.

78 NLS, Ms 3187, ff.170–1.

79 D. Murray Rose, *Historical Notes; or Essays on the '15 and the '45* (Edinburgh, 1897), 188–9. Rose believed that the notorious British spy who called himself Pickle (after Tobias Smollet's 1751 novel, *The Peregrinations of Peregrine Pickle*) was 'James Drummond', whom he referred to as 'James Roy' and thought was a different person from James Mor, Rob Roy's son. But it is generally accepted that A. Lang, *Pickle the Spy, or the Incognito of Prince Charles* (London, 1897) was correct in identifying Pickle as Alasdair MacDonnel, younger of Glengarry.

80 Rose, *Historical Notes*, 189.

81 Rose, *Historical Notes*, 190–4.

82 NLS, Ms 3187, ff.181–2.

83 PRO, SP54/43/76A, 76B, 81; SP54/44/64; Rose, *Historical Notes*, 194–6.

84 NLS, MS 3187, ff.181–2.

85 NLS, Ms 3187, ff.195–6.

86 Omond, 'Some Passages', 51–54; *Clan Gregor*, ii, 434–8.

87 *Scots Magazine*, xvi (1754), 500.

88 In GD50/184/84; in NLS, Ms 305, p.3.

89 *Clan Gregor*, ii, 445.

90 V. Wills (ed.), *Report on the Annexed Estates, 1755–69*, (Edinburgh, 1973), 3.

91 *Clan Gregor*, ii, 490–92.
92 E777/161/61(2), 169. I am most grateful to Domhnall Uilleam Stiubhart for giving me access to his transcripts to these and other petitions to the annexed estate commissioners.
93 E777/232/1, 2.
94 E777/161/243, 266, 280(1), 280(2), 293. Again my thanks to Domhnall Stiubhart.
95 *Clan Gregor*, ii, 451–55; 15 Geo. III, c.29.
96 *The English and Scottish Popular Ballads*, ed. F.J. Childs (5 vols., London, 1882–1898), iv, 243–54, v, 262–4.

13. Life After Death

1 *The Highland Rogue: being a General History of the Highlanders wherein is given an account of their Country and Manners of living* (London, 1743).
2 *A Short History of the Highland Regiment* (London, 1743; facsimile reprint Cornwallville, N.Y., 1963), 5, 19.
3 E. Burt, *Letters from a Gentleman in the Highlands of Scotland*, ed. R. Jamieson (5th edn, 2 vols., London, 1818), i, xlvi; ii, 350n.
4 J. Ramsay of Ochtertyre, *Scotland and Scotsmen in the Eighteenth Century*, ed. A. Allardyce (2 vols., Edinburgh, 1888), ii, 490–4.
5 A. Campbell, *A Journey from Edinburgh through Parts of North Britain* (2 vols., London, 1802), i, 123–25.
6 D. Wordsworth, *Recollections of a Tour made in Scotland A.D. 1803*, ed. J.C. Shairp (Edinburgh, 1894), 92–93.
7 In a later revision Wordsworth dropped the weak 'one' in the third line, substituting the bolder 'a thief'. D. Wordsworth, *Recollections*, 229; W. Wordsworth, *Poetical Works* (1849–50), xi, 20.
8 Wordsworth, *Poetical Works*, xi, 20–4.
9 Wordsworth, *Recollections*, 229–33, 316.
10 H.P. Bolton, 'Playing Rob Roy as Robin Hood', *Scott in Carnival. Selected Papers from the Fourth International Scott Conference, Edinburgh, 1991*, ed. J.H. Alexander & D. Hewitt (Aberdeen, 1993), 482, 486; H.P. Bolton, *Scott Dramatized* (London, 1992), 162, 257 n1; *The New Grove Dictionary of Music and Musicians*, (2nd end, 29 vols., London, 2001), vii, 82.
11 Wordsworth, *Recollections*, 314.
12 Scott, *Letters*, iii, 99–100.
13 All are currently (2003) on display in Abbotsford House. For some of the many other relics attributed to Rob Roy see A.L. Miller, *History of Rob Roy* (Dundee, 1883), appendix, pp. iii-iv.
14 E. Johnson, *Sir Walter Scott, the Great Unknown* (2 vols., London, 1970), i, 603.
15 Scott, *Rob Roy*, i, xvii.
16 Johnson, *Sir Walter Scott, the Great Unknown*, i, 570.
17 Dicaledon, 'Memoir of Rob Roy Macgregor, and some Branches of his Family', *Blackwood's Magazine*, ii (Oct–Dec 1817), 74–80, 145–55, 288–95.
18 J.G. Lockhart, *Life of Sir Walter Scott* (10 vols., Edinburgh, 1903), v, 243, 245.
19 W.B. Todd & A. Bowden, *Sir Walter Scott. A Bibliographical History* (New Castle, DE, 1998), 447–8 (nos. 112Dk, 112Dm).

20 Bolton, *Scott Dramatised*, 166–8; Lockhart, *Life of Sir Walter Scott*, vi, 26–7, 57–8, 59–61.

21 W. Scott, *Rob Roy*, ed. I. Duncan (Oxford, 1988), xiii-xiv.

22 J. Mitchell, *The Walter Scott Operas* (Alabama, 1977), 64–8; J. Mitchell, *More Scott Operas* (London, 1996), 136–7.

23 Of these two works the first is often dated *c.* 1801, and in the second the date 1824 has often been misread as 1812. Both works in fact quote from Scott's novel, so are obviously post–1818. Such inaccurate datings have led to the suggestion that Scott may have read chapbooks on Rob Roy before writing his novel (Bolton, 'Playing Rob Roy as Robin Hood', 490). In fact none of the chapbooks can be dated before 1818.

24 *Bold Rob Roy*, Bodleian Library, Oxford, Firth b. 34 (276). Pocock had followed Wordsworth in labelling Rob Roy a 'thief', but the ballad version reads 'chief', though the change may be accidental.

25 *Rob Roy MacGregor*, Bodleian Library, Oxford, Harding B 11(315).

26 *Rob Roy*, Bodleian Library, Oxford, Harding B 25 (1635).

27 [T. Hood & J.H. Reynolds], *Odes and Addresses to Great People* (London, 1825), 46.

28 H.P. Bolton, *Scott Dramatised* (London, 1992), 165–66.

29 W.H.C. Hosmer, *Poetical Works* (1854), 146.

30 W. Thornbury, *Historical and Legendary Ballads and Songs* (1876), 271.

31 J.S. Blackie, 1809–1895 *Lays of the Highlands and Islands* (1872), 130.

32 *Portraits Illustrative of the Novels, Tales, and Romances of the Author of Waverley* (1820s).

33 J.S.S. Stuart [or J. Hay, or J.H. Allan], *The Costume of the Clans* (Edinburgh, 1845, facsimile reprint 1892), 111–14; J.T. Dunbar, *History of Highland Dress* (London, 1962), 59. The 'portrait' of Rob by Margaret Stewart Black which forms the frontispiece of Howlett's *Highland Constable* is yet another version of the Grant picture.

34 In GD50/184/84/4N (dating from 1870).

35 J.T. Dunbar, *History of Highland Dress* (2nd edn, London, 1978), 148–9, & colour plate section following p.66, portrait of the earl of Wemyss.

36 F. Wyness, *More Spots from the Leopard* (Aberdeen, 1973), 42–43.

37 The original plaster statue is in Perth Museum and Art Gallery. The finished marble version based on it was sold at auction in Edinburgh in 2002.

38 Schotz recorded much friction between himself and Adam McGregor Dick, who commissioned the statue, but 'It is best to draw a veil over our transactions.' Rising costs and tax increases left the sculptor much out of pocket, as Dick would pay no more than the price originally agreed. 'Mr Dick certainly lacked the largesse and humour of his forebear,' B. Schotz, *Bronze in My Blood* (Edinburgh, (1981), 192–93.

39 *The Bioscope*, 14 Sept. 1911, 534–35. I am grateful to the Scottish Film Archive for this reference.

40 D. Cloy, *Scotland in Silent Cinema: a Commemorative Catalogue to accompany the Scottish Reels' Programme at the Pordenone Silent Film Festival, Italy* (Glasgow, 1998), 7, 27.

41 D. Wordsworth, *Recollections*, 82–83.

42 *Journals of Dorothy Wordsworth*, ed. E. de Selincourt (2 vols., London 1952), ii, 353–54.

43 J.C. Holt, *Robin Hood* (London, 1982).

44 J. Millgate, *Scott's Last Edition* (Edinburgh, 1987), 82.

45 Bolton, *Scott Dramatised*, 163.

46 Scott, *Letters*, xii, 7.
47 This of course parallels the way in which those involved in treason against the crown traditionally tended to claim that they were not plotting against the king himself, but against evil advisers who had led him astray.
48 E.J. Hobsbawm, *Bandits* (Harmondsworth, 1972), 43–5.

14. Man versus Myth

1 F. Watson, *The Braes of Balquhidder* (Edinburgh, 1914), 45. For non-British readers the reference to 'public schools' may seem confusing. In Britain the term denoted the private schools to which those rich enough sent their sons to learn to be 'gentlemen'.

INDEX

Surnames have been standardised, and MacGregors listed under that name, with cross references from their adopted names. This provides consistency, but at the expense of some oddities. Thus James Graham of Glengyle is indexed as Gregor MacGregor, a name he only used in early childhood and brief Jacobite episodes in 1715–16 and 1745–6. But the alternative consistency, listing MacGregors under the adopted names they used for most of their lives, would have led to Rob Roy being indexed as Campbell, a crime that would have brought MacGregor wrath upon the unfortunate indexer. Under each surname, individuals are listed in alphabetical order of first names, ignoring titles etc. which may precede them.

BIRLINN LTD (incorporating John Donald and Polygon) is one of Scotland's leading publishers with over four hundred titles in print. Should you wish to be put on our catalogue mailing list **contact**:

Catalogue Request
Birlinn Ltd
West Newington House
10 Newington Road
Edinburgh EH9 1QS
Scotland, UK

Tel: + 44 (0) 131 668 4371
Fax: + 44 (0) 131 668 4466
e-mail: info@birlinn.co.uk

Postage and packing is free within the UK. For overseas orders, postage and packing (airmail) will be charged at 30% of the total order value.

For more information, or to order online, visit our website at **www.birlinn.co.uk**

Birlinn Limited
IMPRINTS: JOHN DONALD · POLYGON